THE FLOOR OF HEAVEN

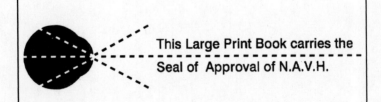

THE FLOOR OF HEAVEN

A TRUE TALE OF THE LAST FRONTIER AND THE YUKON GOLD RUSH

HOWARD BLUM

THORNDIKE PRESS

A part of Gale, Cengage Learning

GALE
CENGAGE Learning™

Detroit • New York • San Francisco • New Haven, Conn • Waterville, Maine • London

GALE
CENGAGE Learning

Copyright © 2011 by Howard Blum.
Thorndike Press, a part of Gale, Cengage Learning.

ALL RIGHTS RESERVED
Thorndike Press® Large Print Nonfiction.
The text of this Large Print edition is unabridged.
Other aspects of the book may vary from the original edition.
Set in 16 pt. Plantin.

LIBRARY OF CONGRESS CATALOGING-IN-PUBLICATION DATA

Blum, Howard.
    The floor of heaven : a true tale of the last frontier and the
Yukon gold rush / Howard Blum. (thorndike press nonfiction)
        p. cm.
    Originally published: New York : Crown Trade, c2011.
    Includes bibliographical references.
    Summary: Using primary source materials from three
individuals around whom the narrative revolves, best-selling
author Blum tells a story of the 1897 Klondike Gold Rush.
    ISBN-13: 978-1-4104-4125-6 (hardback)
    ISBN-10: 1-4104-4125-3 (hardcover)
    1. Yukon River Valley (Yukon and Alaska)—Gold discoveries.
2. West (U.S.)—History—1860–1890. 3. Gold mines and
mining—Yukon River Valley (Yukon and
Alaska)—History—19th century. 4. Siringo, Charles A.,
1855–1928. 5. Smith, Jefferson Randolph, 1860–1898. 6.
Carmack, George W. (George Washington), 1860–1922. 7.
Yukon River Valley (Yukon and Alaska)—Biography. 8. West
(U.S.)—Biography. I. Title.
F912.Y9B58 2011b
978'.02—dc22   2011024158

Published in 2011 by arrangement with Crown Publishers, a division of
Random House, Inc.

Printed in the United States of America
1 2 3 4 5 6 7 15 14 13 12 11

For my sister Marcy,
who has a heart of gold

Here we will sit, and
let the sounds of music
Creep in our ears:
soft stillness, and the night,
Becomes the touches
of sweet harmony.
Sit, Jessica: look,
how the floor of heaven
Is thick inlaid with
patterns of bright gold.

— William Shakespeare,
The Merchant of Venice

They were a rough bunch, rough in dress,
rough in speech and rough handed, but just
as great hearted and manly as they were
rough. Real men, every one of them, with
muscles and sinews like iron bands, devel-
oped by continuous and arduous exercise.
There was no real adventure too strenuous
or dangerous for them to undertake. They
possessed the kind of power and strength

that make men invincible, with characters broadened and strengthened by the hardships and privations they had been forced to endure, in their unequal struggle with the mighty forces of Nature in the unknown and desolate wilds.

— George Carmack,
My Experiences in the Yukon

A NOTE TO THE READER

This is a true story. It is a history of the last years of the Old West and of the Yukon gold rush. It is also a narrative that recounts the lives of three unique men — Charles Siringo, the cowboy detective; Jefferson "Soapy" Smith, the gambler who built an underworld empire; and George Carmack, the prospector whose discovery set off the stampede to the Yukon. In the telling of their interweaving tales, I have benefited from several firsthand accounts. Without these invaluable tools, I would not have been able to portray these men and what they were doing, saying, and even thinking with either accuracy or vividness.

Therefore, the reader should know that I am greatly indebted to the following sources: Charlie Siringo wrote four first-person accounts of his life. These are remarkable documents — folksy, witty, suspenseful, and perceptive. Soapy Smith was shot down before he could fulfill his often-made promise

— or threat, considering the secrets he knew — to record his life story. Jeff Smith, his great-grandson, however, has taken Soapy's letters, correspondence from other family members, diary entries, legal records, as well as the albums of newspaper clippings Soapy collected, and written a smart and exhaustive biography that was published by Klondike Research, in Juneau, Alaska. It was James Albert Johnson who in 1957 discovered an apple crate in a secondhand Seattle bookstore filled with the George Carmack papers. No one was certain how the collection had made its way to the Shorey Book Store, but there was no doubt it was a treasure trove: decades of letters from George to his sister, Rose; handwritten descriptions of his prospecting days; pages of his own romantic poetry; and family photographs. Johnson bought the contents of the apple crate for $500, and he willed the papers to the University of Washington. I am grateful to the university and its Special Collections Division for sharing this invaluable resource with me.

A chapter-by-chapter note on sources appears at the conclusion of this book.

PROLOGUE: UP THE YUKON RIVER

As the millionaire's steamboat chugged north against the current, up the Yukon River, and sidled past the distant Mackenzie Mountains that late-summer day in 1882, the river remained smooth and wide, easy to navigate, but the water had suddenly turned gray and opaque. It was as if the blades — buckets, the builder had called them — of the *New Racket*'s paddle wheel were pushing through a fog. The sun shined high in a big dome of blue sky; nevertheless, Edward Schieffelin stood on the deck staring out at a long stretch of water that held the color of a storm cloud. It was a puzzlement. But as Schieffelin sorted it out in his mind, he came to believe — and not for the first time on his long expedition into the Alaskan wilderness — that he'd stumbled onto a clue. When he was finally convinced, he gave the order to pull the *New Racket* close to shore and drop anchor. Gold, he predicted with an absolute certainty to his team, lay in this dark channel.

13

Schieffelin's instincts had served him well before. Six years earlier he'd been a penniless Indian scout at Camp Huachuca in the Arizona Territory when on a similar hunch he'd ventured deep into Apache country. The soldiers had tried to warn him off; Geronimo's renegade braves still roamed the cracked, treeless flatlands surrounding the Dragoon Mountains. "The only rock you'll find out there," he was told, "will be your own tombstone." But Schieffelin paid them no mind.

He'd always been a willful, independent sort. Odd, too, if you asked some of the soldiers. His thick black hair and beard fell in a tangle past his shoulders, he was thin as a scarecrow, and his getup was homespun. Day after day, he wore the same slouch hat decorated with squirrel fur, its brim pulled straight back as though blown by a sudden gust of wind, and the same pair of deerskin trousers, which he'd patched over the years with scraps of flannel and corduroy. It was his eyes, though, that made folks jumpy. Schieffelin didn't look so much as stare; his soft gray eyes always seemed to be focused on some distant place that he alone could see. Now that he'd gotten it into his mind that there was a "big strike" waiting to be found in the San Pedro Valley, he wasn't about to let the threat of marauding Apaches scare him off. He went off into this rough country

— and found a mountain loaded with silver ore. He also enjoyed a mischievous last laugh on the people who'd tried to discourage him: He named the town built on the mesa adjacent to his treasure-trove mine Tombstone. And by the time Wyatt Earp and Doc Holliday had their shoot-out with the Clanton brothers in the town's O.K. Corral, Schieffelin had shrewdly sold out to a group of Philadelphia investors for well over $1 million.

The money, however, didn't change the nature of Schieffelin's dreams. It stoked them. Visions of a new, distant treasure had taken hold of his imagination, and now he had the bankroll to pursue it. It had been his prospector's habit to study maps, and this practice had led to a theory. A mineral belt, he'd deduced from just a smattering of evidence, circled the globe from Cape Horn to the far reaches of Asia, a highway through the core of the earth paved with gold and silver that crossed North America near the Continental Divide and went on down to the Andes. According to this theory, Alaska's Yukon Valley stretched directly across its glittering path.

The maps he consulted were primitive. Much of the world, after all, was still waiting to be explored. And many geographers were insisting that the Yukon River flowed north into the Arctic Ocean, not west into the Bering Sea. But with his customary confidence, Schieffelin had no doubts that a fortune, a colossal golden windfall many times the size of his Tombstone discovery, had lain hidden for millions of years in the long Yukon River Valley. It was Nature's gift, waiting to be claimed by the prospector with the requisite courage, daring, and knowledge. Edward Schieffelin decided it would be his.

Dressed in his slouch hat and deerskins but with the newly acquired authority that great wealth imparts, Schieffelin walked into a San Francisco shipyard in the winter of 1881 and commissioned a steamboat. As the 175-foot, three-decked *New Racket* was being built, he recruited a team to accompany him to Alaska. Two of the men had sweated alongside him in his Tombstone mine, his brother Effingham and Jack Young. The fourth, Charles Farciot, was a Swiss-born Civil War veteran who'd been traveling around the Arizona Territory for years, taking photographs of soldiers, miners, settlers, and Indians. Schieffelin presumed posterity would want a photographic record of his momentous expedition, too.

In the first days of the spring of 1882, a schooner dragged the *New Racket* by a stout towline from San Francisco up the Pacific to St. Michael, a port the Russians had established on the Bering Sea. After their supplies were loaded, the prospectors did not want to

16

waste any time. Schieffelin and his team boarded the little boat and quickly went to work feeding cords of wood and shovelfuls of coal into the boilers, and before long an explosion of fresh, hot steam was roiling. Suddenly, a deep, guttural rumble shook the ship's hold, but then the engines settled into their steady, noisy grind and the two paddle wheels at the stern of the boat started turning in monotonous circles as they sliced through the water. With a great plume of dark smoke rising from its two tall smokestacks into the perfect blue sky, the *New Racket* began its journey across Norton Sound, heading toward the uncharted meandering labyrinth of the vast Yukon River and into the heart of Alaska.

It was a voyage where every moment seemed a discovery. All was new to their eyes; and, in fact, few if any white men had ever gone here before. The sun remained high in the sky day and night, illuminating a majestic wilderness that seemed as mysterious and exciting to the team of prospectors as a fantasy kingdom in a children's storybook. They kept a fascinated watch as their boat chugged up the twisting river past ramparts of brawny snow-capped mountains, dense green-iced glaciers glowing in the strong light, forests of tall spruce and formidable evergreens that stretched on thick and endless like secret worlds, then through

17

deep green valleys sparkling with brier rose and bluebells, and on and still on past brackish primordial marshes, and a hundred, no, a thousand unexplored and unnamed brooding islands. Dangers, real and imagined, gathered on every shore. Intricately carved totems rose on the riverbanks to mark Indian graves, and there were occasions when the more sharp-eyed of the men saw figures, no doubt Indian braves, darting through the forests, keeping watch on them and perhaps, they feared, planning to attack the invaders. There were also the stories they'd heard in San Francisco of what roamed out there, tales of woolly man-eating prehistoric beasts as large as hills and giant ferocious bears with razor-sharp talons the length of pickaxes. As they looked out into this fresh strange land, a wild kingdom, all the large stories seemed eerily possible. And each new twist of the river brought new challenges and new decisions; you could give the order to head in one direction and you might very well disappear into a maze of countless channels, lost forever in the winding tentacles of the great and unpredictable river.

Yet it wasn't whim that was determining the course of their journey. Schieffelin had a plan. He was not a trained geologist, but he'd picked up a good deal of practical knowledge over the many years, both as a boy and a man, he'd hunted for gold. He knew what he

18

was looking for in Alaska.

Gold, he understood, was a very singular metal. It had been formed over the course of millions of years in the cauldron of the earth's core and had then moved upward, toward the surface, into crevices and fissures, as the aging planet shifted about. You could get at it by mining, by sinking a deep shaft into the stony heart of the planet's underground, shoring this tunnel with a backbone of timbers that would hopefully hold back a suffocating avalanche of dirt and rock; and then with judicious dynamiting and backbreaking shovel work in a dark, narrow, nearly airless hole, someday, if your luck held, the glimmer of a subterranean vein would be revealed. It was a grim, tedious, and dangerous enterprise. And success was as rare as an answered prayer. But there was also another more adventuresome way to find gold.

Gold traveled. As the earth stretched and heaved over the eons of time, rocks containing veins of gold rose up to the surface in this volcanic turmoil. Winds and rains, sleets and snows, streams and rivers, the abrasion of five million active years ground these rocks, honing them, until the gold was set free. And the gold traveled. The light metal was carried along by torrents of water, by fast-moving streams and mighty rivers. It traveled to gorges cut into ancient valleys, to riverbeds and sandbars, across gravel beaches, and down churning streams and quiet creeks. Nature would determine where it was driven, and gravity would dictate where it settled. But it all eventually came to rest, golden specks as fine as sand and tawny nuggets as big as knuckles, a legacy accumulating since the beginning of time that lay like a bright yellow carpet across the planet's floor.

The prospectors called this, Schieffelin knew, placer gold. To get it, you panned. You stuck your tin pan into the water, gave the muck and gravel you brought up a careful, well-practiced shake followed by an earnest wash, and if you spotted colors, flecks of gold, or, even better, a nugget, you knew you were on to something. You had found your spot. All you had to do was dig down a bit past the bedrock, often just a foot or two, and a bonanza was yours for the taking.

Of course, knowing where to pan was essential to success. A prospector's instincts were part science and part pure wishful thinking. You had to follow moving water, tracing in your mind the logical course of a bounty of fast-moving gold, and then decide where this millennium-old journey would've come to a halt. But since this pathway might very well have been altered over the ages, since a raging stream might once have raced through a now bone-dry valley or a placid creek might one million years ago have been a meandering river, guesswork was a large part of the process. You had to imagine how the earth once was; and in those reckonings, science could guide the prospector only so far. His hunches had to inform him.

And so throughout that spring and summer, as the *New Racket* had moved up river, Schieffelin had been scouting for placer gold fields and playing his hunches. Time after time, Schieffelin, bursting with his usual confidence, had seen something that had sparked an unshakable prediction. He'd order the boat to drop anchor and then they'd spend an energetic day or two panning near a sandbar, poking around the mosses of a riverbank, or wading through a stream rushing with glistening, ice-cold water. Each of these forays had ended in disappointment. No colors had ever shined in his pan. After each excursion, all Schieffelin could do was to find the faith to swallow his frustration and give the order to hoist anchor and steam north.

But now, staring at this dark stretch of river, he knew in his heart and in his mind that destiny had indeed been leading him all along. Nature had churned this channel, tossing dark sand and alluvial silt up from the depths, whirling it all about in a turmoil until the water was heavy with sediment and ash — and had turned color. Perhaps there had been a volcanic disturbance; the mountains in the distance, Schieffelin judged, certainly

21

looked ominous. Or maybe it was the effects of a relentless, pounding rainstorm. Ultimately, Schieffelin did not care about the reasons; he would let other men dwell on the science. His attention focused on the result. With all the forceful heaving, with all the shifting about of the riverbed, he knew: Gold had been pried and loosened from its primeval resting places and had floated toward the surface. He had not an iota of doubt: This channel would be his bonanza.

They panned for three days. It was orderly, meticulous work. Standing against the terraced bank, he'd submerge his pan into the dark water that ran along the river's sandy floor; wash off the larger rocks and bits of moss with a gentle, well-practiced circular twist of his wrists, leveling the pan from time to time as he shook it; and then, just to be sure, he'd repeat the entire process before looking for a telltale golden color in the grist of dank sand. Hour after hour, day after day, he kept at it. His success in Arizona had taught him that perseverance was as crucial a tool as luck. He refused to move on. He knew this channel held his next big strike.

On the third day, he found it. A yellow nugget as big as a Yankee dollar lay in his pan. Bursting with excitement, he took it out of the pan and held it up toward the sun. In the bright daylight, it glittered with promise. But common sense required that he give the rock

a strong scratch or two with his thumb —
and the bright color rubbed off. It was just
another big, worthless rock. And with that
realization, all his remaining hope might just
as well have been squeezed out of him.

Later that day, Schieffelin gave the order to
up anchor. Under a fresh head of steam, the
New Racket was soon once again puffing up
the long, twisting river.

Schieffelin had more hunches; and more
disappointments. And when the sun was no
longer so high on the horizon and a sharp
chill was in the air, he realized they'd better
find a place to settle in for winter.

They had been steaming up the fast-moving
Tanana River, a tributary of the Yukon, when
they saw to their astonishment a trading post.
It faced a mossy, high-grassed inlet that was
a natural harbor, and when they rowed ashore
a wizened trapper greeted them with the announcement that he was the proprietor as
well as, for that matter, the king of all they
surveyed. The Indians called the place
Nuklayaket, the trapper said. Schieffelin
looked around and decided it was as good a
place as any to hunker down.

He set the men to work building a cabin
while each day he went off with his pan. He
was not ready to quit. He knew gold was out
there waiting for him. But measuring out his
days in what had become an unremittingly

frustrating exercise began to take its toll. Like the deep, darkening autumn sky that was swiftly beginning to hide the sun, doubts were starting to blot his confidence. Mistake, miscalculation, even folly — a vocabulary of defeat was taking form in his mind.

Then winter came. It didn't arrive so much as attack. The wind grabbed at you and the snow pummeled, but the cold was the truly vindictive adversary. Schieffelin would wrap his newly purchased polar bear skin over his parka and yet could still feel the frost taking him in its death grip. His body shook as much from terror as from the chill; and all he could do in self-defense was to recall the dry, heavy heat of the Arizona desert. But the cold was never out of his mind for long. The trapper had rigged up a thermometer of sorts: four bottles, each one containing a different fluid. The bottle that held mercury would freeze at forty degrees below zero Fahrenheit, the coal oil at fifty below, and the jamaica ginger extract at sixty below; the Perry Davis' Painkiller didn't turn solid until it hit seventy-five below. There were many brutal nights when Schieffelin looked at the Perry Davis bottle and saw a dark mass.

Another sort of cruelty was the trapper's constant taunting. He said Schieffelin had embarked on a fool's mission: There was no gold up in the high north country. Sure, hard rock gold had been discovered a few years back in the Alaska Panhandle, near Juneau. But that was ore buried deep beneath the earth. Mining engineers had to dynamite their way near to China to get at it. Anyways, Juneau was near the coast, over a thousand miles from this inland river valley. And, Schieffelin learned to his surprise, he was not the first prospector to roam about the Yukon Valley. The trapper told him in that back in 1873 Arthur Harper had done a fair share of prospecting along the river, and five years later George Holt had crossed over the Chilkoot Pass to look for placer gold. Both men had come up empty-handed. And so would Schieffelin, the trapper assured him. Can't find what isn't there, he said flatly.

Spring at last came. A thin ray of light pierced the southern sky, and finally the sun itself rose on the horizon. With the new, fresh season, Schieffelin once more found his will. He made up his mind to set out again.

The *New Racket* steamed upriver. Fortified by this renewed confidence, Schieffelin found encouraging signs. Days were spent panning. Yet the results were always the same: nothing. It was dispiriting; the expedition had turned into a grim exercise. And a second winter would be worse than the first. Schieffelin now knew what to expect, and the prospect was more torment than any sane man could endure.

25

He gave each of the men $200 as a gratuity for their loyal service, and before the summer was over he arranged for the sale of the steamboat. The Oregon Territory, he'd come around to thinking, was a surefire treasure field.

I was wrong, Schieffelin announced to his team with a weary resignation on the day he departed Alaska for Portland. My theory, my instincts — all were ill-conceived ditherings, foolish mistakes. There is no gold to be panned in this godforsaken frozen wasteland. There's not a single nugget to be found in the entire Yukon River Valley.

■ ■ ■ ■

PART I
PREMONITIONS

■ ■ ■ ■

ONE

After a good deal of thought, Charlie Siringo decided to hang his sign on the new iron bridge spanning Bluff Creek. It would take a bit of doing; he'd need to link chains to the top of the bridge's battlement and then run 'em through a couple of holes he'd punch in the corners of the painted board that, to his great delight, had turned out "as pretty as a picture." Sure, Kansas, he'd come to realize, had more than its fair share of weather; on a gusty day the oval-shaped sign would be flaying about. Nevertheless, Charlie was certain. This was the perfect spot.

He remembered that two years earlier — two years? It might as well have been in another lifetime — when he'd led the LX outfit and eight hundred fat steers up the Chisholm Trail, the sight of muddy Bluff Creek had filled the worn-out cowboys with excitement and anticipation. It had been a long, slow drive up from the Texas Panhandle during the uncommonly hot summer of

1882, day after day as dry as the piles of bleached chalk-white buffalo bones they saw scattered across the flat plains. Nights took their time coming, but the thin, cool evening whistling through the scrubland was a blessing — for a while. Once they crossed the Red River, the darkness brought new concerns. They were in Indian Territory. Most of the old chiefs had made their peace, but there was always the fear of half-starved Kiowa or Cherokee renegades swooping in from out of the thickening shadows to pick off cattle from the herd, or some ponies from the remuda, and, for good measure, lift a few fresh scalps. But Bluff Creek was the landmark that told the cowboys their ordeal was over. They were coming out of Indian Territory and heading up the end of the trail. Sporting girls, whiskey, and the railroad were only a short, hard ride away in Caldwell.

The Santa Fe Railroad had come to Caldwell, Kansas, in 1880, and now that there was a shipping point to the eastern markets days closer to the Texas ranches than either Wichita or Dodge City, Caldwell quickly became a hurrah cow town. The "Queen City of the Border" the cowboys called it. And once the LX outfit got near Bluff Creek, it was as if whoring and drinking and gambling was all anyone could think about. Around the campfire, there was a lot of hot talk about the rattling good time the boys were looking

forward to at Mag Wood's celebrated Red
Light Saloon.

Charlie, too, had every intention of finding
himself a bottle of whiskey and a sweetheart
to share it. The way he saw it, after more than
two dusty months driving a herd, a cowboy
had earned himself a howling night. But he
was also the trail boss; a leader had a duty to
his men to impart a few words of commonsense restraint. Besides, at twenty-seven he
was older and more experienced than most
of the outfit. He had seen the trouble a fellow could ride into when coming off the
range. So as they were heading up on Bluff
Creek and the talk was getting pretty feverish, Charlie decided it'd be a good time to
tell the hands about the scrape he had gotten
into in Dodge City.

It had been a few years back, the day before
Independence Day 1877, and Charlie, a
twenty-two-year-old cowpuncher, had completed a long drive up the Chisholm Trail
with the Littlefield herd. Sitting with his
chum Wess Adams, he'd been happily drinking the night and his pay away in the Lone
Star dance hall. The place was rollicking,
crowded with buffalo hunters, cowboys, and
flirting ladies hoping to take some money off
them. Bat Masterson, who usually could be
found at one of the poker tables, was working
that night as the barkeeper.

By around eleven P.M., though, things started getting strained; buffalo hunters and cowboys had a tendency to taunt one another, and the liquor helped to erode any inclinations toward indulgence. Wess, particularly, had grown vexed by the disrespectful words. He told Charlie that Jim White needed to be taught some manners, and he wanted to know if Charlie would stand by him in a fight. White was a long-haired, greasy hard case of a buffalo hunter, and about the size of a mountain to boot. Yet Charlie wasn't one to quit on a fellow cowboy. "Start the ball rolling," he agreed.

Wess threw the first punch, and in an instant cowboys and buffalo hunters were going at it. But it was Bat Masterson who drew first blood.

From behind the bar, Masterson hurled one heavy beer mug after another at Charlie. A mug slammed hard into his head, another cracked against a mirror, and suddenly shards of flying glass cut into Charlie's face. With blood streaming down his cheek, Charlie watched as Masterson charged into the fracas armed with an ice mallet. As if he were hammering a fence post into the ground, Masterson pounded away at the face of a big Dutch cowboy. With each solid blow, blood spurted from the Dutchman's face. Charlie wanted to go to the cowboy's aid, but he was too busy trading punches, trying to keep on his feet; if a buffalo hunter took you down, his friends were certain to pile on, and then all would be lost.

Jim White was soon lying on the floor, blood oozing from his head, dying, and the Dutchman's face was raw meat. Then Charlie saw a buffalo hunter plunge a knife into Wess's back, driving the blade in up to the handle and giving it a mean, punishing twist. At once his friend collapsed to his knees. Dodging a flying chair, Charlie hurried over and somehow managed to drag Wess out the saloon door. A deep horseshoe-shaped wound had soaked the back of Wess's shirt red, but he had not lost consciousness. Charlie got Wess on his horse, and he'd just mounted Whiskey Pete, his cow pony, when the sheriff ran over and indignantly barked that they were under arrest. Without a word, Charlie drew his big silver-plated, pearl-handled Colt .45 and charged Whiskey Pete up the wooden steps right at the lawman. The sheriff turned and ran. So with Wess slumped in the saddle and Charlie letting loose a triumphant cowboy yell, the two men put spurs to their horses and galloped east out of Dodge.

Telling the story to the LX hands, he said his point was "to illustrate what fools cowboys were after long drives up the trail." "Had a shot been fired that night in the dance hall," he lectured with an uncustomary earnestness, "the chances are several new mounds would have been added to Boot Hill," Dodge City's graveyard.

Sure enough, Charlie's warning worked. None of his men landed in any real trouble in Caldwell. Instead, to the amusement of the whole outfit, it was Charlie who stumbled; and it was a fall that even an experienced hand like Charlie himself would never have anticipated.

After the cattle had been chuted onto stock cars and were on the rail to Chicago, Charlie passed a pleasant winter in Caldwell. Throughout the cold months he kept warm with festive nights and accommodating ladies. But in March Charlie received a letter from David Thomas Beals, the Boston-based owner of the sprawling LX Ranch. He was ordered to lead more than one hundred head of cow ponies and a crew of cowboys back down to the panhandle. As fate would have it, the same day the letter arrived he also received an invitation from Miss May Beals, the boss's niece, to accompany her to church. And it was after the evening service, while they were standing on the church steps, that it happened.

Miss Beals introduced Charlie to her new friend, Mamie Lloyd. Charlie would always insist that he could not remember a word that passed between them. No doubt there must've been some conversation about the impression the raucous "Queen City of the Border" had made on Miss Lloyd; along with her parents, she'd only recently moved to Caldwell from their home in sedate Shelbyville, Illinois. Still, all Charlie could remember with any certainty was the impression the fifteen-year-old black-eyed Mamie made on him. Though she was still a ruddy-cheeked teenager, he detected a precocious maturity, an impressive promise of authority and confidence. She charmed him, too. Mamie presented herself with a self-conscious shyness, but even in those few moments on the church steps this well-bred reticence would without warning give way to a magnificently mischievous smile. Their one brief, seemingly inconsequential conversation that March evening had an immediate effect on Charlie: "I was a sure-enough locoed cowboy — up to my ears in love."

It was a whirlwind courtship. Mamie's father, H. Clay Lloyd, was, however, a bit of an impediment. The prospect of his only daughter taking up with a freewheeling Texas-born cowpuncher a dozen years her senior did not strike him as a promising match. But Charlie, as he would recall in his typically straightforward way, "wanted her and wanted her badly." He went to work "with a brave heart and a face lined with brass." Charlie pointed out to the old Yankee gent that while there was no denying that since his eleventh birthday he had spent a good deal of his days cowboying and living an adventuresome life on the range, he had managed to work his way up to being a top hand. You don't achieve that position without earning respect, or becoming comfortable with responsibility. With no less diligence, he also convinced Mamie that his love was not simply impetuous but genuine.

Three days after they met, Mamie and Charlie were engaged. Three days after the engagement, they were married. With both Charlie's mother and Mamie's parents attending, the wedding dinner was held in the Phillips Hotel in Wellington, Kansas, a town not much bigger than Caldwell but with a decidedly more respectable reputation. And three days after the ceremony, Charlie saddled up to lead an outfit of twenty-five men, one hundred horses, and six wagons back down to the LX ranch in the Texas Panhandle. He left his new "girl-wife," as he affectionately liked to call young Mamie, behind with her parents.

The abruptness of their separation — not even time for much of a honeymoon — did not sit too well with Charlie. He was torn. He needed a job, especially now that he was a married man. Staying in town, he'd have no way to make a living. Besides, David Beals was the best man he had ever worked for, an honest, broad-gauge cattle man. Mr. Beals was counting on him; it wouldn't do to let him down. Resigned, Charlie rode off.

He spent a hardworking spring down in the southeastern corner of the panhandle in charge of a roundup crew roping and branding some three thousand cows that had been grazing along the Pease River. When he could, he wrote to Mamie. Her letters were more frequent, but their arrival was always bittersweet, each crisp page lying in his hand as if it were a tangible piece of the unlived life he'd left behind. It was an anxious, unsettled time, and the thought increasingly crossed his mind that the cowboy life had lost its charm.

Late in July, he started back to Caldwell with a new herd bound for the stockyards, and he had never ridden up the trail with such a sense of eagerness or anticipation. His reunion with Mamie that September was pure joy; she was even prettier than she had loomed in his campfire memories.

But no sooner was he reunited with his bride than the order came from Mr. Beals to take the outfit back to the panhandle and get another drove. Charlie didn't want to go. The pleasures of sharing a feather mattress with Mamie were a lot more appealing than the prospect of bunking down with a herd of foul-smelling big-horned steers. Still, Charlie decided he'd better obey.

Brooding, his mood growing more and

more keyed up, he went to town and supervised as the cook and a few hands loaded the wagon up with chuck. When it was done, he gave the order to move out, and men and horses started toward the territory line. It was a tense, largely silent departure.

Yet it was only as the outfit approached Bluff Creek that Charlie fully realized the extent of his displeasure. He couldn't go west. He couldn't bring himself to lead his horse across the creek bed and out of Kansas. He felt no need to explain himself to anyone. He simply told Charlie Sprague, a good, responsible hand, that he was turning everything over to him. Then he gave the boys a farewell wave, circled his horse around, and galloped back to Mamie.

Charlie decided he'd become a merchant. First morning back, he woke up next to Mamie, and the comfortable warmth of her body curved around his made him realize he'd never return to his itinerant cowpunching life. Yet he knew he still had to earn a living. And then, before he had time even to worry too much about things, a thought popped into his head: Why not open a store? He mulled the possibility for only a few moments and, satisfied, judged that it offered as good a prospect as any job he'd get in town.

After breakfast, as the rash plan took deeper hold, he strung together some wishful logic and shared it with his wife. Rough as Caldwell was, he explained, eager to convince himself as much as Mamie, there was no denying the town was growing rapidly. A storekeeper who didn't mind a bit of hard work should be able to find himself plenty of customers.

Full of confidence, he rented a vacant room on Main Street and only then began to set about trying to determine what he might sell. He was sitting in the empty space, puffing with a focused, pensive concentration on one of his adored brown cigars, when a flash of inspiration struck.

Other than whiskey and women, what was the one thing you could always count on a cowboy's having a taste for? The answer was, literally, right on his lips: cigars! What would a night of celebrating in a good-time cow town be without a cigar or two? And it wasn't, he raced on with a building enthusiasm, just the cattlemen he could count on as customers. The army was a growing presence in Caldwell. Cavalry brigades had originally arrived to patrol the nearby Indian Territory; keeping the peace between the Texas ranchers who were leasing grazing land to fatten their steers before shipping them east and the renegades intent on poaching required a good deal of diligence. Now additional troops were arriving in Caldwell to turn back the wagons loaded down with homesteaders hoping to sneak over the border and stake their claims to farmland in the Oklahoma Territory. Charlie was certain both the soldiers and the "Oklahoma boomers" flocking to town would also have a hankering for a good cigar.

He scraped together a few hundred dollars to get started and, aided by the seemingly unlimited credit obliging bankers made available, ordered a large shipment of cigars from an eastern factory. The cigars sold quickly, so an excited Charlie decided to offer his customers something more special. Just as cattlemen branded their herd, Charlie got the notion that he should display his own brand name, too. He grandly ordered 100,000 cigars with a trademark phrase, THE OKLAHOMA BOOMER, printed on a distinctive wrapper. It was a colossal shipment; on the day of delivery, boxes on top of boxes of cigars were crammed into the small store. For an uneasy moment, even Charlie wondered if his expectations had been extravagant. But his inventive marketing gamble worked. "They sold like hot cakes," he bragged. In less than a year, Charlie had become, he announced with a self-made man's unrestrained pride, "the Oklahoma border cigar king."

Enjoying his newfound success, Charlie, always bold, decided to expand. He rented the adjoining store, cut an archway between the two rooms, and, once again guided by his own whimful appetitites, announced that he was opening an ice cream and oyster parlor.

It was a bit of an undertaking and, in addition, a costly one. The oysters, packed into deep wooden crates cushioned by sawdust and thick blocks of ice, would need to be shipped by railroad from the East. The ice cream could be churned locally, but people would need to be hired to do the time-consuming work. And since electricity had not yet made its way across the plains to Caldwell, the store's freezers, loaded down with the vats of ice cream and crates of oysters, would require nearly constant hand-cranking. But Charlie was not discouraged by either the complications or the expense. He had been raised in Matagorda County, Texas Gulf Coast country, and fresh, fruit-studded ice cream and briny oysters had been his most coveted childhood treats. He had no doubts that fully grown cowboys and dirt farmers and cavalry men would also have a taste for his boyhood delicacies. And he was right. His Main Street ice cream and oyster parlor was an exotic success. He soon had a staff of five full-time clerks assisting him.

But Charlie was not complacent. He was always — or so it seemed to a bemused Mamie — thinking. And now, two years after stepping into a new life as a merchant, he'd commissioned a sign that he hoped would further expand his already prospering cigar business. He'd found an oil painter in town and hired him to create an advertisement for his Oklahoma Boomer brand. When the painter asked if he had an image in mind, without too much reflection Charlie answered that a scene depicting the rough-and-tumble cowboy life should get the attention of the boys coming off the trail.

Executed in bright colors on a oval board, the finished painting turned out better than Charlie had anticipated: Rearing back in the saddle of a sturdy gray mare, a cowboy had lassoed the hind hoofs of a long-horned steer. But what caught Charlie's excited eye was the recognition that the man in the saddle was the spitting image of him in his heyday. It was his long, rather mournful face, his drooping mustache, his gay red sash twisted around his narrow waist, and his high-heeled Texas boots in the stirrups. I might as well as have posed for it, Charlie rejoiced.

Now he had to decide where to hang his sign. At first he considered placing it above the counter inside his store. It certainly would make the dim place a lot more inviting. But he rejected that location after it occurred to him that it would serve no commercial purpose; if people were inside, he already had their business. There was no sense in wasting such a surefire advertisement on them. And that's how he got to thinking about the Bluff

42

Creek bridge.

The sight of the creek had always stirred him and the boys riding up the trail. It was the gateway to the promised land. What better place to inform a hand coming in from rough country and looking forward to spending his pay that there was a genuine cowboy cigar store in Caldwell?

But once the sign was finally hanging from the top of the bridge, Charlie took one long look and an intense feeling of disappointment set in. He was, he abruptly recognized, no longer the man depicted in the painting. Standing there in his shirtsleeves and suspenders, he had become something less. His merchant's life had grown, as the cowboys liked to say when things turned wrong, scaly. Days that had once been spent with great adventure and the prospect of unforeseen excitement were now uniformly small and dull. He had tried on the settled life, but it had become a tight, uncomfortable fit. Standing on Bluff Creek bridge looking up at the painted sign, he realized the narrowness of his so-called success with a suddenness that was as jarring as it was admonitory. He knew: A storekeeper's life had left him diminished.

Locked deep into this wistful mood, he returned home. In the morning, it had all suited him fine. But now something had shifted. Life on the range should have taught him the fragility of plans; it had been a mistake to allow himself to take to his merchant's calling with so much uncritical determination and resolve. He still loved Mamie, and the fact that she was pregnant held the promise of a further blessing; those feelings were real and beyond doubts. But for Mamie's sake and for his unborn child's, as much as for his own self-esteem, he needed to move on into a life they all could be proud of. He would need to think of something else, another way to support Mamie and the baby that would not leave him so downhearted or, it hurt him to acknowledge, embarrassed. He had been grazing for too long.

As for the sign, it did its job. Like the blue-green waters of Bluff Creek, the hanging oval painting of the cowpuncher roping his steer became in time a landmark, too. And cowboys being cowboys, once the first mischief-maker put a bullet through the sign as he charged across the bridge on horseback, the other hands couldn't help but use it as a target. It remained hanging, but it was soon riddled with bullet holes. Charlie, though, was in no mind to complain. Truth was, it was as if the whole experience of hanging the damn sign had torn a hole through his very being big enough for someone to crawl through.

Two

Like Charlie Siringo, Jefferson Smith was another cowboy who had come in off the range, only there had been nothing tentative or regretful in his decision. Jeff — or Soapy, as most people would later take to calling him — had spent two miserable years in the saddle; driving herds north from Texas up the Chisholm Trail had turned out to be relentless and irritating work. All the busy, dusty days under a baking sun and the dull, quiet nights in lonesome country had ground down what he quickly realized had simply been an ill-conceived, youthful notion. He found nothing to admire or value in the cowpuncher's hard life.

Soapy had been a good rider, though, always sitting well in the saddle, and he drew assignments near the front of the herd. That suited him fine; he'd give the cattle plenty of room to move at their own pace through the stretches of open country while he took to daydreaming. His imagination would drift to thoughts about a way of life that was a bit more leisurely, more suited to the whims of a genial, fun-loving man. His ambitions were vague, but he was certain there had to be an enterprise that held out the prospect of allowing him to make his fortune without the inconvenience of hard labor.

At the end of the long day, sitting with his fellow hands in camp, a tin plate covered with a stew thick with brown beans for dinner, Soapy would boast that he was the son of a southern gentleman, a lawyer. That the family had hit on hard times after the war, moved from Georgia to Round Rock, a dry-as-hay Texas town, that his embittered father had given up the law for drink, and that his mother, a crusty, hot-tempered volcano, supported his brothers and sisters by running a down-at-the-heels hotel famous for the foul-mouthed parrot caged on the front porch, well, those were corners of the family history that Soapy never found reason to share. To hear him tell it — and with all the long nights in camp, the boys had plenty of occasions — he was by birth and breeding cut out for something better than cowboying. His self-esteem was unshakable. And he sure could talk. When Soapy got going, he had a rich way of stringing words together that brought to mind a preacher's Sunday sermon. Yet despite all his eloquence and all his prideful genealogy, a lot of the crew felt there was something about Soapy that didn't quite measure up. The unspoken truth, they soon came around to thinking, was that Soapy just didn't have the backbone for the cowpuncher's demanding life.

But what people thought didn't touch him much. Soapy kept his determination very close, a well-guarded armory of strength. He had his own plans. And so in the summer of 1879, one evening after the cattle had settled into a good bed-ground, Soapy bundled up his bedroll, tied it to his saddle, and took off. He was a strapping nineteen-year-old, cocky about his prospects and, in his breezy, philosophical way, unencumbered by any restraining scruples.

He held no illusions. Soapy anticipated that in his pursuit of easy money he'd need to tread a bit lightly around some people's conception of what was lawful. Not that he was setting out to be an outlaw; robbing banks or horse thieving was bold work and, more troublesome, could get a man hung. And gunplay, too, was something he wanted to avoid. Last year he had seen a vengeful posse shoot down Sam Bass, the notorious train robber, and the frightful scene — the desperado groaning for mercy, his gushing wounds spilling a river of wet, red blood into the sandy Texas street — still stuck in his mind. There had to be easier ways to strike it rich in the West. A quick-thinking, enterprising man, he felt, should be able to rely on the gifts God had given him to make his way. Of course, a little gumption, even a card up the sleeve if it came down to that, would certainly help things along, too. He rode out of camp without hesitation, already imagining the fortune he'd make and the bracing good times he'd enjoy.

Navigating his way in the moonlight across the dark prairie, Soapy was startled to hear the faint, whistling sounds of a calliope playing somewhere in the distance. It was a merry, lighthearted tune, and for lack of any better plan, he followed it. The syncopated clatter led him through the deep shadows that enveloped the unfamiliar country, into the heart of Abilene, Kansas, and on a bit farther, to the outskirts of town. When he crossed the railroad tracks the noise was suddenly booming, and he saw the calliope as well as the pitched tent and wagons of a traveling circus. Years later, after the course of his life had been firmly set, he would look back on this journey and, puffing up his biography another self-important notch, insist that the festive music of a steam organ had guided him through the lonely night to his destiny, as surely as if he had been a wise man following a shining star toward Bethlehem. At the time, though, he just hitched his horse and went off to see if the circus was hiring.

Clubfoot Hall, who ran the shell game in the circus midway, took approving measure of the innocent-looking, smooth-faced young man and was further encouraged by his grand and eloquent way of talking. Here was a boy who with a little instruction might have the makings of a good roper, Clubfoot judged. And moving on his gambler's instinct, he offered Soapy a job on the spot.

Clubfoot had learned the grifter's craft on riverboats decades earlier, and, unencumbered by his deformity, he still practiced it with both dash and skill. Yet to his own considerable surprise, he also proved to be an inspired teacher. Of course, he had to concede, it helped that Soapy was such a gifted and eager pupil. It wasn't long before his protégé had mastered the roper's conversational gambit of steering the marks to the game, as well as the more subtle ploy of encouraging misguided bets. To Clubfoot's prideful amusement, he saw that when Soapy got to talking he could be as persuasive as a six-gun aimed at a victim's heart, and nearly as dangerous. He sure could, as the grifters said, "tell the tale." Another of the young man's natural gifts was his dexterity. Soapy quickly learned to mimic Clubfoot's fast-handed way of keeping the pea deceptively moving from walnut shell to walnut shell. It didn't take long before the pupil's hand, too, was quicker than the sucker's eye.

And from the start Soapy appreciated the one fundamental truth that puts any con into play: A mark desperately wants something for nothing. It was the grifter's sport and challenge to keep the victim believing he'd receive a payoff that was too good to be true. Soapy relished this tense, often inventively complicated game. Even better, he was good at it.

For a while, Soapy traveled with the circus to the prairie cow towns. It was a comprehensive education. He learned the value of bribing the local sheriff; "putting in the fix," Clubfoot lectured, was a business expense that prevented the more costly inconvenience of jail and also provided protection in case a seething victim came looking to get his money back. And while sitting in with Clubfoot as the day's take was divvied up between a half dozen or so players — steerers, inside men, and the requisite muscle — Soapy began to appreciate that the confidence racket was a fraternal enterprise. To pull off the more lucrative and complicated capers, a gang was necessary.

But after more than a year with the circus, Soapy grew restless. He felt he had learned all he could from Clubfoot. The shell game was nimble sport, but he also wanted new, more complex challenges. Besides, Clubfoot would always be the "fixer," the ringleader of the circus gang. Soapy envisioned a world where he'd be running the show. His mind was brimming with potentially lucrative scams. And so with heartfelt thanks, he said good-bye to his mentor and moved on. At twenty-one, he was now a seasoned bunco man.

Soapy drifted through a few cow towns before deciding to join the crowds heading up into Leadville, Colorado. Ten thousand feet high in the Rockies, without even a railroad spur to tie it to the big western towns, Leadville, nevertheless, was roaring. In the summer of 1879 the promise of fortune glittered in the thin mountain air. The town's Matchless Mine was yielding an extraordinary $100,000 a month in silver, and prospectors flocked to the surrounding gulches to try to find their own rich veins. Hotels, saloons, whorehouses, and even an opera house sprang up as if overnight along a muddy stretch of the unruly main street. Each day new arrivals jammed the makeshift town, all chasing after the opportunity to strike it rich. Soapy felt confident that prospectors, men whose trade was the most optimistic of professions, would have a predilection for his kind of speculations, too. They'd be partial to taking a gamble, particularly if it held the promise of an exorbitant return. They'd make the perfect marks.

His instinct was pure cunning. He hit one rich vein after another. But as the silver petered out, so did new prospects for fleecing. Soapy began to realize that continuing to play the same crowd could become a reckless, even fatal enterprise. For the time being people had simply taken to giving him contemptuous looks as he walked the streets. Still, that was enough to make him jumpy. After all, a lot of the miners had a Colt stuck in their belts or a Winchester in their packs. Feeling the moment had turned, he quietly moved on.

Everything Soapy had heard about Denver was promising. In his mind it loomed as a bit more substantial and established version of Leadville, a boomtown that had kept booming. But when he arrived in 1881, the reality proved even more exciting. Denver was on its way to becoming a full-grown city. Its scale, hustle, and already imposing stony grandeur went way beyond anything in his imagination.

Like Leadville, there were streets filled with a seemingly constant buzz of raucous activity. The Larimer Street and Market Street saloons, dance halls, and gambling parlors kept their doors open around the clock. And on Blake Street the sporting girls provocatively worked their trade. Never had he encountered such throngs — an always flowing sea of people looking for good times. Yet, Soapy discovered to his fascination, a sturdy prosperity had wrapped itself around other parts of the far-spread city. Denver was filled with handsome red brick and yellow stone residences, grand public buildings, and wide, elm-shaded streets under piercing blue skies. It was a city where families were digging roots.

Each new day the Union Pacific brought in farmers and merchants from around the country, all hoping to start their lives again out West. Many would continue on to the mountain mines or head off to California, but others looked around and decided to stay. By 1886, there would be nearly 70,000 people living in Denver. And the town was growing rich. Flush with its share of the treasures of gold, silver, coal, iron, and lead that had been ripped from the surrounding mountains — in the mid-1880s, ores worth about $26 million annually were being carted off from the Colorado mines — Denver promised to be the future capital city of the West. Soapy reckoned Denver would be fertile ground for his own ripe future, too. Touring the bustling city left Soapy brimming with an excited, nearly giddy joy. At last, he decided, he had found his home.

THREE

Not every boy growing up in the West in the years after the Civil War, though, wanted to be a cowboy like Charlie Siringo and the young Soapy Smith. That notion never took hold of George Washington Carmack. True, he wound up spending some years in the hill country herding sheep, but that wasn't of his own choosing. And, of course, tending a grazing flock was an entirely different vocation than sitting in the saddle of a sloped-back pony, punching an ornery herd of long-horned cattle. Unlike steers, sheep tended to run together, and one man and his dog would have no trouble moving a herd of considerable size. Cows required much more control, and a crew of mounted cowboys was needed to drive a herd. But it wasn't the solitary nature of sheepherding that troubled George; that part suited him fine. It was just that he had grander aspirations. All George ever really wanted to do was to follow proudly in his father's footsteps. He wanted to find gold.

Like so many other dreamers of the golden dream, Perry Carmack had traveled across the continent in 1849 by covered wagon from the farmlands of Pennsylvania to the gold fields of California. It proved to be a feckless adventure. All his energy, all his high hopes, all his deprivations, all his sweaty, backbreaking ambition — and in the end, only frustration and an overwhelming sense of failure. He never panned a nugget worth bragging about.

Perry didn't have the funds to return to the East, and anyway, he doubted there'd be any work waiting for him. So he found himself homesteading a rocky, inhospitable bit of land in the foothills above the small wheat-shipping center of Port Costa, about thirty-five miles north of San Francisco. The wind coming off San Pablo Bay would lash like a mule skinner's whip, and there was always the unsettling threat of marauders like the Joaquin Murrieta gang preying on lonely ranchers. It was a demanding, unsatisfying life, but he did his best to make a go of it.

He met Hannah Shiles, an Illinois native so sour-faced that it appeared as if all the fun had been wrung out of her, and very quickly they married. They had a daughter, Rose, and then five years later, in September 1860, George was born. In the hot summer before her mother took ill, Rose would remember, the young family would picnic on the grassy banks of the winding San Joaquin River. But even these dalliances could not have brought Perry much amusement. The San Joaquin was busy with swift side-wheeler steamships carrying gold from the Sierra mines to San Francisco. The specially constructed "treasure rooms" in these gold ships famously held millions of dollars of newly mined metal, and the sighting of each big vessel no doubt stung Perry like a rebuke — a reminder of his failure and, no less cruel a taunt, what other, more fortunate prospectors had achieved.

The couple's life together was short, and perhaps that was a mercy. Hannah took to bed a year after George was born and never left. When she finally died, it was as if Perry, too, had been struck down. The burdens of two young, motherless children and a hardscrabble ranch left him overwhelmed. Rose, a thin, sad-eyed girl of fourteen with tight black braids that reached past her waist, escaped by marrying James Watson, who at thirty-eight was the same age as her father. The photograph of the couple on their wedding day shows a seated Watson, dressed for the occasion in a black suit with a somber waistcoat, his thin, dark hair slicked down and a straggly walrus mustache dangling beneath a prominent nose. He's not smiling, merely looking puffed up and self-important. Young Rose, in a calico dress with a bustling petticoat, stands next to him, her hand resting on her new husband's shoulder as if to steady herself. She is staring out at the camera with a look of pure, wild-eyed fear.

Two years later, days after turning forty, Perry just seemed to have had enough of life and fell down dead. George's sole inheritance was his father's broken dream: One day he'd strike the mother lode.

George moved in with Rose and her husband, and although he was just eleven, a fifth grader, this was the end of his childhood. He had a sharp, inquisitive mind, voraciously reading whatever he could get his hands on, devouring dime novels and Shakespeare with equal zeal. He also liked to write poetry; it was his habit to wander off into the hills and then return with an earnest, if rather sentimental ode to the beauty and majesty of the rugged northern California countryside. And somewhere along the way he'd learned to play the piano. But once he moved in with his sister, his formal education came to an end.

Protective of her brother and proud of his talents, Rose tried to convince her husband that the boy should be allowed to continue his schooling. Her hope was that one day George would become a Baptist minister. To Watson's way of thinking, however, school was just an idler's pastime. Days were meant to be spent earning one's keep, and now that he had turned eleven it was high time George started earning his. He put the boy to work tending his flock of sheep.

It was a lonely occupation, a life where George needed to depend on his thoughts for company if he were to pass the time without giving in to despair. What did he think about day after solitary day? The secrets that jump through a young boy's active mind are forever stored in another sort of treasure room. However, there is a clue to at least one wishful daydream.

On George's twelfth birthday, Watson allowed the boy to celebrate by holding a handful of gold nuggets; Watson had received them as payment for a freight shipment he had delivered in his wagon to a mine in the Sierra Nevada. Excited, his eyes shining, George cradled the pieces of gold. In their heft he felt the promise of a larger fortune. "When I grow up," he vowed as though making a birthday wish, "I'm going to be a gold miner."

Birthday or not, Watson had no mind to indulge any foolishness. "Well, son," he said, quickly reminding George of the boy's outstanding debt to him, "you'll do exactly as I tell you until you're twenty-one. After that you can do as you please."

George obeyed. He measured out nearly a decade in dutiful service to the burly, self-confident man who had taken him in as a homeless child. When Watson arranged for neighboring ranches to hire the boy as a sheepherder for $15 a month, George did his work with a convict's forlorn resignation. He grew to hate sheep. He loathed the foul smell, the incessant bleating, the constant shitting. He forced himself to find the reserves of character that would allow him to survive this particular hell. He was already living in the future, an imagined time and place where he'd be his own man, on his own journey, in pursuit of his own fortune. His father's son.

A month after his twenty-first birthday, his debt finally paid in full, George made his long-anticipated move. His immediate concern was to find a way to earn the grubstake that would allow him to support himself while he lived the prospector's uncertain life. He decided on what was, under the narrow circumstances, he told himself, a reasonable plan. George went to the nearby naval base on Mare Island, a skinny strip of land across from the northern California city of Vallejo, and announced that he wanted to join the marines.

The medical exam proved to be nothing more than a quick formality. The blanks on his chart were duly filled: Height: 5'9". Weight: 160 pounds. Eyes: blue. Hair: brown. Complexion: light. The two months of training that followed were rigorous, but George, who had spent an active outdoor life, handled the challenges with skill and little complaint.

Marine discipline, however, chaffed. For someone who had been on his own, who had fixed the meandering course of his shepherd's days largely according to his whims, the constant barking orders and enforced schedule were a torture. Military life went completely against his grain. He gave serious consideration to sneaking out of the barracks late one night as his fellow marines slept their exhausted sleep. He'd get off the island and never return. Let them come looking. He knew places in the hills where nobody, not even the marines, would find him.

But as his basic training came to an end and his plans to become a fugitive took firmer shape in his mind, he learned something that overrode all his previous misgivings. In fact, what he discovered immediately convinced him that he had made the correct, even a providential, decision by enlisting. He was filled with a sudden but deep and irrepressible joy. His platoon, he was informed, was to set sail for Alaska.

FOUR

If George Carmack sailed north to Alaska for adventure, Charlie Siringo had only to walk down Main Street and into the parlor of the Leland Hotel to find himself in a momentous, life-altering experience. Posters had been appearing around Caldwell for days heralding the arrival of a celebrated phrenologist. A man of scientific distinction! A disciple of the famous Fowler! A public demonstration! All were invited! Your true character revealed through an analysis of the lumps, bumps, and configurations on your head!

Normally, Charlie had no truck with this kind of shenanigans. It struck him as the worst manner of tomfoolery, nothing but, as he put it, "wind and graft." Despite all the fancy talk, phrenology, he was certain, was simply one more sly game, and a phrenologist just another bunco man trying to exploit the gullibility of rubes. (Of course, this mild, good-spirited comparison would be knocked for a vengeful loop once Charlie crossed paths with Soapy Smith and his life was on the line; but that encounter was still down the road.)

Yet on this afternoon Charlie, without so much as even a grumble, found himself heading into the spacious parlor of the Leland Hotel. He was still downright skeptical, but two strong reasons had persuaded him that he might as well see what the celebrated visitor to his town was up to.

First, there was his downhearted mood. Charlie was at a crossroads: A merchant's sedentary routine, he'd come to realize, was the wrong fit for his heart. Charlie missed his previous life — his, as he was proud of boasting, "fifteen years on the hurricane deck of a Spanish pony." And yet a cowboy's rough-and-tumble existence sure wasn't suitable for a man with the responsibilities of a wife and young daughter. Each new day behind a counter selling oysters and cigars in bustling Caldwell brought him further proof that the West he'd known was rapidly disappearing. He felt a vast unhappiness over what had been taken from him; and, churning this painful loss, he had a desperate feeling that he would be unable to find his way in a changing, unfamiliar world. It wasn't that he was expecting a phrenologist to provide the answer that would show him a path through his predicament. Rather, Charlie was looking for something, anything, to fill at least an anxious hour or two, and maybe in the process ease for a short spell the turmoil he was going through.

The other compelling reason was a lot simpler: Mamie had her heart set on watching the performance. And no matter how low his mood had sunk, Charlie was still head over heels for his child bride. If Mamie wanted to go, he'd take her on his arm.

So with Mamie by his side, Charlie found two seats in the rows of chairs that had been arranged in the hotel parlor. In the center of the room a single wooden chair had been placed like a throne, only there was no sign of the phrenologist. But just when the crowd — and it seemed to Charlie as if all of Caldwell had turned out — was getting restless, the great man made his entrance.

He had taken only a few steps into the room, his cane tapping as he made his tentative way, before Charlie realized he was blind. Charlie was taken by surprise; and this was, he told himself, one more reason not to have much confidence in what lay ahead. But as the fine-looking old man began to address the crowd in his ringing, confident voice, Charlie decided that it really didn't matter much whether he could see or not. The speaker clearly possessed an immense vitality. And his skill, after all, involved feeling the bumps on people's heads, not looking at them. Besides, the phrenologist seemed well cast for the part. He wore an eastern suit with a watch chain strung across his vest and had a thick hatch of white hair. The man had a respectable appearance; like a college professor, Charlie immediately decided, although he had never met one.

After finishing his preliminary remarks extolling the "science of phrenology," the speaker found his way unassisted to the chair that had been placed in the center of the parlor. Grasping its back with his two hands, he announced in his clear, rich voice that he would like someone to come forward and sit down in front of him. A volunteer? he asked.

"Henry Brown," a voice shouted, and at once many in the audience chimed in to second the suggestion. "Henry Brown, Henry Brown," the animated chorus continued to chant. However, Henry Brown, Caldwell's marshal, was reluctant to come forward. Shaking his head with an obstinate conviction, the marshal made it clear he didn't want to volunteer. The prospect of anyone "feeling" his head and getting an inkling of what was stored inside was not for him. And Charlie was the only person in the room who understood why.

Most of the town's citizens thought Brown was a genuine hero. They'd eagerly pinned the marshal's gold star on his chest after Brown, a newcomer to Caldwell, had demonstrated his courage and his lethal skill in just a few busy weeks. Not only had he killed a couple of hell-raising gunnies who'd been in the process of shooting up a saloon, but he'd also ridden with the posse that had hunted down Spotted Horse, after the Indian chief had attacked a family of settlers. The whole town seemed to think they had found the perfect man for a dangerous job. But when Charlie had first landed in Caldwell back in '82, the sight of Henry Brown wearing a shiny gold star had struck him as damn peculiar.

He knew Henry Brown. Only the Henry Brown he had met had been riding with the outlaw Billy the Kid. Back in '78, when Charlie was foreman at the LX spread down in the Texas Panhandle, Billy and his gang had camped out on the ranch for a while while they were selling a herd of ponies they had stolen in New Mexico. During that time, the Kid and Charlie had grown chummy. Of course, Charlie wasn't under any illusions. He knew the Kid was a killer; in the blink of an eye this jovial young man could suddenly turn terse and steely, and then murderous. But there'd been a target-shooting contest at the ranch and Charlie, to the Kid's surprise, had matched the outlaw shot for shot. And when the Kid had taken a cotton to Charlie's new ten-dollar meerschaum cigar holder, Charlie had let him try it, and then offered it as a present. In return, Billy had presented Charlie with the finely bound novel he'd just finished reading, and in a further gesture of friendship he'd written an inscription on the title page and signed his name. It was this new friend who had introduced Charlie to several of his men — including Henry Brown. That winter, though, Brown and a half-breed Indian had quit the gang and ridden on to Indian Territory.

Come spring, Billy and the rest of the gang had headed out, too. But in October, after branding season was over, they'd returned to the LX and made off with a passel of cattle. Friend or no friend, Charlie wasn't about to let anyone get away with rustling Mr. Beal's cattle. He picked five "fighting cowboys" and went after the Kid and his gang.

The LX crew headed for the mining town of White Oaks, where, Charlie reckoned, the lure of rich prospectors would attract the Kid. But as they made camp after a hard day's ride, Pat Garrett, the sheriff of Lincoln County, New Mexico, rode in. He was forming a posse to go south, down the Pecos River, in search of Billy and his gang. Charlie reckoned this was the wrong direction. Neverthless, he respected Garrett; Charlie had once seen the sheriff wing a drunk in the arm rather than shoot him down. So he turned over two men of his men to the posse and wished Garrett luck.

By the time Charlie and his outfit got to White Oaks, the Kid had fought off an angry mob, killed a deputy sheriff, and escaped. And it was just a week later that Pat Garrett trapped the Kid and his gang in a one-room stone cabin up by the Los Portales road. After a day without food and water, the Kid surrendered.

Charlie hadn't given Brown another thought until he rode into Caldwell and saw the outlaw sporting a lawman's gold star. Figuring it would be best to deal directly with this odd turn of events, Charlie went straight up to Brown and shook his hand. Next thing Charlie knew, Brown was asking — begging him, really — not to give him away. I'm a reformed man, he insisted.

Charlie listened, not saying a word. It wasn't his nature to judge people too harshly. He knew that in the West a man down on his luck might find himself doing a lot of things he'd one day regret; and besides, Brown hadn't been part of the gang that had stolen LX cattle.

Your secret's safe, Henry, he finally told the marshal. No need to worry about any kind of loose talk from me. For more than two years, Charlie had kept his promise. Still, that afternoon he could understand full well the marshal's hesitation.

So Charlie was taken aback when Brown jumped up from his seat and headed for the chair in the center of the room. Perhaps the marshal didn't want to seem as if he had anything to hide. Or perhaps he'd decided he really didn't have much of a choice; they'd keep yelling his name until he "volunteered." Whatever the reason, Charlie watched with a curious anticipation as Brown took his place in front of the blind phrenologist.

Playing to the audience, Brown made an exaggerated bow, then slouched in the chair with an indulgent grin on his face. Without any further preliminaries, the phrenologist began touching the marshal's head. He moved his fingers with a careful, deliberate slowness. Each probing was a journey, a small, intense drama. The phrenologist seemed as if he'd fallen into a trance. As the examination continued, Brown grew increasingly uncomfortable. He was no longer amused. He squirmed in his seat, but he did not attempt to get up.

When the phrenologist finally spoke, his tone was solemn, and as condemning as a judge's decree. You are a man who does not mind bending the truth, he announced. A man of deeply flawed character. A man who should not be trusted.

A collective gasp went up from the audience. There were exclamations of disbelief. The marshal's face had turned a bright crimson. He started to rise from the chair. But with surprising strength, the old man put his two hands on the marshal's shoulders and held him in place. He was not done. He had a final revelation.

You will meet an untimely death, he predicted. A most unfortunate and ignominious demise. "You will die with your neck in a hangman's noose."

The crowd hooted derisively. The joke was on the phrenologist. He was as blind as a bat, so how was he to know he had impugned the character of and predicted an outlaw's death for none other than the town marshal? With his own words, the man had proved himself to be a fraud.

The performance, however, continued. Public entertainment was a rarity in Caldwell, and so any diversion, no matter how farfetched, was appreciated. An indignant Marshal Brown stormed out of the hotel parlor, but everyone else remained in their seats. Only now the townspeople's mood had shifted. They were openly skeptical. Without doubt, the man was a charlatan. They had no faith in the phrenologist's revealing any hidden truths or making any reliable predictions. They simply wanted to have a good time.

So they laughed and catcalled when Theodore Baufman, the portly Oklahoma scout, waddled to the chair in the center of the parlor. Baufman sat there with the proud air of a king as the blind man studiously ran his hand over his head. At last the phrenologist declared, "Ladies and gentlemen, here is a man who, if the Indians were on the warpath and he should run across one lone Indian on the plains, would tell his friends that he had seen a thousand warriors." The crowd whooped in agreement. And a roar of rowdy laughter followed the deflated scout as he trundled back to his seat.

Mamie, although usually shy, went next. When she sat down, Charlie had already made up his mind to intervene if the phrenologist started to cast aspersions on his wife. But there was no need. The blind man ran his hand over Mamie's head just once and then said, "Here is a good-natured little somebody who cannot tell a lie or do a wrong."

Then it was Charlie's turn. He volunteered because he had grown intrigued. It wasn't all guff, as he'd expected. In fact, Charlie had to admit, the phrenologist had said some things that were pretty accurate. Now Charlie was curious to hear what the blind man would say about him.

The phrenologist laid his hands on the top of Charlie's head, found a spot, and began rubbing it as energetically as a bartender polishing a glass. "Ladies and gentleman," he finally said after a good deal of determined rubbing, "here is a mule's head." When he went on to explain that his subject had a large stubborn bump and therefore undoubtedly was as stubborn as a mule, Charlie hooted merrily along with the rest of the audience.

But the phrenologist was not done. He added that the subject had "a fine head." A head that indicated he would one day make a very successful detective.

A detective? Like some desperate character in a dime novel? What a darn ridiculous idea, Charlie silently raged; he might as well have predicted that I'm going to be president. Having some fun was one thing, but Charlie was touchy about anyone thinking they could play him for a fool. He got up so abruptly that the chair he'd been sitting in nearly toppled over. Whatever spark of interest he'd previously had in the performance had been extinguished. The blind man, he informed Mamie with a renewed conviction as he led her out of the hotel, was just another of the West's army of con men, and not a very good one, at that.

Yet Charlie soon would find himself recalling the blind man's words. And wondering.

Five months after the performance in the Leland Hotel, Marshal Henry Brown, along with his deputy, Ben Wheeler, and two cowboys rode into Medicine Lodge, Kansas, and held up the First National Bank. They charged into the bank with their six-guns drawn, and when both the bank president

71

and the cashier refused to open the vault, they shot the two men in cold blood. Then they grabbed whatever cash they could find and rode off. It didn't take long for a hard-charging posse to catch up with them. Before sundown the gang was locked up in the Medicine Lodge jail. And later that night an angry mob stormed the jail and dragged the four men out. The cowboys and the deputy made a break for it, but they didn't get far before they were cut down by blasts of buckshot. Henry Brown didn't try to escape. So a noose was slipped over his head, and he was strung up from a nearby tree until his neck broke. They left him there, the rope squeaking against the bark of the heavy limb as his body swung in the night.

Just as the blind phrenologist had predicted.

FIVE

"Hear ye! Hear ye! Come gather round me, fellow citizens, and rejoice, for I am going to invite you to a feast where money is served with every course," Soapy would typically bellow, as loud as a trumpet, when shortly before noon as he'd drive the light buggy pulled by his big bay horse up to the Union Depot clock tower. As a bemused crowd, mostly travelers coming off an arriving train or waiting for the next one to take them out of Denver, would begin to mill about, he'd hitch the bay to a post. With elaborate ceremony, a performer taking his place on center stage, Soapy would remove his tripe and keister — as he called the stand and suitcase that were the essential tools of his grifter's trade — and set them up on the cobblestones. Finally, when he felt the moment was right, when the audience's curiosity was running hot, he'd stand tall and speak to the crowd with an authority inspired by his memories of his old trail boss setting the day's agenda for the outfit. "This morning," he'd announce, "it will be my pleasure to distribute several hundred dollars among those who gather here."

It was 1883, a time when Charlie Siringo was growing dispirited and George Carmack had in desperation joined the marines. But for Soapy Smith, life had taken a more promising turn. After near on two years in Denver, he'd transformed himself from the dazzled young pup who had stumbled into town. Now he cut quite an imposing figure. He habitually wore a well-cut black frock coat and had a somber black four-in-hand knotted tightly around the high collar of his immaculate white shirt. A wide-brimmed black hat sat flat on his head. His face was no less severe: a carefully trimmed coal-black beard, initially grown to disguise his youth, a thick ridge of black eyebrows, and deep-set, shining dark eyes — a grave and somber countenance. He was a man in black, the image calculated to suggest sober, ecclesiastical propriety as well as both position and expensively tailored success; and yet there was still a hint of menace. Soapy was dressed to do business.

Selling soap was his game, and playing to the crowd, he'd throw himself day after day into the task. "My soap is a universal blessing," he'd proclaim with a booming and fulsome sincerity, "and my untarnished name

74

its heritage. It will cleanse your conscience. It will relieve your life's burdens. It's more than meat and drink in my scheme of the brotherhood of man."

Soapy, though, was too shrewd to bank on either his grandiose rhetoric or a circus barker's promises to persuade customers to spend $10 or even more to buy a nickel cake of soap. Instead, he'd hit on a surefire inducement: money. In many of his bars of soap, he went on, a piece of currency, perhaps a hundred-dollar bill, or a fifty, or, worst come to worst, a ten or twenty, had been placed in the wrapper. As explanation for this startling generosity, he pleaded simple Christian kindness: "The profits from my soap sold in all lands will enable me to beat Old Nick and have 365 Christmas days every year." Loaded down with his self-made bundle, Soapy now wanted to share his wealth. And "plain homely countrymen like yourselves," he'd earnestly assure the rapidly expanding circle of onlookers, should by natural right be the recipients of his good fortune.

Of course, it was all a scam. But shameless, and a born showman, Soapy played his grifter's game with unhesitating sincerity. "Now, my friends," he'd say to the marks as he slipped into his tale, "watch me while I fold the bills in the wrappers." He'd extract a hundred from his wallet; he'd hold it high over his head like a sacred totem; then, each small gesture a performance, he'd fold the bill once, twice, and for good measure a third time; and finally he'd insert the currency deep into the soap wrapper so that it was a well-hidden prize. He'd repeat the process with a fifty and, often, a twenty and a ten, until the moment when, his instincts told him, he had his audience at a boil. They'd be near to bursting with curiosity, eager to get a notion about how those bills might end up in their own pockets.

But Soapy still did not jump into his con. Instead, he paused; and the crowd turned quiet, too, in response. The silence was sudden, and as enveloping as a shared embrace.

When he finally spoke, Soapy found a tone that was pure delicacy. He knew that it was crucial to soften the concerns of anyone who was still feeling a bit ticklish. He needed to win the doubters over. "Gentlemen," he'd say, "if there is any man here in absolute need, let him come up. And if I find him worthy, I will give him a stake."

Some days a prospector down on his luck would shuffle forward, and Soapy, without hesitation, would hand him a bill. This was, he knew, the price of doing business. But it wasn't just that. Soapy, especially when he was flush, had a generous nature. After all, he had done his fair share of hard traveling and could sympathize with someone else's misfortune.

76

Regardless of whether a supplicant stepped forward, though, the crowd would never fail to appreciate this act of kindness. A thunder of respectful applause would break out. And that would be Soapy's signal. The hook had been baited, and now it was high time to reel the suckers in.

"Well, I see that there are no other beggars here, and that you are all worthy men," he'd say. But that left him with a dilemma, Soapy would continue on, but with a newfound hesitancy meant to suggest that he'd spent many a sleepless night grappling with this problem. How was he to settle on a fair "method for distribution"? How should he choose the recipients of his cakes of money-laden soap?

The only sensible solution, he'd explain, answering his own question with a measured, Solomonic wisdom, was to allow people to bid for the bars of soap. "If your eye is keen and your brain alert, you will buy the cake wrapped in the money. While if you are slow and stupid, you will at least secure a valuable soap that will let you ride on its lather over the Rockies and through the deepest mines."

"How much am I offered for this cake of soap?" he'd at last demand in a booming voice, all the time cradling the item in his two hands with an immense solemnity. He wanted the prospectors in the crowd to feel as if a shiny bar of gold had been put before them for their acquisition.

And so the auction would begin. Competing bids would be shouted out in loud, insistent voices, a rapidly building frenzy of greed. It would sound as rough and tumble as a bar fight. But it was all a sham. It was only Soapy's confederates in the crowd vying with one another, just his men going back and forth, raising the price another notch.

When the bidding reached a lofty $40, that was the signal for the shills to sigh with regret and for Soapy to declare a winner. Jumpy with excitement, the lucky man would rush forward to claim his prize cake of soap. In a flurry, he'd unwrap the bar as the crowd watched with a shared anticipation. Lo and behold — a hundred-dollar bill! The winner's whoop of delight would be loud enough to make many in the throng wonder if it was the whistle of an arriving train that had startled them. His joy was sheer ecstasy. And he could not give his benefactor — who, of course, was also his boss — enough thanks; encomiums that Soapy, gentleman that he was, politely dismissed with visible embarrassment.

This hundred, as the grifters put it, was the "convincer." The bidding for the next bar was "solid" — the real thing. Only this time the winner would find nothing in the wrapper but a flat cake of soap. Soapy would reassure the crowd that this unlucky man's loss was their gain; the bars with the hidden green-backs were still waiting to be claimed.

And so it would go. More sales of soap at wildly inflated prices, more disappointed winners, more money going into Soapy's pocket; and, before long, more disgruntled voices beginning to shout from the crowd that this was "a put-up job." When the mood had sufficiently shifted, when the catcalls had turned truly threatening — and another of Soapy's gifts was his ability to gauge the temperature of a crowd — he would promptly put an end to the festivities. "Since so few of you care for money," Soapy, bristling with indignation, would reprimand the assembly, "then I will simply bid you good day."

Now all pretense of ceremony would be gone. His tripe and keister would be packed up with a well-practiced speed. Then Soapy would jump up into his buggy, give the bay the whip, and practically gallop away across the cobblestones. He'd pay no mind to the rude and angry shouts chasing after him. He was already comforted by his confidence that he'd soon enough find a fresh crowd of marks to fleece.

With his soap game, Soapy struck it rich. New arrivals flocked to Denver each day, and the prospect of virtually free money never failed to attract a gullible crowd. He worked nearly all the downtown street corners. It was in the course of putting together this con, recruiting the shills who'd pose as feverish bidders and the intimidating hulks who'd provide the muscle to, as the grifters say, "blow off the mark" if the losers starting showing too much temper, that Soapy built his gang.

Since his days with Clubfoot Hall, it had been one of Soapy's ambitions to be the fixer, the ringleader of his own crew. Now, as crooks and bunco men from across the West drifted into the shiny city of Denver, it wouldn't be long before they'd hear about Soapy Smith. He was a man, rumor had it, who always had a con or two in play. And so they'd track him down in a saloon or at a faro table with the hope of finding work. Soapy, taking to his kingpin role, would make a show of buying the applicant a glass of "the best Irish" and in the short course of the drink would take measure of the man. If he liked what he saw and heard, Soapy would explain that he demanded only one quality from his associates: total loyalty. They must be willing to lie, cheat, steal, or, if the occasion warranted it, kill on his command. If that didn't strike the prospective gang member as too onerous an obligation, he'd welcome the fellow on board. There was no contract, or even a discussion about how large a share of the weekly take they could expect. A firm handshake would be sufficient to seal the vague but tightly binding deal. If you entered Soapy's world, the expectation was that there'd be honor among thieves — and bloodshed if there wasn't.

The recruits became known as the Soap Gang, and what a collection of cunning, broken, and just plain criminal sorts they were. Reverend — the title, naturally, was one more con — John Bowers was their "grip man." By nature a bookish individual, the self-ordained good reverend had put in some long but ultimately valuable time memorizing the fraternal greetings and handshakes of a large variety of secret societies. Now he would patrol the hotels and train stations looking for the telltale lapel pin or ring that identified the bearer as a Mason, or an Odd Fellow, or a Knight of Pythias, or any of a half dozen other orders. Offering the prescribed salutation and the appropriate handshake, the pious-looking man of the cloth would greet his fellow brother. In the course of the ensuing conversation, he would volunteer that he would be only too eager, one brother to another, to show his new friend around Denver. Inevitably, their destination would be a con or a rigged card game that Soapy had in play.

Syd Dixon's role was to give the mark the breakdown. He'd pose as a man of means and he'd encourage the mark to invest, as he already had, in an opportunity that was too good to miss. It was a part for which Dixon was well cast since, like all the best cover stories, it was grounded in a small bit of truth. There had been a time when handsome, bright, smiling Syd, the pampered son of a wealthy father, had lived a cushy life back east as a well-heeled lawyer. His reputation as a ladies' man had been famous. But in the twisting course of the long downward spiral that eventually brought him to Denver, he'd squandered his inheritance, gotten disbarred, and had acquired a taste for opium. These days his remaining Jim Crow eastern suits were shiny from wear, and he looked to Soapy to help him earn the money that would buy him his next opium pipe.

"Judge" Norman Van Horn was another disbarred lawyer, and, like Soapy, he had the smooth gift of telling the tale with eloquence. He also had a impressive knowledge of the law and, no less handy, was an expert on how to wiggle his way around it. His specialty was fixing juries and bribing the police.

"Old Man Tripp" — Van B. Tripplet was his proper name, but it had been long forgotten — was a white-bearded prospector with a weary face as creased as the seat of a hard-ridden leather saddle. He had spent a lifetime looking for gold and silver, but had never managed to strike the mother lode until he had hooked up with Soapy. Now he had great success as a roper, steering his fellow prospectors into Soapy's conniving clutches.

Then there was "Professor" Turner Jackson. While the academic title was an unwarranted boast, there was no denying that the professor knew a great deal about mineral deposits and mines and, more important, how to talk authoritatively about these subjects. Prospectors new to the West would put great stock in his advice — and only realize too late that they were being gamed.

With so many cons in play, it was to be expected that a few of the resentful, gun-toting marks might come looking for Soapy with the hope of evening the score. But Soapy had enlisted a small army to protect him. The chief enforcer was a dull, brutish thug known throughout Denver as "Ice Box" Murphy. He'd earned the nickname (and a lifetime of ridicule) after his attempt to rob the payroll of a local meat market. His plan had been to sneak into the building in the dead of night and then blow the safe. In the darkness, however, Murphy had inadvertently fixed his sticks of dynamite to the door of the meat locker. The force of the explosion left sides of beef scattered about, while the payroll remained locked tightly away across the room in the solid steel safe.

Working under "Ice Box" was a hard crew of veteran gunslingers. "Big Ed" Burns and "Texas Jack" Vermillion wore their holsters low on their hips, and were as coiled and dangerous as a pair of rattlers. They had fought beside Wyatt Earp in bloody Tombstone, Arizona, and the fact that they had survived was proof of their talent. "Shotgun" Tom Collins had earned his nickname from the cannon of a shotgun he toted; one blast could blow a man in half. While "Sure Shot" Tom Cady was a beautiful pistol shot; his draw was quick, and his aim perfect.

It was a very efficient organization. Soapy would set the cons in motion, and his gang would help make sure they came off without a hitch. The opportunities were enormous. "Denver," as Soapy would boast with a larcenous pride, "never had a chance."

But it wasn't all scheming and scamming. Denver was a bright, good-time city, and Soapy, accompanied by his deferential retinue, liked to strut through the downtown saloons and dance halls and have himself a hurrah or two. One of his passions was faro. Many evenings he'd join the other punters "bucking the tiger," as the faro players called their sport, sitting at the long baize-covered table at Big Ed Chase's Arcade. He didn't play with chips, like the rest of the bettors. Instead, he'd dig deep into his pockets and pull out the day's earnings. Then he'd wager twenty-dollar gold pieces on each draw from the box as if they were nothing more than bars of soap; which, of course, they might as well have been, considering how Soapy was making his money. But as fast as he was raking it in on the streets, Soapy was squandering it at the faro table. His huge losses had people talking. Soapy, however, never seemed to complain. A few hours before dawn he'd walk out of the Arcade with his pockets empty, nod a polite good night to Chase, and by noon that day he'd be out again with his tripe and keister.

Fortunately for Soapy, he wasn't recklessly spending money at the faro tables every night. On Blake Street, Chase, who had a keen sense of what people craved, had used some of the profits from his gambling parlor to build a large red brick building for the Palace Theater. The Palace had 750 seats, and most nights they were filled. There were comics and vaudeville acts, but the real draw was the parade of young women who opened each show in frilly skirts short enough to expose their knees. When they kicked their legs up high in unison, many of the men in the crowd sighed as if they were catching their breath. When they weren't performing, the ladies were required to mingle with the audience; and if the mood and the gratuity were agreeable, there were heavily curtained boxes flanking the stage where the mingling could run its course in private. The West was a lonely place for the men who had come in droves from somewhere else to create new lives and find their fortunes; unattached women were in short supply. In Denver, the frolicking pretty ladies of the Palace caused quite a sensation.

Suitors flocked to the stage door, and fellows with dash, wit, money, or simply luck would often find an evening's company. Sometimes, though, the attractions would run deep, and marriages would ensue. No less a longtime womanizer than Ed Chase would marry Frances Minerva Barbour, one of the glamorous Barbour sisters, after first listening to her sing at his theater. Bat Masterson — the very man who years earlier had hurled a beer mug at Charlie Siringo's skull — had followed the money to Denver and wound up marrying Emma Walters, a long-limbed Palace dancer.

Soapy's affections, however, never moved in such a direction. He was content simply to pursue his fancies. And unlike his fortunes at the faro tables, here his luck ran strong. Then one night he was standing, as was his sly practice, in the wings off the Palace stage when he witnessed an event that caused his temper to rise. A gambler he knew from the Arcade backhanded one of the singers as she was heading backstage. It wasn't a hard blow, just a mean, quick slap. But Soapy didn't like men who mistreated women. On instinct, he rushed over and, with a single punch, knocked the gambler down. The man scrambled to his feet, but the wild, resolute look on Soapy's face discouraged him from pursuing the matter. He simply turned and walked away.

That night Soapy accompanied the grateful singer to the boardinghouse where she was staying. Her stage name was Allie, but she told him that her friends called by her real name, Mary. Mary Noonan had long blond hair, which she wore wrapped in a high bun, and a face that was friendly and reassuring rather than beautiful. Yet while many of the pretty dancers and singers Soapy had courted from the Palace were seemingly uncomplicated women, frank about their hopes to the point of brazenness, Mary was a different sort. She was reserved, even a bit standoffish. She behaved as if she had no time for or interest in Soapy. She didn't respond to his attentions with the immediate intensity of feelings that Mamie had so freely offered to Charlie Siringo. Then again, Mamie had been a sheltered fifteen-year-old without either experience or guile; Mary had met enough of the West's lonely men to be guarded. Besides, a showgirl learns not to put too much trust in romance.

Mary made it clear that she wanted nothing from Soapy and that, in fact, she would find the offer of a "present" insulting. Perhaps those rebuffs were what attracted Soapy and first set his mind spinning. Whatever the reason, he intensified his pursuit. And in time Soapy came to realize that she had taken hold of his heart in a way no other woman ever had.

They were married in February 1886. Within a year, their first child, a son, was born. Soapy's life, he understood, had changed dramatically. Yet he attempted to navigate through the responsibilities of love and fatherhood as he did the rest of his tangled enterprises: He played a complicated con. He settled with his bride and baby in a house on Curtis Street in one of Denver's new residential neighborhoods, but he still spent his days and nights working the downtown streets with his crew. There was, as a consequence, an aspect to his life that was seeped in larceny, corruption, and, when necessary, a casual but effective violence. And there was another filled with family happiness, a place that was comforting and where he was comforted. In the end, though, this was one con that was too difficult for even Soapy to play for very long.

Years later, Soapy, ranting with bitter thunder, would still put all the blame for his comeuppance on Colonel John Arkins. And it is true that Arkins possessed several qualities that made him a relentless and effective adversary.

First, he was motivated by a "vision," to

use the colonel's own ardent, deliberately ecclesiastical word, of what Denver could grow to become. He'd realized that the Wild West was rapidly becoming a memory, a reckless and violent era that would live on only in the pages of dime novels. If Denver were to grab its place as the premier city in the new West, it needed to become a destination where newcomers could go about without being harassed, where working men did not need to fear that they would be preyed on by unscrupulous gangs, where families would not have their peace disturbed by louts and villains.

Second, the colonel was a dedicated newspaperman, an editor who, he'd boast with pride, might just as well as have been born with printer's ink running through his veins. After serving in the Civil War as a corporal — "Colonel" was only an honorific title — Arkins had traveled around the Midwest working as a printer. Following the prospectors to Leadville, he'd established the *Evening Chronicle.* By 1880, however, he had realized that the boomtown's time had come and gone. He sold the *Chronicle* and used the proceeds to buy a piece of the *Rocky Mountain News,* Denver's oldest newspaper. The *News* had started out in a rickety log cabin, but it was now housed in a substantial brick building downtown on Patterson Street and had distinguished itself as a crusading civic voice. Yet the colonel had still larger ambitions for his paper, and he saw in Soapy a way to help realize this success. Bandits, he appreciated, were never boring, and front-page stories reporting the exploits of the Soap Gang and its kingpin were a surefire way to sell copies. The nearly daily articles boosted the *News*' circulation, and in the process they made Soapy a larger-than-life villain.

Finally, and not least, the colonel was fearless. When, for example, an argument at Joey's barroom on Curtis Street turned heated and his adversary drew a nickel-plated revolver, Arkins did not hesitate. He stepped forward and, quick and decisive, knocked the man's silk top hat off with a dismissive wave of his hand. Intimidated, the man backed off. The colonel explained with a smirk, "Any man who carries a nickel-plated revolver will not fire it at anybody."

And so the pages of the *News* beat a loud and insistent editorial drum: "Soapy, in the language of the fly-by-night fraternity 'has' Denver"; "The city is absolutely under the control of this prince of knaves"; "His skin games in town are flourishing, he gets his percentage from those to whom he furnishes protection"; "There is not a confidence man, a sneak thief, or any other parasite upon the public who does not pursue his avocation under license from the man"; and on and relentlessly on.

But while there's no getting around that the colonel had it in for him, in the end it was all largely Soapy's own doing. Soapy had no one to blame but himself for the raw anger that overwhelmed his customary calculating and coolheaded demeanor. What happened was that Arkins, trying to keep his long-running story alive, came up with a new angle. He reported that Mrs. Mary Smith was summering with her three children in Idaho Springs under false pretenses. The families in this pleasant summer colony believed that the popular Mrs. Smith was the wife of a prosperous Denver businessman. However, the reality, Arkins gleefully revealed, was that she was married to the notorious Soapy Smith.

As soon as he read the story, Soapy flew into a rage. He immediately rushed over to the newspaper and went directly to the colonel's office. Without a word of explanation, he raised his walking stick and hammered it into the startled editor's skull with so much force that the impact could be heard outside in the newsroom. A punishing fusillade of blows rained down before the astonished pressmen could hurry over and, with some trouble, drag off a wild Soapy. Arkins lay motionless and prostrate on the floor, blood streaming down his face. But he was not dead.

Soapy was arrested and charged with attempted murder. After a little politicking, this was reduced to assault. He was freed on a $1,000 bond. As soon as he got out of jail, Soapy took Mary and the children to the Union Depot and bought them tickets to St. Louis. They would stay with her mother. As he watched the train pull away from the station, he realized with a resigned practicality that his carefully constructed life in Denver had collapsed all around him. He left the city the next day, not bothered at all about jumping bail.

On the run, accompanied by members of his gang who still had faith in his resourcefulness, Soapy drifted through the smaller cow towns. They tried to get scams going in Cheyenne, Salt Lake City, and Ogden. But after Denver, the pickings seemed very small.

Pocatello, Idaho, though, held out a bit of promise since it was a railroad company town and that meant workers would be flush with weekly wages. Yet as soon as the Soap Gang hit town and settled down in a Main Street saloon, the Rincon Kid and his crew came looking for them. Pocatello was his turf, and he had no intention of sharing it. Shots were fired, and two men were killed. In a letter to Mary, Soapy tried to laugh at the incident, joking that he nearly "got his moustache shot off." "The smoke of the pistol blinded me for a moment, but I returned the fire and shot both my assailants. One through the thigh, and the other through the calf of the leg and the heel."

The next day the sheriff escorted the Soap Gang to the station. With a gambler's doggish philosophy, Soapy boarded the first train without protest. Yet he was uncertain of where he was going. He silently longed for the opportunities he had found in Denver, and the comforts he had enjoyed there, too.

Six

George Carmack, meanwhile, had already embarked on his own journey. It had been a rough fifteen-day voyage through choppy ocean waters, but unlike his fellow seasick marines on the USS *Wachusett,* George didn't complain. Day after day he would lean against the rail on the rolling deck of the three-masted ship and look out over a white-capped, gunmetal-gray sea toward the horizon. It was February, a season when the North Pacific was a heavy curtain of dense fog and pelting rain; nevertheless, George's eyes strained against the darkness as if at any moment he would be rewarded with the first sighting of land. He was unsure about what he could expect once his platoon disembarked, but he could not help feeling a building excitement. He was on his way to Alaska.

On orders of the secretary of war, George and the contingent of marines on board the sailing ship were being deployed on a peace-keeping mission to the coastal harbor town of Sitka, the commercial trading and shipping center of the Alaska Territory. Of course, the War Department did not seriously believe that a small garrison of young marines could effectively put down another Tlingit Indian uprising, rein in the rum and whiskey smugglers, enforce the laws protecting the extermination of walruses, whales, seals, and sea otters by marauding trading vessels, or even effectively police the muddy streets of Sitka. In the fifteen years since the United States Congress had reluctantly finalized its purchase of Alaska from Russia for $7.2 million, the official policy toward the district had been one of neglect.

At the time of the sale, feelings had run high in the House and the Senate that Secretary of State William Seward had engineered a frivolous and expensive deal simply to repay a cash-strapped Russia for its support of the North during the Civil War. The sale was loudly dismissed as "Seward's Folly," the half-million-square-mile wilderness mocked in congressional debate as "Seward's Icebox" and "a polar bear garden." The *New York World* compared the territory to "a sucked orange," insisting "It contained nothing of value but furbearing animals, and these had been hunted until they were nearly extinct." Horace Greeley, in the *New York Tribune*, grumbled that Alaska was a "burden . . . not worth taking as a gift." Similarly, one congressman spoke for many prominent and influential national voices when, brimming with frustration, he ranted, "Why didn't we give her [Russia] the seven million and tell her to keep her damned colony? It'll never be of any use to us." In 1877 the territory had been officially declared the Alaska Customs District, but this deliberately vague designation brought no formalized civil government to the area. There were, it was estimated, 33,000 people, largely Indians and Eskimos, spread throughout a wilderness that was nearly one-third the size of the entire continental United States at the time, and for all practical purposes they lived in a state of lawlessness. It was an unruly and untamed land, and the preoccupied lawmakers in Washington accepted this with a philosophical shrug of disinterest. After all, Alaska was undeniably a distant, frozen, and worthless place. The marines on board the *Wachusett* had been sent as a token force, and, it was openly acknowledged, they were a slight token at that.

Yet it was Alaska's very remoteness, the promise of a vast, virgin, and uncivilized country, that attracted a certain kind of individual. As the Wild West grew civilized, as the vanquished Indian tribes settled with dour resignation on government reservations, as the wheels of steam engines clicked and clacked against the metal tracks that stretched across plains where short generations ago herds of buffalo had thundered, and as homesteaders pounded sturdy fence posts and plowed the rich brown earth, stubborn men flocked to this newly acquired territory. Wanderers, trappers, Indian fighters, cowboys, and lawmen, the very men whose fierce, independent, courageous, and often violent ways had shaped the West, now moved on to another lonely and challenging American outpost. They had succeeded in taming one frontier, only to become victims of their own success. They were heroes who had outlived their usefulness. Their spirits found neither joy or comfort in the routine; and — a curse? a blessing? — they had grown accustomed to the sharp edge of uncertainty that shaped an active, dangerous, self-sufficient life. They wanted to grow old boldly, and in the company of new adventures. And so they packed their saddlebags and, as if driven by some natural instinct, began to migrate. They turned their backs on the towns they'd helped build, on the Main Streets where families now strolled, and journeyed north to the last American wilderness.

Along with this legion of daring, restless men came the prospectors. These indomitable sorts had tried their luck in the California gold fields; then, hearing news of fresh strikes, they'd hurried off to the mountain mines in Colorado, Nevada, and Idaho; and now, still dreamers of the elusive golden dream, they arrived undaunted in a new big and promising country. Armed with picks, short-stemmed shovels, and gold pans, they believed their luck would at last change, and that they would finally make the strike that would enable them to purchase new lives. With a faith that was rooted beyond all reason, they knew that somewhere in the icy, desolate silence of this immense, unexplored land, perhaps in the bed of a frozen waterway, possibly in a rocky cave deep in the snow-fields of a dark spruce forest, or in the core of some towering mountain capped by thick, glistening layers of snow and ice, lay what they had been searching for all their working lives. It would take a miracle to find their boodle; but, like all zealots, they knew in their hearts that they were individuals whose lives would in time be blessed by the miraculous. And when in 1880 hard rock gold was discovered near what quickly grew into the mining town of Juneau, there was a collective burst of feverish excitement among this resilient fraternity. This was not the mother lode, but, many were easily convinced, it was a providential sign. Their instincts and calculations had been correct. This last frontier held hidden treasure. Alaska was rich with gold.

In California, George Carmack had heard the rumors of the fortune that was to be found in the harsh and distant north. When the *Wachusett* anchored amid the flotilla of tiny forested islands that dotted Sitka Harbor, George immediately stared out toward the gloomy thicket of mountains with their armor of dark ice that rose high behind the small coastal settlement like the walls of an impregnable fortress. He tried to imagine what lay beyond, out in the wild. He had arrived in Alaska in a marine's blue uniform, but his mind and spirit were seeking another, more heartfelt occupation. Beyond Sitka, in the unexplored snowbound high north county, an empire of unknown dangers and challenges, he would at last fulfill the hopeful destiny his father had passed on to him. George Washington Carmack would strike it rich.

Should I make a run for it?

From the moment of his arrival in Sitka, George began thinking about his escape. His daily life, the U.S. Navy made certain, was rigidly prescribed. Each morning in the numbing cold, his breath nearly freezing in the dawn air, he would turn out with his platoon for inspection. Afternoons would be spent with his fellow marines perfecting endless marching drills on the parade ground across from Sitka's crescent-shaped beach, the late-winter wind too often howling off the Pacific like a discordant military band. And at the end of each exhausting day, tiredness clinging to his bones, he would wrap himself in scratchy U.S. Navy–issued wool blankets and lay in his cot among the rows of beds in the drafty three-story barracks and fall quickly asleep.

Yet even while a busy marine, George remained tightly locked in his own private world. The shepherd's lonely life had taught him how to take shelter in a castle built out of ruminations, and this discipline was once more serving him well. In his active mind, George was so deeply immersed in explorations beyond Sitka's ring of granite mountains that it was as if he'd already fled. The prospect was very sweet.

It would be, he told himself, so easy. Leave his uniform on his cot, walk out of the barracks, and disappear into the seamless pitch-black curtain that fell on a starless subartic night. And yet he hesitated.

There was also — perhaps this, too, a product of his many years of youthful diligence — a practical side to this most optimistic of dreamers. George needed, he realized, to be prepared for what lay out there. If he were to make his solitary way through Alaska, he would need to know how to survive when the cold set in.

He had arrived in Sitka in February, and a month later there were still storms raging, with pelting ice and driving snow so fierce that they shook the little collection of shacks that made up the marine base to their foundations. When storms erupted, the marines had no choice but to slam the shutters tight, stoke the wood fires, and remain inside, praying that the dark weather would pass before they were all blown into the Pacific. How could a man on his own make it through the full blast of a northern winter?

Another anxious realization: As long as he was a marine, George never had to worry about where he'd get his next meal; it was more often than not salt pork and beans, but the cook doled it out regularly and with a generous ladle. In the wilderness, he'd need to make do with what nature offered — provided he had the skill to hunt in bleak or frozen country.

George was shrewd enough to understand that he needed an education in a way of life that was foreign and, by instinct, even unnatural to him. And so while the other marines made it a point to steer clear of the Indians who lived outside Sitka in a compound set off by a high wicker gate, snarling rudely about their god-awful smell and poking fun at the scraggly wisps of mustaches many of the braves sported, George decided he wouldn't be so finicky. He would seek out the Tlingits. He would go through the gate.

It was Aleksandr Baranov, a heavy-drinking, bulbous-nosed merchant and the first administrator of Russian America, who, back in the early 1800s, had originally ordered the construction of a sturdy cedar fence along the outskirts of what was then called New Archangel. "Russians inside the wall, Tlingits outside" was his official edict.

There were three major Indian tribes in Alaska: the Athabascans, hunters who had settled in the harsh interior; the Haida, seafarers and whale hunters who inhabited the islands south of Juneau; and the Tlingits, who numbered about 12,000 and were spread in a variety of clans along the southern coast. The Tlingits were different from the other tribes. They were artists, skilled in carving masks and totems. By instinct they were competitive and ambitious. And as Baranov had discovered when he'd tried to take their land and claim their hilltop fortress, they were warriors.

Swinging stone-headed hammers, the Indians had smashed open the heads of the invading Russian sailors as easily as if they were cracking summer melons. Three separate attacks on their fort had been quickly repulsed. Yet after the failure of the third charge, Baranov, with a cruel practicality, came up with another plan. He directed the captains of the four Russian naval ships in the harbor to fire their cannons at will. The cannonade was relentless and devastating. Booming barrage after barrage of heavy iron balls pounded into the fortress and its small log houses. They whistled through the air and landed with a thudding power that mocked the swing of a Tlingit hammer. The earth shook. Buildings broke apart. And bodies cracked in this thick hail of hard iron balls. Warriors, women, children — all were victims. There was no refuge, and there was no escape.

It was after the Tlingits had surrendered, after Baranov had barked the order that the remains of their fort be burned to the ground, and after he'd begun building his own ample cottage, forever known as Baranov's Castle, on the commanding site of the old Indian fortress, that he decided it would be prudent to keep the Tlingits outside the heart of the settlement. He was still scared. He feared that led by a new bold chief they would arm themselves with their stone hammers and try to reclaim all that had been taken from them. Yet except for a short-lived attack in 1836 and another rebellion following the rape of a squaw by some drunken marines in 1877, the Tlingits, once a tribe of legendary warriors, accepted their defeat with passive resignation.

Each morning many of the Indians would walk past the guards at the fence's wicker gate and enter the settlement. They would trade furs, sell dried salmon, or report to the servants jobs they had at the homes and offices of the white administrators. And by nightfall, they would trudge back to the other side of the fence. Indians on one side; white men on the other. The wicker gate would be solidly bolted. It was a routine that, with few deviations and certainly no debate, had been part of the daily rhythm of life in Sitka for more than seventy-five years.

Only now George decided to break it. He went through the wicker gate, and walked into the Indian camp.

The first thing that struck him was the smell. The air was thick with the acrid odor of smoke, cooking whale blubber, and dried salmon. His nostrils felt as if they were on fire. It was such a high, foul odor that for a moment he decided he'd made a colossal mistake. He did not belong on this side of the fence. But he reminded himself of what was at stake, of what he was trying to accomplish, and then he continued on into the heart of the camp.

The Indians lived in small cabins made from cedar logs, and the homes seemed to have been placed about the camp on whim; he could not detect any logic or art in their arrangement. Some were almost touching each other; others were remote, as isolated as if they were foreign countries. As he got farther into the encampment, word must have spread about the stranger because Indians emerged from the cabins and began to surround him. They looked at him quizzically and, he realized, with suspicion.

He was soon standing in the center of a haphazard circle. He stared back at their brown faces with their flat noses and deep-set dark eyes and did his best to offer up a reassuring smile. There was a long, tense moment when no one moved. The Tlingits studied the intruder. George, feeling more ridiculous than frightened, stood at rigid attention with a happy grin fixed on his face.

At last, when he thought the moment was right, he reached into the pockets of his heavy blue marine coat. With each hand he extracted a bottle of whiskey. It was strictly forbidden to sell whiskey to the Indians; the punishment was a month in the stockade. And George had no idea what sentence would be doled out to the marine who, asking nothing in return, freely gave liquor to the Indians. He doubted, in fact, that his superiors had even contemplated such an unlikely situation. But with gestures and his nonsensical smile, George made it clear to the Indians that he was doing just that. Here was whiskey, yours for the taking.

It took several moments before the Indians were convinced this was not a white man's trick of some kind. But once the first brave took a long swig from the bottle and there were no unexpected consequences, they all stepped forward. Soon the bottles were drained dry.

During that unexpectedly warm summer, George made many trips through the wicker gate and on into the Indian compound. He never appeared without a bottle or two. And in return, he began his education.

It was a more difficult process than he'd previously imagined. Before he could acquire any valuable knowledge or learn the Tlingits' ways, he realized, he had to learn their language. In this he was methodical. And, he discovered to his delight, he had a genuine gift. He would leave the compound and hurry back to the barracks to transcribe what he'd learned that day. His Chinook — as the white men offhandedly lumped together the many dialects spoken by the hundreds of Indian clans — kept growing.

He was proud of this accomplishment, and he could not wait to share his newfound knowledge with the person who mattered most to him. In a letter to his sister, Rose, he was careful not to reveal his ultimate plan, but he did not hesitate to give her a feel of all that he was learning. In two neat columns on a single piece of white paper he created a practical dictionary:

CHINOOK	ENGLISH
Nika sick tumtum nik tika nanitch mika.	I am lonesome for I want to see you.
Spoke nika iskum Nika illahee nanitch Mika.	If some money I will go home to see you.
Spose mika tika Cultus coolie klosh Mika chako kopa Juneau nanitch nika.	I want to go on a pleasure trip you come to Juneau to see me.

It was just a small glossary of phrases, but it was a revealing one. *I am lonesome . . . a pleasure trip.* In his dreams, George was already justifying his escape, already living his great adventure.

In the fall, when herds of gigantic whales returned to plow through the ice-blue waters beyond Sitka Bay, George and his platoon boarded the *Wachusett* and sailed back to Mare Island. He'd decided not to stay in Alaska; he was wise enough to know that he was not ready for the wilderness.

Yet he had not abandoned his plan. He had no doubt that before long he would be making another trip to Alaska. Or that he would return to the Tlingits. He'd grown accustomed to their ways. He felt comfortable in their company. He'd forced himself to swallow chunks of mottled, foul-smelling gray fish without grimacing. He could speak their language. He was becoming one of them.

However, to survive in the wilderness, he would need money to buy supplies. To find gold, he would need to purchase mining tools. It would do him no good to go AWOL from the marines, to head off to Alaska as a wanted man with a federal warrant on his head.

But George had not anticipated the letter that was waiting for him in early November, when his ship finally anchored off the marine base. It was from James Watson, his brother-in-law. His sister, Rose, was gravely ill with pneumonia.

George went immediately to Commander Frederick Pearson, the *Wachusett*'s captain, and asked for shore leave to visit his sick sister. Commander Pearson summarily denied the marine's request. Nevertheless, that afternoon George snuck onto a navy trawler that had delivered supplies and was now returning to the harbor. His days as a marine, George had decided, were over.

SEVEN

Fleeing, warrants issued in their names and, for all they knew, lawmen on their trails, Soapy Smith and George Carmack were on the run. And Charlie Siringo was ready to head off, too. He had made up his mind to flee from his days of wearing suspenders and waiting on customers, from a merchant's life that had never truly fit. But there was more urging him on. His mood had changed. He had outgrown Caldwell, and cowpunching, too, for that matter. His previous lives had worn out, and he was itching for something new.

But what next? He couldn't just saddle up, as he'd done in the past, and head off to wherever Whiskey Pete, his old cow pony, would lead him. Now there was Mamie and little Viola to do right by. They'd need a bit of civilization. And that concern led his thoughts to an unexpected place: Since he no longer felt at home in town or on the trail, then perhaps he should try the big city. The more he mulled it over, the more an idea that had at first been surprising took hold. So in the spring of 1886, along with his wife and their baby daughter, he boarded a train bound for the bustling metropolis of Chicago.

Always full of ambitious notions, Charlie went east with a plan he fully expected would make him rich. And this wasn't some sudden scheme; it had been brewing for a while, all the way back to the winter of '82. In those days he had been the boss of the Beals' horse spread in Indian Territory just across the line from Caldwell, and to help pass the long nights during the Kansas winter the cowboys had decided to subscribe to the *National Police Gazette.* Some of the hands had never had any school learning, but they put a quarter in the pot, too. "We can read the pictures," they said amicably. Charlie, however, could read the words, and a story in the *Gazette* had grabbed his imagination and stayed with him over the years. It was a report about a New York preacher named Potts who had written a successful novel that had earned him "several hundred thousand dollars" and who now was "turning Paris inside out." The image of a writer hurrahing around gay Paree with a fortune in the bank kept building in Charlie's envious mind all the years he was chucking oysters and selling cigars in Caldwell.

Shortly after the birth of his daughter he

had, as he put it, "hit upon the idea of writing a history of my own short, but rugged life." He was a confident man, and diligent, too; he'd written hundreds of pages in his scraggly cursive (one day they would be published as *A Texas Cow Boy*). Now his plan was to arrive in Chicago toting his manuscript, enjoy the acclaim, and then settle into the well-paid writer's life.

It didn't work out that way. There was no denying that Charlie's sprightly sentences and keen eye made him a surefire storyteller, but despite these writerly gifts, neither money nor assignments came his way. Instead he found himself an outsider in a strange, often bewildering city, living in a single crammed room in a hectic Chicago boardinghouse with his wife and baby daughter. Meanwhile, his money was running low.

Charlie needed a way out. And as he was reading the newspaper, he found one. That spring Chicago was a tense, frightened city. He'd arrived just days before a bomb had exploded near his boardinghouse in Haymarket Square; eight policemen assigned to control a labor rally would eventually die from the wounds caused by the explosion, and more than one hundred more, both officers and protesters, had been wounded in the shoot-out that followed. Fears spread that new terror plots were brewing, that Chicago had become a city of targets. A state of anxious vigilance gripped the local business owners, and private detectives were in sudden demand. To keep pace with the boom times, the Pinkerton Detective Agency ran notices in the Chicago papers asking prospective employees to apply.

Charlie was intrigued. The restlessness that had persuaded him to pick up and leave Caldwell was still gnawing at him. Yet here was an opportunity to do something satisfying; a chance, he decided, "to see the world and learn human nature." And joining the ranks of Pinkerton operatives? This would be like, he speculated as his excitement rose, "entering the greatest detective school on earth." The agency was celebrated, christened in the pages of his beloved *Police Gazette* as "the American Scotland Yard."

Founded a decade before the Civil War by Allan Pinkerton, an immigrant from Glasgow who while working as a special agent of the U.S. Mail had received acclaim after going undercover to solve a case involving pilfered bank notes and money orders, the agency had grown into a nationwide operation. While local police, sheriffs, and marshals could not operate outside state lines and were often corrupt, the Pinkertons were a hired army that would travel anywhere to get their man. Tough, tenacious, and at times unscrupulous, they hunted down bank robbers, swindlers, and the gangs that targeted the railroads. An all-seeing eye was the agency's symbol, and the popular newspapers eagerly played along, publishing stories of cases miraclulously solved.

There also was, however, a dark, violent side to the agency's operations. That Pinkerton men had often been employed as brutal, hard-nosed strikebreakers or as spies to infiltrate union meetings — these were complications that didn't intrude on Charlie's evaluation of the detective's mission. He held to the cowboy's harsh code, that right was right and wrong was wrong, and that sometimes a tight noose or a Colt fired in vengeful retribution was needed if law and order were to be enforced. The prospect of hunting down criminals — whether anarchist bomb throwers or rank bank robbers — restored something that seemed to have vanished from his dull life: a sense of purpose.

Once he up his mind to apply for the job, Charlie was methodical in his preparation. He decided he'd need a letter of introduction, so his first stop was the local bank where he had a small (and rapidly dwindling) account. The cashier obliged him:

June 29th, 1886
Gentlemen: The bearer, Mr. Chas. A. Siringo, we know to be a person of good character, and having been a cowboy and

113

brought up on the plains, his services and ability are commendable to you.

S. A. Kean & Co., Bankers

That should do the trick, Charlie decided. But later on that warm morning, when Charlie entered the crowded downtown Pinkerton offices on the seventh floor of the Boyce Building and presented the envelope containing the typed letter to a heavyset man at a desk, it was simply deposited unopened on top of a high pile; and then the clerk, without even a grunt of acknowledgment, returned to whatever it was that was keeping him so busy.

Charlie was not one to wait patiently, or to be ignored. He explained that he'd like the letter delivered to "Billy" Pinkerton.

Now the clerk looked up. You a friend of Mr. Pinkerton's? he inquired carefully.

There was a bite to the man's tone that Charlie found rankling. He was of a mind to teach the fat man some respect. But he also realized his own mistake: While the head of the Chicago office might be called "Billy" in the pages of the *Police Gazette,* that didn't mean he should've have taken the liberty. Still, Charlie wasn't accustomed to apologizing; it struck him as not much better than groveling, and no man who possessed a backbone *ever* groveled. I'd appreciate you giving him the letter, Charlie said. He was frosty, but still straining to be polite.

114

Charlie waited for nearly two hours, all the time getting sharp looks from the constant parade traipsing through the anteroom. People eyed him as though he had been carrying a ticking bomb rather than a banker's introduction. His tiger blood, as he called it, was starting to boil, and he was pretty close to walking out and giving up the whole improbable idea of becoming a detective. But finally he was led into the office of a red-faced man called Captain Farley.

The captain read the letter without comment and returned it to Charlie. After several questions about how Charlie had been earning his living in recent years, the captain decided he was satisfied. Let's go see Mr. Pinkerton, he announced.

William Pinkerton had taken over the Chicago office after the death of his famous father two years earlier. In that time he had made his own name for himself in the press as the indefatigable pursuer of murderers, bank robbers, and arsonists, once following a suspect to Europe and staying on his trail for six dogged months before bringing the culprit home in handcuffs. He was a big, strapping fellow with a bushy walrus mustache and a booming hail-fellow voice. Even seated behind a desk, he seemed bursting with energy, raring to go, the physical embodiment of the Pinkerton motto: "We never sleep." Around the Chicago saloons, he had a well-earned reputation as a burly, bare-knuckled bruiser; after throwing back a whiskey or two, he'd shed his suit jacket, roll up his sleeves, and take on all challengers.

Charlie took an immediate liking to him. Pinkerton, too, felt easy in Charlie's company. Perhaps the detective sensed a spirit similar to his, hard-driving yet at the same time affable, often gregarious. Or maybe he was taken with Charlie's trail boss manner, a quiet authority that came from his having led men through some prickly scrapes. Whatever the reason, Pinkerton apparently made up his mind in a flash. After only a short preliminary conversation, he asked if Charlie could provide the names and addresses of a few references.

Charlie had already given this some thought. The previous night he had sat at a table in the boardinghouse writing down what he hoped would be an impressive list, and now he reeled it off. It included David Beals, his boss at the LX ranch, who had recently become the president of the Union National Bank of Kansas City; Jim East, a celebrated Texas lawman with whom Charlie had cowboyed in the days before East had put on a tin star; and Pat Garrett, the man who had slain Billy the Kid after the outlaw had escaped from jail. Never one to be shy about his own accomplishments — or to hesitate, for that matter, to give them an aggrandizing twist — Charlie couldn't help mentioning that Sheriff Garrett would remember the time he had ridden with him into New Mexico in pursuit of the Kid and a few hundred stolen head of LX cattle. The way he embroidered the tale, Charlie left the impression that not only had he been with Garrett the day the Kid had surrendered, but that the sheriff would've come up empty-handed if Charlie hadn't been around.

Pinkerton dutifully wrote down all the names and addresses. Soon as I hear back from them, we can make things official, he said. But as if to demonstrate that he considered the letters of reference a small formality, he shared what he'd been thinking since the moment Charlie had sat down.

The agency, he revealed, had plans to open a new office in Denver, Colorado. Now that the West was growing civilized and attracting families and men of substance, it would need some serious policing. "A cowboy detective," he said, "might be just the sort of man who can get the job done."

A cowboy detective? Charlie had resigned himself to working out of stuffy offices in Chicago or maybe even New York, an operative in a suit and a black homburg riding streetcars in pursuit of big-city scallywags. But now the prospect of galloping over the plains in his Texas boots and spurs, his big Colt resting on his hip, a cowboy detective, to use William Pinkerton's immediately appealing phrase, chasing down bandits and cattle thieves, well, Charlie was near to rejoicing. This was shaping up better than he could have previously suspected. Still, he wanted to sound professional, like the Pinkerton man he hoped to become. He wanted to say something that he could imagine reading in the *Police Gazette.* "The East is too tame for me," he agreed. "No doubt 'bout it. The West would better suit my wild cowboy ways."

And so it was settled. Once it was established that there was nothing troubling in the replies from Charlie's references, he would begin training. Pinkerton explained that Charlie would need to learn how to tail a suspect without being spotted and how to assume undercover identities. He further expected Charlie to study the agency's *Principles,* a pamphlet that outlined the rules of an operative's conduct; for example, "the ends justified the means" as long as the actions were "for the accomplishment of justice" and that it was forbidden for a Pinkerton to take on a divorce investigation. *Principles* also instructed the operative on how to submit his expenses. And it made clear there was no salary, only a per diem fee while on a case. Within two months, Pinkerton predicted, Charlie would be cleared to report to the new Denver office.

Excited, Charlie rushed back to the board-

118

inghouse. It was only as he was playing out in his mind how he'd break the news to Mamie about their leaving Chicago and heading back west on a new adventure that something else occurred to him. Sure, maybe he had given fate a shove or two by taking it upon himself to walk into the Pinkerton offices and by having had the foresight to have secured a banker's testimonial. But still, there was no getting around it: He was about to become a detective. And that was precisely what the blind phrenologist had predicted.

EIGHT

Actually, Charlie Siringo's arrival in Denver might not have happened without Soapy Smith's help. It seemed that months before Soapy had fled town in the aftermath of his caning of Colonel Arkins, he and his gang had put the screws to a couple of local private detectives. And it was the bloody beating of those detectives that had convinced the Pinkertons to open an office in Denver.

Soapy, of course, had no inkling of the repercussions from his violent outburst. To him, all that mattered was that his actions were entirely justifable.

In his world, the only man worse than a cop was a private detective. Police, whether patrolman or chief, could be bought, and Soapy had paid many a divvy in his time. He'd also put a fair share of private detectives on his payroll. He had no trouble buying them, too. The problem, though, was the cost. Experience had taught him that a private detective would always be wanting a fat wad in return for looking the other way or joining up with the Soap Gang for a little dicker. For that expensive reason, he'd not truck with them at all. Their greed irked him. So when he learned that some skunk detective was spreading a disrespectful tale about him, Soapy was doubly agitated. He went straight off to settle the score.

It all came about because Joe Matthews wanted to make a name for himself. Matthews had just been hired by the Glasson Detective Agency, and his first assignment was to assist the city patrolmen in reining in the bunco men and gamblers crowding downtown Denver. The police had no heart for this work; and, anyway, Soapy was paying them to be lackadaisical. But Matthews was new to the job and full of grit. And when an enterprising reporter for the civic-minded *Rocky Mountain News* interviewed the detective for a story about the crackdown, Matthews couldn't help himself. He bragged about a beating he'd given the notorious gambler: "Smith was finally thumped until he had been condemned by the meat inspector."

That it was not true, that he had never landed a blow on Soapy, let alone pounded him so badly that Soapy's face resembled a piece of raw meat, was one thing. But that some of Soapy's sporting friends were relishing this tall tale, that Soapy couldn't walk down Seventeenth Street without being teased, without, as one of the fellows smirked, "having the life guyed out of him," was another. That was unforgivable. It scarred his pride. And it threatened his business; intimidation was another ace carried up his gambler's sleeve. Furious, Soapy assembled his army and went to war.

John Bowers was the gang's "grip man." Wearing a reverend's collar and an ingratiating smile, he'd spot a mark displaying a fraternal pin or ring, greet him with the prescribed handshake, and then steer the sucker to a gaffed game of chance. Yet when the need arose, Bowers, compact but sparky like a terrier, was handy with his fists and with a blade. "Cap" Light, though, was a full-time hard case; he'd hurt people if given the opportunity, and kill 'em if his blood was boiling. Cap was married to Soapy's sister and had come to Denver leaving a trail of murderous gunfights and brawls behind him. On a Saturday night, Soapy had Cap and Bowers follow him up the stairs to the second-floor Glasson Detective Agency offices. Another three of his gang were ordered to wait nearby, outside the opera house. He'd signal if help was needed.

It wasn't necessary. Soapy charged through the unlocked door hurling curses at Matthews. Before the astonished detective could get his hands up in self-defense, Soapy threw

the first punch. He continued hitting Matthews, going at him with his fists and his feet;
and very quickly Matthews was too beaten to
fight back. Then the real punishment began.
Soapy pounded away until the skin was torn
off his own knuckles. The detective lay in a
pool of blood like a dead animal. In the next
room, Cap and Bowers had pulled Detective
Gavitt from his bed and gone after him
savagely. He, too, was left crumpled on the
floor. Yet their fury remained undiminished.
There were no other detectives present, so
they attacked the offices. Ledgers, files,
lamps, desks — all were subjected to their
spiteful rage.

Nearly an hour after they'd burst into the
Glasson agency, the trio was strolling down
Seventeenth Street, blood staining their
clothes and boots, tin detective stars pinned
to their coats. They took their time. Soapy
wanted the sporting crowd to see him; he
wanted them to understand that disrespect
was a matter that would provoke serious consequences.

Three days later William Glasson officially
closed his offices. He left Denver and never
returned. And it was the absence of any
detective agency in a fast-growing city like
Denver that helped convince William Pinkerton and his brother, Robert, that they'd
found the perfect location for a new branch
office. In fact, when they discovered that the

old Glasson agency offices were available and, since they were a bit worse for wear, could be rented on the cheap, the brothers quickly signed the lease for the second-floor suite. Fresh paint, new furniture, and the Pinkerton name on the door — they were confident that this would make all the difference.

"Let this Mr. Soapy Smith come calling," Charlie Siringo told his new boss, William Pinkerton, after he was informed of the events leading to the abrupt shuttering of the Glasson Detective Agency. "He wants to make a war dance, he'll find himself a partner." But by the time Charlie and his family had taken a Pullman sleeper out of Chicago and arrived at Union Station in Denver, Soapy, with the assault charge on Colonel Arkins hanging over him and a shoot-out in an Idaho train depot giving him further concerns, was on the run. And anyway, Charlie was too busy to give him much thought.

That winter Charlie rented a house on the other side of town from the Pinkerton offices, and Mamie began to unpack and order fabric for curtains. William Pinkerton had instructed the superintendent of the Denver office to break the new operative in slowly, to get him accustomed to acting and thinking like a detective. So Charlie was assigned to investigate a ring of streetcar conductors who were suspected of duplicating their punched tickets. The practice allowed the shady conductors to pocket an extra ten to twenty dollars each day — until Charlie, riding the horse-drawn streetcars across Denver for weeks while all the time keeping watch with a keen eye, documented how the conductors worked the scam.

Of course, riding streetcars wasn't Charlie's idea of high adventure. But he did his best to show enthusiasm and to be tolerant of this tutelage. He was confident the agency would have more challenging cases in store for him once he proved his mettle. So he did what he was told; bided his time; and in secret proceeded with a plan of his own that was much more to his liking.

Charlie's first step was to give himself an alias; he didn't think a Pinkerton operative should attract attention by taking part in what he had in mind. On the Texas cattle ranges, his nickname had been "Dull Knife." The boys had settled on it because when they borrowed his pearl-handled bowie knife, the blade was barely sharp enough, they complained, to slice a fried breakfast egg. Charlie would explain that he used the bowie to kill rattlesnakes. Perched high on his saddle, he'd hold the point between his thumb and forefinger, then throw it down at the snake. He'd pin the snake, but he'd also wind up burying his knife in the ground, too. It was a practice that was certain to dull a blade, he told the boys. After a demonstration, they believed him. But the nickname still stuck. So now, when he was searching for an alias to use when registering for the Cowboy Tournament at River Side Park in Denver, it popped into his mind.

He entered the steer-roping and wild-horse-riding contests, and he gave the crowd quite a show. A newspaper reported: "When Dull Knife rode in armed with pearl-handled pistol and knife, a gold embroidered Mexican sombrero on his head and mounted on a beautiful, quick-reined, white pony he was such a perfect and graceful type of Texas cowboy that the audience gave one spontaneous Ah-h-h! of admiration."

Charlie was the only man that afternoon to succeed in roping and throwing his bronco on horseback, and he wound up winning a $15 check for "Skillful Cowboy Performance." But more important to Charlie than the crowd's cheers or the money was whom he had become in his own mind. As if in an instant, he'd finally shed all the lingering embarrassments and melancholy of his merchant's life. Galloping on his white pony, lasso twirling in the air, he was once again the cow-roping top hand depicted on the sign he had hung from the battlement of the Bluff Creek bridge. Once again he was a man who could walk tall.

■ ■ ■ ■

It wasn't long after the rodeo that Charlie was back in the saddle: The agency sent him out on his first cowboy operation. Bill Mc-Coy had been set to hang after shooting a deputy in Lusk, Wyoming, but had broken out of jail. The outlaw was on the run, and Charlie's assignment was to bring him in.

In Cheyenne, Kalter Skoll, the district attorney, told Charlie he'd a pretty good idea where McCoy might be hiding. Before his arrest, McCoy had been riding with Tom Hall and the gang of Texas outlaws who were holed up at the Keeline Ranch, a vast spread on the Laramie River. One problem, though, was that the Keeline cut through some rugged, high-peaked terrain. A man could hide out forever in those hills without fear of being found. An even more troubling concern, the district attorney explained, was that Charlie was going up against a hard proposition. Three men had already been sent off to get in with the gang, and two of them had turned up dead. The third had hightailed it back to New Mexico.

The next day Charlie bought a horse and saddle and let people at the Cheyenne livery know that he was striking out for Fort Douglas, about a hundred miles north. But that was just what he wanted people to think.

He'd no intention of going anywhere near Fort Douglas. In fact, a plan had already started churning in his mind. It involved getting drunk, and then breaking his leg.

Getting drunk was the easy part. On his second day riding north, when the snow lay deep on the ground and the trail took him near the Laramie River, Charlie stopped for lunch at the Round Up No. 5 Saloon. The place was run by an ex-policeman and prizefighter from Cheyenne and his wife, a former dance hall girl back in the rip-roaring Black Hill days. Both Mr. and Mrs. Howard were growing old, but they hadn't lost either their fondness for drink or, as Charlie soon discovered, their ability to hold their liquor. When Charlie suggested they share a bottle with him after his meal to kill the time, they gladly brought two glasses over to his table.

As the bottle was being drained, Charlie shared his "story." He was, he said, a Texas outlaw on the run and heading north. His hope was to meet up with some friends in Fort Douglas. He knew the Keeline Ranch lay over a small range of mountains some five miles to the east, but Charlie deliberately never asked about it. He just kept up with the Howards glass for glass. When the bottle was done, he said his good-byes, shook hands politely with the couple, and then rose to saddle his horse.

"How 'bout I buy you a glass?" asked Mr.

Howard.

"I wouldn't refuse," said Charlie as he sat back down.

Then it was Charlie's turn to reciprocate. They kept this up for a spell, the two men alternating treating the other to a round. Finally Charlie, starting to feel a little queasy, announced that he better be riding off. But first he bought a quart of whiskey. Charlie said it would keep him company on the trail, though he wound up taking a couple of quick swigs before he made it out the door.

It didn't require much acting to demonstrate that getting on his horse under the circumstances was a complicated undertaking. Still, Charlie did his best to seem drunker than even he already was. He was listing like a boat in a storm, but he somehow managed to keep his seat in the saddle.

"You going to be all right?" the saloonkeeper asked his new friend.

"Soon as I run across my Texas boys, I'll be fine," said Charlie. All he had to do was ride on to Fort Douglas. Course, Douglas was a good fifty miles away. It would make things a mite easier, he suggested, if there were some Texans in this part of the country. Know any I might bunk with? asked Charlie, seemingly full of drunken innocence.

"There are several Texas fellers not far from here, but they're in trouble," Howard offered. "No use going there. They'll kill you. The officers have been trying to get detectives in with them. There are fourteen or so and they all swear they'll kill the next son o' bitch that looks suspicious."

Charlie wheeled his horse around. "If they're from Texas," he answered, "I'm not afraid of them. Just tell me where they are and I'll take my chances on the killing part."

In the distance, Howard pointed out a bridle path that twisted around a high peak. The outlaw camp was on the other side, near a clump of cottonwood timber. But, he warned again, "I wouldn't go there."

Charlie responded by burying his spurs in his horse's flanks and whooping a cowboy yell. Then he galloped off through a thick grove of cottonwoods. There was no trail, and his horse had to jump fallen logs while at the same time Charlie was ducking to avoid tree limbs. It was quite a display of drunken cowboy recklessness — which, despite the whiskey that had his head swirling, was what Charlie had worked out he wanted the Howards to witness.

Riding off toward the mountain, he began thinking through the plan to break his leg — or at least giving the impression that he'd busted it. Charlie got his horse into a gallop as he followed the bridle trail cutting across the mountain that the saloonkeeper had indicated. He figured the outlaws would check his story and that there'd better be a flurry of fast-moving horse tracks. When the narrow trail curved sharply and there was no way a galloping horse, whether the rider was sober or drunk, could've kept his feet, Charlie dismounted. Then he shoved his horse over the rocky bluff.

Whining with surprise, the animal fell twenty feet. It landed on its side in the soft sand of the dry arroyo, just as Charlie had been aiming. It lay there with its wind knocked out, but after a few moments it jumped up to its feet. And Charlie was just as pleased to see that the impact had left a clear impression of the horse and saddle in the sand.

Now it was Charlie's turn. After tying his horse, he climbed high up into the rocks and then jumped. He landed in the arroyo on his left side. Once again there was a distinct impression in the sand. As he led his horse by its bridle back up to the trail, he dragged his left leg across the sand; he wanted to make sure the boot and horseshoe prints would be easy to follow.

Once he was back on the rocky trail, Charlie went to work on his "crippled" left leg. He pulled off his left boot and ripped the seam of his pants leg nearly to his knee. He had a pair of woolen drawers on underneath and he rolled the left leg up above his knee, making sure that it was as tight as possible. This checked the flow of blood, and in only a minute or two his knee swelled and turned red. Satisfied, he gave his "crippled" knee a harsh rubbing with dry grass before, for good measure, pouring some of the whiskey from the bottle he had purchased over the damage. Then he tied his left boot to his saddle, mounted, and rode slowly toward a large grove of cottonwood timber on the Laramie River.

It was open, flat land, and at the edge of the grove Charlie spotted a clutter of log houses. Smoke was swirling out of the chimneys and rising up into a gray evening sky heavy with snow clouds. Charlie couldn't help thinking that if anyone had a mind to shoot, he'd be an easy target.

But no shots were fired. Instead, as Charlie got closer, one man emerged from the cabin and walked to the fence by the front gate. He leaned against it nice and casual, but all the time he kept his eyes locked on the approaching rider. Soon enough he was joined by about a dozen others. Charlie held the horse to a steady, slow pace and kept riding toward the cowboys. He reeled a bit in the saddle as though drunk, but at this point it was all acting. The long row of outlaws was a sight that had sobered him up in a flash.

When Charlie was about sixty yards from the gate, he drew rein as one of the cowboys stepped forward. He was a fine-looking six-footer, and apparently he was the boss; later Charlie would learn that this indeed was Tom Hall. "What the hell are you doing here?" he barked. At the same time Hall held up a hand signaling that Charlie had gone far enough.

"Broke my leg," Charlie explained somewhat plaintively. "I could sure use some help."

Curious, the whole gang rushed forward and gathered round him. The next thing Charlie knew, arms were gingerly lifting him off his horse, while Hall, his voice full of concern, was asking how it had happened. They carried Charlie into the main house and seated him in front of a log blazing in a large stone fireplace. The light lit up the room, and in the glow Charlie couldn't help noticing that each of his saviors wore a pistol on his hip.

They were suspicious. Soon as Charlie was seated, Hall crouched down to examine the damage. The tightly rolled-up long johns were keeping Charlie's knee swollen, and in the glowing firelight Hall also noticed the long scar a large-caliber bullet had traced across Charlie's knee years earlier. When Hall asked about it, Charlie truthfully told him, "You should've seen what happened to the shooter." That brought a small, approving smile to Hall's face.

Nevertheless, with a great concentration the outlaw continued probing and pressing Charlie's knee. He asked Charlie to wiggle his toes, and Charlie obeyed. After all, the last thing he wanted was for them to take him to a doctor. There was some more energetic pressing of the leg muscle, along with a good deal of bending and twisting of Charlie's knee, and in the end Hall finally came around to deciding that nothing was broken. The leg was either badly sprained or out of joint. He instructed one of his men to fetch some hot water and a towel.

As he was carefully wrapping Charlie's knee with the towel, he continued his questioning. How'd you happen to leave the Douglas trail and find your way here? Hall demanded.

Charlie explained that his clumsy horse had stumbled off the trail. Course, he added, with some embarrassment, my having a drink or two might've played a part. Hall listened; his face revealed nothing. Why'd you leave Texas anyway? he went on.

"Why," said Charlie with a sly smile, "the people of Texas tried to get me to stay. They even followed me to the Red River on the Indian Territory border, they were so determined that I stay." The image of Charlie's being chased to the state line by a posse got some sympathetic laughs from the outlaws.

But Hall had already dealt with three detectives, and while they surely weren't cowboys like this stranger, they'd told some good stories, too. He still had his doubts. He dispatched two men with a lantern to examine the spot where Charlie claimed his horse had taken a tumble. Another two rode off to the Howards' saloon to see if that part of Charlie's story was also true.

While they waited for the men to return, Hall applied a dose of liniment to Charlie's damaged leg and then proceeded to roll several bandages so tightly around the knee that now walking was truly impossible. And all the time, Charlie's heart was racing. No one had removed his big Colt from the holster on his hip, but he didn't relish the prospect of shooting it out with a pack of Texas outlaws. His only hope if things got scaly would be to nail Hall with his first bullet and then maybe the rest would lose their will. But looking at those hard faces, Charlie knew it was a hope that had no real chance of playing out. He'd just have to kill as many of them as he could before they got around to shooting him dead.

At about ten o'clock the boys returned. They'd found the tracks where Charlie's horse had gone over the edge. Lucky he hadn't broke his neck, they told Hall. The Howards had confirmed Charlie's story, too. Judging by the foolish manner in which Charlie had ridden off through the woods, the saloonkeeper said, he was not at all surprised to hear about the busted leg. Hell, he'd expected to learn that the drunken cowboy had gotten himself killed.

Hall listened to the two reports, and then invited Charlie to stay until his leg healed. "If you're a detective," he said without a hint of threat in his voice, "you won't be able to keep from showing it. Course, then we'll just take you out to a tree and hang you up by the neck."

Accustomed to cowboy ways, Charlie settled without difficulty into the gang's workday routine. A few of the boys, though, couldn't put their suspicions aside. Johnny Franklin, a bowlegged Texan who had escaped from the Huntsville penitentiary, was the worst. He was always giving Charlie hard looks, waving his pistol in Charlie's face, and warning how he wouldn't think twice about shooting a scheming detective right between the eyes. Hall's tact was to play foxy. He had a habit of feeling Charlie out, trying to find out more about him. Since Charlie had spent a large part of his life riding the Texas plains, he didn't need to invent too much.

Truth was, Charlie loved the subterfuge. He'd always displayed a disregard for danger; it went hand in hand with a natural confidence that bordered on being downright cocky. He felt that living in close quarters with a gang of killers required nothing more than some careful playacting. Not that he wasn't cautious; he slept with his Colt under his pillow and a belt loaded with bullets slung across one shoulder, beneath his long johns. But he was never agitated. And being the cowboy detective, going undercover to infiltrate a gang of outlaws — well, Charlie relished his new calling. Making his way each day on the Keeline Ranch through the tight situations gave him a measure of prideful satisfaction.

Yet there was still no sign of Bill McCoy, the fugitive who had gunned down the deputy. When the gang rode the forty miles into Fort Laramie for a ranch dance, Charlie told 'em his bum leg ruled out any possibility of his dragging a gal around the floor. Instead he bought a bottle of whiskey and checked into a hotel.

He spent most of the night writing letters. The first was his report to the Denver office. He explained that he'd infiltrated the gang and had won their confidence. But he would need more time, months perhaps, to get them to reveal the whereabouts of McCoy. Anyways, the ranch was crawling with fugitives with prices on their heads. The agency could collect some sizable reward money by the time this case was completed. He asked the superintendent to authorize an extended operation, saying he should write back care of the hotel in Fort Laramie. Charlie promised he'd return in two weeks to receive the reply.

After sealing the letter, he found a new

piece of paper and began, "My dearest Mamie." His wife's absence was the single unsatisfactory part of his new life. It pierced him, affecting him in a way he not anticipated. Bullet wounds, he knew from experience, stung like the dickens, but they had always healed. This pain lingered, flashing through his mind without warning and leaving him suddenly unsettled. Nights, though, were the worst. He also felt guilty about leaving Mamie on her own in Denver to care for their little daughter. A husband had a responsibility to be with his family. He ached to give his child bride and daughter a hug. And so he composed a letter that even as he wrote the words left him feeling that he was doing something reckless. Perhaps it was even a mistake. But he didn't consider putting down his pen. If the consequences proved dangerous, he told himself, he and his big Colt would just have to put things right.

He instructed Mamie to take the train to Fort Laramie, along with Viola, and check into the hotel. She was to pretend that she was a widow. He'd be coming by in two weeks to the day. Either he'd have received instructions to return to Denver and they'd make the trip back home together or Mamie and the baby could stay in Fort Laramie for a spell and he'd figure out a way to visit.

With a pang of anticipation, he sealed the letter to his wife. Early the next morning, while the gang was still sleeping off its drunk, he went down to the post office and mailed the two letters. Careful to favor his supposedly crippled left leg, he walked slowly back to the hotel and his fellow outlaws. Soon as everyone sobered up, they'd be riding back to the ranch. Charlie's mind, though, was focused on Denver and a woman with long black hair, which she brushed with a diligent one hundred strokes each night before she went to bed. It would be a long two weeks.

It was little Viola who nearly gave him away. She had been instructed not to call Charlie "Papa," but the child kept making the mistake. No one in Fort Laramie thought it strange that Charlie would be courting the pretty young widow, but when Viola called him "Papa" in the hotel dining room, a few eyebrows were raised. "Girl's rushing things a bit, I reckon," Charlie exclaimed with a good-natured grin, and that seemed to amuse everyone, as well as put an end to any questions.

And getting to Fort Laramie had proved to be no problem. The first time he rode off, he told Hall the truth: He was heading in to pick up his mail. Of course, he didn't say that the letter he expected would be from the superintendent of the Denver Pinkerton office. Nor, upon reading the letter, did he he explain that he'd received authorization for an extended operation: He'd been instructed to stay undercover for as long as was required to ascertain McCoy's whereabouts. And after Charlie had the good fortune to make the acquaintance in the hotel parlor of the pretty widow with the young daughter, none of the gang was the least suspicious about his weekly trips to town. They were simply jealous.

The hard part for Charlie was all the nocturnal sneaking about. He felt it was a funny business for a man to have to tiptoe through a dark hotel hallway to his wife's bedroom. But he knew it would cause a scandal if he got caught going into the young widow's room. As it was, the landlady of the hotel was advising Mamie that Charlie was part of a gang of outlaws and dance hall loafers and she would do well not to associate with him. Mamie and Charlie had a good laugh over that.

They enjoyed a lot of other laughs, too, in their days and nights together. It was as if in Fort Laramie they'd become two different people, the tough outlaw and the young widow, and all the playacting gave their time together a new spark. It was a very happy interlude. Yet Charlie couldn't help growing a bit anxious about Mamie's cough. She said it was just a spring cold, but it didn't seem to be getting any better. He made her promise to consult a doctor as soon as she was back in Denver.

When he wasn't in Fort Laramie, Charlie was leading another life back at the ranch. The gang had come to accept him as one more Texan on the run from the law. They bragged to him about the crimes they'd committed and the jails they'd broken out of. Hall confided that he had ridden with Joe Fowler, a cold-blooded outlaw who had shot a cowboy in the head in Bill Hudgen's Pioneer Saloon and who'd wound up being hung by a mob in Socorro, New Mexico. They would've strung him up too, Hall explained, but his horse was too fast. And Hall finally got around to telling him about his friend Bill McCoy's great escape. It was Hall's plan, and it was an escapade he was mighty proud of.

Once McCoy was sentenced to hang, Hall contacted a slick jailbreaker from back east he'd come across in his travels. He paid him $500. The easterner then went off to commit a petty crime and got himself locked up in the Cheyenne jail. Which was also part of the plan, because the easterner had secreted a pair of saw blades in the soles of his shoes. Late at night as the sheriff slept, he sawed through the bars of the jailhouse window. McCoy squeezed through, and then ran to the horse Hall had left saddled for him in an alleyway. He rode straight out to the Keeline Ranch, picked up some provisions, and then hid out in the surrounding hills. There was a sheriff's posse with one hundred men scouring the territory, but they never found McCoy. He even snuck up on their camp one night and made off with a large bay. Few days after that, Hall went on, McCoy mounted Hall's pet roan racehorse and, using the bay as a packhorse, he rode on to New Orleans. From there, McCoy boarded a sailing ship to Buenos Aires.

Charlie didn't know whether to believe Hall. An outlaw hightailing it all the way to South America to avoid the sheriff struck him as a pretty fanciful notion. But a week later Hall showed him a letter he had received from his old buddy postmarked Buenos Aires, and Charlie realized he wasn't being snookered. McCoy had written to ask Hall to join him; they'd ride together like in the old days. McCoy had hooked up with some outlaws in cattle country, and he provided the name of a dentist in Buenos Aires who could lead Hall to their camp. When Hall asked Charlie if he'd like to head out with him and some of the other boys to try their luck at the rich pickings in Argentina, Charlie realized he had to act quickly.

He rode into Fort Laramie that day and told Mamie it was time to head on back to Denver. And he sent a telegram to the Denver office.

Three days later at daybreak, a large posse

on horseback surrounded the Keeline Ranch. At the same time, a group of deputies had crawled up to the cabins and had their Winchesters cocked and ready. Hall considered the situation, and ordered his men to surrender. Along with the others, Charlie walked out of the cabin with his hands high in the air.

At the Cheyenne jail, though, they let Charlie go. When Hall saw Charlie walking off, he suddenly understood. He flew into a rage, screaming how he'd get even, how he'd hunt Charlie down if it was the last thing he did. He just couldn't believe he'd been taken in by a detective.

Charlie spent a week in Cheyenne making his report to District Attorney Skoll. He had collected a good deal of information over the months, and the district attorney needed all of it to prepare his case for the grand jury.

When he finished up with Skoll, Charlie sold his horse and saddle and boarded a train for Denver. His reunion with Mamie and Viola was a happy one, and he and his wife shared a laugh about the illicit romance between the young widow and the outlaw in Fort Laramie. Still, Charlie was troubled. Mamie's cough had grown more persistent. And now there was blood in her sputum. Whenever she coughed, her handkerchief carried a deep red stain.

NINE

During his long months vagabonding about the West, Soapy had ample opportunity to think about his time in Denver. These memories were instructive. With hindsight, he began to understand his mistakes. Soapy decided his ambitions had been too trivial. The schemes of a circus grifter like his mentor Clubfoot Hall had been tawdry inspirations. It was no longer sufficient, he came to realize, to control a gang of petty thieves.

Like Charlie Siringo, Soapy saw that the West had changed. Certainly, people would always be fools; there'd be no end to the marks who'd believe they could get something for nothing. But all across the civilized new West you could also count on some snooty clique of merchants or do-gooders who'd get the ear of the mayor or the district attorney, and then life for a sporting gentleman like himself would become a continual series of annoyances, harassments, and arrests. There was only one way to guarantee real security and real prosperity: You had to own the entire town. City hall, the police, the courts, as well as the gambling parlors — everything had be under your control.

With these imperial principles occupying his mind, Soapy's life on the run took him to a remote winding canyon high up in the San Juan Mountains, about 250 miles southwest of Denver. He surveyed the spreading assemblies of tents. He strode through the muddy main street. He heard the constant pounding of hammers and the grinding of saws. He observed the army of hopeful men crowding the narrow valley, prospectors whose dreams were inspired by glittering visions similar to the ones that filled George Carmack's head. And Soapy knew: He'd found the perfect place to realize the culmination of all his previous endeavors. He would build his empire.

When Soapy came to Creede in 1890, there was no government, no law. There were just people flocking in, as many as three hundred every day, and money pouring out; in a month, as much as $1 million in silver ore could be mined. The town was wild and booming, and it had all started less than a year earlier with the Holy Moses.

"Holy Moses!" Nicholas Creede had exclaimed when he saw the gleaming vein of silver his pickax had unearthed. Along with his partner, he'd spent the summer working a mine above Wagon Wheel Gap, a steep, twisting river canyon, but he'd never before seen anything like this. By the time the mine was sold that winter for $75,000 to the president of the Denver & Rio Grande Railroad, the claim had become known as the Holy Moses, the town had been renamed Creede, a railroad bed was being laid up the valley, and prospectors were charging in. It seemed as if whenever a miner cleared away a layer of rock from any of the nearby cliffs, silver was discovered. Or at least that was the story, remarkably more truth than rumor, spreading throughout the West.

In the midst of all this tumult, as new fortunes were being made every day, Soapy arrived. He found a makeshift town that to his excited eyes seemed to glow. The business district was nothing more than a field of mud that backed straight up to the rocky face of the canyon. And since there was nowhere else to go, the mountain served as the back wall for the many structures that were being hastily erected. With the clutter of lanterns hanging in these buildings, and with their bright kerosene light reflecting off the slick canyon walls, it struck Soapy as if a glowing sun were shining round the clock. "It's all day in the daytime and there is no night in Creede," he said happily. It was just his sort of wide-open, always jingling town. He had no illusion that it would grow to be another Denver. But he recognized what it could become, and he was determined to make it his.

In the weeks that followed, Soapy's plan to make himself nothing less than the monarch of this high valley proceeded on several fronts. But his first order of business was to commission a map. It was an essential piece of intelligence. In order to take control, he'd need to know as accurately as possible all that lay out there.

On a sheet of Denver & Rio Grande Railroad stationery, a gang member dutifully sketched the layout of the town's mines, stores, and gambling parlors, as well as the names of their owners. And on the top of this crude diagram, he penciled in the observation "Last chance / everything taken." Yet neither this information nor the long list of owners discouraged Soapy. Rather, he took the warning in stride. It just meant that now Soapy knew whom he need to trump.

And largely he did. He employed a variety of slippery methods. In a town where most prospectors believed that they were on the verge of a big strike if only they could find the funds to carry them through another six months, anyone with cash could make an opportune deal. But a swindler with large promises and a stack of phony checks could make a real killing. Soapy would target down-at-the-heels mine owners, convince them to sign over a controlling interest in return for a generous sum, and dutifully write an exorbitant check on a nonexistent account. When they discovered the check couldn't be cashed, he'd offer up a flock of intricate excuses until Cap Light and a few other bruisers would come calling. At that tense point in the negotiations, even the most enraged miner would realize that it would be better to walk away holding a quarter interest in the claim than not to walk away at all. Another well-practiced ploy was to lure the unsuspecting miner into a gaffed game of cards or dice. Inevitably, the mark would lose all his money; and Soapy, a gracious winner, would offer to wager his entire pile against a single scrap of paper — the deed to the mine. Talk about a lucky streak! Once more Soapy would draw the winning hand. These gambits, along with some actual cash purchases, helped Soapy acquire not only mines and tracts of wilderness acres but several dozen additional properties — most of Cliff and Wall streets, a hotel, at least a dozen saloons and gambling parlors, and a dwelling lot where he one day hoped to build a home for his wife and children.

But it was when the state officials arrived in Creede to auction off large parcels of school land — properties owned by Colorado whose sale would fund statewide school construction — that Soapy proved his most ingenious.

A forty-foot circus tent had been erected, and it was crowded with investors from all over the West who'd come to take advantage of the opportunity to purchase land on the cheap in a boomtown. The sale went quickly; there was a good deal of hot, competitive bidding. It was only when a particularly choice lot was offered that one of the handful of attractive women scattered about the crowd would join in. Soon as she made her bid, shouts would break out. "Give it to the woman!" "Let her have it!" "Don't overbid her!" And the well-heeled out-of-towners, gallant as well as fearful of the consequences of any perceived ungentlemanly behavior in a rough-and-tumble mining camp, would acquiesce. The ladies succeeded in purchasing every parcel on which they bid. Only after the leases were signed and delivered did the losing bidders learn that both the women and their vocal supporters were employees of Soapy's. As the *Rocky Mountain News* reported, "Soapy outwitted the authorities, buncoed the state and school fund, and pulled the wool over the keen eye of Governor John L. Routt to the tune of several thousand dollars. The women in loose flowing scarlet robes and glib tongues were acting as cappers for the far-sighted Soapy, and the title of the cream of Creede realty will soon be vested in Jeff T. Smith."

Now that he was the town's largest property owner, Soapy naturally enough wanted assurances that the police and city government would work diligently to protect his investments. So he stuffed ballot boxes, called in favors, grandly canceled several gambling debts, and even padded a few pockets. As a result of these artful manipulations, Creede wound up having officials whose first and foremost allegiance was to Soapy.

Cap Light, a longtime Soap gang tough guy, was appointed the town marshal. He had two obvious qualifications for the job: He had gunned down four men in Texas, and he was Soapy's brother-in-law. It was a pedigree that discouraged most arguments. Just the sight of Cap, his chest puffed out like a barrel, striding into a rowdy saloon would quiet down the hip-pocket brigade, as the gun-toting miners in town were known. But Cap's blood had a tendency to heat, and when it did there were consequences. There was, for example, the night he caught up with Reddy McCann in the Branch Saloon. In fairness, Reddy had done much to irritate the marshal even before their paths had crossed that snowy evening. Not only was Reddy making a play for one of the showgirls for whom Cap had a hankering, but he was a faro dealer at a newly opened establishment meant to compete with Soapy's string of clubs. Add to that, on the icy night in question Cap was already in bad humor after having had to trudge his way through mounds of dark snow as he made his rounds. So when Cap sauntered into the Branch and spotted Reddy at the bar, he couldn't help himself. He let loose with a bombastic and downright rude greeting. His judgment tilted by hours of drink, Reedy responded with a few mean-spirited remarks of his own. Before he could finish, the marshal decided he'd suffered enough humiliation. He drew his gun and shot the faro dealer five times in the chest. There was an inquest, but the ruling was self-defense. So Cap continued to wear his star and, in his fashion, keep the peace.

There were camp meetings to elect aldermen and a judge, but these were sham proceedings. The ballot boxes were as guyed as one of Soapy's faro dealing boxes. And just to make certain there'd be no surprises, Soapy himself did the counting. Landslide victories were the order of the day, and members of the Soap Gang, oafs who had never gotten around to learning to read or write, were sworn in to office.

Yet Soapy wasn't just grabbing with both thick fists. As he thought befit a man in his lofty position, Soapy affected a sense of municipal responsibility. When Reverend

E. A. Paddock came to Creede to build the town's first church, it was Soapy who, in one swift, magnanimous gesture, provided the bulk of the funds. And he could be downright visionary, especially since he appreciated that his vision would help solidify the value of his own investments. Soapy understood that if Creede were to have a future beyond its mining days, the town would need to attract men of substance and commerce. The way to accomplish this, he reasoned, was to elect a mayor whose reputation would inspire confidence.

With that idea in mind, he contacted Herman Strauss of the Levi Strauss dry goods company in Denver. He knew Strauss from his shop on Larimer Street and in a blunt letter offered him the job. That the votes would need to be tallied to make it official, Soapy assured the merchant, should give him no concern. Without going into details, Soapy simply guaranteed that the mayoralty would be Strauss's if he desired it. Intrigued, Strauss came to Creede, looked the town over, but then decided he wasn't interested. Perhaps he recognized that no matter what position he held, the real power in Creede would always reside in Soapy's self-serving authority.

Yet in his heart, Soapy was above all else a gambler, and he transformed Creede into a sporting town. Wedged along a stretch that wasn't even as long as many a freight train, in tents, dim rooms illuminated by kerosene lanterns, and gaudy storefronts with red plush on the walls and crystal chandeliers and piano music and dancing girls, at least sixty establishments flourished. These "clubs," as they were known, operated as saloons, gambling parlors, brothels, and, on Sunday mornings, houses of worship. Day or night, they were always jumping.

Soapy owned at least a third of the clubs outright and had an interest in an equal number. But the centerpiece of his empire and the home for him and his gang was the Orleans Club. Standing in the middle of Main Street, it was a long, narrow building with a large American flag flying from its corniced roof. Faro, dice, and poker were the games, and a wooden bar offered a buffet of free eats featuring bowls of hard-boiled eggs and vats of pickled pigs' trotters. The games were rigged, the decks were stacked, and the food was so unappetizing that it lay untouched until it turned a dingy gray similar to the color of the cliffs outside; when the platters were scraped and the remnants hauled off to the livery, even the burros wouldn't touch it. Yet no one seemed to mind. Most nights, Soapy could count on four hundred or more hurrahing miners filling the Orleans Club.

Hoping to keep the crowds coming, Soapy brought in a trio of musicians from Denver and they had a gay sound that the gamblers enjoyed. He paid them in silver and gold currency, and the gamblers were generous, too, with their tips. But one cold, snowy night a miner playing faro decided the draw was rigged and reached for his Colt. Guns started blasting and a yell went up: "Down on the floor, everybody!" One musician hid behind a potbellied stove; another crouched behind a beer barrel. The shooting went on for what seemed like an eternity, people firing at close range across the room toward one another. Then, with their guns drawn, the men ran out into the street, and the crack of pistol shots echoed off the canyon walls. The musicians had hidden themselves well; they were out of the line of fire, and none of the three was hurt. But in the morning, they decided that Creede was not to their liking and boarded the first train to Denver. Soapy was disappointed, but he appreciated their concerns. After that Soapy made do with only a piano player, and that worked out more successfully since most of the time the musician was too drunk to be perturbed by any gunplay.

Soapy's achievement was swift and total. In about three months, he had fulfilled his plan. He was king of Creede. Everyone he encountered deferred to him. Merchants asked for his advice and hoped for his approval. Women were eager to be in his company. He'd succeeded in an enterprise the likes of which Clubfoot would not have been able to imagine. Yet, he discovered to his bewilderment, it brought him little satisfaction. This troubled him, and set him brooding. Perhaps, he wondered, he was not cut out for this sort of power. Perhaps he required the excitement of a gambler's more uncertain adventures. Though he still wore his old wide-brimmed black hat, heavy lay the crown these days. He controlled an entire town, but there was not one man in his gang worthy of his friendship. He could barely look at them, let alone share a sensible conversation. He would spend days alone in his room reading the Bible. The travails of the ancient Hebrew kings filled him with a sense of recognition. Monarchs like Solomon and David, he felt, were his natural predecessors. He was a cutter with the dance hall girls, yet he missed his wife. Still, he couldn't imagine Mary living here; nor could he blame her. And raising children in Creede? The notion was absurd.

At the same time, he was unprepared to abandon all he had schemed and plotted so energetically to obtain. It went against his grain. His instinct, in fact, was to acquire more, to tighten his control.

Wrestling with these warring thoughts,

Soapy's mood was often skittish. One day he'd be sentimental, filled with a generosity that was almost philanthropic. The next he'd act with a tyrant's stony heart. His gang never knew what to expect, so they gave up trying. They just obeyed.

When, for example, "Gambler Joe" Simmons died from pneumonia, Soapy was knocked for a twister. Simmons and Soapy went back quite a ways; as boys they'd punched cows up the Chisholm Trail. But their friendship had never run deep. Simmons's death, however, left Soapy bereft. Despite a raging snowstorm, Soapy led a procession of mourners up the steep hill to Sunnyside Cemetery. It was a difficult journey. Less than halfway up, the wagon skidded and the casket shot out the back and landed in a snowbank. As a tearful Soapy supervised, his boys carried it back into the wagon. Now the horses resisted; they couldn't pull the load through the drifts of snow. There was talk of turning back, but Soapy wouldn't hear it. He ordered the boys to carry the casket and the case of Pommery he had provided the rest of the way.

By the time they reached the cemetery, the storm had intensified. Soapy, however, insisted on delivering a eulogy. "Did any of you ever know him to do a thing that wasn't square . . . ?" Soapy challenged as thick curtains of snow came down. Of course Simmons, like most of the gamblers at the Orleans, had routinely dealt from a gaffed deck, but no one felt like challenging Soapy in his wound-up state. "The best we can do now is drink to his health and wish him the best there is in the land beyond the range," he continued. At last, on Soapy's command, the twelve bottles of champagne were opened and a toast was drunk to "the health of Joe Simmons in the hereafter, if there is a hereafter." There was a mournful chorus of "Auld Lang Syne," and then the crowd started the long trek down the hill. But Soapy wouldn't leave the grave site. He sat in the falling snow, a limp bundle crying heartfelt tears that only those who knew him well suspected were not just for his departed friend.

Yet when another acquaintance from Denver came to Creede and, with Soapy's approval, opened a dance hall, Soapy had no regard for their years of friendship. He became incensed. The more he brooded, the larger the insult grew in his mind. Friend or not, prior permission or not, Soapy decided an example had to be delivered to the town. If he didn't act, how long would it be before other greedy scoundrels arrived to horn in on his livelihood? He determined that he'd better kill Bob Ford.

Soapy, though, wanted it to seem like a fair fight. A decade earlier Ford had shot Jesse James in the back, and Soapy now decided he would use this history to provoke Ford into drawing on one of Soapy's hired guns. Gunslingers took to following Ford around Creede, taunting him in booming singsong voices with the words of a popular ditty: "Jesse had a wife / A lady all her life / Three children, they were brave. / But that dirty little coward / That shot Mr. Howard / Has laid Jesse James in his grave." Ford had heard it all too many times before. He kept walking.

It was frustrating. Soapy imagined his gunnies would go hoarse before Ford would draw on any of them. What more was he supposed to do? He'd given Ford his chance to show a bit of gumption. If he didn't have it in him, well, Soapy decided, Ford deserved what he got.

Soapy hired an ex-marshal from nearby Bachelor City, Ed O'Kelley. Carrying a double-barreled shotgun, O'Kelley walked into the tent where Ford did business. "Hello, Bob," he said. As Ford turned to acknowledge the greeting, O'Kelley pulled both triggers of the big gun. The blast ripped apart Ford's throat. Gurgling on his own blood, Ford choked to death.

A day or two later, papers were signed that legally transferred the dance hall to one of Soapy's associates.

As the months passed, it got so that the gang

felt they would not be surprised by anything their boss did. But they were mistaken. When Soapy introduced them to McGinty, the boys, for once, didn't know what to make of it. They couldn't decide what was more incredible: the fact that Soapy was brazen enough to try this scam or that the rubes ate it up.

McGinty was nearly six feet tall, weighed a good four hundred pounds, had a bluish-gray complexion, and to the touch was as hard as stone. He was a petrified man.

According to the excited story in the *Creede Candle,* a prospector, J. J. Dore, had been working a claim about seven miles southeast of Creede on a ridge east of the Rio Grande "when he came to a piece of stone shaped like a man's foot protruding from a bank of soil." "Dore," the paper announced, "had found the body of a man turned to stone.

"It is probable that this is the most perfect and interesting petrifaction ever found." The article went on to proclaim: "The man in life had been a well-proportioned and perfect specimen of manhood. Every detail of flesh and muscle is shown in the stone just as it was in life. There is no sign of emaciation. . . . The muscles are as round and finely formed and the surface has the mark of the skin as well as a living man."

On the same front page that reported on the amazing discovery, the paper ran a "news flash": For $3,000, Soapy Smith had purchased the petrified man. He had christened the find "McGinty" and planned to exhibit the body throughout the nation.

"I don't begrudge having invested my three thousand dollars in this piece of stone," Soapy solemnly explained to a reporter the following day. "From all the evidences I have secured I am implicitly convinced that it is a genuine case of petrifaction and that not only myself and the medical world will be benefited by exhibition of it, but also the entire civilized world because of its anatomical perfections."

Of course, Soapy was lying. He had not paid a single dollar for McGinty, let alone three thousand. Then again, Dore had not dug up the petrified man. Soapy had had him manufactured by a California firm that specialized in the ancient Egyptian art of petrifaction. A cadaver had been shipped from Creede (where there were ample unclaimed bodies to choose from), and when the process was completed, Soapy had enlisted Dore. The story of stumbling initially on the exposed foot, then feverishly digging up the stony body, and finally carting it triumphantly into town — all that was Soapy's invention.

It was a showman's fable and, in Soapy's hands, an effective one. From the start, people were curious. Of course, prospectors were by nature a gullible crowd; their profession required that they have faith in the tallest of tales. And when McGinty was laid out on a table in the Orleans Club, the news traveled excitedly around the town.

At Soapy's direction, rows of kerosene lamps with their flues painted black were arranged around the body. The flicker of the many lamps cast ominous shadows across the corpse's gray countenance. It was a strange and disquieting presentation, and it reinforced people's belief that they were observing something wondrous. The price of admission was twenty-five cents, but the line of people snaked down Main Street. It seemed as if everyone in Creede wanted to see the petrified man.

There were precedents for this moneymaking ruse, and these "discoveries" worked to give credibility to Soapy's claim. In 1869, for example, the "Cardiff Giant," a ten-foot stone man, had been "happened upon" on an upstate New York farm. For years it had attracted crowds up and down the East Coast. And "Solid Muldoon" had proved to be an even more profitable "discovery." Unearthed near Pueblo, Colorado, in 1877, it was a perfectly preserved seven-and-a-half-foot-tall apelike creature whose backbone ended in a long tail. After it had been exhibited in Pueblo, P. T. Barnum purchased the 450-pound creature. Authoritatively pronouncing that it was "strongly suggestive of the Darwinian theory," Barnum added Muldoon to his sideshow, and it became one of his most popular attractions.

Soapy, too, had large hopes for McGinty. With the assistance of his gang, he exhibited the stone cadaver in towns throughout Colorado. There were always long lines, and this further encouraged him. Soon he even began to think about returning to Denver.

For a while he'd been feeling as if he had accomplished all that he possibly could in Creede. His exile, he felt, had dragged on for long enough. He had told his gang, The warrant for my arrest is ancient history. Nobody in Denver will remember. Now McGinty helped give his resolutions a tangible justification. With an uncharacteristic measure of anxiety, he placed an advertisement in the *Rocky Mountain News:*

"A petrifaction as natural as life . . . analyzed by the most skeptical, and it has been pronounced genuine by all. $1,000 to any one proving to the contrary. Skeptics, doctors, and all scientific men are especially invited. On exhibition at 914 Seventeenth Street."

It was the ad's concluding words that Soapy had struggled with the most. Finally, he decided: "Admissions 10 cents."

This was less than he had charged in Creede or any of the other towns, but Soapy

162

felt it was essential to all his future plans that the exhibition be a success. He wanted a crowd. He wanted his arrival into Denver to be triumphant.

People came in droves.

Soapy rejoiced. His instincts had been proved correct. Returning to Denver had been the right course of action. And even as people continued to flock to the exhibition on Seventeenth Street, he received what he felt was further confirmation of his wisdom: Creede burned to the ground. A fire had broken out in John Kinneavy's saloon and then spread through the business district. His Orleans Club, as well as the town's other saloons and dance halls and gambling parlors, had been consumed by this inferno.

Right away there was talk in Creede of rebuilding. But Soapy knew he no longer had the heart to stay in that high, lonely valley. He'd sign over control of the Orleans and his other properties to some of his gang and hope they'd be too afraid to skim too much from the earnings. But he wouldn't go back. Soapy had come home, and now that he had finally returned he was resolute. In the morning he'd send a telegram to Mary, in St. Louis, and tell her it was time to come back, too. They'd never have to leave Denver again.

TEN

George Carmack was back home, too. Only unlike Soapy Smith in Denver, his return brought him no peace. George had settled in at his sister's ranch in California, but he couldn't get out of his mind how he had jumped ship and run off from the marines. It had been a spur-of-the moment decision, a rash, angry act provoked by Commander Pearson's refusal to demonstrate an iota of Christian kindheartedness. The commander should've sympathized. A brother, after all, had a right to a visit the ailing sister who raised him. But even as he built the argument in his mind, George knew his justifications amounted to only so much sand. They'd be blown away in an instant by the stern winds of military retribution. The navy wouldn't bother to sort through the circumstances. He was a deserter. They would come looking for him; and when they found him, he'd be led off in chains and then court-martialed. His sentence: four years in the brig, followed by two more at sea. He'd never get back to Alaska.

Alaska! If he was going to desert, he would've done well to have gone through the gate to the Tlingits' camp and not come back. The Indians would've helped, traded him the provisions to make a go of it. They would've guided him over the wall of steep snow-capped mountains and into the wilderness of the high north country. Not even the marines could find him out there, or would they likely have dared. By now he'd have been far up the Yukon River. Hell, he'd probably would've panned his first golden nuggets. He rued the day he had left Sitka.

George's surly mood, however, was softened by the continued improvement to his sister's health. With each passing week, Rose's lungs began to clear, her breathing grew less labored, and her strength returned. It wasn't long before Rose was well enough to get out of bed. She'd lock her arm through his and, as in the old days, they would take a slow walk together down the dirt road to the creek.

Adoring, more a mother than a sister, Rose offered up a constant litany of advice. She urged George to surrender to the authorities. There would be a punishment, to be sure, but the navy, she predicted, would not be vindictive. It would all be resolved, and then he could return to the ranch without the burden of fears and concerns that, she perceived, were now troubling him. "I wish you would hurry and sow your wild oats and settle down with me, for I am proud of my big brother when he is good," she told him. "You don't know how earnestly I pray that you will not walk in forbidden paths."

When Rose wasn't giving George advice, she talked about the ranch. "James has got a good deal of grains in this year and it is looking very well. He is fencing our place with barb wire and he has a good deal of it up. I thought I would have an organ before this time but the fencing took so much money," she confided.

George listened. It was not his way to talk too much; he didn't see the point. In the barracks, everyone would be jabbering, but no one cared what anyone else said. George reckoned Rose would listen to him, but he knew she wouldn't like what he had to say. He didn't want to get into an argument with her. Anyway, how could he explain something he knew she would never understand? So he kept his peace. He didn't share his plan. George just made Rose a promise: After he earned his fortune, he'd buy her an organ.

George liked to be alone and think things out. And he needed money if he was to return to Alaska. When a rancher in Modesto offered him a chance to do some shepherding, George put aside all his old qualms about living with a herd of bleating, shitting sheep and took the job.

The salary turned out to be better than he'd expected. After George's first weeks with the herd, the rancher, satisfied with the new shepherd's way with the sheep, gave him a raise. He was now earning $25 a month — nearly $8 more than the marines had paid him. At that rate, George figured, it wouldn't take him long to put together a stake.

In the meantime, the soft, green roll of the hill country, the fresh spring smells, the sharp colors of dogwood blossoms and rosebushes, and the chatter of birdsong became his companions. The solitude was a comfort; he enjoyed his private worlds. George kept a diary, and in its pages he wrote the log of the sentimental journeys he, alone but not lonely, traveled.

MY THOUGHTS
On Tulare plains amongst alkaline weeds
Or rich wet grass where the wild goose feeds,
My mind far o'er the hills does roam.

In his resolute mind, a compass of desire always pointed north, steady and true.

Then George's will faltered. He met Becky. She was the Modesto rancher's blond-haired daughter, and she made him feel keen in a way he had never felt before. He could even talk to her. They would go walking up into the hills, and being with her, having her next to him, brought George a comfort that left him blissful. He felt it was no longer necessary to put everything down in his diary. He could share the vivid expeditions he was taking in his mind with another person. He could confide in her.

George told Becky about Alaska. He spoke with a conviction that was religious in its intensity. He said it was his intention to go out into the wilderness and discover gold. There would be days of hardship, the challenges of a vast, cold land, a country bigger than Becky, than anyone in Modesto, could imagine. But he was firm. He would go out there — and return a millionaire.

In her wisdom, Becky did not try to argue. Perhaps she understood that there was little point in admonishing someone when they already knew that what they were saying made little sense. Of course George had to realize that finding gold in Alaska was a pipe dream, a pursuit as feckless as the proverbial hunt for the needle in the haystack. Yet if she were to point this out, her carping would only make him stubborn. Or maybe she felt that her presence was argument enough: I am offering you *this*. Another life.

Whatever her reasoning, it was an effective strategy. For the first time, George began to imagine another way of living. He'd never expected to find anyone he would want to be with. Truth was, he seldom spoke to anyone but his sister, and he didn't have all that much to say to Rose. Yet what only weeks ago had been unimaginable now grew increasingly real in his mind: A shared life. A life with Becky.

George called them "my chest of memories." The trove included his recollections of his father, a beaten man, telling him about the days of '49. Or his dad going on about how things would have been different for the whole family if he'd struck it rich. Another was his memory of the heft of the shiny gold nuggets his brother-in-law had allowed him to hold in his hand on his twelfth birthday and the excitement, the animal desire, that had coursed through him. And still another: in Sitka, a young marine staring off beyond the rim of mountains into an unknown world, a realm of adventure.

In the end, the pull of these memories proved too strong. They were as demanding as destiny itself. He could not stay.

When the sting of winter had passed, and before the dogwoods could bloom and a new California spring could work on his resolve, George decided it was time to leave. He'd already saved what he hoped would be a sufficient amount. Besides, he feared that if he delayed any longer, the navy would be bound to find him. On March 29, he said good-bye to Rose and James. He told his sister he'd return soon enough to buy her the organ she wanted so much. As for Becky, he wrote her a note, but then ripped it into pieces. There was nothing he found himself able to say, nothing he could explain. It would always be something that might have been, a life that died before it could be born, a future that never had a chance to unfold. He hoped she would understand that at least; and if she didn't, no words in a letter would be any solace.

He took a train to San Francisco, and there he booked a steerage ticket on the *Queen of the Pacific.* The *Queen* was a new ship, its brass shiny and its mahogany well polished. George made sure he was standing on deck as she glided through the Golden Gate and into the waters of the North Pacific, and the experience left him thrilled. Yet at the same time he found that he couldn't help thinking about the choice he'd made. He was confident that he had done the right thing. Still, he missed Becky more than he'd expected to. Though he was glad to be going, he also felt regret; he'd left something precious behind.

It was a long journey, but the seas were pleasant. The *Queen*'s first stop was Astoria, Oregon. Next, it sailed to Victoria, British

Columbia, where the cargo it had picked up in San Francisco was unloaded from its hold: 3,000 pounds of opium, an equal amount of tobacco, 12,500 pounds of gunpowder, as well as 54,000 pounds of sugar. Lighter, the ship made swift time to Port Townsend, in Washington Territory. George disembarked and boarded the *Idaho*. It was a steamer, a small, old boat that had none of the *Queen*'s polish. But George hardly noticed. He was too excited. The wind blew in his face. Gray-and-white herring gulls screeched overhead. Seals glided slickly in the ship's wake. Dark herds of walruses pounded through the water like a freight train. And beyond the horizon, coming closer each day, straight ahead up the dark, icy Inland Passage, was the gold town of Juneau, Alaska.

ELEVEN

The blast hurled a sleeping George Pelling, the co-owner of the rich Tuscarora silver mine, through the roof. Wrapped in his quilt and blankets, Pelling, along with his mattress, landed in the middle of the Nevada street. He was in shock and both his legs were badly broken, but he was the lucky one. Across town, another explosion had left his partner, C. W. Prinz, in a bad way. Without a mattress to cushion the force of the dynamite, Prinz had been slammed pretty hard. The doctor was certain Prinz was going to die. But somehow he, too, pulled through.

When the men were strong enough, they resettled in the safety of San Francisco, leaving a foreman to supervise the Nevada mine. Yet even before they had fully recovered, they made up their minds to bring whoever had attempted to kill them to justice. They offered a sizable reward for evidence that would lead to the arrest and conviction of "our desperate enemies." When this failed to produce any results, they hired a San Francisco detective agency to track down the bombers. Two operatives went to Tuscarora, but after working undercover for several months, they were unable to produce a single pertinent clue. Dismissing the San Francisco firm, a frustrated and very anxious Pelling went to Denver to hire the Pinkerton Detective Agency.

It will be a ticklish operation, Superintendent James McParland told Charlie when he assigned him to the case. A stranger poking around Tuscarora is bound to attract scrutiny from some tough characters. You must take care not to give yourself away. Remember, McParland warned, there has already been an attempt to murder two men. They won't hesitate to target a third.

Before heading to Nevada, Charlie was instructed to go to San Francisco to consult with the two partners. A ticket had been booked in his name on the Union Pacific, and a room was waiting for him at the Palace Hotel. Pelling and Prinz had thought $250 in expense money should be adequate.

Normally, Charlie would've been elated. A challenging case, and the chance to go carousing around Frisco at somebody else's expense. It was the prospect of opportunities like this one that had persuaded him to become a detective. But Charlie couldn't bring himself to find enjoyment in either new work or the anticipation of travel. Mamie's pleurisy had progressed, and her suffering — each new cough shot through her with a sharp, swift pain — had brought him to the point of despair. He had always been resourceful, but now for the first time in his life he felt truly powerless, unable to take control of the situation.

The tissue surrounding her lungs had become so inflamed, and her breathing had become such a struggle, that the doctors in Denver had determined that only an operation would save her life. Mamie's father begged that it be performed in Springfield, Missouri, where he was living with his new wife. Mamie thought that was a good idea, too; that way there'd be someone to care for little Viola while she recovered. Meanwhile, Charlie could get back to work. Her illness had already built up a mountain of doctors' bills; the expense of an operation would only add to the daunting pile. You can't afford to give up your job, she admonished her husband.

The thought of his child bride undergoing a difficult operation without his being around to comfort her left Charlie at a loss. It did not seem the way things should be done. Charlie did not want to let Mamie leave. But he also understood that Mamie's argument made good sense. Viola needed to be looked after, and money certainly had to be earned.

Still, as he put Mamie and Viola on an east-bound train, he couldn't help feeling disap-pointed in himself, as if he'd betrayed some unwritten code. That same morning, raw with guilt about his decision, Charlie boarded a flyer heading west.

The next nine months stretched Charlie's nerves. There were a passel of dangerous men in Tuscarora; they were aligned with labor and they were determined to give the forces of capital — which the two mine owners, Pel-ling and Prinz, represented — a solid thump-ing. But once again the cowboy detective proved up to the task. He presented himself as a Texan with a rich father, a scoundrel who'd skipped out from his fancy home after getting involved in a scrape that had ended in a killing. It was an easy role for Charlie to play because all the time he was in Nevada he felt like a cavalier villain. The remorse he suffered over allowing Mamie to go to Spring-field on her own weighed him down.

In time, he became a confidant of some hard characters. He went with them on hunt-ing trips into Indian Territory, and did some gold prospecting with them, too. And in the process, he acquired the names of the men who had hired the bombers, as well as learn-ing the identities of the men who had cut the fuses to an exact length and touched them off at the same time with the intention of simultaneously blowing the two mine owners to bits.

As the case had moved forward, the letters Charlie received from Springfield brought him encouragement and helped steady his mood. Mamie's operation had been a success and her recovery was rapid, even encouraging. The last letter that arrived in Nevada, however, left him positively jubilant: When Charlie returned to Denver, Mamie and Viola would be there to welcome him.

It seemed nothing short of a miracle. Mamie was her old active self. In his cowpunching days, Charlie had on several occasions ridden herds of longhorns through lightning storms. Once the thunder started cracking and the sky flashing, all a cowboy could do was to try to keep his mount. He'd seen too many good hands get knocked to the ground and then trampled by a runaway herd of frightened steers before the storm played itself out. Well, he'd kept his saddle, and this storm, too, had finally passed. Now it was beautiful sunny weather and he and his family could ride on. When Superintendent McParland offered him another cowboy operation, he consulted with Mamie. At her urging, he signed on.

Charlie was on the trail of a counterfeiter who'd etched an ingenious steel plate for manufacturing twenty-dollar bills when, as was his habit, he checked in at a telegraph office. In Salt Lake City there was a telegram waiting for him. It was from McParland: Return soonest. Mamie sick.

Charlie got back to Denver in time. He was holding Mamie upright by an open window, supporting her as she tried to swallow a taste of fresh air, when the struggle proved too much for her. Mamie died in his arms.

The next week there was much to keep Charlie busy, what with people to notify, then the funeral, and always little Viola to watch after. He was able to pretend to himself that this was one more rough storm he'd simply have to ride through. After the funeral, when Mamie's aunt, Mrs. Will Read, pleaded that she be allowed to take the child back with her to Shelbyville, Illinois, Charlie resisted. But in the end, he realized the wisdom of this plan. Mrs. Read was a noble woman and she had no children of her own to raise; certainly Viola would be better off with her than in the care of a cowboy detective ready to hit the trail with the announcement of his next case. As soon as Viola left, however, Charlie had no choice but stare into the eye of this storm. And he understood: There'd be no riding this one out.

The next year passed in a blur. One day he got the notion to ride down to New Mexico; he'd always been partial to the weather in those parts. But after he arrived, he let his horse rest for a day and then started the long trip back to Denver. And all the time he was drinking, draining bottle after bottle, a sea of whiskey that, he'd confess without an iota of guilt, "would have made the angels weep."

Superintendent James McParland, the head of the Denver Pinkerton office, had also noticed the change that had taken hold of his star operative. McParland was not insensitive; he appreciated the pain the loss of a young, beloved spouse could inflict. But McParland was also a practical man. He decided that something had to be done to lift Siringo out of his doldrums, or else the agency had better find someone to take the fellow's place. And so when none other than Mr. Robert Pinkerton himself came to him with a case that had left the Portland office perplexed, McParland realized this was the perfect opportunity to get his cowboy detective back in the saddle. He summoned Siringo to his office.

The agency had signed on to investigate a robbery, McParland began. Quite a puzzling case.

Before the superintendent could get any further, Charlie cut him off. I'm not interested, he said. He didn't want to work. He didn't want to do anything, except sit in his room and drain another bottle of whiskey.

McParland was both cross and exasperated. It was impossible to run a detective agency when one of the operatives — his best man, to boot! — kept refusing assignments. He was of a mind to wash his hands of the whole matter. But he genuinely liked Siringo; the fellow had previously shown a lot of grit. And there were operational reasons to consider, too: This would be a dangerous, unpredictable case. The operative would need to work for weeks, or perhaps even longer, in an isolated and lawless frontier. He would be at great risk; and the odds of his succeeding were, as the Portland office had discovered, small if not nil. Siringo, he judged, was the only Pinkerton detective who might prove resourceful enough to make his way through such demanding circumstances. As much as Siringo needed to move on from his deep bereavement, McParland also found himself conceding that he, no less emphatically, needed Siringo to take the case.

But it wasn't McParland's way to beg; and besides, he knew it would prove to be a futile tactic. Instead, McParland shrewdly played his best card: He revealed where the robbery had occurred.

Alaska? interrupted Charlie. Why, that's all the ways up at the ends of the earth.

It's a ways, agreed McParland. Now that the seed had been planted, he offered Siringo one final chance. Why don't you take a day to think about things. Come back tomorrow, and if you still don't want the job, I'll assign someone else. But McParland's crisp tone made clear what went unsaid: You can also be certain I'll never contact you again.

Over the years, Charlie had come to appreciate that McParland was not an arbitrary man; and he was affected by his boss's concern. He agreed to give the matter some consideration.

That night Charlie thought it all through: Up in the high north, a man might find that he'd outrun all his past troubles.

"Alaska it is then," agreed Charlie the next morning in McParland's office. He reached out and shook the superintendent's hand to seal the deal.

Troubles, too, plagued Soapy on his return to Denver. He'd been correct in his prediction that the furor over his attack on Colonel Arkins would've died down. It cost him a tidy sum, but Soapy succeeded in getting the charge reduced from attempted murder to assault. And then the courts showed no inclination to bring such a trivial matter to trial. Unfortunately, Soapy's instincts about the West's becoming a less hospitable place for old-time gamblers like himself was also proving accurate. Too many people didn't want him in Denver anymore.

Defiant, Soapy opened the Tivoli Club, on the corner of Seventeenth and Market streets. He advertised it as a "headquarters for gentlemen, offering first class goods and first class attention" and "serving wines, liquors, and cigars." Upstairs, hidden from the scrutiny of passing policemen, were roulette, faro, and card tables — all of them braced. Soapy, in fact, as much as conceded that the games were rigged. Above the stairs that led to the gambling parlor, he'd posted a cautionary notice: CAVEAT EMPTOR. Let the buyer beware.

It was a sly wisdom, and an ineffective one. The tables were always jammed. Yet after a disastrous night, some gamblers would turn indignant and complain that the odds had been stacked against them. Then they would stomp off to the police and demand that Soapy be arrested. On one such occasion, Soapy was charged with swindling $1,500 from two men at his tables and taken before the Fire and Police Commission. He served as his own attorney, and his defense had wit. Brimming with a bracing confidence, he began:

"As a matter of fact, gentleman, I wish to assure you that we should not be classed as gamblers. We do not conduct a gambling establishment. We are reformers in the true sense of the word."

Now that he had the court's attention, he shared a rascal's winking logic:

"At the Tivoli I am running an educational institution. The famous Keely institute provides a cure for the drinking habit. At the

Tivoli I have a cure for the gambling habit. . . . Why should we tell him it is useless to buck our tables? Let him learn for himself from actual experience. . . . He has, of course, no chance of winning a cent because in my games the player cannot win. When he leaves . . . he is disappointed naturally, but he has had experience of the greatest value. In fact, gentlemen, I should be recognized as a public benefactor!"

It was an impertinent argument, and it helped fuel people's anger. Reformers organized into the Law and Order League with the goal of the closing the city's saloons and gambling houses. Merchants circulated petitions demanding the arrest of the parade of confidence men and bunco steerers working Seventeenth Street. Police raids on the Tivoli became more frequent, and Soapy's men were hurled into jail on a variety of petty charges. Day after day, the harassment continued.

Soapy tried to fight back. He organized the city's gamblers, men like Big Ed Chase and Bat Masterson, into a political organization of their own. They agreed to provide money and muscle to whatever political party would protect their interests. But it was too late to stem the swelling tide of reform. In 1892, Davis Waite was elected governor of Colorado.

Waite was a revolutionist, a man with a

strong sense of mission who, more significantly, didn't mind a good tussle. During the campaign, he had vowed to "fight iniquity until the blood runs as deep as the cavalry's bridles." After his election, he set out to demonstrate that this had not been idle talk.

One of his first acts was to order the resignation of the Denver Fire and Police Commission. It was well known that the commissioners were on the gamblers' payroll; it was high time, Waite declared, that they be replaced. The commissioners, however, were an autocratic group. They'd enjoyed their power and their boodle for too long to give it up. They refused to step down. Instead, they barricaded themselves in city hall. Waite, fierce and vengeful, called out the militia. And so the confrontation that would become famous as the "City Hall War" played out on March 15, 1894.

The commissioners reviewed their situation and after some discussion decided to appoint Soapy as their "general." They appreciated that he had as much reason to fight as they did. If the reformers were to succeed, he would be run out of town, too. Also, he had an army, a confederation of bunco men, thieves, gamblers, hard cases, and dickered policemen and deputy sheriffs.

With two .45s in holsters strapped around his waist and carrying two kegs of dynamite in his hands, Soapy marched a heavily armed force of about 150 men to city hall. Giving quick orders, he shrewdly deployed his troops: Men with shotguns and rifles were placed at every entrance and in the corridors of every floor; a newly christened "bomb brigade" prepared missiles fashioned out of dynamite, powder, fuses, and caps on the third floor; and on the top floor and in the tower were the sharpshooters, crack shots with a pistol or Winchester.

Commanded by Brigadier General E. J. Brooks, the militia proudly marched up Larimer Street and formed an offensive line on Fourteenth Street across from city hall. It was nearly 200 strong, both infantrymen and a cavalry brigade. "I got a dozen men who can shoot," promised a saber-waving Captain Barlett, chief of the army sharpshooters, to a reporter. "I can depend on them to pick the heads out of those windows."

As the troops fell into position, a battering ram mounted on an express wagon was moved to the front of their line. It looked rickety and, regardless of its condition, would seem to have no practical purpose in a firefight. The troops pushing the contraption would surely be cut down before they could reach the front door. Soapy's men stood at the windows laughing and taunting as it was dragged into position.

But the jesting came to an end when the First Regiment pulled its light artillery up to the front line. It was an intimidating display: two twelve-pound Napoleon cannons and two Gatling guns. "We can tumble that building on their heads with a dozen shots," an artillery officer warned.

Soapy, fearful that his men might be wavering, seized the initiative. With a stick of dynamite in his hand, he leaned out the window and shouted to the soldiers, "I've got enough of the stuff to send us all to Hell, and as I am nearer to Heaven than any of you, I'll not be the first to die." His men cheered, reaffirming their support. They were again united under Soapy's leadership.

It was a standoff. All that seemed certain was that once the first shot was fired, dozens — perhaps hundreds — would die.

"If you say fire, we'll fire," General Brooke wrote in a note he had delivered to Governor Waite at his mansion, only a few blocks from city hall. It was five P.M. and the skies were turning dark. Inside the residence, the governor was meeting with a committee of citizens from the chamber of commerce. They were pleading with him to let the state supreme court decide on the ousting of the Fire and Police Commission. If he didn't reconsider, the loss of life would be catastrophic. Waite was adamant. "I shall order the militia to fire," he insisted. "The people may assassinate me if they will, but I propose to have it my way."

Nonetheless, the governor did not respond to the general's note. Instead, he sent a telegram to Brigadier General Cook of the regular U.S. Army. "Property of the United States . . . now in serious jeopardy," he reported. Within an hour, five companies from Fort Logan with one hundred rounds of ammunition per man and rations for twenty-four hours were dispatched by special train.

In the darkness of the cold Denver night, city hall remained illuminated, the building blazing with lights. There were armed men at every window, sharpshooters at the ready in the tower. The dynamite bombs had been assembled; all that was required was the order to ignite the fuses. Soapy had pulled his army together in short order, and they had embraced him. It was a force that shared a unifying self-awareness: They were fighting for their futures. No one was prepared to back down.

But at eight forty-five that evening Soapy looked out from his third-floor window and was startled. He watched with a stern concentration as the companies of U.S. Army troops moved into the front line. At once, he realized his bluff had been called. With a gambler's long-practiced practicality, he folded his hand. Move out, he ordered his men.

Not a shot had been fired. The only casualty was a spectator who had fallen from his perch on a storm door and cracked his head on the pavement. But in the weeks that followed, the courts reiterated the governor's order that the commissioners resign, the Waite administration continued to put pressure on what the papers were now calling the "fly-by-night fraternity," and Soapy realized he'd better leave Denver before he wound up in jail.

The *Denver Times* reported on his travel plans:

Jeff. R. Smith, the Reverend Bowers, and Doctor W. H. Jackson have announced their intention to go to Japan. . . . They announce their object is a pleasure and sightseeing trip, but judging from the props they were seen carrying, they intend to be prepared for emergencies.

Fourteen packs of new cards, a dice box, a set of "ivories," full sets of poker chips, a small square frame covered with canvas, half shells of English walnuts, and quart bottles of good whiskey along with several boxes of fine cigars.

The article correctly reported the items Soapy had packed for his travels. But the reporter had been misled as to his destination. He'd never had any intention to sail to Japan. Soapy was going to Alaska. "This is my last opportunity to make a big haul," he told his gang as he supervised the packing at the Tivoli Club. "Alaska is the last West."

There were three strong toots from the ship's whistle as the *Idaho* puffed down the Tlingit fishing ground of Gastineau Channel and headed into Juneau's harbor on a thickly gray, wet April day. George Carmack stood on deck and looked past a narrow, sandy beach and toward the handful of ramshackle log cabins and wood-frame buildings that made up the small gold-mining camp. In the distance, high mountains formed a steep natural barrier. The mountains were snow-capped, but the rain and fog had painted them gray, too, like the sky. It was an uninviting vista.

He waited impatiently as sailors tied the steamboat up to the wharf. Then, hauling his heavy pack onto his back, George walked down the slippery gangplank and into Alaska.

PART II
GOLD

TWELVE

On their separate ways up to Alaska, the three men encountered many others heading to the north country to leave their old lives behind. Times had been hard back home. The sudden Panic of 1893 had grown into a full-blown economic depression, and two years later it continued to hold the nation in its tight grip. All across the country banks had failed, railroads had gone into receivership, farms had been foreclosed, and jobs had disappeared. The Gay Nineties had turned angry and combative. Sullen mobs roamed city streets searching for food. Fistfights broke out on the floor of the New York Stock Exchange as companies went bust and fortunes turned to dust. Strikes erupted into bloody battles, the forces of labor and capital charging at one another without mercy. Coxey's army, as the resolute thousands who rallied around Ohio businessman Jacob Coxey were known, marched on Washington to demand jobs. Throughout the country there was the feeling that something fundamental had gone wrong. Despair had become a national malaise. Desperate, eager to leave all their disappointments behind, a new wave of pioneers began the journey to the far north. They wanted to believe that in Alaska there would be opportunities to change their luck and, if they were resourceful, to forge new lives.

What had brought America to its knees? Congress certainly deserved a large share of the blame. These legislators had, in their reckless wisdom, created an opportunity to buy dollars at nearly half price. When Soapy set up his keister, he, too, would excite crowds with the come-on that for fifty cents they could buy a bar of soap that'd be worth at least a dollar. But his generosity was just an enticement; he was way too sly to engage in a transaction where there might be a chance that he could take a loss. Congress, though, was more cavalier. It had a sporting attitude toward the nation's treasury. In 1890 it had passed the Sherman Silver Purchase Act, which obligated the government to buy 4.5 million ounces of silver each month — and to pay for these purchases at a set price with an equal amount of notes backed by either silver or gold. Gold had a market value of nearly twice that of silver, so it didn't take considerable financial acumen to prefer a payout in gold dollars. And for once a deal that seemed too good to be true really was true — at least for a while. A silver dollar worth only 58 cents could be exchanged for a dollar certificate backed by gold worth a full 100 cents. But greed being what it is, and human nature, too, it soon transpired that the western mines produced — and then avidly sold to the government — more silver than Congress had ever anticipated. As a result, the U.S. Treasury began running through its gold supplies. When a despairing secretary of the Treasury confessed that the nation's gold reserves had plunged below the traditionally acceptable level of $100 million, he might just as well have been a punter at the Orleans Club who, nearly wiped out, at last realized the faro box had been gaffed.

With the secretary's revelation that the Republic's nest egg was in jeopardy, panic spread. It galloped pell-mell through the national marketplace, destroying illusions, toppling empires, and jamming the machinery that operated everyday life. The forebodings of disaster had become prophecy. Yet even as the country was sent reeling, there remained one economic certainty: gold. Its value was sacrosanct. Its worth held steady. It was the one true thing. So governments demanded it. Investors hoarded it. And prospectors went to great lengths to discover it.

Now gold, too, helped to establish the allure of faraway Alaska in people's minds. Back in the 1840s Russian trappers had reported that they'd stumbled upon traces of the yellow metal in the jagged spits of rocky land fronting the icy blue-green waters of the Cook Inlet. For these trappers, however, this discovery was just a curiosity; they were too occupied with the fortunes that could be made selling the soft, thick furs of minks, lynxes, beavers, and Arctic foxes to fashionable aristocrats at the court in St. Petersburg.

More recently, in the 1880s, American prospectors had experienced some luck panning in the tidewater Tlingit Indian fishing grounds that ran along the territory's coastal panhandle. These were small strikes, but they were sufficient to spark large hopes. In fact, the possibility of further discoveries led George Pilz, an engineer who was already working a claim near Sitka, to come up with an entrepreneurial plan. He offered several bottles of whiskey to any Indian who could lead him to a gold-bearing vein. Soon enough, Chief Kowee of the Auk Tlingit tribe showed up with a piece of quartz rock laced with streaks of gold. There were more yellow-veined rocks like this one, the chief promised, along the banks of a fast-moving creek that lay beyond the Gastineau Channel.

Pilz handed over the whiskey, but he didn't put too much stock in the Indian's information. Although he was the one who had proposed the trade, Pilz now realized he just didn't have it in him to trust any Indian. Besides, he knew that an expedition to search for a specific creek among the dozens, or perhaps even hundreds, of creeks that ran north of the channel would have its difficulties. That was rain-forest country, a dense, inhospitable region that stretched seemingly to the horizon in a maze of tall trees, razor-sharp ferns, and dark, murky swamps. A man could easily lose his bearings and never be seen again.

On the other hand, Pilz didn't relish missing out on a chance to make a windfall discovery. The prospect, however unlikely, was still too tempting.

He recruited two vagabond prospectors, Joe Juneau and Dick Harris, to investigate. When they returned empty-handed, it simply confirmed to Pilz that his initial instinct had been correct. He should never have paid an Indian any mind. Chief Kowee, though, turned belligerent. He thundered: The two men's search had failed because of a lack of heart. They had been lazy. They had not journeyed far enough beyond the head of the channel. The Indian's vehemence took Pilz by surprise; it was the indignant tone of a man defending his honor. And that got Pilz to thinking.

He sent the two prospectors out again, telling them to hack their way through the rain forest and the underbrush if they had to. They were gone for over a month, but when they returned they were proud and gleeful. They had seen some colors in a roaring, spring-fed creek and then, on a hunch, had followed its course back several miles to a steep gulch. And there they'd found gold. "Little lumps as large as peas and beans," Harris rejoiced.

It was a major strike, the first one in Alaska. Around what they took to calling Gold Creek and Snow Slide Gulch, in October 1880 the two men staked out a 160-acre townsite. Word spread quickly, and within a year a tent-city mining camp had been transformed into a shacktown crowded with prospectors, tenderfeet, hurdy-gurdy girls, and tinhorn gamblers. It was the first town to be founded in the nearly two decades since the United States had taken control of the territory. At a high-spirited, celebratory meeting, the miners voted to name it Juneau.

In 1895, while a great depression ravaged America, Juneau prospered. There were a half dozen hard rock mines scattered around the area, and each one was steadily producing large quantities of gold ore. These were loud and clanking industrial operations employing hundreds of workers and engineers. Each day the thick gray smoke from their smelting furnaces would float in an eerie mist above the town, visible testimony to the new fortunes that were being made. In booming Juneau, it was possible to believe that finding gold in Alaska was not simply a figment of the imagination, and that a new, more satisfying future was somewhere out there, another hidden treasure just waiting to be discovered.

A grainy photograph taken in 1895 shows a ragtag group of new arrivals coming off a small one-smokestack steamer tied up to the dock in Juneau. It is a rainy day, possibly spring, judging by the hip-length coats most of the men are wearing, and they are making their way in a lackadaisical procession along the narrow wooden wharf. Some have packs on their backs, others carry valises. The photographer must have set up his camera stand on Front Street, at the end of the long wharf, and from such a distance the faces are indistinguishable. Anyway, the rain is sheeting, and broad-brimmed hats are pulled low on many of their heads. Yet perhaps it is not necessary to be able to identify the newcomers to know at least the broad strokes of their histories. The tumult of the age had driven them to look for something better in the far north. At the same time, undoubtedly they were also running away from something in their own lives. The bittersweet legacies of high dramas had assuredly played a part in each man's decision that it'd be better to move on. Charlie Siringo, Soapy Smith, and George Carmack had, as it happened, walked in similar circumstances down the wooden planks of this very wharf on their way toward Front Street, and on into Juneau. Traveling north with the flow of history, hardened by disquieting events, eager to leave hurtful memories behind, they'd come to Alaska. Like so many of the other newcomers, they were intrepid. They embraced large ambitions. And they, too, had no way of anticipating the mystery, danger, and adventure that lay ahead in such a wild and unknown big country.

THIRTEEN

Charlie missed Mamie every day. He had agreed to take the case and go to Alaska for one reason: to forget. He wanted to put distance between himself and his memories, to separate himself definitively from all that had come before. Alaska, he'd reckoned, promised experiences that would overpower his lingering sense of loss. The truth was, even before his meeting with McParland Charlie had realized something had to be done. He knew it wasn't his nature to keep to himself, or to spend his days all hangdog and steeped in melancholy. He was a garrulous sort, a man who'd spent a lifetime spouting off to whomever he encountered in a loud, cheery, self-confident voice. Why, all through his married days, he'd indulged in a cowboy's weakness for the company a man could find in saloons and dance halls; a lot of his nights, he freely conceded with a bemused grin, had been spent carrying on in a manner that "would make Rome howl." But after Mamie's death he'd retreated to a lonely, private place, and despite his growing recognition of his predicament, he'd found he couldn't manufacture the will necessary to extricate himself. He just couldn't see the point.

Then he had met with McParland; and later, in the course of a long night, he'd come to grasp the full measure of what the superintendent was offering. He was being given not only the chance to solve a mystery that had stymied the Portland office, but also the opportunity to reclaim his life. In Alaska he could escape the constant torment of his memories. He could make a fresh start. Newly hopeful, looking forward to reconnecting to his work, he'd agreed to take the case.

Yet as soon as he boarded the SS *City of Topeka* in Tacoma, Washington, Charlie felt he'd made a colossal mistake. He was being disloyal. Escape, Charlie now decided, was a coward's play. He was disgusted with himself for trying to steer a course that would leave Mamie behind. Even worse, his plan failed completely. His journey brought him no comfort. The memory of his departed wife was as steady as the hard gray rain that followed the steamship each day on its way north. It clung to him. It would be part of him forever, like the long scar that ran down from his knee, the result of a bullet wound suffered in the course of a foolish night in Dodge.

Charlie, same as any hand who'd cowboyed about the frontier, had been witness to his share of sudden, untimely deaths. Marauding Indians, stray bullets, feisty rattlesnakes, even lightning bolts — all had struck with a lethal arbitrariness that he'd learned to accept as simply bad luck. Nine out of ten times a cowboy could be in that exact spot and nothing would happen — only this time it did. On the plains and prairies either you learn to shrug off the unpredictability of life or else its dangers become too overwhelming. But now each day he would find himself once again dwelling on Mamie's death, the unfairness of such a kindhearted soul's dying so young and leaving their daughter motherless. It took all the discipline he could muster to prevent himself from standing on the deck and screaming in raw anger at the vast slate-gray sky above. He desperately wanted to ask for her back; yet he knew that would never happen. He wanted to turn back time and once again be the rascal outlaw sneaking down the hallway to the lonely widow's bedroom in a Fort Laramie boardinghouse. He wanted to be traveling off to this new case with Mamie at his side. But he was alone.

It was a bad way to head into an investigation, he understood, and he knew he needed to get his thoughts fixed on the case at hand. This proved difficult. Charlie remained mired in a finality he could not bring himself to accept. Nevertheless, as the cold rain continued to pour down, as the little steamship rose and fell on the choppy, thick sea, as, no less relentless, he battled through his own internal hell, a sense of duty came to prevail. In his years as a trail boss, he had led men through hard times and across rough country. Now he made up his mind to apply the same unforgiving discipline to himself. Without further delay, he focused his attention on the operation, and the mystery he'd need to get to the bottom of.

As Charlie stood on the rain-swept deck, his mind traveled back to his last meeting in Mc-Parland's office in Denver. The superintendent was a heavyset man, and it was his habit even indoors to wear a bowler hat with the brim pulled so low that it nearly covered his eyes. No less oddly, the room was always as dark as a tomb. The superintendent had once explained to Charlie that he kept the curtains drawn tight and his desktop kerosene lamp at only a faint glow because he didn't want to be spied on. He claimed he was fearful that someone from across the street or on a nearby rooftop might be watching the goings-on in his office. "Lots of people make it their business to know Mr. Pinkerton's business," he'd said. But Charlie suspected that both the bowler pulled low enough to veil the eyes and the cavelike office were ploys inspired by a more playful calculation. These were an actor's affectations. McParland, Charlie had come to recognize, had cast himself as nothing less than the master Pinkerton sleuth, and his shadow-filled lair was center stage for the role he so clearly enjoyed performing. Not that Charlie was of a mind to be critical of such brazen showmanship; after all, he was the rodeo rider who had loped about Denver's River Side Park corral sporting a large white sombrero, leather-fringed chaparejos, a flaming red kerchief, a sash of a similar bright-red hue tied tight around his waist, and a pearl-handled revolver jutting out of his holster. The way Charlie looked at it, a man could gussy himself up as he saw fit — as long as he could deliver on the fancy promise. And McParland had certainly done that. He was a legend. Before taking control of the Denver office, he'd worked three dangerous years undercover in a Pennsylvania mining town to build a case against a ruthlessly violent and corrupt cabal of union men. As a result of the unshakable evidence McParland had obtained at great personal risk, nineteen of the men, known as the Molly Maguires, were hanged. During Charlie's time working with McParland, the superintendent had earned his respect, too: He was shrewd, thoughtful, and completely honest, a man who did as he'd said. In Charlie's world, there was no higher praise.

That morning in Denver, after Charlie had announced that he'd changed his mind and was prepared to go to Alaska, he'd sat attentively in the straight-backed chair opposite his boss's huge desk and waited to be briefed on the particulars. That was how things had always worked in the past. In his careful, orderly way, McParland would lay out a case without ever commenting on the difficulties or risks involved. He was a man who dealt in hard facts, not opinions. But that morning's briefing had been different. Uncharacteristically, McParland had not proceeded in his typical straightforward fashion. Instead, he'd begun with a statement that was expressed with such heartfelt urgency that Charlie recognized that it was a plea: a plea for his help.

"It is imperative that this case be brought to a successful resolution," McParland exclaimed. He let the words fill the room. When he was apparently satisfied that he had his operative's full attention, he continued: "Nothing less than the reputation of the entire Pinkerton Detective Agency hangs in the balance." Leaning his considerable bulk across the desk and in the same moment fixing Charlie with his sharpshooter's stare, he spoke in a low, harsh whisper: "And that means, Siringo, that my reputation is at stake. *I am counting on you.*"

Charlie was taken aback. McParland had never expressed a personal interest in the outcome of any investigation. Nor, for that matter, had the superintendent ever placed such a singular importance on a specific case. What, Charlie wondered, had he gotten himself into? At the same time, he was excited. His vanity enjoyed a sharp challenge; in fact, he even relished the prospect of heading off into an adventure with so much on the line.

As for McParland, he now seemed a bit embarrassed, as if he had surprised himself, too, by the earnest passion he'd expressed. He quickly settled his large body back into his chair; adjusted — a habitual tic — the tilt of his bowler; and then proceeded in a more measured pitch to explain the string of events that had conspired to put such an unlikely importance on this case.

It had all begun routinely enough. Ten thousand dollars' worth of gold bars had been stolen from the busy Treadwell mine on Douglas Island, just across the harbor from Juneau, Alaska. This was a significant sum. Yet possibly more disturbing was the fact that the mine and its mill were patrolled around the clock by a small army of Winchester-toting guards. If despite all these precautions a thief could somehow smuggle out such a large amount of gold without being detected, what was to stop him from doing it again? And again?

Concerned, angry, and perplexed, Thomas Durkin, the superintendent of the Treadwell mine, sent a letter out the next day on a steamer leaving Juneau for Victoria, British Columbia. Addressed to the Western Union Telegraph Office, it instructed the operator to wire the Pinkerton Detective Agency in Portland, Oregon, in his name. The wire did not reveal the nature of the inquiry the agency was being hired to conduct; Durkin was reluctant to let word get out that a thief was preying on his mine. The wire simply requested that the office send three operatives to Alaska on the first available steamer. Cost, the telegram bluntly stated, was not an issue. A swift response, however, was essential.

The Portland office was a newly opened branch of the agency, and Franklin Wooster served as its superintendent. He had been a deputy in Abilene and then a police officer in Denver before he'd applied to the Pinkertons. He had no investigative experience, but he was middle-aged, possessed a sober demeanor, and had an unblemished, albeit undistinguished, record in law enforcement. That had been sufficient pedigree to earn him the appointment six months earlier to the supervisory position in Portland.

When Wooster read the telegram, he rejoiced. Three operatives! Expense no object! After six uneventful months, he now saw his opportunity to solidify his position in the Pinkerton organization. He hastily rounded up three men and, as had been requested, dispatched them on the next steamer to Juneau. With that accomplished, he triumphantly wired William Pinkerton in Chicago, stating that he'd procured a very lucrative operation for the agency. In all his fulsome excitement, it never occurred to Wooster to inquire from the Treadwell supervisor what manner of investigation his operatives would be asked to pursue. Nor did he pause long enough to consider whether specific skills or traits of character would be required of the men sent out to crack this case.

The three men were all new recruits to detective work; the Portland office was, after all, a recently opened branch of the agency. Still, they proved to be, as even Durkin would later grudgingly concede, models of industry and tenacity. With great authority, they prowled about the mill and mine every day for two months, asking questions, making observations. In that time, they identified no suspects. They uncovered no promising clues. But while they were in Alaska, two more robberies took place at the mine. When a third occurred, a frustrated Durkin angrily ordered the three detectives to leave his mine at once. Then he sent a terse telegram to the Portland office: The agency's services are hereby terminated forthwith.

It was a blemish on Wooster's career and an embarrassment for the Pinkerton agency. Nevertheless, neither William nor Robert Pinkerton, the two brothers who had inherited the agency after their father's death, was overly concerned. It was a reality of detective work, they both recognized, that some cases remained unresolved. During their father's time, for example, the railroads had hired the agency to apprehend Jesse James and his gang. Two Pinkertons had closed in on the outlaws, but Jesse had gunned them both down. And in the end it was Bob Ford (who would later become Soapy's nemesis) who'd snuck up on Jesse and shot him in the back, thus ending the case. The mystery of the thefts at the Treadwell mine would be relegated to a similarly embarrassing category — unsolved. Anyway, the matter was no longer the Pinkerton agency's concern. It had been summarily dismissed.

Then, as fate would have it, a small and seemingly uneventful coincidence occurred. Mr. Robert Pinkerton decided that he and his wife would escape the rigors of a New York winter with a restorative stay at a resort hotel in balmy San Diego. It so happened that there was another guest at the hotel that same week who'd also decided to treat himself to a respite from icy weather: Mr. Thomas

Durkin, the supervisor of the Treadwell mine. The two men met by chance at the hotel bar, and a brief conversation ensued. Pinkerton, intrigued by making the acquaintance of someone who lived in the far north, asked his drinking companion to join him and his wife at their table for dinner that evening. Durkin readily accepted.

The dining room was rather grand, with starched white cloths and heavy silver on the table and crystal chandeliers hanging from the ceiling; at the far end of the room, on a small platform decorated with potted palms, a pianist played soft melodies. The Pinkertons made polite conversation with their guest as course after course was served by attentive liveried waiters. But just before dessert, whether because Durkin's restraint had been liberated by several bottles of red wine or whether he simply chose then to seize the moment he'd been patiently waiting for since he'd by chance first encountered Robert Pinkerton, the mine superintendent revealed his connection to the agency. His words were sharp and his tone was unforgiving. He had paid good money, he harrumphed, and had gotten nothing in return. Rather loudly he insisted that the Pinkerton Detective Agency was staffed by incompetents.

About the room heads turned disapprovingly toward their table, but Robert Pinkerton was not deterred. His Scot blood came to a quick boil; and, truth be told, throughout the evening he'd been imbibing his share of wine, too. Indignant, he forcefully demanded an apology.

"I'll be damned if I will," barked Durkin. His difficult years in Alaska had taught him that nothing of merit ever occurred when a man backed down.

For a moment it seemed as if the two men would come to blows in the dining room. Then Mrs. Pinkerton intervened. Gentlemen, please, she begged, near to tears. This is most unbecoming.

Her distress affected both her husband and his guest. In an instant, decorum was restored. The meal was concluded without incident.

And so it came to pass that later that night, after a few calming brandies, the two men walked along the beach, and in this manner an understanding of sorts was reached. Robert Pinkerton, his tone more subdued, even conciliatory, conceded that an error had been made by the Portland office. Wooster had clearly dispatched three men who were totally unsuitable for the job.

Durkin, for his part, acknowledged that he had been too circumspect. It would have been wiser if in his initial telegram he had revealed the nature of the investigation to be conducted.

Now reconciled, the two men continued

their walk along the moonlit edge of the Pacific Ocean. As the waves lapped against the sand, Robert Pinkerton made an impetuous pledge: A great deal of time had passed since the initial robbery. It was uncertain whether the thief or thieves were still at the mine, or even in Alaska. It was uncertain whether the gold could still be recovered; perhaps it had been spent or, just as likely, perhaps it was safely hidden in a bank vault in Seattle. But, he said, I promise you this: If you will see fit to rehire our agency, I will make certain that this time we will dispatch the proper operatives to Alaska. These men will find whoever took your gold. You have my solemn word: The Pinkerton agency will solve this case.

Durkin considered the proposition. He had no doubt Pinkerton was sincere. But unless the culprits were still working at the mine, the trail would be very cold. If a man wanted to disappear, Alaska offered plenty of hiding places. The expense was a concern, too. During the last go-round, the cost of three operatives working two full months had added up to a pretty penny. Yet the thefts still rankled. Besides, who was to say there wouldn't be new robberies unless there were arrests? And Pinkerton had given him his word. That had to count for something.

But only two men this time, Durkin agreed at last.

And so on his way back to New York from San Diego, Robert Pinkerton detoured to Denver to meet with James McParland. He had known McParland since the time when the big Irishman had infiltrated the Molly Maguires. True, McParland was now a deskman, a few years older and lot heavier than during his days in the field, but Pinkerton had no doubts about the superintendent's abilities or loyalties. He was a man who could get a job done.

Without prelude, he outlined the circumstances of his meeting Durkin and the rash promise he'd made. I gave my word, Pinkerton told the superintendent. He did not want to sound desperate or too imploring, but the circumstances were unique in the history of the agency. The reputation of the entire Pinkerton organization was at stake, and his own personal honor, as well. The case must be solved, he ordered.

"I won't let you down, sir," McParland promised with total conviction.

Still standing in seclusion on the wet deck of the steamship, Charlie reviewed what lay in the balance of his efforts. Robert Pinkerton had given his word. McParland had given his, too. Now it would be up to him to make sure that his two bosses didn't turn out to be liars. And that the agency's reputation would not be besmirched. A lot, he understood, was riding on his solving this case. Which suited him fine.

As for the investigation itself, he already had some thoughts about how he would proceed. He'd been a hard-nosed detective for several years, and even without stepping foot in Alaska he felt certain of several facts. First, this wasn't a one-man operation. It would not have been feasible for a single man to have walked out of the mine unnoticed while transporting $10,000 worth of gold bars. That much gold had to weigh, he estimated, seventy-five to a hundred pounds. There were at least two thieves, perhaps even more. And maybe a gang of accomplices waiting to help them fence their stolen booty. Second, this was an inside job. It would have been impossible for anyone to have managed to grab the gold and get by the guards unless he was very familiar with the mine. Even then, it would have taken a good deal of planning. This meant that everyone who worked at the mine or had recently quit was a suspect. That added up to a long list, more than seven hundred names, he guessed. And third, the men from the Portland office had gone about things in precisely the wrong way. This wasn't the sort of case where you call people in for an interview and scribble their statements down in a notebook. That method of investigation would get you nowhere. You'd simply collect pages filled with self-serving half-truths or outright lies. To crack this case, you'd need to go undercover. You'd need to prowl around with your eyes and ears open, without anyone suspecting you were a detective. You had to be able to see things people didn't want you to see.

As Charlie reviewed the case and a strategy took shape in his mind, he began to grow confident. It would not be easy, many months had passed since the initial robbery, but he also suspected that the thieves would not have hightailed it. They had too good a thing going to want to give it up. He was fairly certain they were still around and planning to strike again. And if that was the case, he'd get them.

One thing McParland had said, however, left him feeling uneasy. On orders from Mr. Pinkerton himself, this was to be a two-man investigation. Charlie had tried to argue, to insist that he worked better on his own, but the superintendent was adamant. This was the specific arrangement Mr. Pinkerton had made with the mine superintendent, he told Charlie, and, therefore, it could not be amended. Once Siringo had established himself in Alaska, he was to wire the Denver office. Another operative would be sent to assist him.

Charlie wasn't pleased by the implication that this job was too big for him. But there was no sense fighting a battle he couldn't win. He promised that as soon as he had the lay of the land, he would let McParland know. You can send the reinforcements after you hear from me, he said sourly.

One month, McParland corrected. I expect to hear from you no later than four weeks after your arrival in Alaska. That understood?

Yes, Charlie agreed. But he still wasn't happy about it.

As Charlie got up to leave, McParland rose, too. He walked his operative to the door and placed a hand on his shoulder. "Be careful, Siringo," he said.

It was only while standing on the deck of the SS *Topeka* that Charlie had a sudden realization. The superintendent had never before sent him off on an operation with similar words of caution. Or were they, Charlie now couldn't help but wonder, a warning?

As soon as the steamship docked, Charlie made his way down Front Street and into the heart of Juneau. He'd been to many a hurrah frontier town in his day, and at first glance this one didn't seem all that different. One thing, though, caught his eye and struck him as odd: Many of the buildings were raised on stilts; you had to climb a makeshift ladder to reach the front door. He'd later learn that was a design necessitated by the fact that the streets had a tendency to flood during the rainy season and — another inconvenience

— were transformed into thick rivers of mud during the spring thaw. Also, elevating the front door reduced the likelihood of a prowling black bear busting in to join you in bed. But that first day, Charlie didn't have this knowledge. It just struck him as mighty peculiar, and further confirmation that he'd arrived in a new, strange land.

He found a hotel and registered using the name Lee R. Davis. It was an old alias from a case in New Mexico, and one he'd no reason to doubt would serve him well this time, too. Then Mr. Davis asked for a bottle of whiskey and took it to his room. He sat in the dark, drinking straight from the bottle, and thinking all the time of Mamie.

FOURTEEN

Charlie heard the men coming up the pitch-dark alleyway before he could see them. There were two of them. With each step, their boots sank deep into the mud and made a clear and distinct noise. Their gait was steady; they weren't attempting to sneak up on him, he noted with some relief. But just to be sure he unbuttoned his mackinaw and kept his right hand fixed on the butt of his Colt revolver. He also remained close to the side of the log building; there was no point in standing in the open and giving a shooter an easy target. He waited until they got closer before he spoke.

Over here, gentlemen, he said, his words a soft whisper in the darkness. He knew they hadn't spotted him yet, and he liked the advantage that gave him.

That you, Mr. Davis? a strong voice called out.

Charlie noted the annoyed tone. He didn't care. He responded just as sharply. Might be wise to keep things down a bit, he said, his words pointed but still hushed. Then he stepped away from the building and found a spot in the middle of the alleyway.

You really think this is necessary? the same voice called out, once again loud and defiant. Charlie's eyes had adjusted to the darkness, and now he could see the two men as they approached. He assumed the feisty fellow doing all the talking was Durkin, the mine superintendent. He was small and compact and had a neatly trimmed beard. His walk was near to a strut, and Charlie decided that the man was very sure of himself. He had no idea of the identity of the taller individual bringing up the rear. Clearly, though, he deferred to Durkin. Still, Charlie had expected only one man, and he didn't like surprises. He figured now was as good a time as any for Durkin to come to appreciate that, as well as to learn to pay heed to his instructions, if they were going to work together.

Yesterday, his first full day in Juneau, Charlie had prowled the town looking for a place where he could settle in for a talk with the mine official without anybody noticing. It wouldn't do to show up at the mine, walk into the superintendent's office, and simply introduce himself. Nor could they meet over a bottle in the one-room saloon Charlie had already discovered. Those circumstances would be bound to get tongues wagging and people speculating. His investigation, Charlie was convinced, had to be kept a secret if he was to solve this case. No one could know he'd a connection to Durkin or, for that matter, to any of the people who ran the mine.

The morning's look-see had been a very unsatisfying expedition. Like many mining towns, Juneau had sprung up pretty much overnight. There was only a single main street, and the buildings lining it were wedged together wall to wall. That didn't make for much privacy. He'd noticed there was a big spruce forest and some impressive snow-capped mountains on the outskirts of town; there'd be plenty of isolated spots in all that wilderness where two men could talk without attracting attention. Only this required that he first do a good scout. He'd need to spend a full day poking around in the woods or, for all he knew, maybe even two or more before he'd find a location that'd suit his needs. And then he'd have to get word to Durkin. Why, near on a week might pass before he would be able to get his investigation moving forward. But, he told himself, if that was the only prudent way, he had no choice. In the long run, secrecy was a good deal more important than going off half-cocked.

Discouraged, he left Main Street and walked down toward the wharf. He was ambling along, listening to the squawking of the gulls overhead, when something caught his eye. There were two peaked-roofed structures, one built with logs, the other a simple wood-framed shack, and in between them stretched a long dirt alleyway. On closer inspection, Charlie learned that one building was the steamship office and the other was used by the harbor's customs tax collector. That, too, was perfect: They would both be vacant at night.

Satisfied, he returned to his hotel and quickly wrote a letter to Thomas Durkin, Superintendent, Treadwell Mine. As per your conversation with the gentleman you met in San Diego, Charlie began with a deliberate circumspection, I have arrived in Juneau. He then requested a meeting with Mr. Durkin at midnight the following evening, carefully describing the location of the alleyway where the rendezvous would take place. That this meeting be kept in strictest confidence is of the utmost importance, Charlie concluded. He signed the note "Lee R. Davis"; wrote "Personal and Confidential" on the envelope; and hurried to deposit it on the next ferry crossing Gastineau Channel to Douglas Island.

Now it was a starry midnight and Durkin, as instructed, had arrived. But clearly the superintendent was none too happy about the arrangements. As soon as he drew face-to-face with Charlie, he became bristling and belligerent. He was not at all convinced that such a degree of caution had been necessary. In fact, he fumed, it was a genuine inconvenience.

Charlie gave him his lead before pulling back sharply on the reins. Who's this? he interrupted, pointing bluntly at the taller man.

Durkin introduced William Bordus, his assistant. And he explained: Bordus knows the workings of the mine and the mill as well as I do. Perhaps even better. I thought it would be valuable for you to meet him, too. He has my complete confidence.

Understood, agreed Charlie. But I was expecting only one man. You should know I don't cotton to surprises. No telling what can happen when a man is surprised. To drive home his point, Charlie pulled back his coat to reveal the big Colt in the holster strapped around his waist.

I see, said Durkin uneasily. But come now, Mr. Davis, do you really believe all this secrecy, all these precautions are necessary?

"Men have been killed for a lot less than a fortune in gold," said Charlie.

Durkin considered that statement; and in the process, all his previous temper seemed to slip away. Instead, Charlie observed, a sudden look of apprehension came over his face.

Satisfied that he had gained the upper hand, Charlie shared his plan. His intention was to get a job at the mine. That way, he'd be able to scrutinize things without attracting any attention. Think you could arrange something for me? he asked.

Bordus will handle that, Durkin answered. Just come to the hiring hall tomorrow morning like any prospective employee, and he'll make sure everything goes without a hitch. Then Durkin turned to his assistant and asked what position he thought Mr. Davis should fill. There were, he explained to Charlie, many different jobs a man could sign on for at the mine.

Bordus gave the matter a few moments of thought. At last, he spoke. An oiler, he said emphatically. A machine oiler would have access to all the various facilities. You'd be called on to service machinery throughout the entire operation.

An oiler it is then, Charlie agreed.

Supposing you need to meet with us again? asked Durkin.

Same procedure as tonight, Charlie said. I'll send a note to your office, and we'll meet up in this alleyway that evening at midnight.

Their business concluded, Charlie instructed the two men that it would be best if they'd leave the alleyway first. He'd hold back a spell. If anyone had followed them from the wharf and still was lurking about, he'd be able to spot 'em.

With some formality, Charlie shook hands with the two mine officials. But before they parted his company, he shared a concern that had been troubling him from the moment he had signed on for the case. He wanted to know if they thought the thieves were at the mine and planning to strike again. Or had the culprits taken their bonanza and moseyed along?

Durkin responded with a short, hard smirk. The government of the United States paid a tad more than seven million dollars to purchase the *entire* Territory of Alaska, he said, a testy edge to his voice. Gold totaling at least four times that sum will be brought out of Treadwell. I'd say that makes "our little mine" — he spoke the words with an odd flash of a smile — a downright tempting target. My guess? They're still around. And planning to strike again.

Without any further discussion, the two men turned and walked in silence back down the long alley. Charlie's eyes followed them until they disappeared into the darkness.

After only a few hours of sleep, Charlie returned to the wharf and boarded a late-morning ferry to Douglas Island. A wet spring snow was swirling about, but when he stood on the deck he could make out the outlines of a large collection of shacks and frame buildings spread across the southeast ridge of the island. "Our little mine?" he thought, recalling Durkin's words. Now he understood the irony in the superintendent's tone. Even from this distance he could see that the Treadwell mine operation was bigger than most — hell, any! — of the cow towns he'd ridden into in his time. And just as quickly, another thought struck: There could be a thousand people working at the mine, all scattered across a rugged spruce-forest island nearly the size, he imagined, of the vast LX spread that'd been his old Texas stomping grounds. What were his chances of finding a single clue, let alone the robbers? He silently apologized to the Portland operatives for all the occasions when, railing, he'd dismissed their efforts. For the first time, he truly understood what they'd been up against. Now his assurances to McParland of his success struck him as simply brazen. He'd been, he nearly moaned, incredibly naive.

But there was no longer any turning back. After the ferry docked, he tried to bury all his sudden doubts and made his way up the snow-covered ridge to the hiring hall. As he trudged up the steep path, he noticed that the plumes of thick black smoke escaping from the many furnace chimneys had clouded the morning sky and left the fresh snow stained with dark soot. The sight did not help his mood.

Entering the hiring hall, he saw Bordus standing in a corner, but to Charlie's relief the mine official neither approached nor gave the slightest indication of recognition. It was only as Charlie was finishing his interview that Bordus intervened. We need an oiler, he told the hiring agent. This man will do. For a moment, it appeared that the agent was about to object, but one stern look from Bordus put an end to any further discussion. And so Charlie became a machine oiler. His starting pay, he was informed, would be $3.25 a day. When he heard that, Charlie couldn't help but think, I don't solve this case, well, at least I'll have a paying job.

Charlie was directed to the machine shop, where a terse foreman handed him a large tin of oil and a metal cylindrical oiling device that narrowed into a long, thin pointed tip that reminded Charlie of a barn rat's tail. The job, as quickly explained, struck Charlie as simple enough: He was to tour the mine and mill operations each day, according to a prescribed rotating pattern that was posted on a wall of the shop, and oil the machines in each of these facilities. It was a ten-hour shift; for the first week he'd work days, the next week, nights. At the conclusion of those brief instructions, the foreman sent Charlie on his way with a bit of advice: You have any questions, come see me. But I was you, I wouldn't have too many questions. Do your work, and we'll get along just fine.

And so Charlie went off. He had had a few occupations in his time — cowpuncher, merchant, and, most recently, detective — but nothing in his experience had prepared him for the strange new industrialized enterprise he was entering. Work in the mine was broken down into different procedures, and each one left Charlie, a man with a curious bent, fascinated. "It was a world of which I had never dreamed," he marveled.

The glory hole — as the deep muddy pit where hundreds of miners were busy digging the ore-bearing rocks from the earth was called — was wider and longer than the steamship that had brought Charlie to Alaska. Charlie would descend into its depths and immediately be unnerved. With an army of men swinging picks and wielding shovels at close quarters, he feared that at any moment he'd be speared. The noise, too, was another sort of assault. It wasn't simply the commotion created by some two hundred diligent miners attacking an underbelly of solid rock. Rising at a sharp angle over the pit, supported by a series of increasingly tall log pillars until it reached higher than the tree line, was a massive wooden flume. A nearly constant flood of water rushed through it with a powerful force, cleansing the excavated rocks, and in the process created a rumbling din that echoed like the reports of a dozen Winchesters off the pit's steep stone walls.

But time spent in the tumult of the glory hole, Charlie came to decide, was a holiday when compared to life below ground. A steel cage elevator descended with a careful, rhythmic slowness deep into the earth, carrying teams of miners to a network of long, narrow, timber-shored tunnels. Each of the candlelit tunnels, known as chambers, was its own community. The men worked their shifts digging and scraping in a tight, nearly airless darkness, isolated in caves of shadows, emerging only into the common corridor when they loaded the piles of heavy rock into wooden wagons drawn by massive horses. The wagon master would lead the horses back to the elevator, where another crew would dump the rocks into a cart, which would be wheeled into the cage; then, on his signal, the elevator would begin its long rise up to the surface.

For Charlie, who'd always treated his mounts like family, the sight of the brawny horses, some weighing as much as two thousand pounds, kicking and bucking wildly, near to crazy with terror, as they were led into the elevator at the start of each shift, filled him with revulsion. As soon as they were out of the cage, the horses would become docile; they could be hitched to the wagons and they'd pull their loads without incident. It was only as they were led back to the cage for the trip up to the surface that they'd again turn wild, snarling and whinnying as though possessed. Having witnessed this one afternoon, Charlie was of half a mind to intervene; his blood boiled at the sight of such willful abuse. In the end, though, he decided that the risk was too great. He didn't want to provoke an incident that would attract attention his way. He was, he reminded himself, working undercover; and — an even more persuasive restraint — he'd made a promise to McParland. The best he could do was to try to gentle the horses as they were led into the cage. Still, he sure would've liked to have punched the wagon master flat on the nose; maybe that would teach him to be little more respectful of the animals he was handling. Truth was, Charlie had no trouble understanding what was spooking the horses. He had spent most of his life in big open country, and his emotions, too, would rage dangerously as soon as he began the slow, dark descent underground.

While the glory hole and the underground chambers were curiosities that, though intriguing, left Charlie uneasy, he had nothing but admiration for the collection of inventive machinery housed in a series of long shacks at the crest of the ridge. Massive quantities of the excavated rocks from the mine would be loaded into low flatbed railroad cars, which then traveled up the ridge on a specially designed narrow-gauge track. There, the rocks were placed on wide rubber conveyor belts, which carried them along to the machines. Each piece of machinery performed a separate step in the process of extracting gold. Hydraulic devices that the men called "squeezers" and "crushers" pounded away, their clamor the equal of a stampeding cattle herd, Charlie complained; these machines separated the pyrite and gold from the waste rock. Next, the valuable ore would be washed by a forest of long hoses constantly squirting water, then moved along on vibrating vanner rollers to the chlorinization vats, a series of deep troughs filled with a sulfuric acid mix. Finally, the ore would continue on to the foundry, where it would be baked in gigantic brick-lined ovens, the flames burning around the clock like the fires of hell itself. The finished product — gold bars — would be loaded onto the railroad cars for the ride to the windowless warehouse on a stumpy hill directly above Gastineau Channel. Once a month, under the protection of a squad of heavily armed guards, the bars would be loaded onto a steamship docked at the island's wharf. This "treasure ship," as the envious prospectors up and down the panhandle dubbed it, would steam nonstop to Tacoma, Washington, carrying a shiny fortune of nearly pure gold bullion bars.

For Charlie, the most fascinating aspect of the entire process was that any fool could be hired to do the work. As the ore moved forward on rolling belts, each worker was required to do only a single simple task. The difficult work was done by the machines. On the range, a cowboy prided himself on being a jack-of-all-trades; he had to ride, brand, lasso, scout, and, on occasion, shoot straight. A top hand carried himself with a well-earned pride. But in this new world of machines, there didn't seem much that could give a man any real satisfaction.

It was while working the night shift, though, that Charlie got to thinking more and more about where the West — the entire country, for that forlorn matter — was heading. His first afternoon on the island, he'd watched as the weak winter sunlight faded, the sky turned dark — and then suddenly the entire horizon glowed with bright electric lights. Charlie had encountered electricity in Chicago, and over the past five years a good many neighborhoods in Denver had been wired for electrical current; but he'd never expected to find electric lights on an island up in the far north. However, the Treadwell people, determined to keep their lucrative operations going around the clock, had brought in engineers to set up a water-powered electric generator, and as a result the entire island blazed at night with a harsh artificial light. Charlie was astonished. And saddened. He had lived too long in a frontier of endless distances and dim horizons illuminated after the sun set by only an immense starry sky. He didn't cotton to people bringing civilization to places that got on just fine without it. Still, he realized that this world of machines and electric lights was the future and there was no stopping it. Once he settled into being resigned, it tickled him that he'd had to come up to the wilds of the far north to see progress firsthand.

Of course, all his time on the island he was looking for clues. There was a dining hall that, he figured, seated as many as two hundred men at a time, and on his meal breaks he'd go out of his way to make conversation. He didn't know precisely what he was trying to discover, and some of the men gave him odd looks, as though he was being a mite forward. But it was the best he could do. The problem was, after a month it hadn't gotten him anywhere, and so he hadn't written McParland, as he had promised. He knew he should, but he wanted to get more of an idea who might've been behind the robberies, and how they'd done it, before he gave the superintendent the okay to send up another man. As it was, Charlie had nothing at all to go on. Except, he decided, for possibly one small notion. He found his mind circling back time after time to this same simple fact. It had first occurred to him as he'd watched a crew unload the gold bars from the beds of the railroad cars and carry them into the warehouse. He wasn't certain how this observation fitted into a solution to the mystery;

nevertheless, instinct told him it was important. And so his detective's mind kept mulling one distinct and certainly undeniable fact: Gold was heavy.

Throughout the Treadwell mine, the stamp room was a source of pride. It was well known as the largest operation of its kind in the world: 240 "stamps" under one roof. Charlie's head, though, would start to ache as soon as he put his foot through the door. Each stamp was a heavy metal rod about the circumference of a fence post and, powered by a hydraulic engine, it would crash down like a hammer on an iron box. Inside this enclosed box — the mortar, it was called — were rocks dug from the mine. On impact, they'd be smashed into pieces that would reveal whether they contained veins of gold. The mechanized coordination of a row of 240 metal stamps repeatedly slamming into 240 iron boxes made the concrete floor vibrate beneath Charlie's feet and created a din so powerful that his head felt ready to explode.

Fortunately, the work required of him was routine. Not much concentration was required. He'd wait until a rod was rising back to the start position, then stoop over and give its mechanism a quick squirt of oil before the rod came crashing down. Since each of the 240 stamps needed to be oiled, it was a long process. All he could do to escape the noise and the monotony was to lose himself in his thoughts. Invariably, it would not be long before his mind focused on Mamie. He was still haunted by her memory.

So there was no warning. He did not even realize what he'd done until it was too late. He had gone a good ways down the line, oiling each mechanism in turn; and now he was on his knees, bending toward the next machine, absently angling the tip of his oil can into the hydraulic mechanism, his thoughts elsewhere, when he tried to remove his hand and move on. He couldn't. He was wedged tightly into a narrow space and he couldn't free himself. Somehow the right-hand sleeve of his mackinaw had gotten stuck in the hydraulic mechanism, while his left sleeve had been caught in the belt of the vanner rollers that delivered the rocks. It was as if he were in a grizzly's merciless grip. Only more dangerous. In a moment the heavy metal stamp would come crashing down on his hand.

Desperately, he tried to move away, to unbutton his heavy coat so that he could escape. But the angle of his entrapment made it impossible. He was crouched in the narrow space between two stamps and the rubber belt. His right arm lay exposed. It was impossible to free it. And the heavy stamp was coming down fast. The best he could do was close his fingers into a fist; maybe that way he could avoid getting them severed.

His mind raced but found no way to stop the descent of the metal stamp. Or to get free. He'd seen the stamp smash into the metal box; the heavy rocks inside were reduced to smithereens. It would crush every bone in his hand to dust.

Suddenly Charlie felt an arm reach in, grab the sleeve of his coat, and with one strong motion pull it free. Immediately he jumped up from his crouch and stepped back. Then the stamp crashed down against the mortar.

Shaken, Charlie turned to see an Indian walking away. There were plenty of them at the mine; they worked for a dollar a day less than white men, so Durkin was glad to hire them. Charlie hurried after him. Maybe he didn't speak English, and that was why he was scurrying off. But Charlie still wanted to thank him. If he hadn't come along, there was no telling what would've happened. 'Cept, for sure, Charlie's hand would've been busted up, if not severed.

It was only when Charlie caught up with the Indian that he realized his mistake. Sure, the man had a few hairs on his chin and one of those drooping black mustaches all the Tlingits wore, and there was a string of green beads around his neck, and his dirty slouch hat had a perky feather in the band; but he was no Indian. The set of his eyes, the shape of his nose, his skin color — all revealed him to be a white man. Charlie had, however, just come too close to disaster to be of a mind to make judgments. He simply extended his hand and asked, Who do I have the pleasure of thanking for saving my skin?

Shaking the offered hand, the man answered, "George Carmack."

FIFTEEN

By the time George Carmack had come to Charlie's rescue, he had been to the Yukon and back. He'd also had abandoned any dreams of ever finding gold. Instead, George was driven by a new ambition: He wanted to be made an Indian chief.

It had been a strange and unpredictable journey that had brought George — now known and dismissed as a Siwash, another red-skinned savage, by most of the men with whom he'd once panned for gold — to the Treadwell mine. Yet it had started off in a seemingly uneventful fashion when, upon first arriving in Juneau four years earlier, George had gotten himself a room in the same hotel where Charlie would later register under an alias. Also just like Charlie, his initial morning in Juneau had started out in disappointment.

With the first light, George had headed up to Gold Creek to get a sense of how the prospectors were faring. The murky waters were high and roiling from the heavy spring rains and melting snow, but he found plenty of men working. Some stood on the banks of the creek shoveling gravel into sluice boxes, and others were panning, knee-deep in the swift, frigid waters. To a man, though, each gave George a similarly despairing report: Gold Creek had been played out. A few years back, a fellow could stick his pan into the creek bed and he could count on seeing some yellow in the siftings. There'd been a time, you could walk away with twenty, sometimes even fifty dollars' worth of nuggets and dust after only a morning's work. But gravel and black sand was all anyone was finding nowadays. You've come too late, young fella, George heard time after time.

On the long downhill walk through the icy slush back to the hotel, George began silently blaming himself. It had been a damn silly indulgence to have dawdled so long in California simply because he'd been taken by Becky's charms. What'd he been thinking? But after a mile or so, his raging, self-accusatory mood began to settle. This was a big country, he reminded himself. There had to be lots of Gold Creeks, lots of opportunities.

In fact George, as naive as he was eager, only had to walk up to the front desk upon his return to the hotel to find reason enough to believe all his reassuring thoughts. That same morning the hotel manager introduced him to the Day brothers, and they had a story to tell. And by the time they'd finished, George's vague plans had a definite direction.

The Day brothers, Hugh and Albert, were a pair of heavyset, lumbering, gray-bearded French-Canadian prospectors with thick mud-stained gum boots and fraying mackinaws, but in George's impressionable eyes they might just as well have been gods. They'd lived the rugged prospector's life he'd only imagined, and — even more reason to admire 'em — they'd enjoyed a fair share of success in the process. After striking it rich in British Columbia, they'd promptly sold their claim and used the money to grubstake a couple of fanciful years prospecting along several of the tributaries that spun off from the upper reaches of the mighty Yukon River. This was unexplored territory, a land of lush green valleys, virgin forests, and raging headwaters, and each day was one of discovery. George listened to their tales with an awe that was near on worshipful. They hadn't, they admitted without a trace of excuse or apology, much to show for two years of panning. Sure, here and there they'd collected nearly enough gold dust to fill their poke, but they'd returned to Juneau without a single nugget worth bragging about. Still, they weren't discouraged. Either a prospector figures his luck's only a brief day away from changing or he might just as well give up the life, they sternly advised the young man. They'd spent the winter making plans for their next expedition, partnering up with Isaac Powers. Soon as they were outfitted, the brothers told George, the three of them would be heading back to the Yukon, and the fortune of gold that was waiting.

Normally quite shy, George listened to the two men and quickly grew too excited to be restrained by his inhibitions. He hurled dozens of questions, and the Day brothers, perhaps flattered by the tenderfoot's interest or simply glad to have an audience after making conversation with only each other for so long, were generous in their responses. Rather matter-of-factly, neither exaggerating nor ignoring the hardships and challenges, the brothers sucked on their pipes and responded to George's rapid-fire interrogation. In the process, the two old sourdoughs offered up what amounted to nothing less than a primer for a *cheechako,* as the Indians called the newcomers to Alaska.

You head out from Juneau, you need to get back before the first snow or you'd better be prepared to spend an entire year in the far north, the brothers began. The snow comes, you ain't going out of your cabin, much less making your way out of the frozen Yukon. They spoke more or less in unison, one jumping in to complete the other's sentences; and George had a private smile thinking how their combined voices, their English accented with a singsong French lilt, brought to mind the choir he had heard sitting next to Becky in church last Christmas Eve in California.

They continued: Prospecting in the Yukon was hard work, day in, day out. A man who was too easily put off by failure shouldn't even think of taking up the life. But panning for Yukon gold, rigorous and frustrating as it was, was nothing when compared to what was required of a man in the course of getting there. It was demanding country; it asked a lot from people. You start out, you'd better be sure you had the gumption to see the journey through.

They were heading to the Stewart River, a big, rolling Yukon waterway that spilled down from the Mackenzie Mountains. Some coarse gold had been found along its banks, and the brothers were convinced these small discoveries were the harbingers of a genuine bonanza. Still, they explained to George with an almost paternal patience, reaching the Stewart would be a real test of a man's resolve.

They'd need to find a boat that'd take them to the mouth of the Taiya River, about 120 miles north of Juneau. That might be easy enough. It was the next stage, going over the Chilkoot Pass, that, Al Day warned, was "a real man-killer." This mountain trail — its summit the boundary line between American Alaska and the Canadian Yukon — was so steep that walking upright while carrying a pack loaded down with the weight of a year's supplies became nearly impossible. The Indian guides could do it, but most white men wound up crawling on their hands and knees for miles, over hard rock and slick glacial ice and through gusting mountain winds. Then, once you'd climbed the twenty-five miles up and down the pass, you'd arrive at Lake Lindeman. Don't matter that it's spring; they told him; we'll still need to wait for the last of the winter ice covering the lake to break. Course we won't just be sitting around watching ice melt. We'll be busy building the boat that'll take us across Lindeman. It'll need to be big enough to carry three men and all our grub. And it'd better be seaworthy enough to navigate the churning white-water rapids that lead on up into the Yukon River. From there, it's on to the lake country; and then if the wind is working with us, it's just a swift sail up to the Stewart.

Soon as the brothers had finished, George blurted out, "Got room for one more man?"

They didn't. But they'd taken a liking to the enthusiastic young tenderfoot, so they offered him an alternative. If George could partner up with some other men, their outfit could travel with the Day brothers to the

Taiya and then on over the Chilkoot Pass and into the Canadian Yukon. The mountain trail would be rough going and, the brothers modestly suggested, their experience might prove useful.

"That's good enough for me," said George. Elated, feeling that his life was once more pointing him toward his long-desired goal, he shook hands with the two men to seal the deal.

It didn't take George long to find three more newcomers to join his expedition to the Yukon. Juneau, it seemed, was full of optimistic and daring men ready to make a dangerous gamble as long as it offered even the slimmest prospect of striking it rich. Hugh Donahue, J. V. Dawson, and Dan Foley agreed to match George's contribution and put $200 each for supplies and equipment into the common pot; still, $800 for four men was a mighty small grubstake. And once the money had been anted up, without much discussion it was settled that George'd be the outfit's leader. It wasn't that George had any more experience or knowledge about prospecting than the others. They just recognized that he was bold, and that alone was sufficient, especially among high-spirited men who were looking for further reason to ignore the daunting impracticalities of what they were setting out to do.

George's first command decision was to initiate a scheme that'd save the team some money while they remained in Juneau completing their outfitting. He checked out of the hotel that was costing $5 a week and settled into a big tent he pegged down on the outskirts of town; and encouraged by his example the three others moved in, too. They were on top of each other and come nightfall the spring cold found ways of curling under the tent flap, but the shared experience helped to meld them into a team. And although they were just a short hike from Juneau's general store, George announced that it wasn't too soon to learn to get by without the cushion of such conveniences. During his time in Sitka, he had heard the Tlingit saying "When the tide goes out, the table is set," so now he put that wisdom to the test on the beaches of Juneau. He had the men digging up clams, prowling for beached fish, or just buying salmon and halibut from the Indians at ten cents a fish. It was a monotonous diet, but George's resourceful economy won their respect.

By the time they were done making all the necessary purchases, they'd laid in near on 800 pounds of supplies. It wasn't just a larder of foodstuffs, items like bacon, flour, beans, and baking powder. They'd also had to buy the tools they'd need to build a boat: a two-man whipsaw, sturdy axes, iron nails, as well as pitch and oakum. And on the advice of the Day brothers, who had continued to keep a watchful eye on George and his team, they'd stored away plenty of gold and silver coins. They'd need clinking change to hire the packers who'd help carry their heavy load over the Chilkoot Pass, into Canadian territory; Indians, the Days had told George, didn't trust the white man's paper money.

Only now that they were finally ready to leave, there was a sudden crimp in their plans — they couldn't find a boat to take them on the first leg of their journey. It was 120 miles up to the mouth of the Taiya, and there was no call for either freight or passenger vessels to schedule a trip into such godforsaken country. There wasn't even a boat for charter. After some thought, George improvised a plan: He'd hire Indians to paddle them up the Lynn Canal, to the mouth of the river. He found a few Auke Indians who were willing, but one look at their narrow dugout canoes made him realize it'd be a doomed voyage. Even if they managed to fit all the team's supplies into the cedar canoes, the overloaded boats would never make it through the choppy waters without capsizing. There had to be another way, he told his partners, though even as he said the words he knew they owed more to a wish than to logic.

Yet it turned out that he was right. A passel

of Indian braves had gotten hold of some bootleg whiskey; and before a raucous night was over, they'd whooped through the small town of Chilkoot with their guns blazing. This incident proved to be just the bit of luck that George needed.

A U.S. Navy gunboat, the USS *Pinta*, stationed at Sitka, was dispatched to apprehend the misbehaving Indians. On its way up to Chilkoot, the *Pinta* sailed into Juneau. As soon as Al Day saw the smoke from the galley's stovepipe rising above the harbor, he had an idea. He boarded the *Pinta*, headed straight for the captain, and he must've made quite a persuasive argument. Or perhaps Lieutenant Commander Henry Nichols, USN, simply had a fondness for men chasing after unlikely causes. Whatever the reason, Al got the captain to agree that on his way to Chilkoot, he'd detour to deliver seven men and their supplies to the Taiya.

Boarding the gunship, the men couldn't believe their good fortune. George, however, took it in stride; it was further proof, he insisted, that their expedition was blessed. Despite all the obstacles, they'd meet with success. But while making a casual tour around the *Pinta*'s deck, he saw a sight that in an instant convinced him he'd never make it to the Yukon. Hell, more likely he'd wind up in jail instead. George recognized two sailors he'd served with on the *Wachusett*.

The way they were heading straight toward him, he had no doubt they'd spotted him, too. And he knew: One word to the captain that there was an AWOL sailor on board, and he'd be led off in shackles to a navy brig.

George prepared himself for the worst. Sure enough, first thing the sailors said was how reckless it was for George, given the circumstances surrounding his hasty departure from the *Wachusett,* to have come aboard a navy gunboat. But Jesus, George, they said in the next whispered breath, good to see you, shipmate. And no need to worry. We can keep a secret.

The rest of the voyage was smooth sailing. In fact, when Commander Nichols learned that Dawson and Donahue were heading into the wild without rifles, he issued Springfields, along with 250 rounds of ball cartridges, to the pair. Just return 'em when you're back in Juneau, the captain ordered.

On a sunny mid-May morning, the seven prospectors climbed down into the *Pinta*'s two steam launches. Along with their supplies, the men were ferried to the quick-moving, glacier-fed headwaters of the Taiya River.

Sitting round the blazing campfire, the Day brothers had gone on about the Chilkoot trail for nights on end. But it wasn't until George had his first close look, until he'd the opportunity to see with his own eyes the thirty-five-hundred-foot climb he'd need to make over the steep, glittering white slope, that he realized the reality was a lot more formidable even than all the grim warnings. For the first time since he'd blithely shaken hands with the Day brothers back in Juneau, his confidence began to slip.

Until that morning, the seven prospectors had trudged north for days, following the winding path of the Taiya, and George had been silently congratulating himself on how well things were going. Employing the smatterings of Tlingit he had learned as a marine based in Sitka, he'd succeeded, after an hour or so of dickering, in coming to pretty fair terms with the Chilkoot Indian packers. The negotiated price was $8 per hundred pounds, and each of the forty-eight Indians recruited — young boys and squaws, as well the powerful, thick-chested braves — would also receive a daily cup of flour. Even the Day brothers were impressed with the deal the tenderfoot had cut; in the past, the Indians had demanded $15 per hundred-pound load, and often gotten it.

Each day on the river trail had been arduous. When they made camp for the night, George let loose with a sigh of relief; even with the hired packers, the rucksack on his back held at least fifty pounds of supplies. Still, the trail had led them through some breathtaking country, past snowcapped sharp-edged peaks, mazes of majestic evergreens, fields of fresh emerald-green grass. A log trading post was the only building in the settlement of Dyea, and its proprietor, John Healy, an aging Indian fighter who as a young scout had smoked pipes with Sitting Bull, was the only white man living in these parts, but George could understand the allure. A high volley of birdsong carried through the pine-scented air, and the post faced an inlet of placid blue-green waters, the shimmering images of chiseled mountains and tall evergreens reflected in its glimmering pools. When George spotted a lone eagle circling overhead, he told himself that he must remember to include the sighting in his diary.

But five miles from Dyea the trail led straight into a canyon. The sun had turned the remaining snow that lay across the floor of this stony, high-walled crevice into a swamp of thick slush. With George's pack weighing heavy on his back, each step felt as if he were in a struggle to escape the unforgiving pull of quicksand; the exertion required was enormous. And no sooner had he somehow made it through the canyon than he discovered that the remainder of the trail was blocked by heavy boulders and fallen trees. All George could do was follow the Indians' example and climb over them as best he could. The grade, too, had begun to rise, and he knew this was only a small promise of what he could expect when they started over the Chilkoot. He was totally spent by the time they made camp. That evening, contrary to all the Days' instructions, he fell asleep without drying his wet socks over the smoky spruce-bough fire. He was flat out, snoring loudly, before even managing to remove his leather boots.

In the early morning, he woke up stiff and aching. He came out of his tent, his boots crunching against the fresh layer of ground frost, and for the first time he had a good look at the mountain he intended to climb that day. The camp lay in a broad basin, and from this perspective the Chilkoot stood out from the surrounding peaks. It seemed to rise higher and more steeply, and the sunlight glinted with harsh menace off the green-iced glaciers that fortified its walls. It would be impossible to cross, George suddenly moaned to himself. He'd barely taken a single step, but the muscles in his thighs and calves were still throbbing from yesterday's ordeal. Yet how could he dare to give up, to turn around and go back? But would that be any less of an embarrassment than surrendering halfway up the mountain? Or, worse, falling to his death, his body lost forever, shrouded each passing year by snow and more snow?

Then George saw the Indians hoisting their

huge sacks — one hundred pounds each! — into their backs. And the Day brothers, too, had lit their cob pipes and were raring to head off. George knew he could not be the only one to quit. He was, he chastised himself, too close to his lifelong goal to give up. So in a tremendous burst of will, he lifted his pack to his back, adjusted the leather shoulder straps, and joined the others.

It was four miles uphill to the summit, and George had not gone far before it became clear to him that he was locked in a battle to the death: Either he would cross the Chilkoot into the Canadian Yukon or he'd die trying. Even if he didn't have the heart, it was no longer possible to turn back.

The snow was thick underfoot. Icy boulders as big as streetcars needed to be traversed. The wind shrieked. A mammoth overhanging glacier reflected the sunlight like a prism, dazzling hues of turquoise, sapphire, and rose bouncing off walls of sheer ice, blinding him, while the huge glacier itself seemed poised to come crashing down at any moment. He sweated under his heavy coat. His socks dripped rivulets of ice. His pack ground down hard on his back as if he were carrying the broad trunk of one of the sturdy evergreens he'd only days before admired. After two miles, the line of bone-weary men reached a flat-ledged slope. The Indians lowered the packs from their backs. It was the signal to rest.

George could now see the pass's white-tipped summit. It was tantalizingly close. Nevertheless, he decided he could walk no farther.

He was right. When the line moved forward for the final ascent, he soon found himself bent over, climbing in an awkward, hunched fashion rather than walking upright. A snow-covered rock slide blocked the trail, and the only way up the increasingly steep path was to pull himself over one icy boulder after another. His legs were cramping. His fingers were numb. In his wet, slick boots, footholds were slippery and brief. By the time he found the muscle and the ingenuity and the will to get over the rock slide, all pride belonged to another life. Crawling on all fours like a beaten animal, George reached the summit. He'd left American Alaska and now was standing in Canadian territory, at the entry-way into the vast Yukon. He felt he should let loose with a triumphant yell, but he just didn't have the strength.

Even in late May, the ice on Lake Lindeman was still more than a foot thick. It'd be ten days or so, the Day brothers estimated, before it'd start to break and a boat could make its way to the headwaters of the Yukon. But George found that there was plenty to do in the meantime, and in their cruel way, these tasks were nearly as demanding as the trek over the Chilkoot.

Following the brothers' instructions, a scaffold known as a saw pit was constructed. Logs were first stripped of their bark, then laid on top of this platform. While one man stood on top of the saw pit grasping one handle of a jag-toothed six-foot whipsaw, another gripped the other handle from below. Back and forth the two men uneasily worked the saw, shavings showering down on the man below, the sinews in their arms straining as with each stroke they fought to raise the saw high above their heads; and, inevitably, tempers flared. It was difficult, backbreaking work, but it was the only way to cut the planks for the boats.

At last, the ice melted. And the new boats, the pitch on their seams barely dry, went to sea. The Day brothers headed straight for the Stewart River. But George and his partners guided their twenty-foot boat toward a nearby creek that emptied into the clear waters of Lake Bennett. George had a hunch.

His hunch didn't pan out. Still, there were more hunches, and more creeks. The team traveled 150 miles up the Yukon. At the end of months of daily panning, George's share of the dust they'd found weighed a slight two ounces.

George was back in Juneau before winter set in. Though he had nothing to show for all his difficult travel and hard work, he wasn't discouraged. No one could ever call him a *cheechako* again. He'd proved himself. At last, he was his father's son. Proudly, he wrote to his sister Rose, "I have done better than I expected the first year."

After almost a year on his own, his confidence remained absolute. His belief was religious in its intensity and its certainty. Although he was unable to point to a single piece of tangible evidence, he had no doubts. He concluded the earnest letter to his sister by revealing the cornerstone of his unshakable faith: "There is a big gold field in the Yukon, and I want my share of it. And am going to have it if the Lord wills it."

SIXTEEN

It was one thing, however, for George to believe he'd strike it rich, and it was another to be broke in Alaska with winter setting in. By October, when even the deer had been driven from the mountain meadows above Juneau by the first heavy snows, George had no choice but to abandon his tent. With great reluctance, he dug into the last of his nest egg and took a closet-sized room in a hotel off Front Street. Food, to his relief, wouldn't be too much of a problem. He'd always been a good rifle shot — truth was, like Charlie Siringo, he could be a little vain about his marksmanship — and there were still ducks and geese bobbing up and down on the waves just beyond the tidal flats. A wing shot, and George would have a feast he could roast over a spruce fire. Netting salmon swimming upstream was even easier. And after the birds flew south and the spawning salmon completed their run, he'd still be able to dig for clams or hook a bottomfish. He wouldn't starve. Of course, if he could get work, that would certainly give his circumstances a lift, and he'd be able to save for the grubstake he'd need to head back up north in the spring. But this time of year, no one was hiring; even the Treadwell mine, across the channel, was turning people away. Money or not, he'd just have to make do. "I think I can wiggle through the winter all right," George wrote to his sister, as much to shore up his own spirits as hers.

But George hadn't anticipated the complete loneliness of the existence he'd be locked in to. Although in his shepherd's life he'd known solitude, it was nothing like the prison he now occupied. In California, he'd found solace simply from being in the hill country; invigoration came from spending days in windswept meadows, from nights lying in a field on his back gazing up at the starry Milky Way sprinkled across the heavens. During the long winter months in Alaska, he was besieged. The snow would not stop falling, and the cold would not desist. All George could do was take refuge in his tiny room. Fully dressed, with a cloak of blankets wrapped over his shoulders for additional warmth, he still found it impossible to escape the howling, frosty wind that whooshed into his room each endless night, forcing its ice-cold way into every fiber of his being. Alone and lonely, he brooded.

It was a well-practiced habit. George had taken refuge in his thoughts during his days and nights while tending to his flock in Modesto, and it had always been a comforting excursion. In his mind, he'd travel to an imagined place where the bonanza he so desperately wanted was within his grasp. He could escape by celebrating the triumph, the fortune of gold, he saw in his mind's eye.

The solitary Alaskan winter, however, chilled his dreams. George could not help reminding himself that he'd actually been to the Yukon — only to return empty-handed. A man alone, the reality of his failure became his constant companion. He revisited it. He nurtured it. And in time, the intensity of his expectations subsided. He lost his faith. It had all been folly, he decided. What sort of vanity had it been to think that he'd somehow be the lucky one to strike it rich in the Yukon? Yes, he told himself, he was his father's son. Only now when George acknowledged this pedigree, it stung like a curse.

He shared his weary resignation in a letter to Rose: "I have not been doing much as I can get nothing to do. . . . Some of the men came back from the Yukon reporting good diggings there. But I don't think I will go back in there again. If I can get good wages here in Juneau I will stay until I can make a grubstake for Becky and me."

Becky! During the hard course of the

winter, one dream had been broken. Yet when it had shattered, another had taken on new significance and had grown more elaborate, more impassioned. The only escape George could make from the constant grinding loneliness was to envision an existence with Becky. It had been, he wrote to Becky in a beseeching letter, the mistake of his life to have left her behind. Together, he proclaimed with the solemn ardor of a convert to a new faith, they could create a life filled with happiness. He asked her to join him in Juneau in the spring.

As soon as George mailed the letter, his days took on a purpose. They were no longer empty. He had something to look forward to. He kept busy by plotting out the future, *their* future, in his mind.

He waited for her response. When the letter didn't come, he blamed the mails. Then he worried that Becky was sick. But he entertained no anxieties about her loyalty or her love. It was all he had left, so he refused to doubt it. He clung to Becky; and in this way, she protected him.

Her letter never came. Finally, it was Rose who answered. Becky, she revealed with a no-nonsense brevity, had found someone else.

George was devastated. In a single winter he'd lost everything; and he was certain there'd never be anything else for him in his life. Defeated, despairing, he instinctively fled his room after reading his sister's news. He trudged out to a street covered in high white drifts and held his face up to the gusts of falling snow. It poured down on him in thick, cold waves, and he surrendered to it. George hoped the snow would keep coming and coming, covering him until he was lost forever.

In the end, a poem restored him. It nudged his heart toward a change of mood. On Christmas Eve, surrounded by his loneliness, he recalled an image from the previous summer and he began to write: "But a whispering comes from the tall old spruce / And my soul from the pain is free." His mind had been yearning, and in its desperation it had found a new destination. He focused on a clear, idyllic picture of the hewn-log trading post in Dyea that looked out on a "tall old spruce" and an inlet of shimmering blue water. The fine, bright beauty of the setting had affected him when he'd first encountered it, and in a burst of sentimental emotion he found himself traveling back to it on Christmas Eve in his poem. Soon his thoughts would often be making the journey to Dyea from his little room. And with each new trip, its perfection grew.

In the process, a plan took hold. He'd no money to speak of, certainly not enough to grubstake another journey over the Chilkoot and into the Yukon, even if he were of a mind to take up prospecting again. But if he pitched his tent near old Healy's place in Dyea, he could live off the land — deer and fish were plentiful — and maybe he'd find work as a guide or a packer. At least, he'd be out of the stifling confines of Juneau and in the open air.

As soon as the snow on Front Street began melting into a muddy slush and the promise of spring could be felt in the warming sun on the beach as he dug for clams, George found an Aleut willing to take him up to Dyea in his canoe. He pitched his tent not more than a stone's throw from the trading post, and he waited with a fair amount of apprehension about how old Healy would take to his presence.

George had heard all the stories: how when J. J. Healy had been the sheriff in Chouteau County, Montana, he'd a tendency to hang whomever he arrested without fussing too much over the severity of the infraction. How Healy'd held off a band of wild prairie Indians by waving his lit cigar over a keg of gunpowder and threatening to blow 'em all, himself included, to kingdom come if they didn't ride off. How he'd shot his way out of at least a couple of dozen other tight scrapes as he loped through Mexico, the West, and Canada. And George had seen enough of J.J. to appreciate that while his hair had turned

259

white, he still was a crusty old bird, his back as ramrod straight as a marine's on the Sitka parade grounds, and his stare as unforgiving as a drill sergeant's. Yet, oddly, Healy never said a word to George about his pitching a tent where the merchant couldn't miss seeing it each day when he sat on his porch. Perhaps Healy'd become resigned; in the course of his far-flung travels he might well've come to learn that a man couldn't outrun civilization. Or maybe Healy enjoyed the prospect of company. In fact, to George's considerable surprise, whenever he had occasion to purchase tea or tobacco at the trading post, Healy was downright pleasant, even friendly.

That was how it happened that on a rainy May afternoon George was in the post chewing the fat with Healy when two Indian trappers carrying a bundle of furs entered. As a rule, Healy didn't have much truck with Indians; he'd spent too many years of his rambling life avoiding getting scalped ever to feel comfortable around 'em. Besides, most of the braves who came to the post were Chilkoots hoping to buy molasses and lemon extract for mixing up some hoochinoo, an alcoholic brew that had a genuine kick to it. Last thing you want to deal with, Healy had once told George after he'd ordered some Chinooks — like most white men up north, he used the word dismissively for all Indians — out of his store, was a drunk red man. So

Charlie was bewildered when Healy gave these two Indians a friendly greeting.

To George's further astonishment, he introduced the two braves as politely as if they were guests arriving for tea. The big one was a broad-shouldered, hawk-nosed man, and with a frank, unnerving curiosity, he fixed two eyes as black as lumps of coal on George. Healy called him Skookum Jim. *Skookum,* George knew, was the Chinook word for "strong," and with just a glance George decided the name was appropriate. The Indian looked to be as tall as a spruce and just as sturdy. Still, Healy felt obliged to explain how Jim had earned his nickname: "He can carry a 150 pound sack 'cross the Chilkoot as if it were a feather." The other Indian, George figured, might've been made up from what little was left after the Indian gods had finished putting Jim together. He was a skinny runt of a fellow with a weaselly look. Healy said he was Jim's nephew and called him Tagish Charley.

George had met a few Tagish Indians when he'd been up in the Yukon lake country last summer. They were mighty good hunters and fishermen, and George was inclined to respect people who led that kind of self-sufficient life. In his experience, the Stick country (as the interior was known) Tagish were not as fierce or, for that matter, as arrogant as the coastal Tlingits he'd met in

Sitka and Juneau.

Tlingits, of course, were warriors; George gave 'em that. Back at the turn of the century, they'd fought hand to hand against the Russians, and until the Russians had brought in artillery, they'd had them on the run. Even today George felt that a lot of the young braves were still looking for a fight. That was, after all, one of the reasons the War Department had dispatched him and his company of marines up to Sitka; the thinking was that a show of force was needed to keep the Tlingits in line.

Still, the Tlingits and the Tagish got on fine with each other; it was pretty common for them to marry up. At the same time, both tribes seemed to have it in for the Chilkoots, which George could understand. A Chilkoot clan had a camp near Dyea and they were always poking around his tent; once he'd had to stand out front with his rifle cocked to show 'em he meant business. Not that he was too worried about the Chilkoots going on the warpath. They were making too much money packing white men over the pass to want to chase them away. They were smart, all right. Like all the tribes, the Chilkoots couldn't be bothered to waste their days looking for gold. Indians just didn't see how a hunk of rock could be worth anything. But more than most of the tribes, the Chilkoots had the savvy to realize that they didn't need to take a gamble and waste their days looking for gold. There was a guaranteed bonanza to be made off all the white men foolish enough to believe they'd strike it rich. He recalled the strident way the Chinook packers had bargained with him last spring, and, although he'd wound up getting a fair price, the heated give-and-take left a sour taste in his mouth. So all in all, George reckoned it made some sense that if old Healy was going to smoke the peace pipe with some tribe, it'd be the Tagish.

George watched as Healy sorted through the furs the two Indians had to offer, separating them into piles of marten, fox, muskrat, and beaver. Next Healy carefully inspected every pelt, running his fingers through each one to gauge the thickness of the fur and holding every skin up to the light to see if it was diseased. When he was satisfied, the bargaining began. It was in Chinook, but George had no trouble understanding. And by the time the give-and-take was concluded, both sides felt they had done well. Healy gave Skookum Jim $125; Tagish Charley received $100, and the only reason for the difference, as far as George could guess, was that Healy felt he could get away with paying less to Charley, but not to big Jim.

Once they put the money in their pockets, though, the mood of the two Indians turned somber. They stood facing Healy awkwardly, as if wanting to say something but unable to find the words. Finally, Jim spoke.

We were thinking about spending the summer working as packers, the big Indian began. Lot of money in taking prospectors over the Chilkoot.

Healy nodded. George noticed that Healy's demeanor had suddenly changed, too. He seemed wary.

The two Indians weren't helping things along. They just stood there as if they had forgotten how to speak. Once again, it was Jim who at last spoke up.

The Chilkoots, he said, spitting the name out with an unmistakable venom. We set up camp, he went on, the Chilkoots will try to run us off. There's just two of us, he added rather helplessly, but there's a whole clan of Chilkoots in these parts.

Don't seem like a fair fight, does it, Carmack? Healy asked. Now that he knew what'd been on the two Indians' minds, he was no longer on guard. In fact, their predicament set his temper boiling.

Can't say it does, George agreed.

The odds so rankled the old Indian fighter's sense of justice that Healy made an impetuous suggestion. Why don't you two make camp with Carmack right by my post? Those Chinooks give you any trouble, Carmack and me'll help you set things right.

So it was settled. Jim and Charley found a bit of level ground facing the inlet, and before long George had helped them erect a spruce-bough lean-to. Now when Healy sat on his porch he'd grumble that he might as well be in Denver, Dyea was getting so crowded. But George didn't mind at all. After last winter's crushing isolation, with only his disappointments to keep him company, it was a real pleasure to be able to sit around a fire at night making conversation, even if it was mostly in Chinook.

No less a blessing, George was soon busy, working and making money. When a group of prospectors came around looking to hire the two Indians to help carry their supplies to Lake Lindeman, Jim, without even speaking to George about it, announced that there were three men in this outfit. So George became the only white man to work as a packer going over the Chilkoot.

The morning of their first job, George was full of dread. He remembered his one climb over the trail, and how he'd wound up crawling on his hands and knees like a dazed and wounded animal. That morning's ascent proved to be no less of a battle. But whenever it felt as if he were about to stumble, Jim would somehow understand and he'd be there to steady George with one of his big hands. In this fashion, George was able to make it to the summit on his own two legs.

As the summer passed and there were more trips up the trail, George grew stronger and cannier. He learned how to balance his pack while scampering over slick rocks, how to keep his footing in a soup of melting snow. It was beyond his powers to handle the climb with the ease that Jim and even Charley (who, after all, was no more than a runt) demonstrated, but George grew pleased with himself. He felt he could do a packer's job. And for once he was able to save some money; the going rate was $10 per hundred pounds that summer. There was also another benefit from all the busy summer's labor: He'd been too occupied to let his mind wander to thoughts of Becky. As the weeks passed, George came to realize that he couldn't even remember the color of her eyes or the sound of her voice, let alone why he'd made such a fuss. Now if her name happened to stray into his thoughts, he'd dismiss it with a quick laugh, and chide himself for having been such a foolish, lovesick boy. She, too, had become part of a buried past.

SEVENTEEN

But come the tail end of August, when the wind blew down from the mountains with a sharper, icy slap and the lakes turned dark under the looming afternoon sky, the careful world George had constructed fell apart. Jim announced that with winter nearing, Charley and he'd be returning to their village in the lake country. They planned to buy some supplies from Healy, and then tomorrow they'd head back over the pass.

Sensible as Jim's plan was, George had never considered their return to the Tagish village as even a possibility. It'd never occurred to him that the two Indians would be leaving Dyea. He didn't know what to say. All at once he felt as if he were suffering from a mortal wound, and in a way he was. He knew he couldn't bear to spend another Alaskan winter on his own. For a moment, he wished he'd died on his way up the Chilkoot. That would've been easier, and a lot less painful than what he knew was in store for him.

Why don't you come with us? Jim suddenly asked. "Hiyu skookum illahee. Hiyu clean, all same sky," he urged.

"Indian country strong, plenty clean like the sky," George agreed.

And with those words it was settled.

In the course of the long journey to the Tagish village, George began to fret about his decision. He didn't speak Tagish, and it'd been hard enough to learn Chinook. He worried that he'd be unable to talk to anyone and that this would make things not much different than being holed up on his own in a room in Juneau. Only now, he'd be smack in the middle of a bunch of wild Indians who'd probably be thinking about how to make off with the sizable sum of money he'd been able to save and had tucked into his rucksack. All the way over the pass and then as the trio canoed down the swift streams that linked Lake Lindeman to Lake Bennett, new concerns took shape in his mind each day. He began to realize that he didn't know what to expect. By the time the three men approached the village, paddling north into the ice-still waters of Nares Lake, George had come around to thinking he'd made a mistake.

On the way up this short, narrow channel, his misgivings spreading like the ripples created by each firm stroke of their paddles dipping into the water, George heard what sounded like cannon fire. It was off in the distance, and he was reminded of the fusillade that'd been shot off on parade days in Sitka.

For a crazy moment all he could think of was that the U.S. Marines had decided to attack Canada. After all, the precise boundaries between American Alaska and the Dominion of Canada were, it was well known, a matter of dispute. Canada had requested a jointly financed survey, but the United States had rejected the plan; the folks in Washington didn't see any reason to spend money to establish boundary lines for such a remote and sparsely settled wilderness. As it was, it was generally agreed that the summit of the Chilkoot Trail was the demarcation between the United States' Alaska Territory and the Canadian Yukon. But George suspected that it wouldn't be long before this vague line, based on a loose interpretation of the 1825 treaty between Russia and Britain defining the borders of their colonial possessions, would become the subject of a diplomatic shouting match. Perhaps, he imagined, tempers between the Canadians and the Americans had gotten so riled that the marines had now been called in.

Listening with some attention, he realized that the noise kept growing larger, moving closer and closer. He was certain: It was coming straight at him. He looked across the channel, toward a field of tall grass, and then in a moment he saw the source of the approaching thunder. It was a herd of galloping caribou, perhaps one thousand or, for all he could tell, as many as two thousand of the animals, big and strong with their glistening winter fur, their pointed antlers held high, their hooves pounding the hard earth in a fierce rhythm as they charged forward in a single wave. The three men stopped paddling and stared with respect. It was wondrous: a spectacle of power, majesty, and beauty. George was awed. And as he watched the wild herd race across the plain, George decided that no matter what was in store for him, it was not a mistake to have made the journey.

The Tagish village was about fifty miles from where they'd spotted the migrating herd. It was nestled along the steep brown banks of a channel that circled around two lakes, the gunmetal-gray water stretching flat and clear to the horizon like a mirror reflecting a high, moody sky. Jim's people were a small clan, no more than twenty families, running to about seventy or eighty Indians in all. On a wide, grassy terrace sat two large, rough-planked community houses, and beyond them about a dozen small log cabins were strung out in a loping semicircle.

Jim led George into one of the big houses and introduced him to his mother. She was a chief's daughter, Jim explained, and therefore she was in charge of this lodge. George wondered how this was possible. The woman was frail and wizened; he doubted she possessed the faculties to care for herself. As soon as the old squaw spoke, however, George found he had to reconsider his smug thoughts. He couldn't understand the words, but her voice was strong and confident. The years had taken their toll, yet she still had a leader's authority. He looked at her with a sudden, newfound respect. In fact, she reminded him of his sister, Rose. Like Rose, she didn't hesitate or seem uncertain in her pronouncements. She knew her heart and, he felt, spoke it clearly. In time, he'd come to understand that all the Tagish squaws possessed this trait. In this tribe, the women made the decisions while the men did the hunting, and that division of labor suited George just fine.

At first George was treated with an elaborate courtesy, and he wondered if the Indians were simply being polite or if there was something ironic in their attitude. Of course, he was the only white man many of them had ever spoken to; he couldn't blame them if they felt as uncomfortable as he did. And if they were enjoying a joke at his expense, laughing when, for example, he insisted on spitting out the coarse hairs on the caribou tongue that they considered a great delicacy, well, how often had he heard white men guffawing at an Injun's peculiar ways?

After he'd spent weeks in the village, however, the barriers began to recede. When he went hunting with the braves, they were excited by his skill with a rifle. They all wanted to learn how to shoot like a white man, and George was only too pleased to try to teach them. For his part, George was impressed that when a moose or a caribou was killed, the hunter didn't claim his prey. The carcass belonged to the entire village, everyone joining in for a communal feast, and the women working together to dry and smoke the surplus. For George, who had been on his own for so long, fending for himself ever since he was eleven and his father had died, the opportunity to be part of a community was unexpected. He hadn't been treated this way for a very long time. It felt like he was being given back something that'd been taken from him years ago.

One morning, he was asked to join the moose hunt; he was by far the best shot in the village. Throughout the fall, the braves had on occasion seen a huge moose loping through the evergreen forest. But it'd proved too shrewd. As soon as an Indian approached, it ran, vanishing into the woods before a shot could be fired. Now a hunting party was setting out to track this great moose.

On the second day, they spotted it. George had never seen an animal like it before. Its rack of antlers spread nearly as wide as Tagish Charley was tall, and it stood as if planted, staring back at them in defiance, full of calm, an animal aware of its formidable power. Slowly, carefully, the hunting party inched forward. The great moose waited until they got within shooting range; then it bolted.

It was astonishingly fast. The animal took the hunting party on quite a chase. For more than a week, it led them through dense forests, up steep, rocky hills, and down into deep valleys. It seemed to be playing with them, and enjoying the taunting game. But the Indians refused to give up; an animal this size could feed the entire village for a month, and its skin would make many garments.

In the end it was George's shot that took the moose down, his bullet traveling a remarkable distance yet still striking the animal square in the head. The giant moose fell with a sudden thud, as if his legs had been chopped from under him. He lay quivering in a powerless heap until a volley of killing shots was delivered.

George had made an impressive shot, and now that the long-hunted animal was dead, he expected to be crowded by congratulating braves. Instead, he watched as the Indians, tears streaming down their faces, danced around the fallen moose, honoring the splendid animal they'd just killed with a high-pitched chant that their fathers and their father's fathers had sung to commemorate noble warriors. George stared in mute astonishment, until, tears in his eyes, he, too, joined the circle of braves.

George had accepted the Tagish ways, and now he was invited to attend the men-only tribal dances. They dressed in painted wooden masks and brightly decorated caribou-skin robes and acted out ancient myths. In the beginning, Yehl, the Great Spirit, had taken two blades of grass and created the Eagle and the Raven. Until the end of time, all people would be the descendants of these two great birds. Eagles were powerful, natural warriors. But the Ravens' strength came from a more valuable gift: They were wise. They possessed the shrewdness that would allow them to defeat their adversaries without fighting. For the Tagish, life was a journey to acquire the wisdom of the Raven.

George, a poet himself, found a strange power in these myths. They affected him deeply. He did not believe in their literal truth, but he valued the ideals the tales expressed. He became convinced that there existed something stronger than simply friendship between himself and the Tagish. It

274

was a bond that grew out of a shared approach to living in the world. He felt as if he'd at last found a home.

By the time winter came to the village, George had abandoned his white man's clothes. He dressed like an Indian: knee-high caribou-skin moccasins; tight-fitting caribou-skin leggings, the fur worn against his skin; and a fur parka that reached below his knees and was decorated with drawings of eagles and ravens. The clothes kept him warm, but George also knew that wearing them was another deliberate act on his part. He understood that he was being observed, and he wanted to make his sentiments clear. He wanted to be a Tagish.

Still, when George was asked if he was willing to accept formal membership in the clan, he was astonished. He'd never expected to receive such a great honor. He agreed immediately. He wanted the new life he was being offered.

At sunrise on the day of the initiation ceremony, George was surrounded by solemn Tagish braves. With a great formality, the Indians divided into two lines and then, with George between them, escorted him to the lodge. A brightly decorated caribou cloak was draped over his shoulders, and a mask with a large yellow raven's beak was placed over his head; then they left him. For several hours, the shaman danced around him, chanting with a fierce intensity. The songs had an undeniable power, but George had no idea what was being said. He wanted to feel different, like a true Tagish, and was troubled that he did not. Even the shaman's powers, he feared, would be insufficient to accomplish such a transformation.

When the chanting stopped, the shaman gave George a dark potion to drink. He tasted berries and blood, but he could not recognize any of the other ingredients. He waited to feel its effect, but there was none. That was a disappointment, too.

The braves who had led him to the lodge now returned. Once again they faced him in two lines. With the shaman leading the way, the procession walked deep into the snowy woods. When they came to an open lean-to, the shaman stopped.

You will stay here, the shaman ordered. It is forbidden to eat or to light a fire, he said.

How long should I stay? George asked. He was genuinely confused. He didn't know what was expected of him.

After the animal spirit speaks to you, then you can return, the shaman answered. He explained: For every Tagish, there is an animal who guides his life. You need to discover the animal who watches over you.

How long does that usually take? George asked, trying not to sound too desperate. Or as if he didn't believe in any of this mumbo jumbo.

The shaman abruptly turned and walked off in silence. The braves, too, did not say a word. In two straight lines they followed the shaman toward the village. The sound of their moccasins against the crusted snow was the only noise in the immense woods.

George was alone. He wondered if his questions had offended the shaman. Perhaps they had been too bold, but he was having a difficult time taking all this seriously. It required quite a stretch of the imagination to believe that an animal would soon be talking to him.

A light snow had started to fall, but George was not concerned. He'd wait and see what happened. Besides, he couldn't return to the village just yet; that'd be insulting. In the meantime, his parka kept him warm, and he'd mittens made of rabbit skin and the rabbit-fur hat that covered his ears. And he had gone without food before. He was no stranger to sleeping in the outdoors. Or, for that matter, to spending time with only his thoughts for company.

He passed the first night without incident. Despite the cold, he was glad that it was winter and the bears were hibernating. He'd rather freeze than have to deal with a grizzly, especially since his only weapon was the knife in the scabbard beneath his parka. He'd used the spruce boughs that lay across the earth floor of the lean-to as a blanket and had settled in. But he did not sleep. He lay awake listening to the night noises and wondering if an animal would really come to speak to him. If it did happen, he hoped it'd be a raven. The more he thought about it, the more he grew to fancy the prospect. Yes, he told himself, that'd be something. A wise ol' raven appearing for a chat with George Carmack.

For two days and two nights, he waited for the raven to speak. George heard nothing. Only now he had grown light-headed. And despite the cold, he was sweating. He remembered the potion the shaman had made him drink, but he quickly dismissed it as the cause of his condition. If it were meant to have any effect, he certainly would've felt it before now. No, he told himself, he was suffering the effects of not having eaten for days. Out in the cold, weak from hunger, it was no wonder he'd caught the grippe.

That night a storm blew in. Snow fell in great white torrents, and a shrieking wind pounded the lean-to like a hammer. With sweat pouring off him, George lay immobilized on the ground. He wanted to get up. Walking would help him keep warm, but he couldn't get to his feet. He did not have the strength. Even thought itself seemed beyond his power. He felt as if he were stretched out flat against the giant glacier that hung over the Chilkoot Pass. His entire body felt that cold. Yet he continued to sweat, too. He lay motionless, unable to move, as drifts of snow began to cover him; and then he fell into a deep, deep sleep.

When the dream came, it seemed too real to be anything but something that had actually occurred. He knew it was impossible for a frog to talk, but he'd been engaged in such a vivid conversation that it was also difficult to believe that his mind could've played such an elaborate trick on him. He remembered: He was sitting cross-legged in the snow, and across from him a green frog not much bigger than his fist spoke to him in a clear and steady voice. It was a woman's caring, patient voice. The words were in Tagish, but for some reason he had no trouble understanding. I am your protector, the squaw frog said. My spirit will guide you to your future.

When George awoke, he was covered in snow. But he was no longer icy cold, and his fever had broken. As he recalled the dream, his first reaction was disappointment. He would've preferred to have been visited by the wise raven or the mighty eagle. Nevertheless, he felt that something out of the ordinary, something beyond all his previous experiences, had occurred. It left him puzzled. But it was time, he decided, to return to the village.

When he entered the lodge, Jim was waiting. You gone long time, Jim said.

A few days, George agreed.

No, said Jim. Six nights.

George was shocked. It hadn't seemed that long at all. A moment passed in silence. Then George revealed that a frog had spoken to him in a dream.

No dream, said Jim.

George considered that, but he was still too much of a white man to believe what Jim was saying. Rather than argue, though, he shared his sense of regret. It would've been much more to my liking, George told his friend, to have an eagle or a raven as a guiding spirit.

No, Jim said, frog very good. You will see. Frog is Wealth Woman.

As a Tagish, George was given a new name: Kahse. It translated to "seeker," but George wasn't sure if it was meant to define him as a prospector or as a white man who had sought out a different way of life. Perhaps, he decided with an easy shrug, it meant both, and that was all right, too.

Now that he was part of the tribe, George thought it would at last be proper to act on an impulse that he'd been restraining with a growing difficulty. Jim's entire family lived in the lodge, his four married sisters, his two married brothers, and all their spouses and children. In the course of the long winter, however, George had come to focus his attention on only one of Jim's siblings: a young unmarried sister. She had large dark eyes and hair as black and shiny as the feathers on a raven's wing. Her name was Shaaw Tiaa, but George took to calling her Kate, and that always made her laugh. Like her mother, she spoke her mind. As with the mother, this trait brought to George's mind his sister, Rose; and that only increased his admiration for the young girl. At night, though, his thoughts would take another turn. Jim's entire clan would huddle down on bearskin sleeping robes in a single compartment in the lodge. George had his corner, too. There was no privacy, but the Tagish did not even try to be discreet about their intercourse. They saw no reason to. Night after night George would lie awake hearing the distinct sounds of their couplings. He'd listen, and look across the way toward Kate. And she'd be staring back at him, her blazing eyes fixing him with an unmistakable frankness.

That spring, as a shining sun melted the snow and the first purple pasqueflowers appeared, George agreed to go back to Dyea with Jim and Charley. Kate announced that she wanted to work as a packer, too. Her mother protested, but Kate, always willful, had her mind set. She lived with her brother and cousin in the lean-to by Healy's trading post. George slept in his tent. The four of them found lots of packing jobs. Working as a single crew, they made many trips over the

Chilkoot Pass that summer.

When the season turned and Jim decided it was time to go back to their Yukon village, George said he wouldn't be returning. Jim couldn't understand until Kate explained that she'd be staying, too.

The two Indians delayed their departure long enough to help George build a ten-by-twelve-foot log cabin. There wasn't a stick of furniture, not even a chair. But Kate had brought with her a bearskin sleeping robe. George spread it out on the dirt floor, and it was all George and Kate seemed to need that winter.

Within a year, their daughter was born. Kate named the baby Ah-gay, "the daughter of the lake." George complained that he had a difficult time pronouncing the Tagish name, but truth was, it didn't feel right to him. He wanted his child to appreciate that she was a white man's daughter, too. So he called the girl Graphie Grace, after a character in a book he'd borrowed from the reverend up at the Protestant church at Fort Selkirk. Graphie Grace — that was a name he could say with a smile.

Now that George had an Indian daughter and Indian wife — although they were never formally married — the white men started calling him "Siwash George" or simply "squawman." It annoyed Kate that George was the object of their derision. He insisted that he didn't mind. In fact, he'd a plan that would one day give him the last laugh. It was a matter of Tagish law that the chief of the tribe was chosen from the female descendants of a chief. Kate's mother had been a chief's daughter, so Kate, of course, was a chief's granddaughter. And that made her spouse a suitable candidate for chief. Those old sourdoughs will still be looking to pan their first nugget, George told Kate, and there I'll be — chief of the Tagish nation.

That kind of talk pleased Kate. She was glad she'd found a white man who accepted her and respected the ways of her people. She might have felt differently, though, if she'd read what George wrote to his sister in Modesto to announce the big changes in his life: "My wife is Irish and talks very broad English, but I have the prettiest little daughter you ever saw."

George needed money. With a wife and child, there were always new expenses. In the harsh months when there were no packing jobs, George had to find other ways to support his family. For a while he worked on the new church that was going up at Fort Selkirk. Then he heard they were at last hiring again at the Treadwell mine.

He got work in the machine shop, and that was how he happened to be around to save

283

some poor fellow from getting his hand busted up by one of the hydraulic stamps. The man was truly grateful; he couldn't seem to thank George enough. All of which made George uneasy. When this Davis fellow made a point of seeking him out in the dining hall the next day, George decided there was something disturbing about him. He asked too many darn questions. George worried that maybe this Lee Davis had seen him in Sitka in his military uniform and now was thinking he'd claim a sizable reward for turning in an AWOL marine. Then who'd take care of Kate and little Gracie? Besides, George told himself, he'd spent enough time in Juneau away from his family. And with spring coming, the prospectors would soon be wanting packers to help 'em across the pass. It was high time, he decided, to head on back to the cabin in Dyea.

EIGHTEEN

And where was Soapy while Carmack and Siringo were meeting up under precarious circumstances at the Treadwell mine? He was just across the channel in Juneau, only he wasn't having a much better time of it than either the undercover detective or the would-be Indian chief. And like Charlie, he, too, was going under an alias. Not that it did him any good. Regardless of the name Soapy was sporting, people were already raring to run him out of town.

Soapy had arrived in Juneau from Tacoma, Washington, on the *General Canby,* a tugboat that had been quickly refitted to take advantage of the newfound interest in the far north by depression-weary Americans and then christened with the name of the officer who'd once commanded the U.S. Alaskan Territory. Even before setting foot on the scruffy boat, Soapy had taken the precaution of instructing the gang members accompanying him to call him John Rudolph; his name and his reputation, he conceded, had become something of an inconvenience. It wasn't just that "Soapy Smith" was printed in big letters on Wanted posters throughout the West. Why, he'd heard there was some coot in Chicago, a Dr. M. A. Holmes, who was attracting crowds of paying customers to lectures titled "Soapy, a Famous Gambler." Maybe, Soapy considered with a playfulness laced with a measure of pride, he should call himself a doctor, too, and rent a hall. People wanted to hear about Soapy Smith, he sure had stories to tell — and some of the most amazing ones were even true. But when it came down to it, Soapy didn't think there was cause to invent any new tricks. Instead, he looked forward to the easy pickings in Juneau. It'd be like the sweet days when he'd first arrived in Denver as a young pup.

Soapy was mistaken. At first, it all played out according to the well-practiced plan. He set out his keister on the wharf across from the customs shack — not more than a short stroll from where Charlie had powwowed with the two mine officials, but of course Soapy didn't know that — and began to offer his soap to the highest bidders. The steerers made sure a curious crowd gathered, and the shills kept the bidding going at an avaricious pitch. But Soapy hadn't auctioned off more than two bars before the crowd turned mean. Perhaps too many of the prospectors milling about Juneau had returned from the Yukon with empty pokes; they'd no patience for a bunco man with the brass to think he could lure 'em into another lopsided gamble. Or perhaps the crotchety sourdoughs simply didn't take to some fancy talker in a shiny store-bought black suit. For certain, though, the crowd's rage had been ignited. A voice shouted, "He's gaffing us!" Next thing, people were yelling, "String him up! String him up!" With the force of a tidal wave, a sea of people surged forward.

Three of Soapy's men rushed to form a cordon in front of their boss, and Soapy quickly had his hand firm on the revolver under his black jacket. He'd no reluctance about firing if need be. Still, if there was a shoot-out, he knew there'd be no telling who'd walk away. These weren't just a bunch of miners. Men who'd spent some time in the wilderness were either handy with their weapons or they were dead. The odds of getting out of this jam without a scratch, he quickly calculated, were stacked against him. "My friends, my friends," he bellowed desperately. But this crowd was beyond listening to what he had to say.

Then a loud shot rang out. A short man with a star on his chest had fired his Colt into the air. It had been a warning shot, but now a U.S. marshal leveled his revolver at the crowd. Let me take care of this, he threatened as he held his six-gun steady. He'd been appointed by the U.S. government in Washington to make sure there was law and order in Juneau, and he was determined to do his job. The crowd paused as if to consider the situation, then backed off.

Soapy had never been so happy to see a lawman. Over the years, he'd dealt with city policemen and with western sheriffs, who were usually elected by the town, and he couldn't help wondering if a federal appointee would be as easy to bribe. But he didn't even try. The fact that he had to spend his first night in Alaska behind bars didn't bother him. He'd grown accepting of the vagaries of the welcome a man in his chosen profession might encounter. True, Juneau had not worked out as he had hoped, but Alaska was certainly a big country and in time he was bound to find his opportunities. A night in a drafty cell, Soapy decided with the grit of a man who had drawn his share of losing hands, was nothing more than an inconvenience. It was sure a hell of a lot better than swinging from the branch of a stout tree with a noose around his neck. And that, he couldn't help but recall, had loomed as a genuine possibility only a few tense hours ago.

Shortly after noon the next day, Soapy was brought before a very stern magistrate. His sentence: a $25 fine as well as one more night in jail. The magistrate also made it clear that Soapy was not welcome in Juneau. It would be to Soapy's considerable personal advantage, the magistrate thundered, if he'd leave Juneau as soon as he was released. Of course, Your Honor, Soapy said obediently.

The next morning Soapy was a free man. He walked into the saloon closest to the jail and, as expected, found his gang members at a poker table. It was a muted reunion; the scrape down by the wharf had been a little too close for comfort, and the mood was low, even a bit hostile. A few of the boys were having second thoughts about Alaska, so Soapy had to spin a tale or two about the paydays that lay ahead. But when pressed, even Soapy had to admit that, at the moment, their prospects were vague.

After a big breakfast, he walked down Main Street. Soapy wasn't just taking the town in; he was on a hunt. He stopped in all the stores until he discovered a copy of the *Alaska Searchlight,* the broadsheet that was Juneau's daily newspaper. He found what he was looking for on the bottom of the front page:

John Rudolph was brought before Commissioner Mellen on the 24th charged with gambling. His mode of procedure was what is termed by the "profesh" as "flim-flaming the guys" — or he would pretend to wrap up ten and twenty dollar bills with a cake of soap and sell it for five or ten dollars as the case might be. . . . And yet they say there are no suckers in Alaska.

With great care, Soapy tore the article from the paper. He took a pencil from his coat pocket and, along the top margin, wrote a message to his wife, Mary: "The money I wrapped up was borrowed. I have nothing. Fined $25.00 cost and stopped from work." Then he went off to find a post office where he could mail the amended article to his wife in St. Louis.

It was important, Soapy felt, for Mary to know where he was and what he was doing, even if the news was often not very encouraging. He had not seen her or the children for over a year, but he wanted her to understand that he hadn't abandoned them. Rather, he was protecting her. He didn't want Mary to be held accountable for how he made his living; it'd been years ago, but the snide reference to his wife in the Denver paper still stung, and he had not the slightest regret for the beating he had inflicted on Colonel Arkins in response. He didn't want her and the boys to be tarred by the sort of vile accusations he'd become accustomed to shrugging off, especially since most of the things people were suggesting were all too true. He wanted his family to be able to live without the burden of his notoriety.

In his practical way — with his heart, if not always with his actions — he was faithful to Mary. He loved her very much. His grand ambitions always took shape with her in mind. He wanted Mary to believe that once money was steadily rolling in and he was finally able to move on to more respectable work, they'd be back together. In his mind he saw a day when he and Mary would be treated with esteem, when they'd live in the biggest house in town, when respectable folks would urge him to run for mayor or even governor. When he was riding a lucky streak, Soapy could see that day very clearly. Sure, at other times, when he was down and out and on the run, such a day seemed mighty wishful. But like any gambler, he never lost hope. And despite their separation, his allegiance to a future with his Mary never faltered.

As soon as the letter was mailed, Soapy felt as if his responsibilities to his family had been fulfilled. Once more, he began thinking of working again. He was too shrewd to risk trying his luck a second time in Juneau; long experience had taught him the wisdom of knowing when it was time to move on. But where should he and the boys put down stakes? He knew next to nothing about

Alaska. He had only his instincts to guide him.

Soapy was sorting through the possibilities in his mind, trying without any success to devise a plan, when his eyes happened to focus on an article in the very same issue of the *Searchlight* that had featured his arrest. In two brief paragraphs, the paper stated that there had been several reports of gold being panned up-country. The paper did not elaborate on either the quality of the ore that had been found or its quantity. The article went on to say, though, that prospectors were excited by this news and were already booking passage on ships leaving Juneau for the Cook Inlet, one of the starting points for an expedition into the interior.

Soapy had not been in Alaska long enough to know that optimistic articles like the one he'd read were commonplace. Unsubstantiated reports of gold being discovered in some godforsaken part of the territory were a mainstay of the local journalism. They helped keep spirits high during the long cold months. And prospectors, a breed that fed their dreams with rumors, were all for rushing off gung ho, determined to stake their claim before a site was overrun.

Still, it was odd that Soapy, given the many occasions on which he'd manipulated the press, accepted what he'd read without even raising an eyebrow in disbelief. Of course, it was an unsettled time, and he was scurrying to find something; that, no doubt, made him more susceptible than usual. But the fact is that from the moment Soapy read the slim newspaper report, a notion started to take hold. He considered it; he played with it; and soon it seemed like a most reasonable course of action. Besides, he'd learned on the voyage up to Juneau that the *General Canby* was scheduled to continue farther up the coast to the Cook Inlet. It'd be steaming off at the end of the week. Now, that was certainly a propitious turn of events. It was further proof that the big scheme coming together in his mind was meant to be. Here was his chance to establish himself early on in a boomtown, same as he'd done in Creede. He'd arrive with the first wave of miners, and when they struck it rich, he would, too. He'd latch on to some real money, long as he wasn't too particular about what he'd need to do.

Boys, he told the gang, his mood bouncy and once again full of resolve, we're moving on.

Two days later they were back on board the *General Canby* as it headed out of Juneau's harbor. Soapy continued to travel under the name John Rudolph, yet he doubted that an alias was still necessary. He'd stand on deck, the boat rolling in empty heavy seas, thousands of miles from Denver — from anywhere, really — and he'd tell himself that an alias was more an act of vanity than one of prudence. There was no likelihood that his renown, such as it was, would extend to this remote corner of the world. But he'd signed on for the first leg of the journey from Tacoma as Mr. Rudolph, and he might be obliged to answer some embarrassing questions from the passengers and crew if he were suddenly to give them another name. Anyways, he hoped that by using a new name he might change the run of bad luck he'd been having. Soapy's feeling was that as John Rudolph he'd have a better chance of building an operation up north before anyone had suspicions about what he and his gang were up to. So no doubt Soapy would've been surprised to learn that even while he was still at sea, a dispatch appeared in the *Rocky Mountain News* stating that the notorious Soapy Smith had been seen boarding a steamer in Juneau. The noted bunco man, the Denver paper authoritatively reported, was moving his varied criminal enterprises to the newly discovered gold fields that lay beyond the headwaters of the Cook Inlet.

NINETEEN

While Soapy was off at sea, in unfamiliar waters, Charlie was still mired on Douglas Island. After three months, his investigation at the Treadwell mine had stalled. It wasn't that he didn't have any suspects; the problem was that he'd too many. Security at the gold warehouse, he'd discovered to his utter dismay, was taken seriously only on the days when the bars were loaded for shipment. Then a whole militia of gunslinger types with cocked Winchesters would be on hand as the wooden crates filled with gold were carried from the warehouse to the train. A second squad of marksmen would ride on board as the train chugged across the island with its precious cargo to the wharf where the treasure ship was docked. On most days, though, two armed guards merely looked in at the warehouse in the course of the rounds that took them over the entire island. The reasoning behind this lackadaisical approach was that nobody was going to scamper off the island unnoticed lugging a crate of gold bars, so why bother paying attention to something that had no chance of happening? Only it had happened — somehow. This whole business was mighty perplexing, Charlie had come to feel. He recalled that when he'd first reported to the Denver office, McParland had taken his new operative under his wing and lectured, "When endeavoring to solve a crime, consider who possesses both opportunity and motive." Well, as far as Charlie could reckon, given the surprising laxness, it seemed as if everyone had an opportunity. Same as everyone had a motive; who wouldn't, after all, be looking to get his hands on a fortune in gold?

Except, of course, the Indian workers. Charlie had eliminated them on principle even before he'd started his investigation. He knew they had no hankering for gold; and while he'd fought in the terrible Red River Indian War and therefore had good reason to respect Indians as damn shrewd strategists, he didn't figure them as master thieves. Grabbing a boodle of gold and then getting it off the island, all without being seen or even leaving a clue, well, Charlie was convinced the red man's mind didn't run in that shifty way. Which then left, he'd calculated with a groan, only five hundred or so white men as the possible culprits.

Though there was one fellow, Charlie knew, who didn't quite fit into either category.

George Carmack seemed to have a foot in both the white man's and red man's worlds. This struck Charlie as a genuine curiosity. But the detective also recognized that if Carmack hadn't come along when he did, Charlie Siringo would now be drawing his old Colt with his left hand. He owed Carmack a large debt, and Charlie was a man who considered small, routine obligations as blood oaths. Charlie had vowed that one day he'd find a way to repay Carmack and erase the slate clean.

Still, there was no getting around the fact that Carmack was a strange one. A quick look and with his beads, caribou trousers, and knee-high moccasins, anyone would reckon he was one of those Stick braves from up north. But give him a second glance or, for that matter, strike up a conversation, and there'd be no doubting he was a white. Story was, he had an Indian wife and a half-breed child, too, and Charlie had heard people up at the mine dining hall having a good laugh about "Siwash George" and sneering that he was just another "squawman." Talk like that had a nasty ring to it, and Charlie felt Carmack had every right to go box the ears of anyone jawing in such a fashion. But Carmack didn't seem to be bothered. It was as if he was proud of his wife and child, as well as his being some sort of Indian, too. No doubt about it, Carmack sang an odd tune. Then again, Charlie noted with some amusement, who was he to be pointing fingers? After all, if he could be a cowboy turned detective, who's to say Carmack couldn't be a prospector turned Indian?

There was, however, one thing about Carmack that didn't lie so easy with Charlie: The man had skedaddled. One day he was working in the machine shop; the next he picked up his pay and left. Told the mine office he was going back up-country to work as a packer, which sounded true enough on the face of it. But Charlie also couldn't help wondering if Carmack's sudden departure had anything to do with his interest. When Charlie had taken the seat next to him in the dining hall, it'd been plain that Carmack didn't want to talk. He couldn't finish his meal fast enough, get out of the dining hall, and hurry on back to work. Two days after that, he'd quit the mine. It was as if he had something to hide — such as, say, a role in the robberies.

Now, lying in his bed and unable to sleep, with only the mystery for company, Charlie turned to Mamie for advice. He knew, of course, that she wasn't there, but he found it a comfort, when there was no one to eavesdrop, to pretend as if she were. Speaking to her, even if the words only ran through his mind like a silent prayer, made him feel less alone. So tonight, when he felt the old sadness coming back, he tried to ease things by conversing (after a fashion) with the woman he missed so much.

Now, isn't this something, Mamie? he said silently, knowing she would've appreciated the irony. I finally get a suspect — and it's the one man in the whole damn territory I'm beholden to.

Mamie, though, wasn't Charlie's only solace. He also kept a bottle on the floor beneath his bed, near his boots, and when the old pain returned, he found it a comfort, too. He'd take a sip; share a silent word with Mamie; and then his thoughts on that long night would return to Carmack. He wasn't sure why. But in his relentless way, with Mamie as his audience, he picked away at Carmack as if the man were offering up some sort of challenge. It was as if Carmack somehow held the key to the case.

Which, Charlie told himself, was unlikely. He was too much an Injun to be a gold thief. Yet even if Carmack was involved, Charlie knew he couldn't have done it on his own. There was no way a single man could've managed it. Why, just getting all that gold off the island would've been quite an undertaking. And now prodded, his mind circled back to something he'd been mulling for weeks, ever since he'd first watched a crew unloading the crates: Gold was heavy.

Like boxcars coupled together on a slow-moving train, these separate thoughts pulled one another along through the course of Charlie's pensive, restless night. He kept trying to sort it all out. And sometime before dawn, things began to clarify. There was no hurrah cowboy shout of "Yippee!" No rushing up to Durkin's office to alert him to the news. Charlie, in fact, understood that he was no closer to identifying the men who had taken the gold than he'd been when the night began. Nor were the precise details clear in his mind; that'd require some further investigation. But now, for the first time, he announced triumphantly to Mamie, he was pretty sure he knew the broad strokes of how they'd done it.

Despite his excitement, Charlie waited until he finished his shift to put his theory to the test. He'd considered not reporting to work, just going off first thing in the morning, but he'd decided such rashness would be a mistake. He'd put in too much time creating the cover of Lee Davis, machine oiler, and it'd be plumb foolishness to wreck it now — especially since he'd still need to round up the thieves and recover the gold. Accomplishing that would be a tall order; he'd have to win the trust of some unsavory sorts, and he wouldn't stand a chance if they even as much as suspected that he was a detective. So that morning, patience ruled.

Yet all through the shift as Charlie, oil can in hand, went about his duties, his mind was elsewhere. Regardless of the tasks he appeared to be performing, Charlie passed the hours laying out in a precise, orderly way what he knew for certain about the thefts.

Fact: Gold bars stamped with the TM mark of the Treadwell mine had been taken from the warehouse. On three occasions.

Fact: The thefts had gone undetected until the weekly routine warehouse inventories.

Fact: The gold was nowhere to be found. Durkin had had teams of men scour the island, digging beneath piles of rocks, poking into rotted tree trunks, tearing apart the ferry — and they'd discover not even a trace of yellow dust. Meanwhile, the banks in Seattle and Tacoma had reported that no one had tried to cash bars marked with the Treadwell stamp.

Fact: It was the perfect crime.

Or it had been, Charlie told himself as his shift ticked slowly on, until he'd sorted it all out.

And then it was six P.M. His shift was over. The previous night the facts had led Charlie to a theory, and now he was at last ready to confirm it. But once again he realized that restraint was necessary. In one more accommodation to his cover, after clocking out he went directly to supper at the dining hall. He

301

feared that his absence might be noted; anyone with reason to be wary would very likely be keeping a sharp eye. Breaking routine, McParland had warned, will get an undercover operative exposed or, no less likely, killed. So for what seemed like an eternity, Charlie ate food he was unaware of swallowing, and made conversation without any notion of what he was saying. He sat at the long refectory table, but in truth he was in another world.

When the men finally began exiting the hall, he lingered at the rear of the crowd. He stayed back until he was all alone; and after he was certain no one was watching, he disappeared into the night shadows. Avoiding the path, he bolted into the spruce forest. Hidden among the tall trees, Charlie felt elated; after the day's excruciating delays, he could at last proceed. Yet in the next moment another realization struck, and he cursed his stupidity. Why hadn't he brought a lantern? But then a gust of wind moved the clouds across the sky to reveal a hunter's moon hanging high and bright in the sky, as if put there to show him the way.

He stayed in the trees, and as the grade grew steeper, he followed it. When he reached the summit of a densely wooded hill, he stopped; he listened to the country to see if he could detect the sound of someone trailing him; and when he was certain he was alone, he took his bearings. The warehouse, Charlie knew, sat on a hilltop on the northeast corner of the island. He had climbed the same hill, but from an opposite direction. With the North Star as his guide, he'd be able to stay unseen, hidden behind the curtain of trees, until he was fairly close. And after an easy ten-minute walk, there it was.

In his mind, Charlie was imagining he was one of the thieves. His plan was to do what they'd done, except, of course, for actually making off with the gold. So he moved up to where the tree line began to thin out and, being careful to stay in the shadows, he began searching. Without having to try too hard, Charlie found what he'd been looking for. A half dozen big rocks had been moved to form a barrier, and a pile of spruce boughs had been scattered on the ground as a buffer against the cold. It reminded Charlie of one of the hunter's blinds he'd occupied in the New Mexico hills, only these hunters weren't after antelopes. When Charlie settled in, he discovered that it provided a perfect sight line through the trees, toward the warehouse. Which was just as he'd expected. So he sat and watched, same as he was certain the thieves had done.

He had to pass a very cold hour, far colder than he'd supposed, until he saw two guards approach the building. They opened the warehouse door, shined their lanterns around for a few curious moments, and, apparently satisfied, then moved off to complete the remainder of their nightly rounds. He'd have about an hour, Charlie judged, before they returned.

When Charlie saw the two men disappear down the hill and into the darkness, he raced from the trees. It was a good thirty yards or so to the warehouse, and all he could do was run as fast as he could and hope no one was lurking about. He reached the front door without a shout ringing out; and, buoyed, Charlie pressed himself flat against the building.

Then he saw it: A big padlock secured the front door. Charlie didn't have a key, but he expected the robbers hadn't had one, either. If they could figure a way in, he confidently told himself, he would, too. He walked slowly around the building looking for access: a window, a gap in the foundation he could wiggle beneath, a back door. But Charlie found nothing. After five minutes, he was back once more staring at the padlock.

Charlie studied it carefully, and then held it in his hand. It was a heavy, irksome hunk of metal; Durkin must've thought a lock of that size and heft would be bound to discourage break-ins. Sure, he knew he could find a rock and split the hasp open. But there'd been no reports of any busted locks, and such an irregularity would surely have been noticed by the guards in the course of their rounds. The alarm would've been immediately sounded. Only the thefts had gone undetected for days. So how had the robbers managed it? How had they gotten into the warehouse without destroying the padlock? Charlie focused all his attention on the lock, aware that if he didn't figure something out soon, the guards would be returning. Then all he'd have to show for his three months on the island would be a lot of useless conjecture. He'd be back where he'd started — utterly dumbfounded. He was trying not to panic, but his mind was racing. Then he hit on an idea.

Charlie reached under his shirt for the scabbard he wore tied across his chest by a leather strap, and removed his knife. Using the blade, he pried off the metal hinge that had been hammered into one side of the door to hold the lock in place. When he was done, the padlock was still closed, only now it was no longer secured to the door; it just dangled ineffectively alongside the hinge. He made sure to gather up the nails that had fallen to the ground and put them in his pocket; he'd need them later. Then he gave the front door a firm push and stepped in. The room was darker than McParland's office, but as his eyes grew accustomed to the darkness Charlie noticed that a lantern had been thoughtfully left on a shelf by the door. He took a match from his pocket, lit the wick, and stared out at a treasure of gold.

Or so he assumed. From his position by the door, it was impossible to be certain. All he knew for sure was what he saw: The room was crammed wall to wall with crates stacked chest-high in neat rows. But when he used his knife to lift the top of one the crates, he wasn't disappointed. It was packed with shiny bars.

Nevertheless — and this was what had dawned on him in his eureka moment the previous night — as long as the crates were nailed shut, there was no telling what was inside. A box might've been picked clean, and then its top nailed back on. The watchmen would stop in every hour or so while on their rounds, give a quick glance to see if the rows of crates were in place and undisturbed, and figure all's right with the world. They never bothered to look inside any of the boxes. Nor could they've been expected to. There were at least two hundred crates; a careful inspection would've taken hours and hours, and they had an entire island to patrol.

Deceiving the watchmen, Charlie had determined, would be simple enough — as long as the thieves weren't greedy. If they didn't walk off with crate after crate but took only the amount of gold that two men could carry before the watchmen circled back, then it'd be as easy as shooting grazing buffaloes. Two men making two trips, say, could grab forty or fifty bars and still have time to nail the crates shut again and fix the hinge on the front door before the guards returned. No one would be the wiser until the weekly warehouse inventories.

Yes, Charlie told himself as he put the lantern back on its shelf, removing the gold from the warehouse without being discovered would be the easy part. The hard part would be figuring out a plan to get the fifty bars down the long hill and then off the island. Well, he quickly corrected, getting the booty off the island wouldn't require too much invention. Best he could make out, there were only two possible ways: Either you swam or you had a boat. But the odds of anyone swimming across the frigid channel waters while dragging a sack of gold bars and surviving to rob the mine another day were too overwhelming. There was just no way that could've happened. So Charlie felt certain they must've had a boat, maybe even a canoe, anchored off some dark cove on the less hectic side of the island.

No, the real mystery was how they'd been able to get fifty bars of gold down the hill and across the island to their boat. And, Charlie didn't need to remind himself, gold was heavy. Fifty bars would weigh, he guessed, near on three hundred pounds. From the front door of the warehouse down to the beach was more than two miles. And it was anyone's guess where along the island's coastline their boat would've been moored; that could add further miles to the escape route. Two men — Charlie had by now come to believe it was a two-man job or more bars would've been stolen — lugging that much gold would need to make several trips. Yet they couldn't load up gunnysacks, or stack it in wheelbarrows, or, for that matter, carry it in their arms. Besides the watchmen, there were a thousand people on the island, and they worked day and night. Someone would be bound to notice. So, Charlie asked himself, how'd the robbers do it? The only answer he could come up with was — I'll be damned if I know.

But Charlie hadn't come this far — or *this close*, he truly believed — only to give up. He hoped that if he continued to put himself in the thieves' shoes, the solution would come to him. So he closed the warehouse door behind him and found a rock to nail the metal hinge back in place. Then, imagining he'd a dozen or so gold bars cradled in his arms, he began to look for a way to get his hoard to the beach without any alarms being sounded or shots fired.

He stood on the hilltop, a sentinel surveying the busy island stretched out below him. Electric lights illuminated many of the buildings, and their glow shimmered in long pools across the swift, dark waters of the channel.

He searched in all directions, hoping to see something that'd reveal the thieves' plan. Yet nothing sparked a notion that made any sense. He dreaded the possibility that he'd fail to sort out this last part of the crime. If he was going to catch the thieves, he'd need to know how they'd made off with the gold. If they got away, he'd be letting McParland down; and he'd given the superintendent his word. But the more Charlie focused his attention, the more he continued to look in all directions, the more futile his search proved. Mamie, he begged in silent desperation, tell me what I'm missing.

A moment later, as if in answer to his question, a loud noise startled him. At first Charlie thought it was the sound of deer running through the woods. But it grew larger; and he realized it wasn't the commotion of scattering animal hooves. It was something more powerful. Like a torrent of rushing water. That was it, he was now certain. He was hearing a raging creek, its waters high from the spring rains. Only there was no creek on the island.

So what could it be? The noise carried easily through the night, and he followed it. As the sound of thrashing, streaming water became clearer and more distinct, he hurried toward it. All his instincts alerted him that the solution he'd been looking for was now at hand. Yet even as the realization took hold,

Charlie had no expectation of what he'd find.

He had gone at most two hundred yards before he was able to stand on the edge of a shallow ravine and gaze down on what looked like a giant twisting black snake. But a moment later Charlie's mind worked out what his eyes were seeing. The long snake was a metal pipeline. With the light of the moon, he could see that the pipeline climbed up one side of the island and then angled down the other. Later, he'd learn that it was eighteen miles long. But even that night he quickly understood why he'd suddenly heard the sound of rushing water. And how the pipeline had allowed the thieves to get away with the gold.

In itself, the pipeline was an ingenious piece of engineering. It carried the water powering the generators that allowed the mill machines to run and the electric lights to shine. Yet its basic operating principles, as Charlie grasped them, were simple enough. With the natural rising tides in the channel, water was carried up through the pipeline to a small reservoir that sat on the high ground adjacent to the warehouse. Depending on the demand for electricity, water would be released from the reservoir. Then it would flood downhill through the pipeline in a torrent, its speed a crucial part of the physics necessary to create hydroelectric power. The roar Charlie had heard was the rush of a new stream of water as it charged through the pipeline. It was also the answer to many of his questions.

With a renewed sense of triumph, Charlie scurried down the ravine and, his eyes to the ground, began his search. He followed the pipeline, and after only a few yards, spotted what he'd anticipated: a pile of mud.

Ignoring the muck, Charlie went down on his knees and began running his fingers along the cold metal of the pipeline. In a moment, he found the rope. He was now convinced that he knew how the thieves had transported the gold, but just to be sure he began to unravel the circles of rope. Once they lay loose, it required just a strong pull for a section of the pipeline to be removed. He ran his hand over the metal edge: It had been carefully sawed. Satisfied, he fitted the two sections back together until they were joined as tightly as two hands in a deal-binding grip. Then he began wrapping the cords of rope back around the metal cylinder so the pieces would stay in place.

While he worked, Charlie couldn't help but admire the thieves' plan. They'd sawed through a section of the pipeline — anyone could lift a hacksaw from the tool shop — and then let the rushing water take the gold down-island. It was the same principle used by the rubber conveyor belts that transported the gold rocks to the various mill shops for processing; perhaps that'd even been their inspiration. Safely hidden, the bars would be carried down to the beach without anyone being the wiser. Oh, there were two tell-tale signs: the mud produced by the water that had rushed out of the pipeline when they'd removed a section; and the rope they'd wrapped around to bind the sections when they were done. But if you hadn't already figured things out, you probably never would've noticed. Sure enough, Charlie told Mamie in an exulting burst of pride, a darn near perfect crime — until we came along.

The rest of the evening moved on quickly. Continuing to follow the pipeline, he hurried down to the beach and set to looking for a section tied with rope. When he saw it, he knew he'd found the spot where they'd removed the gold after its journey down the hill. From there, he walked east, following the shoreline toward a thickly forested corner of the island. In a small cove shaped like a perfect U and surrounded by tall spruces, a rowboat was anchored.

The getaway boat was still here! The thieves were still on the island! Charlie's spirits soared. He now had no doubt that the thieves were planning to strike again. And when they did, Charlie Siringo, the cowboy detective, would catch 'em in the act.

Once again, Charlie forced himself to rein in all his eagerness. He reported to work the next morning at the machine shop and went through the motions. He told himself that maintaining his cover remained essential. There was no way of knowing when the robbers would make their move. It might be tonight, but he could just as well wind up waiting for a week or longer. In the meantime, Charlie understood he must not take any actions that'd make them suspicious. If the thieves fled before he caught them in the act, the case might never be completely resolved. He might never recover the stolen gold. Charlie did, however, make one concession prompted by the previous nights' discoveries. Beneath his mackinaw, he'd tucked his Colt into the waistband of his pants. No one could see it, but as he went about his work he felt it pressing against him, a reminder of what was at stake.

After dinner, he retraced his steps to the spot in the woods where the thieves had constructed the covert to monitor the warehouse. His plan was to conceal himself in the trees near their hideout, watching and waiting in silence until they entered the warehouse. Then he'd charge in with his Colt drawn to make the arrests.

Charlie moved with great alertness. He knew a snapped branch would echo like the crack of a rifle shot in the night. His large hope was that the thieves would be crouched behind the rocks, that they'd break into the warehouse tonight. But as soon as he approached the spot, a sudden sense of dread stabbed his heart. All at once he ran toward the hideout, now unconcerned about the noise. One look had told him it no longer mattered. It was too late. The rocks and the spruce boughs had been scattered. Whether this had been done in an outburst of anger over having been discovered or in an attempt to disguise the hideout, he had no way of knowing. Nor did he have any idea whether he had carelessly left a clue that had betrayed his presence on the previous night or if they had simply decided to call things off.

But even as a flood of frustrations rose up in him, Charlie realized there was still one last hope. He ran as fast as he could through the darkness, nearly stumbling on several occasions as he made his way downhill. Panting, he rushed to the cove where the rowboat had been anchored. It was gone. And, he now knew without a doubt, so were the thieves.

For several minutes, he leaned against a tree. He was out of breath, and felt deeply foolish. He'd protected his cover, but at a large cost. While Lee Davis had been working as an oiler, the thieves had bolted. He'd had his chance to catch them, and had squandered it. All he could do now, he decided, was go back to his room. There was a letter he needed to write. And, he realized with a measure of resignation, the time had come, as well, to send the telegram he'd been putting off.

TWENTY

How'd you know? Durkin asked Charlie as he handed the detective two metal disks about the size and shape of silver dollars.

It was shortly after midnight of the following day, and they were back in the alleyway in Juneau. The mine superintendent had received Charlie's letter requesting a meeting at the usual spot and hour, and he'd obeyed. This time, Charlie observed with satisfaction, Durkin had come alone.

I didn't, Charlie answered. I was just guessing — until now.

Charlie studied the two disks. Each was etched with a three-digit number. When a man reported for his shift at the mine, the supervisor would chalk his name on the board and then give him the numbered metal disk that was hanging on the adjacent peg. It was a safety precaution. If the disk hadn't been returned at the end of the day, the supervisor would assume there'd been an accident; mining, to be sure, had its dangers. A search party would be dispatched at once to look for the missing man. Charlie's letter to Durkin had inquired whether any men had failed to sign out after their shift yesterday. The disks in his hand established that two men had not returned.

You can call off the search, Charlie went on after a moment. You won't find them. These men are not on the island.

Durkin's confusion was apparent. But the detective was in no mood to be helpful. He stared with a mute frustration at the two disks.

The two missing men weren't victims of an accident. They had bolted. He also knew he was the reason for their flight. Perhaps he'd carelessly left behind a sign when he'd occupied their hideout in the woods. Or maybe it was the way he'd retied the ropes around the pipeline; he should've paid more attention to the knot they'd used. Whatever the reason, Charlie had no doubt that he'd alerted the thieves. It was his own dumb fault. They'd fled the island in the middle of their shift because they'd discovered that someone was on to them.

What're their names? Charlie asked.

Durkin pulled a piece of paper from his coat pocket and handed it to Charlie.

Charlie read out loud: Hiram Schell and Charlie Hubbard. He tried to recall their faces, but he couldn't. He was certain he'd never met them, never spoken to them. There were, after all, about a thousand people on the island.

They're your gold thieves, he announced.

Now Durkin had had enough. He demanded that Charlie explain. So at last Charlie did. He told the mine superintendent how he'd worked out how the thefts had occurred, adding that in the course of his investigation he must have inadvertently left a clue that'd alerted the culprits.

So you had 'em, but you let 'em get away, Durkin accused.

Correct, Charlie agreed mildly.

You've no idea where they've hidden the stolen gold? Durkin challenged. Or where they went?

Correct, Charlie repeated.

I'm no better off with you than I was with the three men from the Portland office, Durkin remarked pointedly.

Charlie didn't attempt to argue.

So what in tarnation you gonna do now? Durkin exploded. He was florid with rage.

I'm gonna find them. And then I'm gonna get you your gold, Charlie said with the perfect calm of a resigned anger.

But seven nights passed and the only person Charlie had found was another Pinkerton detective. Sitting across from him in a saloon in Juneau was the man who had just arrived in response to his telegram.

The morning after Charlie had discovered that the thieves' rowboat was gone, he'd finally notified McParland to dispatch the second operative. "At once," he had urged, realizing that he could use the help. There were two men on the run. What if they'd split up? He wouldn't be able to trail them both. Another factor in his finally getting around to obeying McParland's order had been his own pride, always a touchy spot. The arrival of another detective would no longer, Charlie had felt, be a slight. He'd succeeded where three Pinkerton agents had failed: He'd single-handedly worked out how the robberies had occurred. There was no shame in calling in reinforcements to help round up the thieves and recover the gold. Two men, he expected, would be able to accomplish that far better than one. Charlie just hoped McParland would be obliging enough to dispatch someone who'd be useful.

The man across the table was W. O. Sayles, known to all as Billy, and Charlie had taken to him straight off. Although that might not have been expected since Billy, who had been raised in genteel circumstances in London, had a highfalutin accent as well as a bit of the dude in his manner. But like Charlie, he was a fun-loving fellow with, no less appealing, a decided yearn for adventure. Billy had fled to America nearly fifteen years ago, determined to make a life for himself in the Wild West he'd read about, and he'd done just that. There had been some years cowboying on Montana cattle spreads, and then he'd worked as a lawman in those parts, too. It was a hard frontier, and while the army came to be a civilizing presence, there were still renegade Indians on the prowl and horse thieves to deal with. A sheriff had his work cut out for him, but Billy had proved he could get the job done. Things had fallen apart, though, after there'd been some talk that he was keeping company with a shopkeeper's wife. Rather than let her reputation get further besmirched, Billy had hightailed it down to Denver. The Pinkertons had hired him, and the next thing Billy had known, he was on a steamboat to Juneau. Soon as he arrived he'd contacted Charlie, and now they were happily making their way through a bottle of whiskey like old friends.

As they drank, Charlie got around to sharing the progress he'd made since he'd identified the two thieves. His detective work, he explained, had been limited since it was still necessary that he keep his cover; he didn't want any of the thieves' friends — or, worse, their accomplices — spreading the news that Lee Davis, one of the machine oilers, had quit the day after they'd run off. Schell and Hubbard already knew that someone at the mine was on to them. There was no sense in giving them reason to believe that Charlie was the Pinkerton who'd sorted out their scheme. His cover could still come in handy. Nevertheless, while reporting to his shifts as an oiler, he'd done some nosing around. And, Charlie announced to his new friend, he'd learned something pretty interesting: Schell and Hubbard had bought a fast schooner. A boat, he told Billy, that was big enough to carry a hoard of gold.

So Charlie had a plan. He wanted Billy to head down to the wharf in the morning and speak to the man who had sold the schooner. He instructed Billy not to be too direct, but to try to learn where the two man had sailed off to. And while he was at it, Billy should also keep his eye out for a cheap boat. More then likely, Charlie explained, we're going to have to chase after them.

As Charlie gave his instructions, he noticed that he was losing Billy's attention. His companion's eyes were fixed on the Indian women standing in a single line across the room. Charlie had seen them before. They came into the saloon most nights, some even carrying babies wrapped in blankets on their backs. They'd plunk their little ones on a bench and then the squaws would assemble in an orderly row. The piano would be playing and some nights a fiddler would join in, too, and the Indian women would stand in their spots, moving their hips in time to the happy music. If a miner came over and asked them to dance, they'd let him drag them around the floor for a bit and hope to receive a quarter for their company. Course, if the miner and the squaw were of a mind, they might also head to a tent out back for some more-intimate activities.

Think I'd like to try a dance with an Injun maiden, Billy said. He'd turned away from the squaws and now was looking across at Charlie. Perhaps you'd like to accompany me?

No, Charlie said curtly, and left it at that. He didn't want to explain about Mamie; just the thought of reopening that wound was unsettling. You go have yourself a good time, he told Billy. Only don't get too tired out. I'm counting on you to head down to the wharf in the morning.

Billy nodded in agreement. Well, if you'll excuse me then, Billy said with an exaggerated politeness as he rose from his chair. But just before he made his way across the room he paused to ask Charlie what he intended to do tomorrow.

"I'm gonna break my arm," Charlie revealed with a smile.

Actually, Charlie had no intention of breaking his arm. He just wanted people to think he had. He decided that if he was going to quit his job at the mine to go off in pursuit of Schell and Hubbard, he'd need a good excuse. A fake broken leg had quieted a lot of suspicions when he'd gone undercover at the Keeline Ranch in Wyoming. A broken arm, he reckoned, should do the trick up in Alaska.

It was Charlie's first night back on the late shift, and at the midnight "lunch" in the dining hall he made a point of making his presence known. He entertained everyone at his table with tales of his carryings-on with the squaws in Juneau the night before. When the meal was over, he snuck off to the basement.

Once he'd determined that he was alone, he went to work. He removed his shirt and began rubbing his left shoulder with a few wood chips he'd found on the floor. He kept at it fiercely, and before long the skin was covered with a bright red bruise. Then he put his shirt back on and returned to the mill.

He'd already selected the location for his accident. There was a steep stairway up to the second floor in the building where machines that the men called "squeezers" began the process of separating quartz from the gold. He waited until the other workers were hunched over the squeezers with their backs to the staircase, and then he fell. It was quite a tumble. He landed broadside in the mud and slush at the bottom of the stairs. His impact was so hard that the lantern he was carrying shattered into pieces.

The thud of Charlie's landing echoed

through the room, and the men hurried over. It's my shoulder, he complained with a good deal of truth as they lifted him to his feet; he hadn't intended to land that hard. I hit it against a timber post at the foot of the stairs, he went on through gritted teeth.

By the time the doctor arrived, there was no need for Charlie to act. His shoulder was throbbing. The doctor removed his shirt and, with considerable tut-tutting, observed the large red bruise on his shoulder. See if you can raise your arm, the doctor ordered. Playing to his audience, Charlie struggled mightily, but in the end he couldn't lift his arm at all. Still, the doctor diagnosed that the shoulder was not broken, just badly bruised from the crash into the post. A couple of the men helped Charlie to the infirmary, and he moaned all the way. Once Charlie was sitting on the examination table, the doctor rubbed liniment into his shoulder and put his arm into a sling. You'd better spend the night here, the doctor suggested. Charlie readily agreed.

The next day at noon, Charlie showed up at the dining hall with his arm in the sling. There were at least a hundred men at the long table, and Charlie made quite a fuss. He was in pain, and he insisted that someone help him cut his food. The following day at lunch he went through a similar performance, complaining loudly and being needy. So no one at the mine was surprised when, three days after the accident, Lee Davis said his good-byes and drew his final pay. Arm in a sling, trudging along as if each new step was a painful effort, he boarded the ferry for Juneau.

Billy met Charlie on the wharf. I got some news, he announced right away. Schell and Hubbard sailed into Juneau last evening. Their schooner was moored in the harbor all night.

Where're they now? Charlie asked hopefully. If they were still in the harbor, he'd board the boat and, with luck, wrap the case up by nightfall.

They set sail this morning, Billy revealed, his words prickly with frustration. He had no idea where they were headed.

Well, said Charlie as he removed his sling and flung it to the ground, we'd better find out.

TWENTY-ONE

Two days later, an hour before dawn, when the night sky still held Juneau's harbor in a deep and stolid darkness, the two detectives set off in pursuit of the thieves. They had purchased a forty-foot Indian canoe that was painted, Charlie observed with a chuckle, "in all the colors of the rainbow." More to his liking, its bow and stern were built high above the water and that, he judged, would give them some protection if they hit rough waters. So there wouldn't be a constant need to paddle, they had rigged up a tall-masted sail. As a barefoot boy in south Texas, Charlie'd spent summers frolicking on the Gulf of Mexico, chasing crabs, oysters, and seafowl. The waters running along the Alaskan coast might be more tempestuous, Charlie conceded, but he felt confident that he'd sufficient experience to handle a small sailboat in any conditions. Then again, it was Charlie's nature to feel confident about most things he set out to do.

It had also occurred to Charlie that they'd need a cover story to explain why they were traveling up and down the coast. If they caught up with Schell and Hubbard — and there was no guarantee they would; they didn't even know which direction the thieves had sailed — it'd still be necessary to win their confidence in order to learn where they'd hidden the gold. Two strangers had better be able to offer a reasonable explanation for their having paddled to some godforsaken corner of the wilderness in their rainbow canoe, or else things could swiftly turn scaly. Gunplay, Charlie imagined, might very well be inevitable; nevertheless, he'd prefer to sort out the whereabouts of the gold before he had cause to draw his big Colt. He gave the problem considerable thought, but in the end it was Billy who hit on the story that struck them both as perfect. They'd pass themselves off as whiskey peddlers. It was an occupation that would provide reasons enough for stopping into the many Indian villages scattered along the coastal waterways and rivers, and at the same time it'd give them opportunities to inquire if their customers happened to have recently seen their friends' schooner. Along with a newly purchased chart of the Alaskan coast, they'd stowed twenty-five gallons of Canadian rye whiskey on board. Of course, the challenge now would be making sure there'd be any of the whiskey left to sell. In the two days it'd taken to rig the mast, they'd already gone through an impressive number of bottles.

Then, just as they were getting set to sail, Charlie had another idea. This was his case and he was the senior operative, but he'd led men in the past and knew that hard feelings could be the undoing of any expedition. The fact that he liked Billy also prodded his concern. So when they boarded the canoe he offered an arrangement that, he hoped, would ease any problems between the two of them before they occurred. Why don't we, he suggested, take turns being captain of the ship? "When you're the captain," Charlie said, "I'll be your slave and vice versa." Billy swiftly agreed.

With Billy assuming the captain's duties for that first day, they sailed out from Juneau's harbor. They were embarking, both men felt, on a curious undertaking. They'd no knowledge of where Schell and Hubbard had headed, but on a hunch they'd set course toward Admiralty Island. It was only about fifteen miles south of Juneau, and as far as Charlie could learn it was little more than a rugged strip of spruce and hemlock forest populated by Tlingit Indians and packs of big brown bears who feasted like kings on the running salmon. But it was where, Billy had heard, Schell and Hubbard had spent some days before they'd reappeared in Juneau. If they didn't find the thieves moored off the island, then their plan, such as it was, was to sail up and down the panhandle coast until they either spotted the schooner or met someone who had. In their time both detectives had trailed horses, cattle, and men, but never a schooner on water. Still, neither of them found the prospect daunting. The oddity of it sparked their old sense of adventure; it had been, after all, the imagined notion of participating in the unexpected that had provoked Charlie to abandon his merchant's apron and Billy his parents' comfortable London home. In their bold and spirited way, both men were kin to the heroes who'd settled the West. They were self-sufficient men with grit. With the new morning, they sailed south on smooth waters with merry hearts, full of an eager excitement at the thought of what lay ahead.

Two days later, Charlie was convinced that they were doomed. When he had first felt the change in the wind, he hadn't paid it much mind. The day had been still, and from his captain's seat in the stern he'd been busy manipulating the paddle as a rudder to steer the canoe up a wide inlet several miles long that led to Admiralty Island. At least now, Charlie thought, he'd be able to let the wind take the sail and he could sit back and enjoy the scenery. The island was in the far distance, a speck of gray-green forestland, and a herd of honking sea lions had suddenly appeared. The big, glistening animals swam playfully alongside the canoe, causing Charlie to wonder if they intended to escort the boat all the way to shore, a good five miles. Or maybe they'd simply come over for a close look, as curious about him as he was about them.

Minutes later, rain joined in with the wind. There were only large scattered drops at first, but quickly the drops got thicker and rain poured down. Still, Charlie shrugged it off; a cowboy learns to put up with considerable weather and, in fact, prides himself on maintaining a contemptuous attitude toward its inconveniences. Also, he was captain. He felt it'd be improper for him to complain about a little rain. Besides, Charlie could see that Billy was not in a smiling mood. The rain must've surely been bothering him, because this was one of the rare times when Billy, who liked a good conversation, was keeping quiet. This struck Charlie, always competitive, as another good reason to maintain his pretense of disinterest in the soaking they were getting. It'd provide one more occasion for a sturdy Texan to lord it over "Hold Hengland," as he'd taken to calling his English partner.

But then the sky opened up, and Charlie realized he'd larger concerns than taunting

Billy. Rain pounded down in thick sheets, and the wind grew fitful. Cascades of water lashed at their faces, a cold, stinging attack. They couldn't see past the prow of the canoe; the rain was impenetrable. The water poured down so heavily that Charlie thought they might very well drown sitting in their canoe. Billy was attempting to bail out the water splashing into the boat, but Charlie judged it was a futile struggle. A river had settled on the bottom of the canoe and had reached their shins. Their boots sloshed as they moved. At the same time, strong waves continued to bounce the canoe about. When Charlie caught the eye of his "slave," though, he flashed a confident smile. He was the captain. He'd plod on and pray that they'd be able to ride the storm out.

In the next instant, though, Charlie lost hope. The giant gusts propelling the canoe forward had suddenly pushed it directly into another tide. Caught in this tide-riff, at the mercy of two malicious tides that seemed hell-bent on cruelly tossing the canoe back and forth between them on the choppy sea, Charlie decided that they were doomed. There was nothing he could do but accept his death with valor. Still, it struck him as damn peculiar that after all the nasty scrapes he'd been in out west, after all the gunfights, Charlie Siringo would wind up drowning in a canoe. Who'd have predicted that? His only consolation was that he'd soon be reunited with Mamie.

But they were spared. It was the wind that set them free, another ferocious gust nearly picking their canoe out of the water, liberating it from the tide-riff, and hurling it toward shore. Only now they had to worry about crashing against the rocks. Like knuckles jutting out from clenched fists, rows of craggy, sharp-edged rocks blocked the approach to shore.

"Jump!" Charlie ordered, and on his command the two men hit the water feetfirst. It was one miracle when they both came up for air and another when they discovered that the canoe had not capsized. They swam toward it frantically, and managed to grab its bow. It required all their remaining strength, and a good deal of concentration, to push the boat through the whitecaps and between the rocks, toward shore.

As they got closer, an Indian stepped out of the timber. At first Charlie thought his exhausted mind was playing tricks on him, that the Indian was only an apparition brought on by his fatigue. But when the Indian waded into the water, a grateful Charlie understood that help had come. The Indian was a big man and capable, too. With his assistance, they managed to pull the canoe ashore. By the time the rain had stopped, the Indian had a bark fire going and a bottle of

332

rye had been passed around. Wet and cold, totally spent, the two detectives found the dry side of a large spruce tree and quickly fell into a deep sleep on Admiralty Island.

The island was shaped like an egg; at its widest point it was one hundred miles or so from shore to shore, and nearly twice as long. For a week they circled around the island, wriggling up inlets guarded by gloomy granite mountains and exploring wide, smooth bays while eagles soared overhead. They'd hoped to sight the thieves' schooner, but they had no luck. And the Indians who bought their whiskey could offer no assistance.

So they sailed on into unknown waters. It was a strange, frustrating voyage for Charlie. His usual response to a challenge was to charge toward it. He felt most comfortable when he was taking action, even if it required his standing up to unfavorable odds. That'd always been his way. But day after day, and then week after week, he found that all he could do was paddle on aimlessly, and the passivity of this expedition began to take its toll.

The entire country seemed to goad his uneasy mood further. Sure, there was so much of it, and it was all for the taking. And there was no denying the glory in its terraced valleys, its immense forests, its shimmering glacial peaks. Yet it struck Charlie that this was a wilderness not at all like what he'd encountered when, as a teenager, he'd first ridden up the Chisholm Trail. He couldn't imagine settlers taking on this frontier. Why bother? he asked himself. It was one thing to stake out a lonely homestead and risk getting scalped in your bed by the Comanche when you could dream that if you stuck it out, in a generation or so your children would be living in a territory bursting with farms, ranches, and towns. But it was another thing completely if there was just no point. Up here, Charlie couldn't see what was to be gained by a pioneer's sacrifices. It wasn't a question of hard work or courage. The irrefutable fact was that you couldn't defeat nature. Geronimo was as murderous a cuss as any man who'd ever lived, but even he had finally been driven to the reservation. You couldn't clear these forests or level these mountains. And every year come winter, all a man could do was surrender. Charlie was certain there'd never be farms, or ranches, or cities in Alaska. In the end, the country was too powerful. It'd always best you.

As the weeks stretched into months, even the constant diet of fish grew to be an annoyance. At first, it'd been almost a lark. There seemed to be no end to the fish, crabs, and clams that inhabited the coastal waters. They'd bought two halibut lines, each over one hundred feet long, and it was as if as quick as they'd cast them out, the fish would bite. But soon Charlie was complaining that he smelled of fish. He took to bathing every day, but it brought him no comfort. The rank odor, he was convinced, had seeped into his skin.

The constant sunlight, too, was an irritant. The sun would rise at about nine in the morning and then hang high and bright as a beacon in the sky till about an hour and a half after midnight. It was as if the day wouldn't end, and that grew to be a genuine annoyance, since one day was disturbingly like the next.

Yet the two detectives never considered giving up. They sailed on. In an Indian village they'd heard that two strange white men in a schooner had headed westward. All they could think to do was point their rainbow canoe in that direction and go with the current.

No doubt it was the monotony that affected Charlie's judgment, and prompted the display of recklessness that almost got them killed.

It was about eleven at night, but the sun was shining as though it were noon, and the water was like crystal. Their canoe was far from land, and at sea there was a total silence. The stillness made Charlie uncomfortable; at night in the West there'd always be a coyote howling or an owl hooting, and the crickets and insects had their thick buzz of night sounds, too. But this sort of complete noiselessness was new to him, and he found that it fitted around him too tightly. It was unnerving. There was no point complaining, though, so he sat silently with his thoughts in the canoe's stern, using his paddle to steer while Billy slowly stroked them forward.

As Charlie looked ahead, he saw a dark object about five hundred yards in the distance. Reckoning that it must be an island, he steered toward it. It'd be as good a place as any to put up for the night, he told his partner.

After they'd crossed another hundred yards or so of calm water, Billy began to doubt that they were heading to an island. "That might very well be a sleeping whale," he warned. "You wake one of them up, they're apt to turn dangerous. It'll come straight at us," he said. There was no anxiety in his voice. He was simply suggesting that prudence required that Charlie change course.

But Charlie was in no mood to be bossed around or, for that matter, to pay much mind to commonsense advice. He snapped back at Billy, "It's my night to be captain. You've got no right to chip in." Anyway, he was curious.

So Charlie steered closer until there was no doubt. It was a whale. If they kept going on this course, they'd be able to reach out and touch its massive head. Another two canoes lengths or so down the line was its tail.

By now Billy was frantic. He was pulling hard, back-paddling with all his might in an attempt to put some distance between their canoe and this colossal creature. And all the time he was whispering imploringly to Charlie, urging that they had to get away before the whale awoke. If the whale attacked, Billy pleaded with Charlie, it would have them both for dinner.

Charlie was in no mood to exercise caution. After all the flat days, he relished an opportunity to do something out of the ordinary. "Holy smokes, Sayles, here's the chance of my life to shoot big game!" he exclaimed. Grabbing the Winchester that lay by his side, Charlie lifted it to take aim. Sighting carefully, he took a bead on a broad spot right behind where he imagined the gills might be.

"For God's sake, don't do it, Charlie!"

But even as Billy was screaming the words, he heard the crack of the rifle. The bullet struck the whale, and blood spurted out into the water. As the sea turned red, the whale went wild. The massive creature begin turning in circles, faster and faster. It seemed impossible to Charlie that something so large could turn around and around with such speed. The whale circled about in confusion and fury, and the water churned with foam. Large waves shook the canoe mightily.

Suddenly, the whale dived. It went deep, as

though intent on hitting the sandy bottom. As its huge tail lifted up toward the sky, it was as if a gigantic hole was created in the water. The canoe was immediately sucked toward this vacuum. The two men desperately attempted to back-paddle, but the pull of this whooshing vortex was too powerful. They could not escape, and Charlie looked down into its inky blackness and imagined he was staring straight into Hades. It was a destination, he realized, that he richly deserved. It had been sheer willfulness that had provoked him to shoot at the whale, and now he'd pay the price for his impertinence.

But no sooner had it opened than the cascades of foam receded, the hole filled, and the water once again lay as flat and calm as a tabletop. The whale had vanished, and they were saved.

As an apology of sorts, Charlie promised Billy that he'd never go after that kind of big game again. But the Englishman was in no mood to listen. He sulked in angry silence for the rest of the night, and for most of the next day, too.

By the time three more days had passed and they were far from Admiralty Island, the encounter with "Mr. Whale," as Charlie referred to the great creature with a new-found deference, had been told and retold many times between them. It'd taken on the proportions of an epic battle. They'd survived, as Charlie was fond of reminding his friend, with a tale they'd be able to share around many a campfire. Looking back at it that way, Billy was of a mind to agree.

They'd been sailing up the coast for days when, on a whim, they decided to follow the course of a long inlet. A swift inland river pulled them along to the banks of an Indian village. This seemed, both detectives agreed, as good a place as any to stop.

As they dragged their canoe ashore, they were met by a stern-looking passel of braves cradling rifles in their arms. But Charlie quickly got out the "firewater" and even went so far as to offer a free taste. That turned people friendly, and the Indians led the two men up toward their settlement.

The detectives decided to linger at the village the next day because an Indian maiden there had caught Billy's eye. He was off trying to win her over when Charlie, just looking for a way to fill the time, decided to head down to the shore. As he was walking along on the beach, lost in his thoughts, he saw a brave climb out of a birch canoe a few yards in front of him. It took him a moment before he realized that he was staring straight into the face of George Carmack.

TWENTY-TWO

There was no telling who was more surprised. The last person Charlie was expecting to see climbing out of a canoe in the middle of nowhere was the man who'd come to his rescue at the mine. George, meanwhile, would've bet anything that he'd never see that durn inquisitive machine oiler again. But it took only another moment before both men's astonishment turned into suspicion.

Charlie began to wonder if he and his partner had indeed stumbled into Schell and Hubbard's hideout. Perhaps his initial instinct had been correct: Carmack was somehow involved in the robberies. Accomplice? Mastermind? Maybe it was the squawman who'd alerted the two robbers to a detective's presence? Perhaps he'd given them the warning that'd made them bolt? Standing still as a pole, rigid with shock as Carmack gazed back at him, Charlie thought that all of those possibilities made sense. And certainly none of them were as far-fetched as going upriver in a rainbow canoe in pursuit of two gold thieves, only to wind up face-to-face on a isolated sandy beach with Carmack. Hoping to resolve things right then, Charlie quickly turned toward the inlet, expecting that he'd see the schooner sailing into view. But when he looked, the water was flat and empty.

The schooner's absence hit him with the force of a rebuke; and at once his suspicions began to slip. In the next instant Charlie reminded himself that sometimes in life things occur without a connecting rhyme or reason; they just happen.

Howdy, Carmack, he said. And, walking down the long beach toward George, the detective used the time to apply some firm logic to the situation. He remembered that Carmack had quit the mine way before he'd rooted out the crooks' lair in the woods or had deduced the role the pipeline had played. Carmack had grabbed his final pay and been long gone, while Schell and Hubbard had still been hanging around, lying low, planning to strike again. There couldn't be a connection. The timing just didn't add up. Now that Charlie'd thought it through, he started to consider that the joke was on him. Imagine thinking that a thief hoarding a small fortune in gold would be living in the wilderness like some down-at-the-heels Stick Injun. As Charlie stuck out his hand in greeting, he gave himself a stern lecture: Any person who don't spend his days sitting on the front porch, why, he's bound to encounter his fair share of coincidences in his travels.

But the man staring back at Charlie wasn't of a mind to believe in happenstance. George Carmack had something to hide, and as a consequence, a guilty man's fears rose up in him. At the mine he'd suspected that this Davis fellow had been snaking up to him in the dining hall because he'd recognized an AWOL marine. The sneaky oiler, he thought, had hopes of pocketing himself a nice reward courtesy of the United States government for reporting a deserter. But finding him now up along the Dyea River in Chinook country, far from Juneau or any settlement of white men, for that matter, convinced George that Davis was someone a lot more dangerous: He was a U.S. marshal with a federal warrant. The War Department, George figured, must've sent him on a mission to apprehend runaway marines. What other explanation could there be for his suddenly appearing near old Healy's trading post in Dyea just days after George had returned from his short trip into the Yukon? Davis must've been trailing him all along, waiting patiently until he'd left Canada and crossed the border back into American territory so the arrest would be nice and legal. There was no other way to sort it out. People just don't wander up the Dyea for no reason at all. I should've stayed in the Yukon, George complained silently. Though maybe it wouldn't have made a lick of difference. Way my luck has been running, he nearly moaned, misfortune was bound to strike.

When George had come back to Dyea from working at the mine in Juneau months earlier, he'd been a changed man. Perhaps it was the experience of spending time in the white man's world again. Or maybe it was simply the mine itself. Seeing all that glittering gold ore being dug up from the cold ground, day in and day out, had had its effect. Old, sleeping thoughts had stirred. He'd found himself having some mighty fanciful notions about other bonanzas waiting to be discovered in this big country. He'd imagined what life would be like if he struck it rich. And as if they'd never been renounced, the legacy of hopes he'd inherited from his father, the dream that'd brought him to Alaska in the first place, had reclaimed their strong hold. He wasn't of a mind to turn his back on his Tagish ways, but at the same time becoming an Indian chief was no longer a future he'd be setting his heart on. Instead, he was eager to go prospecting. He wanted to return to the Yukon. In fact, he'd just begun mulling the problem of how he'd find a crew to accompany him up north when, as luck would have it, two recruits showed up literally at his front door.

George had only been back with Kate and three-year-old Gracie for a few days, at the cabin in Dyea he'd built two years earlier, when his wife's scream woke him from a lazy afternoon's nap. His first thought was that something terrible had happened to the baby, and in the space of a moment his mind raced with countless dire possibilities. In his bare feet, he hurried outside to find an excited Kate celebrating the arrival of the brother and nephew she'd not seen in over two years. Skookum Jim and Tagish Charley had come to the nearby trading post carrying a load of furs, mostly muskrat and mink pelts that season, hoping to get a good price from old man Healy. Once their business was done, they were looking to get some work packing across the Chilkoot. Another plan, however, had already taken shape in George's mind.

That night, dinner was a feast. Caribou steaks were roasted on an open fire, and to go with the frying-pan bread Kate had baked up, there was bone butter, a rare delicacy since the fixing required plenty of work. First the caribou bones needed to be fleshed and dried, then pounded with a rock. Next, the crushed bones would be simmered until reduced to a liquid that could be strained through a cloth. Kate would let this liquid cool, and in time a fatty marrow would form. She'd skim the marrow off and simmer it again before finally letting it cool and gel. The whole process would take near a week, but when it was completed there'd be a tub of fresh white bone butter. The butter would be brought out only on special occasions, and whenever it appeared George sure had a taste for it. He'd slobber the bone butter on the hot frying-pan bread and eat until he was near to bursting. Tonight, though, he held back. He felt obliged to make sure there was enough for his guests. He wanted them to be of a good mind.

Shrewdly, too, he waited until the dinner was done and pipes were being lit to share his plan. Jim, Charley, he announced now that the moment seemed right, I want you to go prospecting with me. There's gold up in the Yukon. I'm certain of it. We find it, and we'll be rich.

The two Indians were taken aback. The way they looked at it, they were already rich. They could hunt and fish for all the food they needed, and trapping and packing earned them money for whiskey and tobacco. Besides, they knew nothing about prospecting.

I'll teach you, George insisted. Same as you taught me how to pack. Now it'd be my turn to help you. We're brothers, right?

Yes, Jim agreed. George had accepted their ways. He was living with Jim's sister. He was father to Jim's niece. There was a bond. Still, Jim hesitated. Why you so sure we'll find gold? he challenged.

Remember, George shot back at once, Wealth Woman is watching over me.

And so it was settled. The next morning they went to the trading post and bought supplies.

"When are you back?" wondered Healy.

"When we make it big and strike it rich," answered George confidently.

As he had during his first trip to the Yukon, George let his instincts guide him. They went downstream to the Hootalinqua River, and when days of panning failed to reveal any bright colors, they drifted down to the Big Salmon River. This was a broad churning waterway, cold as ice, too, since its waters slithered down from the snowcapped Mackenzie Mountains. They worked the sandbars, and at first they were encouraged. They found colors in nearly every shoveful of sand. But it proved to be only a false promise, nothing but what the sourdoughs called "flour gold." They shoveled and shoveled, but all it got them were specks that looked like tiny grains of yellow flour. And all the specks didn't add up to even a single small nugget of coarse gold.

Still, it was an education. Jim, George observed with a teacher's pride, had learned to be a whale with a rocker. The big Indian could expertly wash down a pan of dirt and sand in just minutes. And Charley, though as

346

lean as a seedling, managed to put lots of muscle into his pick-and-shovel work. Prospecting was an exhausting occupation, but the Indians never complained or slacked off. "There wasn't," George would later recall, "a lazy bone in either of their bodies."

This second expedition into the north country was instructive for George, too. He began to get an understanding of things that previously hadn't been apparent. Prospecting in the Yukon, he decided, was different. This country had hard ways of its own. You couldn't do things same as you would elsewhere.

In California, say, there'd be gold for the panning on the banks of the rivers twisting down from the Sierra Nevadas. But California was just a piddling place when compared to the Yukon Territory. This was a big country, with big mountains and big rivers. By the time the gold had traveled downstream from the Yukon ranges, it'd been worn down to a fine sand. You want to find nuggets, George told himself, you'd better stick to panning creeks and small streams. Thousands of years of journeying down the big rivers had given the rocks too much of a pounding.

His newfound knowledge, though, brought George little comfort. It was only a theory, after all. And how many creeks and streams would he need to wade through before it'd be proved? For all George knew, he could spend months — years? — in the Yukon and still wind up empty-handed. Lying sleepless by the campfire, George chastised himself with the single irrefutable certainty he'd learned in the course of this expedition: Once again he'd tried his hand at prospecting and had failed. Kate and Gracie couldn't count on Wealth Woman to provide for them, and neither could he. If he wanted to earn some money for his family before winter came, he'd better head back to Dyea. Packing work would be better than no work at all.

Full of a bitter resolve after the restless night, that morning he told the Indians he'd be returning to Dyea. He had had enough.

Jim and Charley listened in silence. At last Jim spoke: We stay.

Suit yourself, said George. He shook hands good-bye with each of them. The occasion, he thought, demanded some formality; they were, after all, his pupils. But as he was trudging back to where he'd stowed his canoe, George found himself thinking, Now, don't that beat everything? The Indians get gold fever, while the white man heads back to do packing.

But his surprise at this unexpected turn of events was soon eclipsed. For waiting for him on the beach at Dyea was the pesky oiler from the Treadwell mine.

Theirs was a short conversation. As was his

nature, Charlie would've been of a mind to jaw all day, but he could see Carmack was not so inclined. In fact, he was downright testy. When Charlie inquired as to what he'd been up to lately, George figured there was no point in lying, since his interrogator — who he was now certain was a U.S. marshal — knew damn well. Prospecting, he said tersely. Then he turned and went straight back to his cabin.

That night George waited for the marshal to come arrest him. When he hadn't shown up by morning, George figured he'd better run while he still had a chance. He told Kate that he hoped Reverend Canham up at Fort Selkirk would have some carpentry work for him. Dawn had not yet broken when he slid his canoe into the water. With deep, quick strokes, he paddled off, all the time waiting for the shout ordering him to stop.

There was no work up north. The old Hudson's Bay Company fort was just as bleak and desolate as when it had been burned to the ground back in the 1850s by the Chilkoot Indians. George found himself sitting on the banks of the river wondering what to do next.

Oddly, despite his predicament, he felt hopeful. He'd a hunch, "a premonition," he'd call it, "that something unusual was going to take place." He reached into his pocket and found a silver dollar he'd tucked away. It was near about all that was left of the money he'd earned the previous winter at the Treadwell mine. Cradling the coin in his palm, he formed his plan. Heads, he'd go upriver. Tails, downriver. He flipped the coin high in the air. It came down tails.

Without delay he packed up his canoe and climbed into the stern with his paddle. He sat back and let the swift current take him downstream toward the Fortymile River.

As for Charlie, he wound up acting on a hunch, too. Carmack's disappearance didn't bother him much. Sure, the man had pulled him out of a sticky situation back at the mine; he owed him. But there was still no getting around the fact that the man was an odd sort. Besides, no sooner had Carmack hurried off than an agitated Billy appeared. It seemed there was a problem brewing: The young Indian maiden's father was none too happy about the white man's attentions to his daughter. Unless I want to take me a wife, Billy warned, I think we'd do best to leave.

The two detectives traveled that day. They still had no idea where Schell and Hubbard had sailed. After only a brief review of their chart, they decided to head south down the Dyea River, toward the small settlement at Skagway. But they both knew it was no better a plan than if they'd simply flipped a coin.

TWENTY-THREE

Siringo and Carmack were not the only ones following their hunches as they plied the waters of the far north. Soapy, too, had steamed across the great thousand-mile-wide Gulf of Alaska in pursuit of a sudden whim. But after ten rough days at sea he'd begun to question his decision. What manner of folly, of sheer arrogance, had persuaded me to head farther north? he demanded sourly. Why, he admonished himself, had I even shipped off to Alaska? And the only answer Soapy could find was that for once his instincts had failed him badly.

This was a far cry from the enthusiastic, confident Soapy who, accompanied by his gang, had strutted up the gangplank of the *General Canby*. Despite two nights in a drafty Juneau jail cell, he'd swiftly managed to shed his disappointments. It was of little consequence that Juneau had proved to be intolerant of his profession. His hopes had already moved on. It had taken only a quick glance at a newspaper report to convince him that there were ripe pickings for a man of his skills in the tent camps springing up around the gold fields in Alaska's vast interior. Just reading the names of new settlements like Miller Creek, Rampart, and Resurrection conjured up in Soapy's sly mind images of wide-open frontier towns, of prospectors toting pokes bulging with gold dust. What they'd achieved in Creede, he assured his gang, would soon be repeated in Alaska. Only this go-around, Soapy Smith wouldn't merely control a town. He'd be the king of the whole far north. He'd rule over a rich frontier empire.

But the long voyage across the gulf tested the reality of his giddy proclamations. Raging storms, battering tides, and heaving seas left him with a new, clear appreciation for how formidable the far north could be. It was May — springtime! — and yet on the rare days when the seas were sufficiently calm so that he might stretch his legs with a walk around the deck, the subzero cold drove him straight back to his cabin. And when the little steamboat pushed up close to the coastline, all that Soapy saw added to his mounting sense of dread. This was fierce country, a land of massive glaciers cascading down to the sea, ramparts of impenetrable mountain ranges, and inlet waterways choked with sprawls of thick ice. The hardships facing newcomers to this wilderness were only now becoming apparent; and Soapy, who knew well both his limitations and his intolerances, began to question whether he'd the gumption for such a rugged pioneer life. After all, he was a man partial to lying down each night in a warm feather bed.

Yet when the boat docked at Cook Inlet, the gateway to the interior, he tried to persuade himself that the worst was over. He'd survived the misery of the sea voyage, and soon he'd be heading to the gold fields and to the pockets ripe for fleecing. In steadier spirits, he wrote to his wife.

Cook Inlet near Coal Bay, 600 miles from Juneau on board the Gen. Canby 2500 miles north of San Francisco.

Dear Mary

Am well, will be to my destination tomorrow if nothing goes wrong. Have had a hell of a trip. You can write to Resurrection Creek, Cook Inlet, Alaska . . . Yours Jeff

Love to all

Then, before rushing to deliver the brief note to the southbound steamer that would take it to San Francisco, he had an afterthought. He turned the envelope sideways and wrote across it: "Gold here in big quantities — all country talking up here."

353

Of course, he'd no idea whether that was true. However, if he told Mary that his prospects remained promising, perhaps he'd find further reason to believe, too. He had told so many lies in his life, where was the harm in telling one to himself? It was also important that Mary understand that a big score would soon be within his grasp. He needed Mary to know that he'd traveled to the ends of the earth — twenty-five hundred miles from San Francisco; who knew how many from his family in St. Louis, Missouri? — for her, too. The fortune he'd earn with his ingenuity and boldness would be theirs. He wanted her to know that wherever he went, regardless of how great the distances between them stretched, she was in his thoughts. Without her, there was no point in his journeying on deeper and deeper into this miserable frozen country. In a life shaped by guile and lies, she remained the one true thing. He thought of her, and found the will to plow on.

A short day later, all of Soapy's renewed hopes were forced to scramble over another obstacle. The *Canby* had started up the Turnagain Arm, a narrow twenty-five-mile inlet leading toward the gold fields, when just after midnight there was a loud creaking noise, like a giant groan, and all at once the boat started keeling over. People screamed in panic, and for a terrible moment it looked as if the boat was going to fall flat on its side. But it held steady, tilted at a forty-five-degree angle. What had happened, Soapy learned, was that the tide had abruptly gone out, leaving the boat's prow wedged into the muddy flats. Sailors secured the *Canby* by stout cables to a copse of nearby trees, and the shaken passengers were led off over an improvised gangplank. It was a bit of an inconvenience, but Soapy reckoned it'd be sorted out soon enough. Come high tide, the *Canby* would be back on its way.

He was wrong. The *Canby* was not going anywhere, at least for another three weeks, maybe longer. Word had reached the captain that the ice was too thick farther up the inlet for any travel. In May? Soapy moaned helplessly. But the captain just shrugged. Up north the weather is a mite unpredictable, he offered. Until the ice melted, there was no alternative but to camp on the muddy spit of land across from the beached boat.

And as if that wasn't sufficient to shake Soapy's mood to the point of collapse, the captain had some even more discouraging news. Reports had it that the fields up north were pretty much played out and people were heading off before winter set in. Any man continuing on could very well find a ghost town waiting for him.

When Soapy heard this, he just gave up. A weariness that was pure defeat seeped into his bones. It was as if the tide had gone out on his life, too, and he was stranded. Mired down in muck like the damned steamboat. His luck had finally run out, and Soapy knew that a gambler without his luck was playing against a stacked deck. Better to walk away from the table than to keep tossing coins into a pot he was destined to lose. He now realized that this entire Alaskan expedition had been a mistake. The latest in a life of mistakes, he decided with a new bitterness. He was confused, and sad, and resentful. Soapy didn't know what to do next, and then he realized he didn't have much of a choice. He assembled his dispirited gang, the men circling around him in the soft, oozing mud.

Boys, he announced with the grim resolve of a general announcing a surrender, we're heading back to Seattle.

The first ship making its way south was the steamship *Utopia,* and Soapy and his gang quickly booked passage. Yet once again there was a delay. No sooner had they boarded then they were informed that the captain of the ship was too sick to give the order to raise anchor.

The skipper was Dynamite Johnny O'Brien, a two-fisted Irishman whose exploits were so famous in ports up and down the Pacific coast that his taking ill wasn't simply unexpected, it struck most who knew him as impossible. Why, Dynamite Johnny had fought Chinese pirates, escaped from cannibals, romanced a nubile Tahitian princess, and nearly became emperor of the island of Yap. His nickname was testimony to his explosive temper, and he'd never failed to come out swinging when an impertinent sailor dared to challenge his orders. He'd take on all comers, often two or three old salts at a time, and at the end he'd be the only man standing. But now Dynamite Johnny had collapsed on the deck. Two of the astonished crew carried him to his cabin, and he lay there in agonizing pain.

After a frantic search for a doctor, one of the *Utopia*'s officers managed to locate a prospector who'd once studied medicine. He conducted a hasty examination and diagnosed that the captain's appendix had burst. "About a thousand-to-one shot to pull through," he told the officers hovering around their half-conscious skipper. "I'd operate if I had any tools," the lapsed medical student added. The words came out as an afterthought; there was no real commitment to them.

Dynamite Johnny, however, lifted his head. "Doc, I heard you say I had a long chance to pull through. I'm a sport and God knows I don't want to die in this damn place. Go ahead. All you need is a knife and scissors."

Although anchored, the *Utopia* was rolling

357

on the rough sea, so it was decided that the operation should be performed on land. The captain was carried ashore in brutal cold to a cargo hut. His men laid him across three planks balanced on two packing cartons, and a knife and scissors were honed to a razor sharpness. Whiskey was the only anesthetic, and Dynamite Johnny drank liberally. Still, he remained conscious for most of the surgery. At one point he softly hummed an Irish reel.

Dynamite Johnny survived the operation, but lay burning with fever in the hut for several days. When the fever broke, the captain, wan and weak, was carried back to his ship. Two days later he managed to rouse himself. From his bunk, he gave the orders to raise anchor and get under way.

The first officer hesitated, then gave Dynamite Johnny the news: The coal bunkers were scraped nearly bare. Without coal, the ship wouldn't be able to make the voyage.

It took all of Dynamite Johnny's strength to raise himself up from his supine position. He sat on his bunk and forlornly contemplated the ship's predicament. Then a thought occurred to him. Before he'd taken ill, he'd noticed that when the tide receded, a coal formation had been revealed. He ordered the crew to begin digging up coal from the bottom of the bay. Exhausted, he fell back onto his bunk.

For the next two days, whenever the tide went out, the crew shoveled coal from the bay floor. Knee-deep in mud, whipped by bitter cold, they did backbreaking work. Ten tons of coal were added to the steamboat's coal bunker. But more would be needed if the *Utopia* was to reach Seattle, and on the third day the crew refused to shoulder their shovels and trudge back into the muck of the bay. And since their captain could barely find the strength to sit up in his bunk, they knew no one could force them.

The passengers by this point had grown restless. For Soapy, in particular, the prospect of spending another day anchored in the harbor was a torture. Now that he'd made up his mind to leave Alaska, he was desperate to get under way as soon as possible. He wanted to put distance between himself and this frozen nightmare of a land, the site of his comeuppance. Being moored in the harbor was a constant reminder of his failure. Another grating day sitting here, he thought, and he'd burst more than an appendix. It was in this raw state that Soapy knocked on the captain's door, then entered.

"When do you sail, Skipper?" Soapy demanded.

"No coal, mister, and no money to buy any with, dammit . . ."

"How much do you need?"

The captain said it would cost $300 to fill

the coal bunkers.

Without another word, Soapy reached into his wallet and took out the bills. The fact that he wanted to get under way was one reason for his generosity, but it was not the only one. It was part of his showman's nature to make grand gestures. And, truth be told, after Soapy's run of misfortunes, it restored a bit of his pride to cast himself as the ship's savior.

Over the three days that it took for the coal to be delivered, Soapy spent a good deal of the time in the captain's cabin. The two men traded stories, each vying with the other to prove who'd led the more eventful life. Encouraged by their friendly, albeit competitive conversations, Soapy found himself feeling less rueful about the past and more sanguine about what the future might hold. The dialogue was restorative, too, for Dynamite Johnny; nursed by Soapy's presence and attention, he slowly grew stronger.

At last the coal was loaded on board and the *Utopia* steamed off. Eight hours later it came to a halt in the middle of the gulf. The engines stopped and the anchor was lowered.

Dynamite Johnny was perplexed. He wanted to investigate, but he couldn't lift himself from his bunk. All he could do was summon the mate.

The engineers refuse to burn any more of this coal, the mate explained flatly. The quality's too poor.

The captain couldn't help but notice the boldness in the mate's tone. From his bed, Dynamite Johnny did his best to shoot him a withering look.

The mate was not cowed. "We've decided to anchor here under the lee of Cape Elizabeth and wait for a supply of good coal," he went on defiantly. "The crew agrees with the engineers."

"Why in the devil wasn't I told of this?" the captain bellowed. Once more he tried to rise, but a pain shot through his side as though he'd been stabbed with a bowie knife. "Who do you think is master of this ship?"

"We didn't think you were in any condition to handle the ship, Captain."

Dynamite Johnny exploded: "Call Smith, the bearded passenger. At once."

By the time Soapy entered the cabin, the captain had managed to get to his feet. Without bothering to go into the details, Dynamite Johnny told his new friend that the crew was mutinous. He needed Soapy's help.

Soapy opened his long black coat. Leather holsters were strapped under each armpit, and both held revolvers. "Glad to be of service," Soapy agreed.

It was a struggle for Soapy to lead Dynamite Johnny up the ladder to the deck, and when they arrived, Soapy had to assist the spent and ashen captain into a chair. But the captain's voice had its old boom as he called for the crew to assemble. With Soapy standing next to him, his guns drawn and cocked, a ferocious and loyal sentinel, the captain ordered each member of the crew to swear their allegiance. They'd get the ship into Juneau where a new supply of coal would be purchased, or else.

"I want steam up in this old tub and I want it in a hurry! Understand me?"

The chief engineer responded with a contemptuous stare. He hadn't spoken, but he was clearly reluctant to obey the captain's orders. And if he wouldn't cooperate, there'd be no chance of getting the other men in the engine room to agree.

Dynamite Johnny looked at Soapy and gave him a small nod. It was a swift and graceful gesture. Immediately, Soapy stepped forward. His face was tight with menace as he pressed the barrel of his revolver into the engineer's temple.

"Agreed, agreed," the engineer blurted out at once. And so the mutiny was quelled.

In Juneau, the *Utopia* took on a new batch of coal, and eight days later it docked in Seattle. The captain gripped Soapy's arm for support as he walked slowly down the gangplank. Dynamite Johnny had lost nearly forty pounds in the course of his illness, and was a gaunt and stooped version of the sea captain who'd sailed to Alaska two months earlier. As Soapy assisted his new friend down the gangplank, he couldn't help but feel diminished, too. These were not the circumstances in which he'd expected to return to Seattle.

Soapy checked into the Butler Hotel, on Second Avenue and James Street, in the city's raucous downtown. For days he remained alone in his room, trying to come to terms with what to do next. In the past, he would've simply concocted a new scam and convinced the boys that Easy Street beckoned. They would've followed along obediently. But up in the north he'd lost his sense of purpose. It wasn't that he no longer knew where to set up his tripe and keister or how a man with guile might proceed to find his next mark. The plain truth was, he no longer cared. He'd lived the con man's life for so long that it'd become a habit. But now he felt like taking a rest. He no longer wanted to make new plans or pursue new schemes. All he knew with any certainty was that he'd never, *never* set foot in Alaska again. The whole damn territory could freeze up and disappear, for all he cared.

A month later Soapy was still in Seattle. His old huckster's sense had left him so completely that when he looked at his gang, he wondered how he ever could've had the ingenuity to command such men. Worse, he knew he was losing their respect. If he didn't come up with a score, if he didn't put money in their pockets soon, they'd start drifting off. And he wouldn't blame them.

It was on one of these long, slow days that he received a letter from his wife. She'd used stationery from the Ingersoll Club, another of his old Denver gambling parlors, and the letterhead immediately brought back memories of better times. But as if to remind him that the past remained forever past, Mary had crossed out the address and written, "St. Louis Mo."

Dear Husband,

I would have written to you sooner but Jeff swallowed a fish hook and I did not want to worry you until I found out it would be necessary for him to go under an operation, but he is getting along all right and doesn't seem to suffer. . . .

It is dreadful hot here, suffocating, lots of rain and then intense heat. I nearly went crazy the day Jeffy swallowed that hook but I know now that he will be all right. . . .

When he put down the letter, Soapy was no longer a man filled with questions about what to do next. Instead, he was a father a long way from his family, wondering how his ten-year-old son had managed to swallow a fish hook. And why he wasn't with them.

TWENTY-FOUR

The two detectives were also beginning to have their doubts. They had sailed the rainbow canoe down the Dyea River, crossed wide, choppy waters to Bischoff Island, continued south until the scalloped snow-capped peaks of the immense mountains surrounding Sitka jutted above the horizon, and then abruptly turned east to revisit the heavily forested lee coast of Admiralty Island. They'd abandoned even the pretense that they were following the thieves' trail. Now each new day's course was set by a guess. But despite Charlie's recognition that Alaska's coastline was strewn with uncharted islands and broke off into hundreds of twisting channels, that the prospects of their finding the schooner were slim, he insisted that they continue the search. Most likely it'd been rash to have given McParland his word that he'd corral the thieves and recover the gold, but there was no taking it back. So doggedly they sailed on. Then, on a morning when the chill in the air was brisk enough to cause Charlie to flinch whenever the wind slapped his face, he steered the canoe across the whitecapped waters of Chieke Bay and saw the schooner anchored in front of an Indian village.

When they sidled past the sleek boat, the two detectives got a further surprise. The deck of the schooner was loaded with farm animals, some in crates, others tied to the masts. Charlie joked that it looked like Noah's ark. But there were no signs of the two thieves, so they put their bewilderment aside and headed without delay to the shore-front Indian village.

As they were beaching their canoe, Charlie noticed two men coming down from the cabins to meet them. Even from a distance, Charlie could see they were Schell and Hubbard; they fit the description Durkin, the mine superintendent, had supplied. In another stroke of good luck, Charlie knew straight off that he'd never met them at the mine and he doubted that they'd ever seen him, either. That would certainly make things easier. He whispered to Billy to follow his lead.

Schell came up close, staring at them as if irritated by their presence. He was a large man, as big and threatening as a bear. A scraggly beard running to gray hid most of his wide face, except for two dark, sullen eyes and a nose that looked like it'd once been busted, then never properly reset. A few yards back Hubbard, arms folded across his chest, slouched with a deadly stillness against a tree. He was a runt of a man, with a shiny, bald dome for a head and a belly protruding from his checked shirt. A holster packing a Colt rode low on his hip. Charlie had met many a gunny who didn't look threatening but nevertheless was a crack shot — Billy the Kid quickly came to mind — so he kept a wary eye on Hubbard. It was also plain that Hubbard was drunk; and while drink could affect his draw and his aim, it might also turn him nasty. Very casually, Charlie unbuttoned his mackinaw. If it became necessary, he wanted to be able to reach for the big revolver tucked into his waistband. And as if it were the most natural of things, he moved a few steps away from his partner. Billy eased away, too. Both detectives understood there was no advantage to being bunched close together like grazing buffaloes.

Schell seemed not to notice the cautions the two men were taking. His manner was both confident and insolent. Without a word of greeting, he demanded to know what they were doing in the Indian village. His gruff tone made it clear that it wasn't an idle question; he'd better be satisfied by the answer or there'd be consequences.

Making sure to put plenty of south Texas in

his voice, Charlie played the genial cowboy. Schell had been loud and direct, and in other circumstances Charlie would've taken offense at such rudeness. But Charlie hadn't come this far simply to arrest the two thieves. He wanted to find the stolen gold, and to accomplish that, he reckoned he'd need to win their confidence. He didn't want to gamble on trying to sweat the information out of them. They looked like hard cases, and too much was at stake. Besides, if they stonewalled, Charlie realized, it wasn't just the gold that would be lost. He might not even be able to prove to a judge's satisfaction that they were the thieves.

So he played along. He was all high spirits, as friendly as a cowpuncher jawing with the other hands as they washed away the day's dust at the bar. In this garrulous manner, he dished up the cover story Billy and he had concocted at the start of the voyage. They were whiskey peddlers and they were doing a hurrah business in the Indian villages, while at he same time managing to stay one step ahead of the law. This Chinook camp looked as good a place as any to unload some of our firewater, Charlie went on heartily.

Schell's reaction did not betray anything. He might've believed Charlie, or he might not have.

It was a tense moment. Charlie saw that Hubbard's arms were no longer folded. They now rested by his sides, as if ready to draw. At the same time, Billy had inched backward, toward the canoe; the Winchester lay in its stern.

Reckoning he'd nothing to lose, Charlie decided to improvise. Days earlier, when they'd put into Killisnoo, a nearby settlement, a prospector who'd happily shared their bottle of rye had told them a fanciful tale about the "Lost Rocker" gold mine. According to legend, some forty years ago three old sourdoughs had been working a rich mine somewhere in the rolling hills beyond the waterfall, near the head of Chieke Bay. But before they could register their claim, a passel of renegade Tlinglits had swooped into their camp and smashed their skulls. By the time the bodies were discovered the following spring, all that was left of the camp was a wooden rocker, the handmade device the prospectors had used to "rock" the gravel as they sifted for colors. And so the legend of the Lost Rocker Mine had been born, a tale of a bonanza waiting to be rediscovered. The yarn had tickled Charlie's imagination when he'd heard it, he being an accomplished storyteller, and instinct told him it might now come in handy. After all, Schell and Hubbard surely had gold fever. They might cotton to a couple of prospectors. So he tried it out.

Course, he began to palaver, selling whiskey ain't the only reason we crossed Chieke Bay.

We figure that while we're at it, we might get lucky and find us the Lost Rocker Mine.

You think there's any truth to that story? Schell asked. His tone was now less like that of a man looking for a fight. In fact, he seemed genuinely interested.

Catching his partner's drift, Billy answered: If anyone's gonna find that mine, it'll be us, he snapped. They'd done some prospecting in Nevada and California, he explained, and knew a few things.

Suddenly Hubbard spoke up. All this talk is making me thirsty, he said in a voice so high it reminded Charlie of a child's. How 'bout you fellows gather your wares and we try some of that whiskey you're selling.

In the camp, the two whiskey peddlers did a booming business. It was clear Schell and Hubbard had forged some kind of relationship with the Indian chief. Were they paying him? Had they promised him a share of their gold? Or were they simply giving him whiskey? All Charlie knew for certain was that there was a bond between the two thieves and the chief, and that, he worried, might make for complications when it came time for arrests. He figured he could handle the two men, but a whole village of angry Indians might prove more of a challenge.

For now, though, everything was under control. Although the Indians lined up to buy their bottles of rye, Hubbard proved to be their best customer. Even Charlie had difficulty keeping up with him. Course, Charlie was also being careful. He knew he needed to get the men to talk, and he also had to remain sober enough to listen. But even before the first bottle was drained, Charlie asked the question that'd been on his mind ever since they'd paddled by the schooner. All day it'd been itching his curiosity nearly as much as the whereabouts of the stolen gold. How come, he asked, you've all those animals on your boat?

Hubbard broke out laughing as if it was the funniest question he'd ever heard. You tell him, he finally managed to say, pointing the bottle at Schell.

With a sudden hesitancy, Schell started to explain. He'd come up with the idea of going into the stock business, he began finally. So he'd ordered some chicken, hogs, and cattle from a stock dealer in Seattle and had them shipped by steamer to Killisnoo. Yesterday they'd sailed over in the schooner to pick up the animals. He waited a moment before going on, and Charlie saw that a pained expression suddenly covered the big man's face. The plan had been to breed them, Schell said at last with a shrug.

Breed 'em? Hubbard challenged, and now tears of laughter were running from his eyes. That'd be a good trick all right, he continued derisively. We got a dozen leghorn hens, but no rooster. A big ol' razorback hog, but no sow. And two black muley cows, but no bull. I don't see no stock business coming out of those pickings.

No doubt the liquor had helped fuel Hubbard's amusement, but Charlie had to agree it was a pretty funny situation. He started laughing, too. So did Billy.

Ain't my fault that fool in Seattle didn't pay attention to what I'd ordered, Schell said, nearly whining.

The laughter just got louder.

Well, Schell went on, trying to reclaim his dignity, it ain't like that's our only way of earning. Fact is, we've had a pretty good run as of late.

Immediately Hubbard shot his partner a stern look. Schell acknowledged the reprimand with a small nod. He hurriedly began talking about how'd they'd just have to slaughter the animals. They'd eat like kings this winter.

Charlie listened. He made sure to keep a bemused smile fixed on his face. He was determined not to betray his excitement over the quick exchange he'd just witnessed. But now he knew. After all his months working at the mine, after all the time spent searching the Alaskan coast, he was finally very close.

That night the two detectives pitched their tent on the edge of the woods, across from the village. As Charlie lay in his bedroll, he spoke to Mamie in his mind while at the same time trying to pretend she was lying next to him. You were right, he told her. You told me not to give up, and now we're nearly there. After he'd said his piece, he fell asleep with a lighter heart than he'd known in many months.

Billy shook him awake only hours later. He had the Winchester in his hand, and he told Charlie that he'd better grab his Colt. Think we're about to be attacked, Billy said evenly.

The two armed men hurried outside in their long johns to find a bunch of drunken Indians. In loud, belligerent voices they demanded that the peddlers hand over the rest of their liquor.

Charlie saw that one of the braves had the neck of a whiskey bottle dangling from his hand. He took aim and the bottle shattered. Then he spoke: Come any closer, and I'll put the next bullet right between your eyes. He didn't yell; experience had taught him that a firm, steady voice carried more of a threat.

The Indians backed off, but they didn't go away. They stayed close to the woods, finishing the bottles they had and singing drunkenly. Suddenly they erupted into a volley of war cries.

Charlie listened. When they were done, he cupped his hands together and let out his own long, loud whoop.

Billy, who had fought his share of Indians in Montana, was amazed. The yell cutting through the night was genuine enough to make his blood crawl.

Learned that from an old Comanche in Wichita, Charlie explained with some pride. And for a while, he amused himself by trading war cries with the braves.

Finally, the Indians left. But the two detectives stayed on guard outside their tent, their guns ready. They knew that if they lost their whiskey to the Indians, they'd have no chance of getting on with Hubbard.

The next morning they left the Indian village. It'd been Charlie's idea, and as soon as he shared it with Billy, the other detective agreed that it made sense. Ain't gonna do us any good to linger here, Charlie explained to his partner. Those two are bound to get suspicious. And then there'd be no chance of our learning where they've got the gold. I say we head on over to the Chieke Falls and make camp. Tell Schell and Hubbard we're going off to find the Lost Rocker Mine. I'm betting they'll soon enough come looking for us — long as we got the bait. He pointed to the crates of rye just in case Billy didn't follow.

It was a three-mile canoe journey across placid waters to the head of the bay, and they continued on foot for less than a mile before making camp. They'd thought about pitching their tent closer to the falls, but then they realized they'd never hear anyone sneaking up. The water cascading down from two thousand feet made quite a racket.

In his careful way, Charlie made sure they lived this new cover, too. Each morning they went off looking for the mine, and they brought back rocks to test each night. "We might find the damn mine before Schell and Hubbard get a notion to come by," Billy complained after they'd been prospecting for a week and the thieves had not appeared. "Course then we'll be rich. We won't need to be detectives." Billy was only joshing, but Charlie didn't see the humor in the remark. All the money in the world, and he'd still have to keep his promise to McParland: He'd need to recover the gold. Nevertheless, he was beginning to wonder if he'd overestimated the lure of the whiskey.

On the morning of their tenth day by the falls, Charlie left camp with a new agenda. He'd spotted bear tracks the previous day and he'd convinced Billy to set out with him on a bear hunt. With winter coming, a thick bear-fur robe might come in handy, he'd suggested. But all Billy could think of, as they made their way through thick woods, was how his partner's pursuit of Mr. Whale had nearly cost them their lives.

There were no disasters that day, only disappointments. The tracks led straight up into some granite hills before they lost them. On the long hike back to camp, through rough country, a frustrated Billy recited a list of their failures. They had spent a week looking for a mine that probably didn't exist. They'd chased a bear who'd outsmarted them. And if that wasn't enough, they'd found the gold thieves, only to leave the next day. Charlie listened to this dismal tally and could find no reason to disagree. More troubling, a new consideration had been gnawing at him: For all he knew, the schooner could've upped anchor and sailed off. Then they'd need to track the two thieves again. Only this time, the detectives might never find them. Or if they somehow got lucky again, they'd be hard-pressed to offer a believable excuse for showing up. Billy was right. The entire operation seemed to be heading downhill.

As they got closer to camp, both detectives saw a wisp of smoke rising up into the clear evening sky. Without a word, the two men cocked their weapons. Charlie indicated with his hand that he'd march straight in; Billy should circle around and enter from the tree line. They split up, and Charlie proceeded forward warily.

Hubbard was sitting by a fire. Didn't know when you fellows would return, so I made myself at home, he said. It was getting cold.

Howdy, said Charlie with a big smile. And

he eased back the hammer on his Colt.

Howdy, Billy called out as he entered from the woods. His rifle was cradled lightly in his arms.

I was wondering if you fellows had some whiskey to sell? Hubbard asked with the happy voice of a man who'd already put away his share. He held out the half-empty bottle in his hand and explained that this was the last bottle in the stash he'd been working his way through.

We don't sell whiskey to white men, Charlie said.

Hubbard looked at him ominously.

But you're free to drink with us, Charlie continued. Let me get you a bottle.

It turned out that the only lure better than whiskey was free whiskey. Hubbard took to coming by nearly every night for the next two weeks. Still, Charlie was patient. He didn't rush things. He knew that if Hubbard turned suspicious, he'd run, and then they'd never discover where the thieves had stored the gold. Or, for that matter, have a case that would stand up in court.

So when they sat around the campfire and passed the bottle, Charlie told tales about his many scrapes in Texas and New Mexico. He never came out and said it, but he made it apparent that he'd come north to Alaska to escape some trouble. Considering his shaky frame of mind when he'd left Denver, that was pretty much the truth. Maybe that was why his stories were so convincing. Anyway, Hubbard was impressed. He felt like he was drinking with a real desperado.

And when Charlie wasn't talking about his outlaw adventures, he'd would sit by the campfire and discuss gold. He'd picked up a few things while working in the mine, so, always nice and casual, he'd make a point of throwing bits of his knowledge into conversations. One night he'd be going on about how a prospector who knew his beans would be able to extract ten times more gold from his ore than one who didn't. The next he'd be lecturing about leaching, how it was necessary to use chlorine to process the ore if you hoped to get the contaminants out of the slag. Charlie could tell Hubbard was paying close attention to this sort of talk. In fact, he asked Charlie lots of questions about the chlorinization process.

One night when the detectives returned to camp, both Schell and Hubbard were waiting for them. Schell had never come by their camp before, and Charlie knew his presence could mean only one of two things: Either the big man was there to take care of the two whiskey peddlers once and for all or he'd come to ask a favor. However things played out tonight, Charlie suspected, the successful resolution to the case would hang in the balance. In the distance he could hear the rumble of the falls. At that tense moment, Charlie felt it might have been a drum roll signaling a momentous event. He waited in silence for Schell to speak.

He didn't have to wait long. No sooner had Charlie sat down by the campfire than Schell blurted it out.

Hubbard tells me you boys know a bit about prospecting, he began.

Charlie simply nodded. He'd decided there was no point in overplaying his hand.

Hubbard hesitated. Then: "How'd you like to make $400 by helping us melt down some gold?"

"We'd like that very much," Charlie answered quickly, and for once there was not a trace of an actor's guile in his joy.

TWENTY-FIVE

That momentous night in the camp near the Chieke Falls, the evening seemed to stretch on and on, the sun remaining high in the sky, glowing all the while as brightly as the flames from the campfire. It was a night when Charlie felt that a solution to the case might finally be within his grasp. Then, sometime after ten, the sun went down and a thick darkness enveloped the spruce forest and the night sounds grew thick, the birds and insects chirping in a steady chorus. Hubbard sidled up to Charlie. I want you to come with me, he said.

Where to? Charlie asked evenly.

Hubbard didn't answer the question. Instead he said they would be back in a few hours. In the meantime, Schell would keep his partner company.

Guard him is what you mean, Charlie thought. It immediately occurred to Charlie that this might be a trap, a move to separate the two of them so they'd be easier to overpower. The offer of $400 to melt the gold had been a trick, a ruse to lull them into believing there was nothing to worry about. Or then again, perhaps not. It might just as well have been a genuine business proposition. Yet for a moment Charlie considered that it would be prudent to arrest the two thieves right then and there, while Billy and he had the chance of getting the drop on them. But arrests wouldn't solve the case. In fact, he reminded himself, without the gold it'd be difficult to convict the two men. So when Hubbard got up to leave, Charlie ignored his misgivings, said a cheery good-bye to Billy, grabbed a fresh bottle of rye for the journey, and then, with a calm that was all disguise, followed Hubbard out of the camp. Hubbard led the way to a canoe.

In the canoe crossing Chieke Bay, there was little talk. Hubbard steered, and Charlie listened to the whishing sound of the paddle cutting through the water. His eyes soon adjusted to the dim light thrown off by the stars, and he saw that they were heading back toward the Indian village. He began to wonder whether Hubbard had arranged for a group of braves to be waiting on the beach to waylay him. Charlie had his Colt tucked into the waistband of his pants, but taking on a passel of Chinooks as well as a white gun-slinger would prove difficult. Yet he was not afraid. His mind didn't work like that. Instead, he began to focus on how he'd extricate himself if things turned sticky. He decided straight off he'd need to put one right between Hubbard's eyes and hope that'd put a damper on the Injuns' grit. As the canoe moved closer to shore, he scanned the beach and the tree line; he saw no one.

Once they were on the beach, Charlie kept a watchful eye on the shadows but at the same time tried not to betray his concern. Again he asked Hubbard where they were heading.

You'll know soon enough, Hubbard said tersely. Then he asked for the bottle. Charlie felt that might be a reassuring sign. A man doesn't want to dull his senses before a gunfight. In the next moment, though, Charlie had to concede that he'd known a few hard types who needed help finding the courage to draw on a man. In the end, Charlie decided he'd no choice but to accept what Hubbard had said. He'd know soon enough.

Hubbard led the way through the spruce forest. At night it was a bewildering maze of tall trees and deep shadows, but Hubbard was not deterred. He marched on swiftly and without hesitation. At first Charlie tried to mark the trail in his mind, looking for distinctive limbs or rock outcroppings. But he soon realized that this was impossible. The stars were hiding behind clouds and the darkness was so total that he could not distinguish one big spruce from another and the rocks they passed rose up as vague forms. Still, he dragged his right boot heel as he walked; though the ground was hard, it might leave a trace he'd be able to see in the daylight.

They continued on in silence for what seemed to Charlie to be three miles or so, and then Hubbard raised his hand. "We're here," he announced.

As Charlie watched with a growing excitement, the small man found a shovel that had been leaning against a tree. Then he executed a right turn like a soldier on parade and took a series of measured steps. One, he counted out loud. Two. . . . When he reached ten, he began to dig.

This is it! Charlie told himself. Hubbard's about to dig up the stolen gold!

After shoveling for only a short time, Hubbard reached into the hole. In the darkness Charlie couldn't make out what he was holding in his hand. But when Hubbard approached, he saw the object clearly: It was a frying pan.

A frying pan? Charlie had no idea what was going on. He'd been led through the woods in the dark of night to a secret hiding place, where the master thief had unearthed — a frying pan! It didn't make any sense.

Then Hubbard handed him the pan. Charlie looked closely and saw that it was coated with a yellow substance. He traced his fingers across the plate of the frying pan in a slow examination. The pan was coated with gold.

That's why we need you and Sayles, Hubbard offered in explanation. Charlie still had no idea what Hubbard meant. The whole thing was damn odd. A golden frying pan? But he hadn't been bushwhacked. And he wanted to believe that the frying pan was not the only thing buried somewhere in these woods. It seemed very likely that the gold bars were hidden nearby. If he was patient, Charlie reckoned, Hubbard would get around to making things clear. In the meantime, Charlie would just listen. Besides, he feared that if he did too much talking, he'd reveal how little he actually knew about processing gold.

The whiskey encouraged Hubbard's natural tendency to ramble, but just as Charlie was beginning to lose patience, the thief got back on track. He explained that they'd tried to recast some gold bars into nuggets. The first step, they'd figured, would be simple enough: Melt the gold. We got a good bark fire going, he said. And we made a bellows out of an old raincoat and a cracker box. That kept the fire blazing. Next we plunked a gold bar into that frying pan and held it over the flame. We figured that soon enough we'd have a liquid we could pour into a mold. Only thing — and now Hubbard began waving the frying pan about — when the gold cooled, it stuck to the frying pan. We can't even scrape it off.

Imagine it might raise a few questions, you walking into a bank in Seattle trying to cash in a frying pan, Charlie suggested. He was treading lightly, but at the same time he was also trying to draw Hubbard out.

Hubbard laughed one of his deep, wheezy laughs. That's why we need you and Sayles. We got a lot of bars we need to recast. Don't want any smart-aleck banker running to the sheriff.

At that moment Charlie kept very still. *Go on,* he silently coaxed. *Tell me the whole story. Tell me where the gold is hidden.* He was bursting with questions, but he feared that if he pressed, Hubbard would be spooked. He'd stop talking altogether.

Charlie waited. Then Hubbard asked in a low, soft voice, "I tell you a secret, swear you'll keep it?"

"Yes," Charlie lied.

"The gold. It's stolen from the Treadwell mine."

Over the next three days, the four men seemed to discuss little other than the mechanics of recasting gold bars. Now that the secret about the source of the gold had been revealed, the thieves were no longer cagey about their intentions. They made it clear that they needed to mold the machine-stamped

Treadwell bullion into smaller, unrecognizable bars. It'd be the only way they'd be able to turn the gold into cash at a bank and not get arrested. But other than explaining their need for their two new friends' expertise, the thieves remained guarded, if not downright suspicious. They were very careful not to reveal where the cache of stolen bars was hidden. And whenever Charlie dared to ask what he'd hoped would be seen as an innocent question, wondering, say, how many bars they'd need to recast, the two thieves would immediately shoot each other wary looks and the conversation would come to an abrupt halt. So Charlie decided not to pry. Too much was at stake; he needed to know where the gold was hidden. He would wait and play along.

Guess we'll need to build a furnace to melt the gold, Schell said.

Of course, Charlie agreed, although he had no idea if that was the case.

We do this right, Schell continued, we'll need crucibles to hold the molten gold. And molds. And chloride so we can leach the stuff when we melt it down. Get all the impurities out.

Exactly, Charlie agreed; only once more he had no idea what he was agreeing to. He didn't want Schell to stop talking. He figured that if the thief kept jawing he might inadvertently reveal where the gold was hidden. But as the days of talk went on, Charlie became convinced that the two thieves were too disciplined to make a slip. He'd learn the location of the gold only when the time came to recast the bars. He'd have to wait until then. Except that strategy raised another problem. Despite all his boasting, Charlie had no idea how to melt down the gold. Once he set to work, he'd be exposed as a fraud. And then he'd never learn where the gold was hidden. Instead, the two detectives would need to kill the two thieves before they got killed themselves.

He sat lost in thought over his predicament. And after a while, he came up with an idea. He shared it with Billy that afternoon when they went off alone into the woods to gather firewood. Might work, Billy agreed.

Later that evening, as the four of them were sitting around the campfire and a bottle was being passed, Charlie tried it out on Schell and Hubbard.

If we're gonna build a furnace and recast the gold, then we're gonna need supplies, he said. Sayles will stay here with you, but I'm gonna go to Juneau and get us what we need. What do you think? he asked, hoping his suggestion sounded reasonable.

Hubbard looked questioningly at Schell. The big man thought about it for a moment, then spoke. Sounds like a good idea, he agreed.

But then, Schell had no idea where Charlie intended to get the supplies.

There is a difference, Durkin lectured authoritatively, a *huge* difference, between melting and smelting. You can't just put gold in a frying pan as if it were a hunk of hog lard, like those two fools did.

Earlier, the meeting in the mine superintendent's home on Douglas Island had started off as though it were a war council. As soon as Charlie had announced that he'd caught up with the two thieves, Durkin had jumped to his feet. A log fire roared in a massive limestone fireplace, and Durkin stood silhouetted in front of it, waving his hands and shouting with glee. Charlie wouldn't have been surprised if the man had broken out into a jig. "I knew we'd get the bastards. I knew it," he exalted. "Congratulations, Mr. Davis."

It was then that the detective disclosed for the first time that his name was in reality Charlie Siringo, not Lee Davis. The superintendent considered that for only an instant before proclaiming that he didn't care a dickens about the name. All that mattered was that Davis or Siringo or whatever he wanted to call himself had found the thieves. He wanted Charlie to contact the authorities and make the arrests.

We do that, Charlie countered flatly, it's

more than likely we'll never recover the gold.

Durkin suddenly stood very still. It was as if all his previous joy had in an instant been drained out of him. He stared at Charlie, and when he finally spoke his tone was low and accusatory. "You don't know where the gold is?" he asked.

Charlie suggested that Durkin take a seat; he would explain the situation. In great detail he recounted how, along with his partner, he'd tracked the two thieves, won their confidence, and been offered the job of recasting the stolen gold bars. But, Charlie went on, neither he nor Sayles had the slightest idea how to build a furnace and mold the gold into nuggets.

Well, Durkin said, you've come to the right man. What I don't know about gold ain't worth knowing.

For the next hour or so Durkin delivered a thoughtful and meticulous primer on the art of processing gold. In truth, a lot of it was lost on Charlie, especially when Durkin reeled off the chemical formulas of the solutions involved in removing the impurities from gold. But by the time Durkin had concluded his lecture, Charlie was confident that he'd understood the basic principles. He'd be able to build a furnace with heat-resistant clay bricks. He'd stoke it up with charcoal, not wood, because charcoal was pure carbon and burned at a higher temperature. He'd make sure the fire reached 2,000 degrees; gold melted at 1,943 degrees Fahrenheit, Durkin had specified. And he'd wait until the flame turned blue, an indication that there was sufficient carbon monoxide present for the melting process to proceed. Durkin also trained Charlie in the tricky skills of handling the red-hot crucibles that would hold the molten ore as well as the molds into which the gold would be recast.

It was late when the lecture was finally concluded, and Durkin brought out a celebratory bottle of whiskey and two glasses. Perhaps we'd better wait until we've something to toast, Charlie suggested cautiously. But Durkin wouldn't hear of it. "We got 'em," he kept on repeating. Florid with excitement, he clinked his glass against Charlie's and raised it to his lips. "To the arrests," he toasted.

Charlie spent the night as a guest in Durkin's house. At precisely six-thirty a big breakfast was served in the wood-paneled dining room by an Indian cook. Then the superintendent, still bubbling with the previous night's enthusiasm, escorted Charlie on a tour of the mine and mill buildings. As Charlie followed behind him, Durkin walked swiftly up and down the corridors, picking and choosing items as he went. He wanted to make sure that the detective had all the supplies and materials he needed.

It was quite a load, and Charlie fretted that he wouldn't be able to get it all back to Chieke Bay. Durkin told him not to worry. He gave a flurry of orders, and his assistants packed everything up into a couple of large crates. Then, on Durkin's further command, the crates were taken by ferry to Juneau. They would be put on the next steamer to Killisnoo. A ticket had been booked for Charlie, too. Just go to the shipping office after you arrive in Killisnoo, Durkin instructed. The crates will be waiting for you.

But when the steamer *Topeka* docked in Killisnoo, Charlie didn't go directly to the small shipping shack on the wharf. On his trip to Juneau earlier in the week he'd noticed a U.S. Navy warship anchored in the harbor. On a hunch he hired a rowboat and went out to the man-of-war. He'd suspected there might be a U.S. marshal on board, and he was correct.

Marshal Jim Collins was a discouragingly old man with a scraggly gray mustache. When Charlie introduced himself as a Pinkerton, Collins's attitude was reserved. Like most lawmen, the marshal didn't set much store in private detectives. But as soon as Collins learned the reason for Charlie's visit, his attitude improved.

Putting the cuffs on two gold thieves would be a good day's work, he agreed. Soon as you've learned where they've hidden the gold,

391

get word to me. Just tell me when you're ready, he volunteered, and I'll be there to make it nice and legal.

That pledge of support reassured Charlie, but there was something else that'd been troubling him. He thought it only fair to share it with the marshal before things went any further.

Schell and Hubbard, Charlie began cautiously, have a good deal of Indian friends. The chief of the village is their bosom buddy. We arrest them, and we might find ourselves in a real fight. Whole tribe might come out to protect 'em.

The old marshal replied without the slightest hesitation. "Then I imagine another gun will come in mighty handy," he said firmly.

So it was with a renewed feeling of confidence about his prospects that Charlie had the crates loaded into a hired Indian canoe and began the trip back to Chieke Bay. A storm blew up as the canoe entered the long strait leading into the bay, and for an unsteady hour Charlie worried that the overloaded canoe might capsize in rough waters. But the storm finally passed and the sea calmed. The rest of the trip was uneventful.

He left the crates on the beach and, exhausted, walked up toward the camp. As he got closer he could smell bacon frying, and his stomach began to growl. He hadn't eaten since breakfast. He was looking forward to some hot grub, a few pulls from the bottle, and then a good night's sleep. In the morning he'd start constructing the furnace, and if all went according to plan, he'd soon have his hands on the stolen gold. Charlie was feeling very good about things as he walked into the camp.

There was Billy, cooking over the fire. Across the way sat Hubbard, nursing a bottle. And right off Charlie knew that something was very wrong.

When Billy saw his partner, he didn't say anything; he just walked into the tent. When he emerged a few moments later, he waited until Hubbard's head was turned and then, without a word, slipped a small piece of paper into Charlie's hand.

Charlie quickly put it into his pocket, and went over to talk to Hubbard. The small man was in a sullen mood. He sat hunched, a tight, grim expression on his face. Charlie pretended not to notice. He went on in his spirited way about the high time he'd had in Juneau and how he'd picked up all the supplies. Hubbard listened with a fierce silence. Finally Charlie said he needed a drink. He was going to fetch a fresh bottle. A man in no hurry, he went off to the tent.

But once inside, he immediately took Billy's note from his pocket. He read: "It's all off. They are suspicious of us and say they won't dig up the gold."

TWENTY-SIX

As Charlie's careful strategy collapsed, George Carmack was sitting idly farther north in Fortymile, a small, lonely settlement on the high banks on the Yukon River forty miles downstream from Fort Reliance. A decision made by the impetuous toss of a coin had pointed him toward this destination. But now that George had arrived, he'd no idea of what he'd do; unlike the detective, he didn't even possess a plan that could fall apart. He was a man alone, and without prospects. Oddly, though, he wasn't concerned. In fact, his blood, he would say, was tingling. The previous day's premonition remained strong. He knew that something unusual was about to take place.

That night George slept in his tent, and very quickly he fell into a dream as intense as if he were living it. Events unfolded in vivid detail. There he was sitting on the banks of a small stream, watching grayling shoot the rapids. Suddenly the grayling scattered in fright as two large king salmon burst up-stream in a torrent of white, foaming water. The two enormous fish came to a stop below him. He gazed down and was immediately stirred by their golden beauty. When he looked closer, he saw that their sparkling skin was covered not in scales but with bright gold nuggets. Their eyes were shiny twenty-dollar gold pieces. Excited, he reached into the icy water to grasp one of the salmon, and it was at that moment he awoke.

The dream had been so compelling, so fantastic yet at the same time so real, that sleep was no longer possible. George spent the remainder of the restless night lying under his blanket trying to make some sense of the experience. Living with the Tagish had taught him that dreams were not accidents but communications from the guiding spirits. Yet George could not decipher the message in this strange dream. It was very frustrating, like a letter that could not be read because the ink had faded.

By the morning, however, the implications of the dream grew clear: He must go fishing for salmon. There was a good market for dried salmon, and the dream was telling him that he'd be able to earn some money by sell-ing his catch. The spirits, he felt, were look-ing out for him.

After breakfast, George went to the trading post run by old Jack McQuesten, another frustrated prospector, and bought a spool of net twine. He spent the morning stringing together the long gill net he'd anchor down with willow poles and use as a weir to catch the salmon. As he worked in the strong sun, he gave some thought to where he'd set his net. He'd hunted and fished with the Tagish along many of the streams that emptied into the Yukon. There were plenty of rich fishing grounds. But as soon as he began to consider the possibilities, one location took an iron hold in his mind. About fifty miles to the north, in Canadian territory, a small, swift stream of placid blue-green waters cut off from the roaring Yukon River. The Indians called it Throndiuk; the name meant "Hammer Water," in recognition of the fence of stakes they'd hammer across its shallow waters to hold their gill nets. Trappers and prospectors had taken to netting salmon there, too. But they found the guttural Indian word unpronounceable. Mangled by the white man, it came out "Klondike," and the new name stuck.

George now had a plan. To his surprise, his life had been given a new and resolute direction. He'd fish for salmon, and grow rich from selling his catch. On the first day of July 1896, George loaded his boat and started up-river for the Klondike.

The Indians blamed the white man's steamboats. They believed that the constant churning of the paddle wheels as the boats chugged downstream had disturbed the pattern of the currents flowing through the Yukon River. George had no idea whether this explanation was correct. All he knew was that this year the salmon weren't running on the Klondike. He'd hammered in the stakes and stretched his fish trap across the shallow water at the mouth of the river. He'd built a birch frame where he'd hang the fish to dry in the sun. But there was little to catch or dry. In all his years in the north, George had never seen a poorer run of fish.

The weather was working against him, too. Torrential rains fell day after day, and when, at last, the daily drenchings subsided, cold moved in. He'd wake up in the morning to find that the heavy dew glistening on the riverbank had frozen into a solid icy coat. But George didn't break camp. He had faith in the guiding wisdom of his dream. He'd stay on and the salmon run would soon increase.

One afternoon, after spending a disappointing month on the Klondike, George waded into the cold, shallow water to check his traps. This was monotonous work; each square of netting needed to be inspected and, more bothersome, the long immersion in the chilly water made his legs cramp. He was pulling a small salmon from the net when he heard a booming voice: "Kla-how-ya, George." He looked up to see Skookum Jim calling to him; Tagish Charley was beside him.

Surprised, George hurried out of the water to greet them. He hadn't seen the two Indians since their time prospecting together in the Yukon, and now the sudden memory struck him as an experience from another, distant life. Their appearance also nudged his thoughts to Kate — she was, he reminded himself, Jim's sister — and little Gracie. In pursuit of his new ambition, he had left his family behind. And by now the wilderness had crept around him so completely that they also seemed to belong to another time. He didn't miss them; it was not his way. The years on his own had taught George to find comfort in solitude.

After shaking hands, George asked what had brought the two Indians so far down-river.

We've had nothing but bad luck since you left, Jim explained. We find no gold. And this —

Jim rolled up his sleeve and displayed a row of long, deep scars. George recognized that they'd been made by a bear. George had always feared bears, and it was unsettling to listen as Jim described the attack.

He'd been in the woods when, without warning, a big brown bear had charged. He got off two quick shots with his rifle and both bullets hit, but the wounds seemed only to enrage the great creature. Growling with fury, the bear rose up on its hind legs and swiped with its sharp claws like a boxer throwing punches. Desperate, Jim clubbed at the bear with his empty rifle. But he was no match for the angry beast. Jim's caribou-skin shirt was in tatters, his arms and chest were dripping with blood, when suddenly the bear collapsed from its wounds. As the animal lay helpless on its back, Jim repeatedly smashed a large rock against its head until he was sure the bear was dead.

Bad luck, George agreed; just hearing the tale had left him with shivers. But he still didn't understand why the two Indians had turned up on the Klondike.

We speak with the medicine man in the village, Jim went on. He said we want to rid evil spirits, we need to find George. He said George make good medicine for us.

"Well, you've hunted me up," George said. "You're welcome to stay." But he also told them that maybe the shaman was wrong: "I'm not having much luck myself. Don't see how I can help you."

All afternoon, George pondered what Jim had said. He knew the shaman's medicine was strong. There had to be a reason the two Indians were instructed to find him. All his life he'd been on his own, and he'd grown accustomed to sorting through things. So George kept at it, and soon he felt he understood. He'd stumbled off the path the spirits had determined for him. The shaman had sent Jim and Charley to warn him. But what about his dream? George let it unfold again in his mind, and now it occurred to him that he'd misinterpreted the message. The spirits hadn't wanted him to fish for salmon. That wasn't what it was about at all.

That night after dinner he sat with Jim and Charley and held a council. "The fish aren't coming," George began. "We got to do something else."

Jim suggested that they go lumbering. They could float the logs down the river. The saw mill at Fortymile was paying $25 a thousand feet.

George considered the idea. Been told there're some big spruce trees up the Klondike, he said. Maybe we do a little logging, he agreed.

The Indians nodded. A new path had been set. Their luck would change. The shaman had been wise to send them to George.

George, however, was not finished. There was something he needed to tell them, he announced with a measure of gravity. Sitting by the campfire across from his two friends, he shared his dream.

The spirits talking to you, George, Charley said with certainty.

George concurred. And at last, George explained, he understood what he was being told. The dream wasn't about salmon fishing. The spirits weren't telling him to go logging, either. George said, "We head up the Klondike and go prospecting."

The Klondike was unexplored country, a wilderness new to all three of the men, and George decided that it made sense first to scout out a good route north. In the morning George and Jim shouldered their packs and started up the Klondike on foot; Tagish Charley stayed behind to begin packing up the camp.

The two men hiked along the north bank of the river for several miles. The brush was not thick, and it was an easy journey. Soft green willows bent low toward the smooth water, and martens scattered at the sound of their approach. The birdsong of thrushes and yellow warblers filled the air. Shortly before noon, George spotted a high butte rising in the west. From its top, he told Jim, they'd be able to see the entire countryside. Jim agreed, and George led the way.

The climb to the summit was steep and exhausting. When they reached the top, George was eager to drop his pack. He wanted to sit down and catch his breath. But as he began to remove the leather strap from his shoulder, his eyes peered out into the distance; and then he no longer was aware of his fatigue.

The view was glorious. At that instant George was, he'd remember for the rest of his life, "deeply moved." As far as he could see was a procession of fat hills, one after another, an undulating carpet woven in a pattern of green and brown shades. Instinctively, George turned to see what was behind him. Now he looked out at a solid wall of mountains, their snow-capped peaks reaching up into the blue sky. He turned his head again, looking eastward, and he saw another range of low, dome-shaped hills. As he studied this rolling landscape, each hill nearly identical in height, he noticed a series of long, broad furrows cutting across the length of the entire range. For a moment he was reminded of the red claw marks scarring Jim's arm. But then he grasped what he was looking at it. The clefts were deep stream beds. Over the course of untold centuries, their fast waters had gouged their way down from the hilltops, carving out steep valleys and breaking off into a lace of twisting creeks as they'd rumbled toward the Klondike River. And at once George knew. These were the streams in his dream. The fish in these waters would have twenty-dollar coins for eyes, and the stream beds would be shining with gold nuggets. It'd be like panning on the floor of heaven. Standing on that high butte and looking east, he had another unshakable premonition: He'd strike gold in those distant streams.

They didn't get back to camp until late that night. But still George was up with the dawn. Now that his mind was set, there was a great deal to do. If they were going to head up the Klondike, they'd need to build a canoe big enough to hold three men and their supplies.

A day later, as George was hollowing out a long birch log that would become their canoe, he watched as a tall, lean man poled a flat-bottomed boat down the Yukon, toward their camp. It wasn't until the man was drawing the bow of his boat up onto the beach that George saw the bushy red mustache and recognized him. It was Robert Henderson, a dour Scot who'd been drifting through the Yukon for years in a futile search for gold. George didn't know Henderson well at all, but he admired any man who had the gumption to be undeterred by years of failure.

"Hello, Bob!" George called as the Scotsman walked slowly toward him. "Where in the world did you drop from?"

"I just came down from Ogilvie. I'm going up the Klondike."

"What's the idea, Bob?"

"There's been a prospect found in a small creek. I think it empties into the Klondike, about fifteen miles up. I'm looking for a better way to get there than going over the mountains from Indian Creek."

Now George was curious. This was near the country he was setting out to explore. "Got any kind of prospect?" he asked, hoping he didn't betray too much interest.

"We don't know yet. We can get a prospect on the surface. When I left, the boys were running up an open cut to get in the bedrock."

George mulled this news. Since he'd already decided to head that way, it might makes sense to partner up with an outfit that knew the country. "What are the chances to locate up there?" he asked. "Everything staked?"

Henderson glanced at the two Indians who'd been standing nearby and listening to the conversation. "There's a chance for you, George, but I don't want any damn Siwashes staking on that creek."

George's anger quickly started to rise. The insult had been directed at Jim and Charley, but it affected George as deeply as if he'd been the target, too. He realized that it had been a mistake for him to have considered working with a white man.

But George didn't relish confrontations. He simply turned his back on Henderson and went to work on his canoe. It wasn't long before the Scotsman pushed his boat into the water and started up the Klondike.

When Henderson was gone, Jim spoke up. "What's the matter with that white man?" he asked loudly, speaking Chinook. "Him kill

Indian moose, Indian caribou. Look for gold in Indian country. No like Indian stake claim. What for, no good?"

George thought about trying to explain to his friend, but he knew no argument he might use would be sufficient. Some people had a narrow way of looking at the world, and that would always be that. And since you couldn't change things, it made more sense to George to let some things go. That had always been his way.

"Never mind, Jim," George said easily. "This is a big country. We'll go and find a creek of our own."

TWENTY-SEVEN

The next morning at daylight George and the two Indians loaded the canoe and began poling up the Klondike. A light breeze carried the crisp fragrance of the spruce forests as the boat followed the river toward the glow of the rising sun. After about two miles, George guided them into a backwater and they beached their canoe at a spot where the hard summer rains had flattened the left bank.

They would continue on foot, so they shouldered their packs and grabbed their pans and shovels from the stern. Stretching in front of them was a dense underbrush of sharp-edged ferns and tangles of wet moss. "Where you go now?" Jim asked.

In the past when there had been no apparent trail, George had let the Indians take the lead. He felt they'd be better able to find the way through rough country. Today, however, George understood that he needed to set the course. He alone could lead the way to the waters where the golden salmon of his dream ran. "You come, I go first," George said emphatically.

Instinct told him to head to the right, and he set off. For more than a mile they trudged through soft black river mud, their moccasins sinking deep into the muck with each new step. Then the ground became firmer, and George guided them through some thick timber until they came out at the mouth of a creek.

The water was clear and glistening, the sunlight beaming on a stream bed speckled with tiny bright-white pebbles. That was a promising sign; George had never seen such a clear indication of quartz in any of his previous expeditions into the Yukon Valley. And where there was quartz, he knew, there often was gold. He threw down his pack and grabbed his pan and shovel.

The creek bent left, and he followed it to a small sandbar. Deciding that this was as good a spot as any, George filled his pan with gravel. Then he got down on his haunches and began tilting and twirling the pan in the sunlit water. From time to time, he used his hand to softly stir the mix of dirt. When there was not more than a handful of dark silt remaining in the pan, George paused.

How many times in his lifetime had he lived this moment? How many times had he waited to learn if a prospect would show in his pan?

Yet George couldn't help feeling that this occasion was different. The intensity of his expectations was unique. "To be or not to be," he found himself saying out loud, as if Hamlet's soliloquy were an incantation. "That is the question."

Why you talking in that strange way? Charley demanded. The Indians were looking over George's shoulder, an audience caught up in his every word and gesture. "I no see um gold," Charley observed with disappointment.

"That's all right, Charley," George told him. "I makum Boston man's medicine."

He lifted the pan with its small residue of black sand toward the Indians. "Spit in it, boys, for good luck."

They did, and George put the pan in the water. Gently, he twirled it; and tilted it; and a streak of bright yellow gold appeared. It was very fine, like soft golden sand, but it lay heavy in the pan. This flour gold had weight.

George's hopes leaped. If there were colors in this low creek, he could only imagine what he'd find when he panned the distant higher waters he'd seen from the summit.

He gave the order to shoulder their packs. They were moving on.

They hiked up a mossy incline, still following the path of the frothing creek. The sun was warm and bright. The chirping lilt of birdsong filled the air. George felt, he would recall years later, as if the guiding spirits were welcoming him into "a valley of golden dreams."

After walking on for about an hour, George stopped at a rocky crest abutting the creek's left bank. A rock formation had attracted him, and he decided to dig. With only a little effort, he broke through the rain-soaked bedrock, dug up a shoveful of dirt, and emptied it into his pan. This time he found not only fine gold but also two coarse pieces, each about the size of a BB shot.

George had washed only a single small pan of dirt, but it had revealed a fine prospect. Jim thought they should locate here, and George weighed the idea.

Hunting for gold was a gamble, an occupation where ultimately luck played a greater role than either skill or hard work. Nevertheless, a canny prospector, George had learned, can help shift the odds a bit in his favor by paying close attention to the signs in his pan. And two coarse yellow pieces, however tiny, held out a persuasive promise. It was entirely feasible that if they dug deep, they'd find long veins of gold running beneath the rocky banks fronting this stretch of the creek. Yet from the start this expedition had been driven by George's strong premonitions, and now his instincts told him to continue on. To appease Jim, he agreed that if they found no better site they would return here. But even as he offered the compromise, George was certain he'd never be staking this run of the creek. He knew there were richer prospects ahead.

Once again the trio shouldered their packs. "Mush on!" George said, enjoying a small joke. He led the way about a mile farther up the creek, and they came to a flat grassy plain. It'd been a long day, and he gave the order to make camp.

It was a cold camp, and they ate some of the dried salmon they had carried in their packs. Later that night George lay underneath his blanket, too excited to sleep. But his sleeplessness gave him no concerns. He knew he'd be prepared for tomorrow. He'd already experienced his guiding dream.

With the new morning, George was, as he'd anticipated, refreshed. He led the way once again, sticking close to the creek bed. They continued upstream until they arrived at a fork. A small creek twisted off to the south; a longer and wider branch rose straight on up, hugging the rising contours of the valley.

George hesitated. For the first time on this trip he was uncertain about which way to proceed. A prospector's logic advised that he hold to the broader, faster-running branch; the bedrock along its banks should be similar in composition to the gravel that yesterday

410

had yielded flour gold as well as two coarse pieces. But something about the tributary tugged at all his instincts. He walked along it for just a yard or so, and his heart raced. A peculiar sensation coursed through him.

Which way, George? Jim asked impatiently.

George thought about it further, then chose to respect the mineralogical wisdom he'd accumulated during his time panning in the Yukon. He said they'd follow the broad, wide fork.

It was a reasonable choice, but it was the wrong one. For once George had ignored his intuition, and as a result he lost the opportunity to make a startling discovery. When he'd started up the bank of the south fork he'd been walking on the richest ground in the world. There was gold scattered along the creek bed, in the bedrock beneath the sloping banks, and buried like an abandoned treasure deep in the surrounding hills. Millions and millions of dollars' worth of gold were waiting to be claimed along the creek that would soon become aptly known as Eldorado. But that morning George turned away, and trudged on up through the narrow valley.

He continued past the head of the creek and came to the top of a grassy ridge. George decided that they'd turn east; his new plan was to circle back to the headwaters of the main creek and prospect all the way down.

They had gone only a short distance along

the ridge when a black bear emerged from a thicket of blueberry bushes. George stood as if paralyzed. His secret fear had suddenly become real. All he could do was stare at the bear. The big animal stared back. George was certain that in the next instant the bear would charge. But even as he had that thought, he could feel the presence of Jim standing behind him and leveling the long barrel of a Winchester on his shoulder. Then Jim fired, the rifle bouncing on George's shoulder. Jim fired again. And again. And the bear fell down dead.

The Indians skinned the bear. The fur would be used for a sleeping robe, and Jim kept the claws for a necklace he'd make for his wife. The meat was divided among the three men. They'd roast it that night over a campfire. The Indians felt the spirits had blessed them by giving them the bear; it was a sign that their luck was changing. But the encounter had left George unnerved. He saw it as a warning. In the wilderness, anything might happen. He needed to fulfill his destiny while he was still able. The next bear might not be so docile. George insisted that they continue on.

At the head of a series of small creeks that ran toward the mightier Klondike and Indian rivers, George spotted a high, dome-shaped hill. Let's climb to the top, he suggested. We'll be able to see the whole country.

The view reached to the horizon. The early frosts had tinted the foothills into a weave of fiery crimsons, emerald greens, and golden yellows, and the ripe colors glowed in the high afternoon sun. This same sharp light also caught the many streams rushing in a shiny crystal tumble down the flanks of the distant hills and mountains. Looking at this panorama, George was affected not just by its beauty but also by its energy. The Great Spirit who had created this wondrous valley had led him here for a reason.

As he continued to peer out into the distance, he noticed a wisp of pale smoke. It was rising up from a small canyon. They were not alone! He was startled for a moment, and then he realized it must be Henderson's campfire.

"Well, boys," George told the Indians, "we've got this far. Let's go down and see what they got."

Jim refused. He had not forgotten Henderson's insult, and he was too proud to forgive. "No liket go," he said flatly.

"Oh come on, Jim," George tried. "We've found more good country than we want. Have a good tum-tum, Jim, and come along."

It irritated Jim that George was willing to pretend that nothing had happened. Jim decided that although George believed he'd become a Tagish, the reality was that he would never be an Indian. A Tagish brave would never surrender his honor so easily. No, Jim repeated. He wouldn't go to the camp of the man who'd scorned him.

But George was persistent. He explained that it was a matter of honor for him, too. The sourdough's code required that he tell Henderson about the creek where they'd panned the pieces of coarse gold. In a wilderness without the government's laws, the unwritten rules between men were all the prospectors had. These were commandments that must be obeyed.

It was a standoff. Both men believed they had to act with honor, but the concept held a different meaning for each of them. However, when George started down to Henderson's camp and Charley followed, Jim realized he'd better go along. He was part of George's crew, and it wouldn't be right to abandon his partners. That was a matter of honor, too. Perhaps, he even began to wonder as he trailed slowly behind them, George was right. Maybe he should give the white man one more chance.

"Hello, George," greeted Henderson as they entered the camp on what would become known as Gold Bottom Creek. "You found us at last, eh?"

"Well, yes. Although it was accidental," George explained.

He was not a man to make small talk, so he

got straight to the purpose of his visit. "We found some good prospects in a creek over on the other side of that range. And seeing your camp from up on that mountain we came around out of our way to tell you about it."

Henderson said he was much obliged, but he and his partners were encouraged by what they'd panned on this creek. He led the way downstream to where his three partners — Frank Swanson, Al Dalton, and Charley Monson — were working an open cut. They were going to keep at it with their shovels until they got down to bedrock. Then they'd know if the gold ran deep.

George was intrigued. If Henderson and his crew were ready to stake here, maybe the creek was rich. He asked permission to try a few pans.

"Be my guest," Henderson offered grandly.

George sifted several pans of gravel, first from the creek and then from down in the cut. There were a few colors, but they were not heavy like the gold he'd panned earlier in the day.

When George had finished panning, he was ready to leave. He wouldn't stay the night in this camp; Henderson's rudeness still rankled. But Henderson was a fellow prospector, and the code must be obeyed. So George decided to give him one more chance.

"Take a look at what I found on that creek

of ours," George said, showing him the two tiny pieces of coarse gold. "You'd better come have a look."

"I'm staying here until we get down to bedrock," Henderson replied stubbornly.

"Suit yourself," George said.

They were about to head off when Jim saw Henderson take a bulging pouch of tobacco out of his pocket and begin to pack his pipe. Their own supply of tobacco was nearly gone, so Jim asked the prospector if he could buy some.

No, snapped Henderson, and he gave Jim an insolent look. Its meaning was clear: I don't do business with Indians.

Without another word, the three men walked off. They maintained a tense silence as they headed out of the canyon and back up the hill.

George felt he'd given Henderson his chance, as the code required. But after this last insult, he was done trying to do right by the man. Henderson and his outfit could go their way; he and his partners would go theirs.

Jim was resigned, too. But his anger was not confined to Henderson. He'd never again trust any white man. Fuming, he was even beginning to have doubts about George.

As for Henderson, no doubt he forgot about the incident over the tobacco moments after it happened. But in time he'd have reason to recall it, and then it would haunt him for the rest of his life.

Twenty-Eight

Six hundred or so miles south of the Yukon Valley, the mood in the detectives' camp on Chieke Bay had turned tense, too. No sooner had Charlie Siringo returned from Juneau then he had cause to regret that he'd ever left the company of the two thieves.

Charlie had been tipped off by his partner that their operation had fallen apart, but even if he hadn't read Billy's note it wouldn't have taken much detective work to figure out that things had turned scaly. All through dinner Hubbard kept shooting him scowling looks; Charlie pretended not to notice. There was no advantage in letting on that he knew the thieves had grown suspicious; he'd wait for Hubbard to make his move.

It was dusk by the time the meal was over, and that was when Hubbard finally spoke up. "Let's walk," he said to Charlie. "I want to talk to you."

Charlie rose and followed him. He saw that Hubbard was packing, his holster low on his hip as though he meant business. Charlie was glad he had his big Colt under his coat. He reckoned that pretty soon he'd find out if Hubbard was the gunny he wanted people to think he was. And that, Charlie thought, would be a damn shame. It wasn't that the detective had any misgivings about drawing on the thief; he'd shoot him down if need be. It was just irksome that after all this time he still had no notion about where the gold was hidden. If he had to put a bullet or two into Hubbard, it was unlikely he'd ever find out.

When they reached the top of a heavily timbered gulch, Hubbard straightened up to his full height and looked Charlie in the face. Charlie's eyes, though, kept a steady watch on the thief's right hand. Soon as it fell toward the hip, Charlie would draw.

Hubbard's hand didn't move. Instead he began shouting. "That partner of yours is a goddamned policeman," he declared hotly. "Schell and I have concluded not to dig up that gold now."

Hubbard was bristling with rage, and the arrangement to process the gold bars had broken down. But all things considered, Charlie judged, it could've played out worse. After all, no one had yet charged that he was a lawman.

"A policeman? What do you mean by that?" Charlie asked as if he were bewildered by the accusation. He was trying to buy time, to work out a way to salvage things.

"I mean he's a fly-cop — a detective," Hubbard answered.

"Goddamned if that ain't news to me," Charlie said, acting shocked. "If I thought he was, I wouldn't sleep until I had him anchored out in a deep place in the bay where no one would ever find him. Why, he knows things about me that would put me in the pen for the rest of my natural life." Charlie's only hope was that his anger seemed as convincing as Hubbard's.

The thief considered what he'd just heard. Then he asked, "How long have you known Sayles?"

Charlie and Billy had worked out their cover story months ago, and now he retold it: He'd met Sayles a few months previous in Juneau. An old smuggler friend had vouched for him. This friend had assured Charlie that "Sayles could be trusted even with my life." The two had been partners in a smuggling business between Canada and Montana, and they'd gotten into their share of sticky spots with the law. He'd seen Sayles tested.

Still, it was possible, Charlie speculated, that Sayles had turned detective since splitting up with the smuggler. "If Sayles had," Charlie threatened, "I want to know it."

Hubbard seemed to have calmed a bit; perhaps he was even willing to believe the story about the outlaw friend in Juneau. So

420

Charlie decided to attack. "What grounds you got for your suspicions?" he demanded.

"Goddamn him!" Hubbard snarled. "He just looks like a policeman. And he's traveled over the world too much. He's told me all about his travels."

Charlie erupted with laughter. It kept building and building till his whole body was shaking. But now he wasn't acting. He was laughing with relief. And he was laughing at himself. All along he'd assumed that Billy had said or done something to betray that he was working undercover. But this was sheer foolishness on the thieves' part. They had no justification at all for their suspicions.

So now when Charlie tried to calm Hubbard's concerns, he stuck to the truth: Of course Sayles had traveled some. He was born in London, England, for gosh sakes. Hadn't you noticed his accent? Or maybe that's why you thought he was a detective? And sure enough, Billy came from well-off stock. But he's a wild and reckless sort, Charlie said. After he struck off on his own, they plumb cut him off. He ain't no detective, Charlie concluded with genuine exasperation. He's an Englishman!

But — and the Pinkerton case files would later suggest that this was Charlie's masterstroke — although he'd just demolished all of Hubbard's and Schell's suspicions, Charlie didn't turn indignant. A cowpuncher comes to learn that while you might succeed in calming an ornery bull, it don't do well to drive him back to the herd. Better the bull mosey back on his own; otherwise the animal might take it into his head to lower his horns and charge. So now the cowboy detective acted complacent, as if melting down the gold was of little consequence to him. Charlie said that unless Hubbard felt completely convinced that Sayles wasn't a detective, he should let the gold stay hidden.

"Of course," he went on with a small shrug, "it would hurt me a little as I'd spent some money in Juneau on supplies for melting the stuff." But Charlie made it clear that the money he'd be losing was a small matter. All that counted was that Hubbard and Schell do what they thought best.

Hubbard suddenly turned contrite. He bowed his head like a man lost in prayer as he sorted through all he'd just heard. Then he reached out for Charlie's hand and shook it firmly. "I never doubted you for a minute," the thief said. "We will call the deal on again."

He was still cautious, though. "But I'm only going to bring about one-fourth of the stuff at a time," Hubbard added. "When you melt the first batch, you can take $100 worth out for your part. Then I'll cache my part and bring in more. That way there won't be any danger of us losing it all if he's a policeman."

"Suits Sayles and me fine," Charlie said

evenly, while he silently rejoiced. The operation was back on track.

The next day Charlie watched as the two thieves selected a location for the furnace. It was in a timber grove about two hundred yards from the camp. Nice and secluded, both Hubbard and Schell appraised it. "No one will ever find it," Charlie agreed; although for a reckless, mischievous moment he felt like adding, "Except for two Pinkerton operatives."

Then, spouting the knowledge he'd picked up from Durkin, Charlie assumed his role as the expert gold processor. He gave instructions on how to make the clay bricks for the furnace, and he got a fire going in another kiln to burn the charcoal they'd need. Schell and Hubbard put in full days, but they had no complaints. Schell still didn't feel completely easy about Sayles; there was something in the Englishman's manner that put him off. But he had no doubts about Sayles's partner, Lee Davis. It sure was a stroke of luck they'd crossed paths with him. Without his taking charge, they'd still be plunking the gold bars into a frying pan and watching as their fortune melted into a yellow muck over an open fire.

It all went very smoothly. By the afternoon the clay bricks had been molded and set out to dry in the sun. Then Charlie fell sick. His stomach was hurting him something fierce, he complained. He felt like an angry mule was kicking at his insides. And this wasn't the first time he'd been brought low like this, he revealed. It was an old digestive ailment, and there was only one thing that would set him right: Carter's Little Liver Pills. A sawbones in Abilene had prescribed the pills the last time the pain had nearly laid him out, and they'd worked like magic. Since there was little to do for the next few days but wait for the bricks to dry and the charcoal to burn, Charlie said, he might as well head down to Killisnoo. He should be able to rustle up some of the Carter pills from a doctor, or maybe the trading post stocked them.

Shot of whiskey might work just as well, Hubbard suggested.

Let the man get his darn pills, Schell reprimanded. We're counting on Lee. He ain't gonna do us any good if he's feeling poorly.

So clutching his stomach, near to doubled over with pain, Charlie got into his canoe. They helped him shove off, and Charlie made a small drama out of the difficulties involved in paddling while he was suffering so. But once the camp was no longer in sight, he straightened up and began paddling vigorously. He was feeling better than he had for months. Mamie, he silently celebrated to his wife, we're gonna do it! We're gonna get the gold!

In Killisnoo, Charlie didn't search out a doctor or head to the trading post. He went straight to the warship where Marshal Collins was stationed.

The old lawman listened with attention as Charlie shared his plan. He wanted the marshal to make camp at the head of Hood Bay, on the south side of the island, and wait for him. Once the first batch of gold had been melted and the thieves had revealed its hiding place, Charlie would come get him. About five miles, Charlie reckoned, separated the heads of Chieke and Hood bays. He'd sneak out of camp on foot and head out to find the marshal when matters were ripe for arrest.

It wasn't Collins's plan, but as the marshal considered it he couldn't find anything that didn't set right. He asked the detective when he wanted him in Hood Bay.

Five days from now should do the trick, Charlie replied. I imagine I'll come wandering into your camp sometime after midnight. Still, I'd be obliged if, in case I don't show that night, you wait around for two more days.

The marshal nodded in agreement. Then he asked: "What if you don't show after that?"

"Reckon," Charlie said gravely, "you'd better come looking for me with your guns drawn. I'll either be in a heap of trouble or dead."

Three days later, just after the sky had turned dark, Hubbard appeared without warning in the whiskey traders' camp. He was carrying several bars of gold. He tossed a bar to Charlie.

Charlie caught it, and his first thought was that it was damn heavy. Then he remembered that it'd been his appreciation of the weight of the bars that'd helped him work out how the thieves had managed to get their loot from the mine warehouse down to the beach. He hoped Durkin had followed his advice and now had guards patrolling the pipeline. But in the next moment Charlie quickly put that concern aside as Hubbard began to explain the reason for his unexpected arrival.

Schell and me figured we should run a test, Hubbard announced. We want to see if you boys know what you're doing before we bring over any more gold.

Makes sense, Charlie agreed lightly, while at the same time his mind instantly raced with anxieties. *What if I can't follow Durkin's instructions? What if I get it all wrong? What if the damn furnace blows up in my face?*

He was so preoccupied with worry that it didn't occur to him to ask the question Billy finally posed: "Where's Schell?"

"Wouldn't you like to know," Hubbard shot

back snidely. He still hadn't come around to trusting Sayles. But he finally said, "Schell stayed behind to stand guard over our cache."

That news caused Charlie further consternation. He had no idea where the gold was hidden. And he wouldn't have a chance of finding out unless he succeeded in melting down a few bars tomorrow. Meanwhile, tomorrow was also the day he'd told Marshal Collins to make camp at Hood Bay. Only there'd be no point in making arrests unless the detectives knew where Hubbard and Schell had hidden the gold. Charlie cursed his own stupidity. He should never have told the marshal to set out so soon for Hood Bay. All Charlie could do was hope that the marshal wouldn't get antsy, that he'd wait, as they'd agreed, for two additional days before charging in. Of course, Charlie knew, there was no guarantee that even with an extra two days he'd locate the gold. But he was hoping that by then his "two-by-four brain," as he liked to joke, would've figured something out.

The next morning Charlie fired up the charcoal in the furnace and soon had a blue flame burning. He kept watching for signs that the furnace was beginning to crack, for smoke to start pouring out, but it worked like a charm. And hours later, when he easily removed perfectly formed gold nuggets from the molds, he imagined even Durkin would've been proud of him.

There was no need, however, to guess about Hubbard's reaction. He was ecstatic. You boys sure know what you're doing, he rejoiced. After a few drinks to celebrate, he said he'd be going back to tell Schell. Tomorrow he'd come by with a serious batch of gold.

As soon as Hubbard left, Billy wanted to follow him. We play it right, we'll be looking over their shoulders when they dig up the rest of the gold, he insisted with excitement.

Charlie was of a mind to agree. It was more than likely that Hubbard would lead them to Schell and the hiding place. But it was also likely, he reasoned, that Schell and Hubbard would be expecting them to follow. There was no getting around the fact that the thieves remained suspicious. That's why they weren't bringing the gold in a single load. That's why Schell was standing guard. The more Charlie thought about it, the more convinced he grew that this was another test: Hubbard would be on the alert to see if he was being trailed.

No, Charlie said in the end. It's better we hold back.

What about Marshal Collins? He struck camp in Hood Bay today, Billy argued.

He knows to wait, Charlie said. I reckon he will.

And supposing Hubbard doesn't show tomorrow with the gold? Supposing they hightail it during the night? Now that they know about building a furnace and such, they might figure they don't need our help, Billy went on, pressing his argument.

Charlie hadn't considered that possibility. He had to think about it for a few moments. He finally answered. "I don't know," he said truthfully.

But shortly after daybreak, Hubbard paddled into camp with a canoe loaded with gold. As soon as Charlie saw the stack of bars shining in the sun, he smiled at his partner as if to say, Told you so. And the two detectives set in motion the plan they'd worked out during the long, anxious night.

Charlie got a fire burning in the furnace, but this morning he made sure not to add sufficient charcoal. He let the first batch of charcoal burn down before it occurred to him that he best pile on more charcoal to get the necessary blue flame. Then, when the fire was burning blue, Billy had a problem with filling the crucibles. It took hours and hours just to get a single bar of gold reduced to shiny nuggets. And there remained some dozen bars to process.

If Hubbard suspected the two men of deliberately delaying things, he didn't say it. He seemed content with the way things were going. If it took an entire day to melt the bars, he was willing to wait. In his mind he was no doubt imagining walking into a Seattle bank and cashing his pokes full of nuggets.

429

As the day dragged on and the processing proceeded in its slow way, Charlie had a thought. Since we're gonna be at this for a while, he said, as if the notion had just occurred to him, why don't I head back to camp and put some chowder on the fire? A week back he'd prepared his fish chowder, an old Texas Gulf recipe, and Hubbard had wolfed it down. Fact was, the thief had remarked that it was one of the tastiest meals he'd ever eaten. So Charlie was hoping he'd be partial to having a bowl this evening.

Sounds good to me, Hubbard said eagerly. No sense all of us waiting around the furnace. Me and Sayles should be able to handle things.

Charlie hiked back to camp, and quickly went to work preparing the fish chowder. He used his bowie knife like an executioner's ax, chopping off fish heads at a frantic clip, and he didn't take much care with the spices. And quicker than he would've thought possible, Charlie had a slapdash version of the stew simmering over the fire. It wouldn't win any blue ribbons in Matagorda County, but up in Alaska it might do.

Satisfied, he put the next part of his plan into action. He hurried through the woods to the Indian village. Charlie was hoping he'd be able to spot Schell standing guard, and that way he'd learn where the gold was hidden. It stood to reason that Schell wouldn't be expecting him; the thief believed his partner had the two men within his sight at all times. The dicey part, though, was whether Schell would actually be standing watch over the gold. And there was no telling when Hubbard might get a sudden hankering for chowder and head into camp — only to find Charlie gone. That could cause a real disturbance. In that case, Billy had best be able to get to his Winchester mighty quick.

Still, it was the only plan Charlie could think of, and he'd decided it'd have to work. And for once, luck was on his side. He made his way to the Indian camp and had taken a concealed position behind a clump of trees when straight off he spotted Schell. As he'd been running through the woods, Charlie's fear had been that the hideout would be somewhere deep in the forest, perhaps near where Hubbard had buried the frying pan. But now he looked into the camp and understood that that, too, had been a ruse. There was Schell, rifle cradled in his arms, standing guard by the birch racks over where the Indians dried salmon. The smell would be god-awful. It'd be the last place anyone would think to conceal a fortune of gold. That's why it was the perfect hiding place. And if Charlie had any doubts about whether the treasure was buried where Schell was standing, a further look erased them. The ground beneath Schell's boots had been turned over and then hastily trampled down again in an attempt to disguise the digging. Which made sense; this morning Hubbard had delivered a new batch of gold for processing.

Then all at once, Charlie's moment of discovery collapsed into one of panic. Schell appeared to be looking his way. Had the thief spotted him? Charlie pressed his body tight against the side of a giant spruce, and waited. But in the next instant he saw what had caught Schell's eye. A whiskey bottle was leaning against one of the salmon racks, and Schell picked it up to take a pull. Charlie moved slowly back into the deep timber. Soon he was running through the woods, returning as fast as he could to the camp on Chieke Bay. He prayed that Billy had been able to drag out the processing, that Hubbard hadn't left the furnace for a quick taste of chowder.

Charlie had managed to grab a spoon and was stirring his chowder when Hubbard and Billy walked into camp.

Hubbard was smiling. He had a sack full of gold nuggets, and he was looking forward to a bowl of chowder. Been thinking 'bout this meal all day, Hubbard said.

Before they sat down to eat, though, Charlie suggested that they have what he playfully called "appetizers." He passed a bottle of rye to Hubbard and watched the thief take a swallow. Next it was his turn. Charlie took a long, deep pull. After the nerve-racking day, he reckoned, he surely could do with a drink.

That night Charlie took sick. His stomach was acting up again. He moaned softly; he wanted it to sound convincing, though at the same time he hoped he wouldn't wake up Hubbard. That was the latest complication. He'd hadn't counted on the thief's sleeping across from him in the tent, but Hubbard had drunk too many "appetizers" to make his way back to the Indian village. Charlie would now need to slip out of the tent without waking Hubbard. He thought about putting off getting the marshal for one more night, but he felt that would be risky. He'd told Collins that if he didn't show by tonight, the marshal should come in with guns blazing. If it played out that way, anything might happen.

So Charlie got up and put on his clothes and boots. He moved carefully, hoping not to wake the sleeping man.

"Where you going?" Hubbard spoke up, instantly awake.

My stomach, Charlie complained. He said he was going to make a hot toddy. Maybe that would help things.

Charlie went to the campfire and put water on to heat. After it came to a boil, he poured it into a cup and added a good measure of rye. After all, McParland had always stressed the importance of living your cover, he told himself with a smile. Dutifully, he sat by the fire for a while and sipped his toddy.

When he was done, he returned to the tent. For the next hour he tried to sleep, but the pain in his stomach, he wanted Hubbard to believe, was too troubling. He got up to make another toddy. When Hubbard didn't stir, he grabbed his Winchester. This time he didn't pretend to sit by the campfire. Charlie headed out of camp.

He'd never previously hiked over to Hood Bay, and on a starless night the trip through unexplored country proved to be hard going. Fallen timbers unexpectedly blocked his way, and all Charlie could do was crawl on his hands and knees beneath the high piles of thick tree trunks. But that left him at the mercy of the devil's clubs. These were tough briar bushes, and they took hold of his clothes and ripped at his skin like an eagle's claws. It was slow, painful going. Another concern: Charlie had to get to the head of Hood Bay before the marshal broke camp. He doubted he'd make it.

The only way he'd arrive before sunup, he decided with resignation, was to follow the bear trails. There were plenty of trails, all right. The big animals had come down from the mountains and were feasting on the skunk cabbage and berries in the woods. Charlie's fear was that they might wonder whether a cowboy detective would be a mite more tasty than some blueberries. Still, he stuck to the bear trails. To scare off the beasts, he took to singing.

He started in on a song he'd learned while cowboying in the Texas Panhandle: "My lover is a cowboy / He's kind, he's brave, and true / He rides the Spanish pony / And throws the lasso, too . . ." But after a half dozen or so times it got so that even he couldn't tolerate the lyrics. Then he tried just whistling. And when he grew tired of puckering, he let loose with his Comanche yell. He felt damn foolish, but it was better than having some bear come nosing up to him. Charlie could hear the sound of brush cracking as the bears prowled nearby in the darkness. He kept his Winchester cocked, waiting for an animal to come charging out of the shadows. But they never showed. Still, his nerves grew frayed as he continued on his cautious way through the night.

On the top of the mountain range, Charlie came to a lake. He couldn't scout up a bear trail, and the prospect of creeping through fields of sharp devil's clubs was discouraging. So he made his way down the edge of the timber and waded into the lake. He thought if he stuck close to shore, it wouldn't be too bad. But the water was ice-cold and deeper than he'd expected. It reached up to his waist, and he had to make his way carrying his Winchester over his head. His progress was slow, and it was getting late.

When at last he reached the opposite shore of the lake, he discovered that there was a creek running down the side of the mountain toward the bay. Since he was already wet and cold, Charlie figured another soaking wouldn't be of much consequence. No matter what, it'd be better than traipsing through a mess of devil's clubs. As it turned out, the creek was only knee-deep, and Charlie made good time.

It was just turning to daylight when Charlie woke up Marshal Collins in his tent.

"Wondering whether you'd show," the marshal said.

"For a spell, so was I," Charlie replied.

Charlie and the marshal stood on top of a hill and looked down on the camp at Chieke Bay. Hubbard and Sayles were getting breakfast. The smell of fresh coffee was strong.

Charlie led the way through the brush, and they came down behind the tent. They'd stayed away from the campfire and had not been seen. Now they waited. The moment seemed so full of tension that it was about to burst. Then Collins looked at Charlie, and the detective nodded.

Charlie walked out from behind the tent with his rifle leveled.

"You're under arrest," the marshal shouted

as he followed, his pistol drawn.

Hubbard stared. He was quivering with anger, unable to speak. For a second it seemed as if he might draw, but he must've realized it would be suicide. Instead he ignored the marshal and walked straight up to Charlie.

"How in hell can you ever show your face in public again after the way you treated me?" he declared, the words full of fury.

Charlie uttered a small laugh, and at the same time lifted the Colt from Hubbard's holster. "My conscience won't bother me on that score, I can assure you," Charlie said with pride.

Schell was in his tent when he was arrested. His rifle was by his side, but he didn't even consider reaching for it. He just raised his hands in surrender.

As Schell was led out of the tent with his hands cuffed behind his back, the big man finally spoke. He turned toward Charlie and taunted, "You bastards will never find the gold."

Charlie didn't answer. There was a shovel lying near the tent, and he grabbed it. He walked slowly to the salmon racks and began digging, a broad smile on his face all the while.

TWENTY-NINE

Up north in the Canadian Yukon Valley, George Carmack led the two Indians away from Henderson's camp. The encounter had left them dispirited; even in the wilderness it was impossible to escape the pettiness of men. They were a sullen procession as they trudged along the banks of Gold Bottom Creek and then headed up the steep side of the mountain they'd descended only hours ago.

There was no trail, and the climb was a challenge. Like Charlie Siringo during his race to Hood Bay, they had to struggle over fallen trees, through sharp, thorny devil's clubs and thickets of underbrush. It was near the end of a long day, and by now their packs weighed heavy on their backs. George pushed himself forward. He kept telling himself, "A weakling has no business to play in this kind of game." He was determined to prove that he possessed the grit to be a prospector in the Yukon. In that way, goading himself on, he made it to the summit.

They roasted bear steaks that night and drank tea. In the morning, George woke ready to put yesterday's unpleasantness behind him. He weighed the two small pieces of gold they'd found in his hand, and he felt encouraged. A plan quickly formed: They'd return to the creek where they'd panned the specks of coarse gold. Jim and Charley agreed that it was a promising strategy.

With George leading the way, they began hiking down the south side of the mountain. He reckoned it'd be a waste of valuable time to backtrack along the trail they'd previously made from Rabbit Creek, as the stream would soon become known. He'd try a more direct route.

He went west, heading straight into the sun, and led them into a large swamp. Crossing was a nasty business. The only way through was to try to get a footing on the clumps of spongy green underbrush scattered like stepping stones across the thick glacial ooze. But jumping from one clump of vegetation to the next, then keeping balance once you landed, was tricky with a fifty-pound pack on your back. The swarms of attacking mosquitoes and gnats didn't help matters.

The trio was nearly halfway across when George landed in the dark muck. He began sinking quickly. In seconds the ooze had climbed above his thighs. He was convinced he was about to go under when he felt two heavy hands grabbing his shoulder. As if he were hoisting a sack of flour, Jim pulled George out of the muck and gingerly deposited him by his side on a small island of green swamp fronds. George's clothes were dripping and his moccasins were wet and slimy, but otherwise, he began to realize as he caught his breath, he was none the worse for the dunking. He exercised particular caution, concentrating on each step, as he made his slow way across the remainder of the swamp.

They came out on a rocky trail, and with their wet moccasins they had a difficult time getting traction. There were some hard falls, but luck was with them. They managed not to break any bones. In this stumbling, weary way they reached the headwaters of Rabbit Creek.

George decided they should press on, and soon they came to the fork they'd previously encountered. As before, George was pulled toward Eldorado Creek. This time he walked up about a quarter of a mile and tried a few pans. He didn't see any colors, so for the second time he rashly decided that his instincts were misleading him.

With the two Indians following, he retraced his steps and went up the other fork. He panned here, too, but found nothing but black sand. Nevertheless, he hiked along this branch for another quarter of a mile or so, sticking close to the rocky banks as the stream rose up the hillside. As the creek climbed higher, its clear blue waters were reduced to a trickle. But along the way there were several small pools swarming with grayling. Tagish Charley's hands were so swift that he could reach in and grab a squirming fish at will. They made camp on this high ground and roasted grayling over the fire.

George was exhausted, but he didn't go straight to sleep. He lay awake for hours staring up at the big starry sky and listening to the scurrying and chirping noises that twisted through the wilderness at night. This was the land of the Great Spirit and he knew his dream had led him here for a purpose. At last he grew tired, and he fell asleep cushioned by a fine, deep peace.

The new day was August 16, 1896. By midmorning they'd worked their way downstream, toward the fork. George had panned as they'd trudged along, and the results had been promising. There were traces of colors in many of the pans. That'd made George more careful in his prospecting. As he followed each new bend of the creek, he scouted for signs of bedrock. "Looking for gold, look for bedrock" was an old sourdough adage, and George took the wisdom to heart. He kept his eyes peeled.

About half a mile below the fork, Rabbit

Creek broke off in a sharp bend to the right, and George stayed with this tributary. He marched up a steep bank. When he was about fifty feet from the water's edge, he came to a halt. He looked down the bank and saw a strip of black bedrock. It must've been, he guessed, only a hundred feet long and just an arm's length wide. But it was, he knew at once, "the very thing we were looking for."

He waited until the two Indians caught up to him and then pointed excitedly at the dark streak cutting down the bank. "Look down there, boys," he said. "We surely ought to find gold down there."

Throwing off his pack, George scrambled down the bank of the creek. Something in the shallow water immediately caught his eye. It was shining out at him from the rim of the bedrock. Instinctively, he rubbed his eyes with the back of his hand; the moment seemed impossible, as if it were part of a world where salmon had twenty-dollar gold pieces for eyes. But this time when he reached down into the cool water, he didn't abruptly wake up from a dream. He grasped a gold nugget as big as his thumb. Yet he still couldn't believe it. To be sure, he put the nugget between his teeth and bit hard. The nugget bent. It wasn't a yellow rock.

"Hi yu gold!" he bellowed to his partners. "Bring down the pan and shovel. Hurry!"

The gold lay in long flat slabs wedged into

the crevices of rocks. It sparkled in the creek bed. It washed down in their pans. It was a treasure for the taking.

George flung his tin pan heavy with gold high into the air. A fine yellow shower rained down on him like a heavenly mist. And when the pan landed, he spontaneously broke into a dance. He was wild with delight. Jim and Charley joined in, too, the three of them dancing with abandon around the pan. What a time they had! Bursting with happiness, they improvised a war dance that, George would always remember with an unashamed grin, was part "Scotch hornpipe, Indian fox trot, syncopated Irish jig, and a sort of Siwash Hula-Hula." They danced and danced with an unrestrained joy.

That night they gave thanks. The Indians sat around the fire smoking their pipes and gave praise to the Great Spirit. With blankets wrapped around their shoulders, Jim and Charley chanted in Tagish. They sang of the times that had led them to the Great Discovery, of hungry days, of silent, aimless trails, of failed hunts. They thanked the spirits for all the years of hardships because now they understood that these were part of one journey. The Wealth Woman had spoken to George, and the promise she had given him was their fulfilled blessing, too.

George's gratitude ran a different course. He refused to look back at the past. To his mind, all that came before had in an instant been made irrelevant. With a pious conviction, George believed he had "unlocked a treasure chest" and he would show his thanks by freely enjoying what a fortune of gold could buy. All his life he'd run from civilization. There'd been a time when even Juneau had seemed too filled with city ways. His ideal had been sharing with Kate and Gracie a log cabin that faced the shimmering waters of the Dyea River. But wrapped in his blanket on that first night of his new life, he made a mental accounting of his new ambitions: "A trip around the world with a congenial companion. A beautiful home with well kept lawns, shrubbery and flowers. A sum invested in government bonds, the income of which would be sufficient to enable me to enjoy the good things of life in a decent way and keep me comfortable for the balance of my life."

Then he fell into a dreamless sleep.

They were up at the break of day. George brewed coffee, and this morning, rather than complaining about having to take it without sugar or milk, he found himself thinking that he'd soon be sipping out of fine china cups. In high spirits, he took his hand ax and chose a small spruce tree standing in the center of the flat creek bank. He blazed the spruce on both the up- and the downstream sides. Then he wrote on the upstream side with a pencil:

I do, this day, locate and claim, by right of discovery, five hundred feet, running up stream from this notice. Located this 17th day of August, 1896.

G. W. Carmack

Then he staked out his claim. Taking a fifty-foot tape line out of his pack, he measured five hundred feet upstream. The Klondike was in Canada, and under Canadian mining law this was the maximum length allowed for a claim, but it would straddle the creek from rimrock to rimrock. He made the calculations with great care. Every inch held treasure; the slightest error could lose him a fortune. He walked over rocks and flat land and along sandy banks. It was only a small strip of land, but he was convinced that it would allow him to purchase a kingdom.

Where his claim ended, he measured off another five hundred feet for Jim. Then he went back to the starting point and headed downstream. He measured off five hundred feet for Charley. The discoverer was allowed by law to make two claims on a single stream — all other prospectors were allowed only one — so he then marked off an additional five hundred feet downstream for himself. It was a long and meticulous process. It took hours.

Canadian law required that he register the sites he'd staked within sixty days; he'd need to go to the recorder's office in Fortymile. George understood that even once this was done, his hold on the four specific claims still might be disputed. His survey, after all, was not very exact. And he'd only be able to enter an approximate location of the creek bed into the register. Still, George was confident that the North-West Mounted Police would enforce his rights; the Canadian Yukon was better policed than the nearly lawless American Alaska Territory. He also counted on the prospector's code; it was unlikely that any of the old sourdoughs would pull up his wooden stakes and claim the creek bed for their own. But if there was a claim jumper, George was prepared to use his Winchester to settle any argument. He was still a good shot, and the two Indians would join in if things got rough. That was the way things were in the north, and it'd have to do, he told himself.

When he finished pounding in the boundary stakes, George was still not ready to leave. Ahead lay a difficult thirty-mile journey back to the Klondike River, where they'd beached their canoe. But there was one more thing he needed to do.

A tall birch tree stood on the bank above where he'd found the first gold nugget. With his ax, he cut off a piece of bark. Then he took his pencil and wrote on it: "I name this creek Bonanza. George Carmack."

It was the name of the vision that had filled his head as a lonely shepherd in the California hills. It was the legacy he'd been destined to inherit from his father. And now he'd claimed it.

With the back of his ax head, he nailed the bark sign into the tree. He left a pan and shovel beside it, symbols of his achievement. Then he shouldered his pack, and the three men began the long hike to the Klondike.

THIRTY

In the days that followed the arrest of the
two thieves, mine superintendent Durkin sent
a special steam launch to Chieke Bay to
retrieve the stolen gold. As Charlie supervised, a crew carted the bars from the Indian
camp to the launch moored off the beach.
The detective made sure the frying pan was
taken along, too; after all, a couple of hundred
dollars' worth of gold coated the pan. Once
the ship got under way, a burly retinue of
armed guards, rifles cradled in their arms and
six-guns on their hips, stood on deck. Now
that Durkin had his gold back, he was determined not to lose it again.

Along with the marshal, Charlie and Billy
accompanied the two prisoners on the commercial steamer *Lucy* to Juneau. On Charlie's
instructions, the thieves were kept apart, each
at separate ends of the boat. Billy guarded a
snarling Schell; the marshal stayed with a
weepy Hubbard. Throughout the voyage
Charlie stood on deck, keeping watch. His

fear was that Schell had gotten word to his friend the Tlingit chief of the village. If the chief had been promised a cut from the hidden gold, he'd be mighty disappointed by now. So Charlie kept scanning the horizon, expecting to see a flotilla of birch canoes carrying an Indian war party. He'd fought in the bloody Red River Indian War when waves of Comanches allied with Kiowa-Apaches had charged with the murderous skill of trained cavalry brigades. The prospect of just two Pinkertons and a marshal holding off a mess of Indians, even if they weren't on horseback, made sleep impossible. Charlie stayed at his post around the clock, and didn't feel any ease until the *Lucy* docked in Juneau.

Raging with anger, fiercely unrepentant, Schell was led off to the jail in Juneau. But before the marshal took him away, Schell turned to confront Charlie. No jail will hold me, he promised. He'd break out and come looking for the detective. There was a score to be settled.

"I'll be waiting," Charlie said with conviction.

Hubbard wasn't taken straight to jail. Charlie had other plans. Since the arrest, the thief had undergone a transformation. All his previous swagger had disappeared. He was no longer the snide gunny itching to show his prowess. Hubbard had sat hunched and mute in the cabin, sobbing from time to time with deep emotion. He'd barely touched his food. He knew he was facing a long stretch in the Alaska territorial penitentiary, and years in a frontier jail would be hard time. Of course, Charlie also reckoned, going days without a drink must be taking its toll, too. So Charlie decided he'd take advantage of Hubbard's depressed state. He'd job him.

Instead of letting the marshal take Hubbard to jail, Charlie removed his handcuffs. Make a break for it, and I'll shoot you down, Charlie warned. But you behave yourself, and you can stay with me for a spell. Hubbard nodded in resigned agreement; anything was better than jail.

With Charlie, the thief boarded the ferry to Douglas Island. Durkin had provided a cabin, and the two men shared it. They ate meals together. When Charlie opened a bottle of whiskey, he made sure to pour Hubbard a glass. And as he had done throughout the entire case, Charlie continued to act with restraint. At least once each day Durkin would sidle up to the detective and ask whether Hubbard had confessed — was he ready to testify against his partner? And each time Charlie would say he hadn't discussed the matter with Hubbard. What the blazes are you waiting for? Durkin would shout. Charlie would answer in a calm, easy voice that the time wasn't right.

After a week had passed and Hubbard

seemed more accepting of things, Charlie asked him how they'd gotten the gold off the island. He posed the question matter-of-factly, as if he were simply curious.

There was no longer any point in keeping the secret; Hubbard would be going to jail no matter what. Besides, Siringo was his friend. Who else cared if he'd a taste when he felt the need? So Hubbard told him everything — about the blind in the woods, the warehouse lock, and the pipeline. When he finished, Hubbard said he felt proud of what he and Schell had managed to do. It'd been a damn ingenious caper.

Don't blame you, Charlie said amicably. Then, as if it were an afterthought, Charlie asked Hubbard if he'd be willing to write it all down. Maybe put your signature on it, too, he suggested.

Can't see why not at this point, Hubbard went along flatly.

Once Charlie was holding the signed confession, Hubbard was put back in handcuffs and taken to the Juneau jail. And Charlie booked passage on a steamer bound for Seattle.

It was a week's voyage; the steamer stopped in Sitka first. On the trip Charlie had time to reflect on all he'd accomplished. He had hunted down the thieves and reclaimed the gold. He'd done what the Portland operatives had failed to do. He'd restored the honor of

451

the Pinkerton agency. He'd kept his promise to McParland. And yet he knew the operation had not been a total success.

He'd decided to go off to Alaska with the hope that in the north, thousands of miles from Denver, the distance and the new surroundings would separate him from his memories. But this hadn't happened. Mamie loomed in his mind at all times; and the nights alone too often held a more disquieting torment. However, in the course of this long adventure, he'd been able to make a truce of sorts with the demons that continued to rage within him. He no longer tried to escape from his memories. He embraced them. In that way Mamie stayed a part of all he did, and life had grown easier.

In fact, it gave him considerable pleasure to contemplate how Mamie would've enjoyed what happened on the steamer voyage. A German prince, Bismarck's nephew, was on board; he had visited Alaska as part of a world tour. The prince strolled haughtily around the deck in a military uniform decorated with medals. He kept his eyes fixed on the horizon, refusing to look at the other passengers. He ate his meals at a separate table. His imperious attitude rankled Charlie's Texas sensibilities. So whenever he encountered the royal personage on deck or in the dining room, Charlie made sure to greet him with a loud "Howdy, partner."

The prince complained to the captain. "What does that bloody American mean by calling me partner?" he demanded.

The abashed captain explained that Mr. Siringo was a famous detective. He had captured the thieves who had made off with a fortune from Alaska's largest gold mine.

That night the prince clicked his heels when he saw Charlie. He congratulated him for discovering gold in Alaska.

THIRTY-ONE

Now that George Carmack had staked his claims, he couldn't wait to spread the news of his discovery. Along with the two Indians, George had retrieved the canoe and had poled only a short distance down the Klondike when he spotted four men towing a loaded boat in the opposite direction. The men were wading through the knee-deep shoreline mud, and it took some muscle to pull their boat upstream. George judged that they had the look and the tanned, bearded faces of longtime prospectors.

"Hello, boys," George called as he steadied his boat with a pike pole. "Kind of wet traveling, ain't it?"

"Well, it ain't so dry as it might be," one of them answered wearily. It was clear that he was exhausted.

George asked where they were bound for.

Dave McKay, the leader of the outfit, said they'd heard that a prospect had been found on some creek between the Klondike and

Indian rivers. "We came around this way to have a look-see. Do you know anything about it?"

That was Henderson's claim, George realized at once. "I left there three days ago," he said.

"What'd you think about it?"

George gave an indulgent smile. "I don't like to be a knocker, but I don't think much of it," he told them.

The prospectors' faces fell in disappointment. Once again they'd gone off chasing a far-fetched tale. But it was still hard to give up. "Then you wouldn't advise us to go up there?" Dan McGillivery, another of the crew, tried. He hoped George might change his opinion.

"I've got something better for you," George declared with a big grin. He reached into his pocket, pulled out his cartridge case, and emptied the contents into his hand. He held out a handful of golden nuggets.

The prospectors were stunned. George Carmack had accomplished what they'd been trying to achieve for a hard, frustrating decade.

They had a flurry of questions, and George, nearly preening with self-satisfaction, answered them all. Without prodding, he gave the astounded men directions to Bonanza Creek. Why not? he thought. He'd marked off his two five-hundred-foot claims, and under the Canadian regulations that was all he was allowed in a single mining district. The rest of the creek was free pickings, one mining site granted by legal right to any man who staked it and then filed. Besides, he knew he'd enjoy seeing the look on their faces once they heard his news.

Within minutes the four prospectors were on their way. They hurried upriver and now, George observed, "that old tow line was as taut as the E string on a violin." As it happened, their chance encounter with George Carmack would change their lives. They staked four claims on Bonanza, and each of them would become millionaires.

George, meanwhile, continued on to his fishing camp at the mouth of the Klondike. He was sitting by his empty salmon racks, still feeling "as if I had just dealt myself a royal flush in the game of life," when he noticed a small boat coming down the Yukon. The boat would've passed on by, but he was in no mood to let that happen. George hailed it, and two men paddled the boat to shore.

The men introduced themselves as Alphonse Lapierre and George Remillard. They were French-Canadians who'd spent the past eleven years up north searching for gold without anything much to show for it. Two days ago they'd finished off the last of their bacon and flour, and now they were on their way to Fortymile. They hoped McQuesten at the trading post would outfit them on credit, and then they'd head back out.

"If I were you boys I wouldn't go any further," George said mildly. "Haven't you heard of the new strike?"

"Oh, yes, we know all about it," Lapierre replied. "I tink hees wan beeg bluff."

"How's this for a bluff?" George said, bristling as if he'd been insulted. Then he reached into his pocket and held out the handful of gold nuggets.

The two men stared with silent awe. It was as if they were suddenly unable to speak.

"You can put your outfit on my cache and leave your boat here," George went on easily. "You can ford the Klondike at the Bonanza. That's what I've named the new creek."

Within minutes their boat was unloaded and packs were hoisted onto their backs. They nearly ran across the flat ground, gesticulating to each other and talking at the same time in a rush of French and English. They were so excited that they'd forgotten to tie their boat. It would've floated downstream with the current if George hadn't noticed and secured it. They, too, would stake claims on Bonanza and at last strike it rich.

But even as George prepared to go to Fortymile to record his claim, he still made time to spread the news. After supper he paddled across the river to the fishing camp of an old friend, Lou Cooper. Cooper was sitting around the fire with Ed Monahan, and they listened with fascination as George told the story of his great discovery. Monahan didn't believe him. "You're the biggest liar this side of hell," he charged. Without saying another word, George produced the gold nuggets. The next day Cooper and Monahan headed for Bonanza Creek, and they would also stake claims.

Early the next morning, George told Jim to take a pack of provisions and his rifle and go back up to the creek. He reckoned the big Indian would be able to run off any claim jumpers. He'd join him after he recorded his discovery at the registrar's office downriver.

George and Tagish Charley landed in Fortymile late that afternoon. The plan had been to go directly to the Canadian government post and make things official, but George couldn't restrain himself. He wasn't a drinking man, but he knew a crowd of miners would be in Bill McPhee's saloon. It was the time of year when they'd be coming down from their camps at lonely, far-off places like Miller, Glacier, and Davis creeks to place orders for their winter outfit.

"Hello there, you damned old meat-eating Siwash," a miner George knew only as Andy greeted him when he entered the dark one-room saloon. "Got any dried salmon to sell? I don't get something to eat besides that damn yaller sow belly purty soon, I'll sure be way-billed for Hell."

The fish hadn't been running this year, George said. He had no salmon to sell. "Have a drink anyway," someone shouted.

The boys were pretty well lit up, so George reckoned he might as well join them. He'd earned himself a glass of hooch. One drink, though, led to another. George decided he'd better cut it out or he'd never get around to sharing the news. He took a moment to steady himself. Then he turned his back to the bar and held up his hand for quiet.

"Boys, I've got some good news to tell you," he shouted. "There's a big strike up the river."

"Strike, hell!" yelled a husky miner sitting at the card table. "That ain't no news. "That's just a scheme being spread to start a stampede up the river."

"That's where you're off, you big rabbit-eating malamute!" George snapped back. Then he reached across the bar for the "blower," as the gold scales used to weigh a miner's poke were known. Enjoying the moment, his face beaming with triumph, he dumped his gold nuggets onto the scale. "How does that look to you?" he challenged.

The big man strode up to the bar. There was no telling what sorts of stories a squaw-man like Siwash George would invent to get attention. He looked at the gold suspiciously. He poked at it with a thick forefinger. Its texture and shape and color were unlike any gold he'd ever seen before. He picked up a nugget and weighed it in his hand. It was heavy, too.

"Holy Makuluk, boys!" he shouted. "Put it there, George," he said and began shaking George's hand with fervor.

Now all the miners crowded up to the bar to see Carmack's gold. And someone called out, "Say, if it ain't asking too much, where in hell did you get it?"

"Listen, boys, and I'll tell you," George answered. In an instant, the saloon turned completely quiet and all eyes were fixed on George. And he began to tell the story of his great discovery.

By the next morning, when George registered his claim at the police post, Fortymile was a ghost town. The saloons and trading post were empty. The tent camps had vanished. The boats that had been moored on the beach were gone. Everyone had rushed off to the Klondike.

During the next two months, 338 claims would be staked along Bonanza and the nearby creeks. Yet as George continued to spread the news throughout the Yukon Valley, there remained one man he refused to tell. He was determined that Robert Henderson not hear a peep.

THIRTY-TWO

While Charlie Siringo and George Carmack enjoyed their triumphs, Soapy Smith had moved on to Spokane, Washington, and established himself in the Owl Saloon. But this was a scaled-down operation. The folly of his Alaska trip had broken his ambitions. He no longer schemed up high-rolling plays. These days he earned what he could with a gaffed deck at the poker table.

Most of the old gang had moved on. He had no work to give them and, the real rub, his mind was not fixed on new schemes. He let them go with his blessings. "Keep in touch," he told 'em as one by one they headed off to Denver or San Francisco or wherever they thought there were pockets ripe for the fleecing. Many of them would write, their letters reaching Soapy care of the Owl. They hoped that one day his bleak mood would lift, Soapy would be up to his old tricks, and then he'd summon them. Dutifully, Soapy answered their letters. He thought he owed them that much for old times' sake. But he made a point not to mention anything about someday hooking up again. He didn't want to encourage any hopes that things could ever be as they once were.

Oh, now and then he'd hunt up a chance to make some flash, and there'd be a glimmer of the old rascal Soapy Smith. He managed to con an inebriated Martin Murphy into signing over his one-eighth interest in a gold mine located about 150 miles north of Spokane. When a regretful Murphy sobered up, the document proved binding enough to impress a Spokane judge. A few weeks later, though, it was established that the mine itself was worthless. And when Soapy tried to grab title to a mine in Newlin's Gulch, Colorado, with an unsigned check in the amount of $2,500, the check was promptly returned by registered letter "herewith for your signature." They never heard from Soapy again.

These were hard times for Soapy, but he seemed resigned to them. He wrote to his old friend Bat Masterson — the very gambler who had gone after Charlie Siringo with a beer mug during a bar fight years ago in Dodge — and made no bones about the sad state of his life. Yet Masterson, who was suffering through his own troubles after a reform-minded Denver police board had come into power, could do no more than sympathize. "It would have pleased me much better," he wrote back, "had you stated you were prospering."

But while Soapy was frank to his associates about how his life had spiraled down to slim pickings, he could not bear to tell his wife, Mary, the truth. To do so would have been to acknowledge that the prospect of their growing old together, of their one day living in a big house and being respected by their neighbors, was a lie, too. If Mary knew the truth, he feared, she would leave him. And then he'd truly have nothing. So he wrote her a terse note. He provided no specifics; perhaps he hoped her imagination would embroider the optimistic mood he was hoping to impart. And as if to compensate for his brevity, he made the letters large enough to fill the entire page:

Dear Wife
This far on my journey to the North. God bless you.

Jeff
Owl Saloon
Spokane

But Soapy had no intention of going north, or going anywhere, for that matter. He didn't care if he never left the Owl again.

THIRTY-THREE

George Carmack felt like celebrating, so he decided to splurge and buy a can of peaches. On the way back to his cabin from filing the claims at the police post in Fortymile, he stopped at Healy's trading post.

Same as he'd done at Bill McPhee's saloon, George couldn't resist boasting about his discovery. And once again he was treated as if he was making the whole thing up. The white-haired Indian fighter had heard about far-off wilderness creeks sprinkled with gold too many times before. He didn't put much truck in Carmack's tale. But then George said he'd like a can of peaches, and he emptied a hill of gold dust from his caribou poke onto the counter. This should more than cover it, I expect, he said with a gloating smile. All Healy managed to mutter at last was "By golly, Carmack. You gone and done it!" George agreed that he surely had.

Stuffing the can into his pack, George couldn't help feeling that simply by making the purchase he'd done something nearly as extraordinary as what he'd accomplished up on Bonanza Creek. He'd a taste for peaches ever since he was a child, but after coming to Alaska he had learned to do without. Years back, in Juneau, he'd wanted to buy a can, only the price had been alarming. Now it wouldn't be long, he teased himself, before he'd be drinking French champagne like some New York swell in one of the Horatio Alger books he'd borrowed from Reverend Canham at Fort Selkirk. It was an extravagance, no getting around that. At the same time, George felt proud that he could afford such a luxury. Once he started working his claims, George reckoned, he'd become very rich. Might as well get use to the high life, he told himself. Anyways, it wasn't just for him. It was a gift, too.

As he walked toward the cabin, little Gracie spotted him. She ran down the beach to meet her father, her long black hair twisted into a single braid and her dark eyes sparkling. George noticed, with a father's anxious pride, that she'd soon be growing up into a young woman; she was already about mule-high, and although she was still as thin as a seedling, she was a pretty little thing, with an Indian's chiseled face. As Kate approached, he called out, "I brought you something."

George had never given her a present before. She'd no idea what to expect. Perhaps, she hoped, they'd shot a bear up north. Winter was coming, and a bearskin would come in handy.

"A can of peaches," George announced. The way he said it, he might as well have been presenting a diamond.

For a moment all Kate could think was that George had been drinking and the whiskey had led him to go off and do something crazy. But when he handed her the big tin can, he didn't seem drunk. He was just grinning. Then a thought occurred to her, but still she had to struggle to get the words out.

You found gold? she finally dared to ask.

George began to tell the story, only his Chinook couldn't keep up with his galloping excitement. So he wound up grabbing Kate's hand, and then Gracie's, too, and in the next moment he had them dancing around in a circle. He broke out in a wild hoot, and Kate started in with a Tagish chant, and Gracie, not really understanding but still caught up in it all, began making her own happy noises. The jubilant commotion carried on for quite a while.

That night Kate and Gracie ate their first canned peach. The only fruit the girl had previously tried was a dried apricot. Biting into one was like chewing a stone. A peach, she discovered, was nothing like that at all. It was as soft as bone butter, and the syrup trickled down her throat like melted honey. It was the most wonderful taste she'd ever experienced, and even as an old woman she'd still be treasuring the memory.

With the new day, the celebration was over. There was so much to do. George needed to get back to his claim. He'd already been away too long, and the thought of Jim and Charley working on their own left him uneasy. He told Kate to pack up. They'd take whatever they could carry and just leave the rest.

George had built the cabin with his own hands. It was the home where he and Kate had raised their daughter; where they'd taken shelter when gusting winds had hurled the snow so high that the white drifts reached toward the roof; and where they'd lain together warding off the brutal freeze of the subarctic nights. But George had no qualms about abandoning it. That was the way frontier life was lived in the far north. Alaska wasn't like the West. Most pioneers didn't think about putting down roots; this wilderness required too much of a struggle. It was a place in which to seek your fortune, and then ramble on. George walked away from the cabin without a sentimental thought.

In fact, in the aftermath of the first giddy moments when he'd grasped the significance of his discovery on the Klondike, George had started to erase all the hardscrabble years from his memory. There was nothing, he told himself, worth remembering; it had been a time when he simply did what needed to be done to get by. He'd always been a man susceptible to whims, but now he fixed his mind on the future and held it there as steady as a compass needle. He focused on the day when he'd return to California to show his sister, Rose, the fortune he'd earned. But first, George knew, there was plenty of hard work ahead of him, and he hurried north, eager to get on with it.

When he arrived along with his family at Bonanza Creek, George was relieved to see that Jim and Charley had been productive. Over just a few days the two Indians had felled a small forest of trees, hacked the branches off the trunks, and then piled the logs into a high pyramid. George was about to tell them they'd done good work when Jim approached. The big Indian revealed that he'd also put in some time panning on his own claim, and he held out a handful of gold dust for George to admire. Another week, Jim predicted, and he'd to be able to fill an entire poke, maybe even two.

George exploded. The circumstances called for patience, and a bit of instruction, as well. Since the California days of '49, working a claim had evolved into a time-tested craft that'd been passed on by one prospector to another. The Day brothers had tutored George when he'd arrived in Juneau as an ignorant *cheechako*. And there'd been a time when George was of a mind to share all the tricks of the prospector's trade with Jim and Charley; he was the one, after all, who on their first expedition to the Yukon had shown Jim the sourdough's art of panning with a smooth, gentle roll of the wrist. George could have explained that in only another month winter would be blowing in, and before the heavy snows there was a sluice box to build, thick layers of bedrock to uncover, and a deep shaft to dig. Panning would need to wait until the spring. But George felt no need to have a discussion. It was *his* success, and he was beginning to resent having to divvy up his fortune with two Indians just because they'd the good luck to partner up with him. He'd come around to thinking that he should never have gotten involved with those two Chinooks. It had been a mistake. All his time with the Tagish, in fact, now struck him as sheer foolishness, an experience best kept buried. It wouldn't do at all for the man who'd pulled the first nugget out of Bonanza Creek to be known as Siwash George. So in this irritated, put-upon mood, he gave Jim a stern talking-to. He wanted it understood, he barked, that he was in charge. From now on, they'd do what he said. And that meant no more panning.

Jim, prideful as he was, was not a man to complain. If George wanted to be the boss, he'd follow orders. At least that way they'd get the gold out of the ground. But at the same time he pondered the change that'd quickly come over his partner. He'd best be wary, Jim warned himself. Gold made white men unpredictable.

George grew uneasy around Kate, too. She'd always been a formidable woman, willful and commanding. That'd been part of the attraction; George had appreciated that she knew her mind like his sister, Rose. Only now George was unwilling to be subject to a stiff, uncompromising squaw. His accomplishment had convinced George that he shouldn't be letting anyone tell him what to do. He was no squawman, and it was suddenly irksome that people had ever referred to him in such a snide fashion. Full of his newfound confidence, George wouldn't give an inch; and Kate, still the unbending granddaughter of a Tagish chief, wouldn't either.

On their first day at the claim they locked horns. Kate looked at the pile of logs and told George he'd better start in on building a cabin. George snapped back that there was no time for that right now. There were too many more important things to get done before the freeze-up. Then he just walked off. So they slept in a tent, and each night the cold's sting seemed particularly mean since they were no longer sharing the same bearskin robe.

■ ■ ■ ■

Once again, George found that he stood alone. Without his thinking too much more about it, things got so that he barely spoke to Kate and he only bothered to talk to Jim and Charley when he needed to tell them what to do. He threw himself into working the claim, and that suited him fine.

Straight off, he poked around the riverbank until he found a gully that'd do as a saw pit. Then he borrowed a two-man whipsaw from Dave McKay, who'd struck a claim downstream, and he and Jim started in on the pile of logs. Jim was top-saw; even in his self-important mood George had to concede that he was no match for the big Indian's strength and mulish endurance. Standing in the bottom of the gully — the "underbucket," as it was known — George'd grip a handle and do his best to keep up. Stroking back and forth, the two men moving in unison, they sawed one after another of the logs they'd laid across the pit into fairly straight planks.

After a stack of boards had been cut and roughly planed with a sharp knife, George set to work on constructing a sluice box. It was a contraption the early panners in California had devised to mimic nature: Just as the rush of ancient rivers had carried the heavy gold downhill to stream beds, the prospectors would shovel gravel into this raised funnel-like box, and the water shooting through would push the gold along until it was trapped in slow spots created by a peg frame — called a riffle — along the way or in the crossbars and the matting at the far end.

Years of practice had taught miners that a good "box length" was about twelve feet, while the height of the sides should be half that, with an opening at one end wide enough for a long-handled shovel piled high with gravel. A "string" of wooden boxes would be hammered together, forming a continuous waterway; the device, in its makeshift way, held to the same principles that had guided the Treadwell mine engineers when they'd welded together the metal pipeline stretching across Douglas Island. George kept at it; and still it took him more than two weeks to build this twelve-foot funnel.

Positioning the sluice box over a "cut" in the stream bed was a careful business, too. Experience in the California mines had led to a precise formula for achieving the best downhill flow of water. The general rule of thumb, George knew, was a one-inch drop per foot of the length of the box. So from the "lead box," into which the gravel was shoveled, to the "dump box," where the gold would collect, the incline was about a foot. The elevations had to be just so, and although each gust of wind whooshing down from the mountains was a reminder of winter's imminent arrival, George refused to be rushed. He was meticulous in his work. A miscalculation, a slipshod bit of carpentry, and there was no telling how much gold might never complete its journey to the dump box. A small fortune could be as good as lost.

While the sluice box was being completed, George made sure Jim and Charley kept busy. Snapping out his instructions with a terse authority, George had them fill sacks with shovelfuls of dirt and gravel lifted from the cracks and crevices of the exposed bedrock scattered about the site. Although the bulk of the gold would be below the surface, in the core bedrock, the outcroppings might be laced with gold veins, too. There was no wheelbarrow, so the two Indians had to carry the sacks of "paydirt" to the site of the sluice box at the edge of the creek. They emptied the sacks, and soon a gravel hill miners called the "dump" started taking shape. In the spring cleanup, the dump gravel would be shoveled into the sluice box and washed. Until then, a long eight months off, they wouldn't know if they'd dug up a heap of dirt or buried treasure.

As the two Indians continued filling and unloading sacks, George began sinking a shaft on his claim. With the first frost the ground would be as hard as granite, so George had to start work without delay. He'd need to dig a hole wide enough for a man to stand in and that might need to go straight down for forty or even fifty feet; there was no telling how deep the bedrock would be buried. The work required a good deal of muscle: slamming a pickax into stiff ground, then pushing the long-handled miner's shovel through the heavy rocks and thick dirt. By the end of each long day his arms and back would ache, and he'd be so weary that he felt as if couldn't find the strength to make it back to the tent. Still he kept at it, going deeper and deeper, until soon he began to feel as if he were standing in his own grave. He worked surrounded by solid walls of muck and dirt, the air tight in the narrow space, and after a few weeks he'd gone so deep that when he looked up he could see only a tiny patch of sky.

He was determined to keep digging until he reached bedrock; and while this was backbreaking work, George took comfort in the fact that getting the job done was simply a matter of will. Any man who put his mind to it could dig a hole. It'd be the next step that would be tricky.

The subterranean bedrock would be the sign that he'd reached the stream that millennia ago had carried the gold to the floor of Bonanza Creek. This was the path to real riches. The muck and gravel of the buried waterway would contain the greatest concentration of gold ore.

But this was not always easy to find. George would need to read the "dip," or slant, of the bedrock and use that as his guide to decipher the path of ancient stream bed. Then he'd start in tunneling, digging through a wall of dirt.

A stream, though, would more often than not run "spotted"; it could twist and turn at will. Chasing the right direction required a talent where intuition was as important as hard work. A miner could tunnel for weeks, working fifty feet below ground to shovel out a tunnel through a dense mountain of earth, only to realize that he'd lost the path of the stream. Then he'd need to start in on a new "cross-cut."

But once he hit the old creek channel, he'd have found the "paystreak." There'd be yellow nuggets as big as a man's thumb studding the soft creek bed. He could pluck them out with his hand. And every shovelful of clay and gravel would be laced with gold. So George kept digging.

Then on the morning of October 13, George walked out of the tent and discovered that the ground was covered in a fresh white coat of snow. His boots crunched against the hard ice as he walked over to see about the creek. It was frozen solid. Winter had come to the Yukon, and he still hadn't hit bedrock.

THIRTY-FOUR

George swung his pickax, but it didn't even make an indentation. There was only a sharp *clink.* The ground beneath the fresh snow was frozen solid. Still, George was determined not to let the Yukon winter stop him. He was in a hurry to get rich. All his instincts told him he was close to reaching bedrock. He refused to sit idle, staring helplessly at buried treasure as he waited out the months until the spring thaw.

Years back he had heard the old sourdoughs talking about how in '87, up on Franklin Gulch, a prospector by the name of Fred Hutchinson had also grown impatient. When winter came, the notion struck him to build a fire at the bottom of his shaft. He'd let it burn all night, and in the morning he'd clear the ashes, shovel out a swamp of thawed muck, and then he'd be able to keep on digging through soft earth. To hear the sourdoughs tell it, the technique had turned out to be as effective as the spring sun. "Winter burnings," they called it. George made up his mind to give it a try.

He told the two Indians to start cutting cords of wood. At the same time, he went to work building a spruce-log winch — a windlass — over the shaft. Turning the crank would lower into the hole a wooden bucket attached by a spiral hook to a thick rope. That way, once he hit bedrock he'd be able to get the paydirt out of the shaft. Standing on top, the Indians would hoist the filled bucket up and carry the gravel to the dump. The bucket was big enough to hold about eight shovelfuls of dirt, so George figured that one hundred buckets would be a good day's work. Come the spring cleanup, with any luck he'd be rich.

The first time George built a fire in the bottom of the shaft, he piled on too many logs. The roaring blaze thawed the earth, but a fog of gray smoke remained trapped in the narrow shaft. Work was impossible. The next night he used fewer logs; in the morning smoke was still wafting through the hole, stinging his eyes and seeping into his nostrils and throat, but he didn't feel the overpowering need to escape. He could work, and he filled more than fifty buckets. Encouraged, the following night he tried building an even smaller fire. But it proved too weak to thaw the earth, so he resigned himself to working through the smoke. He tied a bandanna over his nose and mouth, and in time he got used to it. He even found that there were advantages to working underground in the winter. The possibility of the shaft's walls crumbling around him and burying him alive had been a constant fear. Now it was no longer a concern. "The ground is frozen and never caves in," he observed with relief.

Only now that winter had arrived, it became clear that they could no longer continue living in tents. They'd freeze; the temperature would hit sixty below when the icy spears of wind came hurling down from the Arctic. As much as he wanted to concentrate solely on working the claim, George knew it was time — way past the time, truth be told — to build the cabins. Besides, that might put an end to some of Kate's complaining.

He picked out sites on flat land, and they set to work. The cabins would be built from logs chinked with moss, and each would be about the width and length of three canoes placed side to side. There'd be a window made out of empty glass jars, but it'd let in only a hazy light. The single room would be a tight, shadow-streaked space. Jim and Charley would share one cabin. About a hundred yards away was another site for George, Kate, and their daughter.

As he started in cutting the logs, just the prospect of settling into the pokey cabin left George feeling as if he were heading off to prison. The confinement would be worse than being wedged into the narrow shaft and surrounded by walls of dirt. In the tiny cabin there'd be no place to escape Kate's constant carping. He mulled building a separate cabin just for himself, but considering all he had to do, he realized this was not a possibility. Instead, he retreated, as he'd done so many times in his solitary life, into the comforting seclusion of his imagination. He lived in the future, and there he built his own home. In his mind he'd left Bonanza Creek and was already in California with Rose, the prodigal brother who'd returned a wealthy man.

Yet as it became clear that the work on the cabins would drag on for a spell, not even the distance he was putting between himself and the others was of much comfort. After three days he was ready to explode from the frustration. He didn't have time for what the sourdoughs called "dead work." He needed to get back to digging his way to the bedrock. There was a fortune within his grasp — only he was sawing logs.

George gave his predicament some thought, and soon he came up with a plan. Why not set the fires in the shaft in the morning? That way he could spend the day finishing up the cabins, and at the same time the shaft would be thawing out. After a quick supper, he'd head off to dig for bedrock.

It became an arduous routine. He'd work

all day; and then at night, he would climb down into the dark, smoky hole and dig by the soft glow of candlelight. He was at the point of utter exhaustion. The shovel felt very heavy in his hands. But he knew he was getting nearer to the bedrock, and that goal drove him on.

Jim, however, was troubled. It wasn't that he was averse to the hard work and the endless hours. And he could tolerate the change in George's attitude; he'd never expected too much from a white man anyways. But the thought that George was exploiting him had begun to take hold. They'd been working the site for over two months, and only one shaft had been dug. And it was on George's claim. He was beginning to suspect that Charley and he were working to make George rich. The white man had no intention of assisting them. When Jim felt he could no longer tolerate the one-sided way things were proceeding, he confronted George.

"When we dig shaft on my claim?" he demanded.

George didn't reply. Instead, he gave Jim a long, cool look. He was the boss of this outfit; he didn't have to answer any questions. And he didn't cotton to the big Indian's tone. It was damn impertinent. Hell, it was one more reason why he should never have partnered up with a couple of scraggly Chinooks in the first place. He was of a mind to let the Indians stew. But in the next moment, George realized it wouldn't do to have them storm off. So he swallowed his pride and told Jim the truth.

"Listen, Jim, and you too, Charley," he said sharply. "We have to work together to get gold out. I can't work my two claims by myself. I need your help. You fellows can't work your claims alone either. You need my help. That way everybody helps, no fighting. Jim, Charley, George — three partners. Savvy?"

Jim gave no sign that he knew what George was talking about. For a moment George thought that the two Indians would indeed return to their village for the winter. For that matter, the way Jim was staring at him, his face hard and full of scorn, George wouldn't have been surprised if the Indian had thrown a punch. George, though, extended his hand. And Jim shook it. Charley did, too. And just like that, an agreement was formalized.

George was true to his word. Over the next four years, more than $1 million worth of gold would be taken from their claims on Bonanza Creek, and they would share it equally. It had never, in fact, been George's intention to exploit the two Indians. His plan had always been to dig one shaft at a time; once he hit bedrock, they'd move on to Jim's site. He'd reckoned there was no need, though, to share his plans with them. Just as there was no reason to explain that while they were still his partners, they were no longer his friends. His accomplishment had shattered the bonds of whatever they once might have had in common.

Even during that first winter, George and his crew were not alone on the Klondike. The outside world still had no idea that gold had been discovered in the Yukon, but the river valley was overrun with veteran prospectors who'd heard the news and rushed north to stake claims. Within days, George had neighbors up and down Bonanza Creek. The next wave of sourdoughs had to settle for sites on nearby Eldorado Creek. "Bonanza's pup," they grudingly called it. They'd soon discover, however, that the short snaking creek held untold riches. The days had turned cold, and yet the wilderness was bustling with miners working claims. At night the strong, bright flames from hundreds of fires rising up from thawing shafts reached toward the starry sky, and the crimson reflections crawled up icy mountainsides lit by the white moon.

It was a heady time. The Yukon River Valley was a snow-covered wilderness populated with men who just six months earlier had been dead broke and who now were intoxicated by the realization that they'd soon be millionaires. At the center of all this merry commotion a tent city began to take shape. A winter ago Dawson had been nothing more than a quiet stretch of frozen swampland near the mouth of the Klondike. There was a sawmill that was shut most of the year; a squalid saloon with the same defeated drunks at the bar day after day; and a trading post famous throughout the north for the credit it routinely extended to prospectors. Now Dawson was the richest community in the world.

Except no one had any money. In the spring, the sourdoughs would wash off the gravel piled in their dumps and sell the accumulated gold in Seattle for cash. But that first winter they were a collection of millionaires with empty pockets. The only tangible resources they possessed were the nuggets and yellow dust they'd scoop from their piles of paydirt. All they had was gold; and they had plenty of it.

So gold became the accepted currency. Dawson, a disorderly ragtag collection of dirty tents in the middle of nowhere, was a more expensive place to live than Paris, London, or New York. A small keg of bent nails cost $800. Salt was literally worth its weight in gold dust. Eggs were traded for nuggets. A Juneau butcher came north with a raftload of beef cattle and in weeks had sold off his small herd for $200,000 in gold. Poker was played for fantastic pots, piles of nuggets and dust that could easily ransom a king. A round of drinks would wind up costing the price of a house in other parts of the world. Every night that winter the saloon would be packed with high-spirited men who couldn't believe their luck.

That winter, George hit bedrock. The weather had turned so cold that some days his mustache became coated with a white frost. But he would still trudge out of the cabin and climb down into the shaft. His bandanna offered only a small protection from the curl of smoke that continued to rise from the embers of the bonfire. After all the weeks, smoke had seeped into the frozen walls of dirt; the sharp, strong smell enveloped him. Yet he didn't hesitate. He'd shovel off the ash, fill the bucket with the melted ooze, and then dig. He'd reached fourteen feet when he heard the clear, unmistakable sound of his shovel banging against solid rock.

George was elated, but there was no time for celebration. Instead, as he'd always planned, he went straight to work sinking a shaft on Jim's claim. They hit bedrock there in no time at all, or so it seemed to George after all the frustrations at his site. Then they went to work putting in a shaft on Charley's section.

By February, they were hoisting up buckets of paydirt laced with veins of gold from all four claims. George couldn't wait to tell Rose how things were working out. He wrote:

I sent you a letter last Fall telling you of the strike I made. Well, it has growed wonderful since then. Everybody here is a millionaire. Eldorado Creek comes into Bonanza about a half mile above me. It is something wonderful. The pay has been located for four miles now and some the claims they think will pay a million and not one of them are blanks. . . . This is only one chance in a lifetime and I must make the best of it.

After they ran the gravel through the sluice box in the spring, then weighed the gold in Dawson, George no longer had any doubts that he was a wealthy man. The yield for that first winter from the four claims totaled about $60,000. Two of the sites were in his name, so his share would be $30,000. That would be sufficient to buy a sizable ranch in Modesto, and there'd still be money left to pay off Rose's mortgage, too. But it wasn't enough for George. He had written his sister that this was "one chance in a lifetime" and he was not prepared to walk away from it.

By June, many of the prospectors along the banks of the Klondike had booked tickets to Seattle. They stuffed their haul of gold into coffee cans, valises, and backpacks and made the trip to St. Michael to board the steamer.

But George was not ready to cash in. When he returned home, he wanted to be *very* rich.

THIRTY-FIVE

Soapy was transformed. He now had his sights set on a new, breathtakingly rich scheme, and he was raring to go. Just three months after he'd mailed the misleading letter to his wife, an event happened that as if by magic restored his wily energy and his old assurance.

The elixir was an article in the *Seattle Post-Intelligencer.* It was a scoop, actually, and an intrepid one to boot. The editors had received a tip that the steamer *Portland* had shipped off a month earlier from the old Alaskan port of St. Michael on the Bering Sea, and was bound for Seattle carrying an incredible cargo. It was filled with prospectors who had rushed to a remote gold field in the Yukon wilderness following a discovery by someone named George Carmack. They'd mined all winter and spring, and now they were loaded down with gold. So the newspaper had charted a tug to intercept the steamer. As soon as the *Portland* entered the sound, newsmen from the *Post-Intelligencer* were scrambling over the ship's rails.

And what a story they found! Times were tough. America was still gripped by a depression. But here were men who less than a year ago had been broke and now were rich. They had gold jammed into their suitcases, in caribou-hide pokes, in jam jars, old tonic bottles, tomato cans, and bundled up in Indian blankets. Gold was stacked on deck, in the purser's office, and piled high in cabins. The *Portland* was a treasure ship.

An extra edition of the *Post-Intelligencer* hit the Seattle streets before the *Portland* docked. The front page screamed in huge type:

GOLD! GOLD! GOLD! GOLD!
68 Rich Men on the Steamer *Portland*
STACKS OF YELLOW METAL!

But while the headline surely grabbed the reader's attention, the opening sentence of the story that ran below was inspired. Beriah Brown wrote that the steamer carried "more than a ton of solid gold aboard."

The reporter had miscalculated. When all the gold on the *Portland* was added up, the total was more than two tons. But "a ton of solid gold" proved sufficiently captivating. The phrase was telegraphed around the world.

In Spokane, Soapy read the report even

before the *Portland* had headed into Seattle's harbor. He took the night train and was part of the throng of five thousand people who crowded the waterfront as the steamer anchored at Schwabacher's dock. It was pandemonium.

"Show us your gold!" screamed the crowd, and in response the miners lined along the boat's rail happily raised suitcases and pokes high into the air. The crowd cheered. Soapy stared at the sea of excited faces all around him, people hot with visions of their own anticipated fortunes, and he was inspired.

He returned to the Owl in Spokane, but now he had no time for poker. That day he wrote to "Reverend" Bowers in Denver. "Call out the troops," he announced, ordering Bowers to round up the old gang. He fired off another letter to a Denver police officer who had taken part in a few of his old swindles. Soapy hoped to persuade him to turn in his badge and sign on for the Big Scheme that would make them all rich. "You will know that there is a good chance for a good talker and a petrified man in Klondyke at this stage of the game," he wrote. Bursting with his former confidence, he continued, "And if I didn't say it myself, there ain't any of them that can out-talk old Jeff. We'll open up a real estate and mining office when we get there, and I'll gamble and they'll tumble like tired doves."

Within days the boys started gathering around. They arrived from San Francisco, Denver, from all parts of the West as soon as they received the word. And as the reunited gang made preparations to head north, if any of them dared to mention their boss's fervent pledge never, never to return to Alaska, Soapy would look them straight in the face. Then he'd earnestly remind them that the only promise a gambler keeps is his vow to break all his promises.

■ ■ ■ ■

PART III
SKAGWAY

■ ■ ■ ■

THIRTY-SIX

The stampede began. Just as George Carmack's handful of gold nuggets deposited on the blower in a one-room wilderness saloon had ignited a dash to the Klondike by a passel of sourdoughs, the arrival of "a ton of gold" in Seattle created a worldwide frenzy. At a time when an economic depression continued to squeeze lives and cloud futures, the prospect of dipping a pan into a cool Yukon stream and — *presto!* — finding a fortune of bright yellow gold dust was an answered prayer. The Klondike suddenly loomed as an enchanted land, a fairy-tale world where wishes would be fulfilled — if one were bold enough to make the journey.

"Klondicitis," as the *New York Herald* dubbed the phenomenon, gripped folks everywhere. A giddy mix of greed, a yearn for adventure, and wishful thinking, Klondicitis convinced people to abandon their old lives in a rash instant and confidently set off for the far north. "Klondike or bust!" pledged tens of thousands, the three words sealing an oath of allegiance to an intrepid fraternity. The lure of gold, people in all walks of life agreed, was too hypnotic to resist.

In Seattle, it was as if the city had been attacked by a devastating plague, so quickly did thousands of its citizens rush to escape. Streetcar service came to a halt as the operators walked away from their jobs. Policemen resigned. Barbers closed shops. Doctors left their patients. The *Seattle Times* lost nearly all its reporters. Even the mayor, W. D. Wood, boarded a steamer to Alaska, wiring his resignation from the ship rather than dallying to say his good-byes at city hall. "Seattle," a *New York Herald* reporter observed, "has gone stark, staring mad on gold."

In California, the Sacramento Valley fruit pickers decided they'd rather pluck gold nuggets from bedrock than oranges from trees. The gold fields near Jackson couldn't keep their miners. At medical schools in Los Angeles and San Francisco, scores of members of the graduating classes announced plans to settle in the Yukon Valley. Those with jobs and those without jobs — people up and down the Pacific coast found a reason to race north.

All across the continent hopes soared. The day after headlines in the New York papers announced the arrival of the treasure ship, two thousand tickets to Alaska were sold. The following day, another twelve hundred people signed up. In Chicago, stockyard workers tossed off their bloodstained aprons and decided to become prospectors; the hunt for gold, they assumed without the slightest evidence, offered a chance at a better life than the gruesome, low-paying occupation with which they passed their days. "I have never seen such a change pass over the faces of people," said Senator C. K. Davis of Minnesota in astonishment.

Throughout the world the time was right for great expectations; people who had nothing were willing to risk all they had. The century had seen previous gold rushes in California, Australia, and South Africa, but none had taken hold of people's imaginations as immediately as this new stampede. Within months men and women were blithely crossing continents and oceans, bound for a rough wilderness of which they had no previous knowledge. Crammed boats sailed from Norway and Australia. A group of Greeks headed out from Jerusalem. Several hundred Italians made their way to California, an advance party, they promised, for thousands more. Three hundred Scots sailed to Montreal and then planned to cross Canada on foot. From England alone, the former prime minister of Canada Sir Charles Tupper estimated with a persuasive authority, 100,000 would-be prospectors set forth. All over the world the lust to become rich sparked glittering dreams.

The opportunity for adventure swayed brave hearts, too. The West had been tamed. The world was largely at peace. For those who craved excitement, an expedition to the far north appeared as a magnificent challenge. Winfield Scott Stratton, already blessed by the fortune he had made at Cripple Creek, outfitted two riverboats to sail up the Yukon. Brigadier General M. E. Carr, mired in a stultifying law practice after a dashing military career, gave it all up to rush to the gold fields. A. J. Balliot, once celebrated as Yale's quarterback but now languishing in a downtown office, headed for Alaska. At a sprightly seventy-one, E. J. "Lucky" Baldwin, flush with millions from hotels and real estate, decided that this was his last chance to wring the most out of his days and joined the stampede. As champagne corks popped and an orchestra played, a clique of well-heeled English aristocrats gaily steamed across the Atlantic in a yacht. Like so many others on their way to the Yukon, they sought to live to the limit; they looked forward to facing up to dangers and returning home with tales of their triumphs.

In the feverish initial ten days, fifteen hundred people had left Seattle and nine more ships were busily boarding passengers. By August, the northwest coast shipping industry had pressed into service all manner of crafts, many of them of dubious seaworthiness, and twenty-eight hundred people would embark each week toward the Lynn Canal. As of September 1, nine thousand passengers and thirty-six thousand tons of freight had sailed off just from Seattle.

The coming of winter had little effect on the enthusiasm of people who had never experienced the far north's penetrating cold or attempted to trudge over a snow-blocked mountain pass when the winds were howling and ice as hard as granite gripped the ground. In mid-August of 1897 a concerned U.S. secretary of the interior issued an official warning to those impetuous enough to set out at this late date. The Canadian minister of the interior released a similar advisory, urging travelers to wait until the spring. The newspapers offered their advice, too. "TIME TO CALL A HALT," pleaded one headline. The accompanying article pointedly admonished: "There are but a few sane men who would deliberately set out to make an Arctic trip in the fall of the year, yet this is exactly what those who now set for the Klondike are doing."

There was no way, though, to dissuade people whose convictions were firmly set. The stampede to the gold fields charged on. In that first winter, at least 100,000 pushed across the world toward the Yukon and another 1 million people made arrangements to go.

Only a few of these travelers, though, had a realistic appreciation of the struggles that awaited them. Most believed that the boats would be dropping them off at the gold fields. The geography of the north, including the long distances from the Alaskan port cities in American territory to the Klondike creeks in Canada, was ignored. And the will that would be required to complete this journey, an expedition over steep, snowcapped mountains furrowed with narrow trails and down twisting rivers with stretches of churning rapids, was not even pondered. The desire to get rich overwhelmed practical considerations. The fact that even after arriving in Alaska travelers would have no chance to reach the Klondike until the following summer — six long months away — did not enter their calculations. They just kept coming.

The shipping companies, pushed by their own strong greed, were happy to keep selling tickets. Glossing over the perils that awaited the travelers, captains crowded any boat that would float and set off on hazardous voyages through increasingly stormy autumnal waters. The *Willamette,* for example, was an old coal ship quickly converted into a passenger vessel by the Pacific Coast Steamship Company. Once eight hundred men and women, as well as three hundred horses, were packed aboard, it sailed from Tacoma. The voyage was a torture. The dining area could hold only sixty-five people, so there were ten seatings on the first day. After that, the food ran out. The second-class hold was a dungeon; the dank, noxious stench of hundreds of bodies crowded into a small space carpeted with layers of coal dust proved nearly suffocating. Those in first class fared no better. Their quarters were directly below the tethered horses, and the animals' excrement slid through the cracks of the deck planks and rained down on them. The only recourse was to spend the ten-day voyage jammed shoulder to shoulder on the open main deck, drenched by the cold, pelting rain that fell for the entire journey. On the Canadian steamer *Amur,* five hundred passengers, all promised and paying for separate berths, were shoved into accommodations designed for one hundred. A victimized traveler described the experience as "a floating bedlam . . . the Black Hole of Calcutta in an Arctic setting." Other boats, like the *Islander,* were little more than floating brothels, their corridors sweet with perfume and long, snaking lines of men chugging from bottles of rye while waiting impatiently for their turn to be entertained. "Half-dressed — and often completely naked — women reeled about the passages . . . laughing, screaming or talking in a drunken babble. Others would dance obscene dances on the dining room tables, while their bullies and pimps took the hat around for subscriptions," primly recalled one irritated passenger after his voyage.

Yet the conditions on these boats were only inconveniences when compared to the mishaps and disasters that plagued more unfortunate vessels. The steamer *Bristol* set off loaded down with so many passengers and horses that the first strong wind nearly turned the boat on its side and it was forced to creep back to port. The *Nancy G.* foundered on the Lynn Canal and then went up in flames. Despite a law prohibiting passenger travel on boats carrying explosives, when the dynamite in the hold of the *Clara Nevada* exploded, sixty-five people were killed. The *City of Mexico* struck Devil's Rock, off Sitka, and sank. Overloaded and manned by an inexperienced crew, the *Anderson* listed to starboard, which caused her rudder to malfunction, and she smashed into the *Glory of the Seas,* a three-masted clipper, leaving both ships badly damaged. The sea voyage to Alaska was invariably a nasty, dangerous trip.

A flotilla of all manner of ships, however, continued to head north, and hordes of passengers continued to push and shove their way to the ticket windows. The most direct route was by steamer to the dismal, weather-beaten port of St. Michael, on the Bering Sea, about twenty-seven hundred miles from Seattle. Upon arrival, the traveler would transfer to a flat-bottomed riverboat for the sixteen-hundred-mile trip up the Yukon to the boomtown of Dawson. From there, it would be an arduous hike to the Klondike. Among alternatives that held only uncertainties and hardships, this was the least challenging route. Still, the icy Yukon was navigable for only four months, from mid-June to early September. For the flurry of gung ho stampeders (as the would-be prospectors rushing north came to be known) who shipped out during this first fall and winter, this route was not a possibility.

Then there was the Canadian route. From Edmonton, the trip would be a start-and-stop twenty-seven-hundred-mile journey over rutted wagon passes and nearly a dozen tricky rivers, often going against hard currents, that eventually led to Dawson. But this circuitous and demanding trail was also impassable for most of the year.

As a result, the steamship companies settled on a route that took ships along the southeastern Alaskan coast and then through the long Lynn Canal. Pointing like an outstretched finger, the canal led directly to the headwaters lapping at the crescent beaches of two new hectic tent towns. The boats would anchor a mile offshore and unload their passengers and cargo in a haphazard flurry of activity.

Terrified horses and mules would be dumped into cold waters. Packing cases loaded with carefully purchased provisions would be heaved onto snub-nosed transport boats only to smash apart on landing, the goods scattering into the sea. And these small makeshift ferries quickly filled to capacity; for many of the new arrivals, there would be no choice but to wade through numbing water to the beach.

The rocky beaches were scenes of constant pandemonium. Hundreds of confused, exhausted people would be searching frantically for their belongings or scrambling to make camp, while yelping dogs and whining horses raced about fitfully. John Muir, the well-known naturalist, made his bewildered way through the high-pitched tumult and compared it to "a nest of ants taken into a strange country and stirred up by a stick."

From the teeming beaches, the stampeders had their choice of two boomtown destinations just six miles apart. One was Dyea, the same spruce-forested inlet where Charlie Siringo had happened upon a suspicious George Carmack. Here prospectors could start out on the dauntingly steep Chilkoot Pass, the very route that had nearly done in Carmack. If they made it to the other side and down to Lake Lindeman, then it was a six-hundred-mile voyage across placid lakes and down the Yukon River to the Klondike.

The other beachfront settlement was Skagway. This was the entry point to the White Pass, another gap over the mountains. The White Pass was ten miles longer then the Chilkoot Trail, but it had the seeming advantage of being far less steep; its summit was six hundred feet below the lofty Chilkoot's and there were trails for pack animals. Still, as one old sourdough who had struggled over both passes reckoned, "There ain't no choice. One's hell. The other's damnation."

But to the newcomers gazing up toward the mountains as they huddled in exhaustion around campfires on the beaches, the distant rolling hills of the lower White Pass seemed an easier passageway. All through that first fall and winter people flocked to Skagway, the settlment whose name was inspired by the Indian word *Skagus* — the home of the North Wind.

It was a idyllic site, a flat patch of windblown land nestled between a beach, clear blue alpine lakes, and a fortress of jagged-peaked mountains. Its only inhabitants were a single self-sufficient frontier family living in a log cabin. But by the spring of 1898, as the thick crust of ice on the trail began to melt, Skagway had been transformed into a rip-roaring tent city bustling with over 10,000 inhabitants, and more were arriving each warm day.

■ ■ ■ ■

A quiet decade before the Klondike gold rush, Skookum Jim had led a surveyor through the undulating hills, canyons, and valleys that became known as the White Pass. And as was the case when he accompanied George Carmack on the momentous expedition that discovered gold on Bonanza Creek, the big Indian's role became only a footnote in the white man's history. It was seventy-one-year-old Captain William Moore who became renowned for charting the long, snaking trail. And it was the sturdy white pioneer who in time grew rich as the sole founding father of Skagway.

Yet even if Moore's achievement has been heralded generously and Jim's largely ignored, there is no denying that the captain was a remarkable man. Arriving from Germany in his teens, he was soon piloting towboats on the Mississippi. But the lust for gold grabbed hold of his dreams, and for the next half century he sought it — in California, Peru, and British Columbia. Along the hard-charging way he made a fortune, built a mansion in Victoria, and lost it all. For a while he ran a fleet of steamboats up the Fraser River, even carrying camels to the Canadian gold fields in an quixotic scheme that in the end turned into a shambles. By the time he arrived in Alaska in 1887, he was dead broke.

Moore's mind, however, was churning. He still dreamed of gold. Only now he became fixated on the Yukon Valley. A lifetime of experiences in gold fields in North and South America had sharpened his intuition. He possessed not a single tangible piece of evidence, yet he was certain: The next big strike would be in the Yukon.

Moore, though, didn't set off with his pack and shovel. Finding gold, he knew too well, was a chancy business. You could spend decades panning and never see a single yellow nugget. Besides, he was in his sixties; traipsing through the wilderness was a younger man's occupation. Instead Moore focused his ambitions on a sure thing: He'd create and own a boomtown.

Moore had heard stories about a pass through the mountains that was less precipitous than the Chilkoot, and with Skookum Jim leading the way, he went out in search of it. It was two months of grueling work. Yet they succeeded in marking the path of a forty-five-mile trail wide enough for men and pack animals. It led through high country that twisted and turned along narrow cliffsides; passed through deep bogs and swampland; crossed and then recrossed fast-moving rivers; and built to a thousand-foot climb over sharp rocks before it scurried down to Lake Bennett and the beginnings of the Yukon

River. Moore named the trail in honor of Sir Thomas White, the Canadian minister of the interior.

But — and this stroke showed the reach of Moore's genius — his activities didn't stop with the creation of this new route to the north country. His visionary intelligence predicted that the little valley below White Pass would one day be filled with prospectors heading off to find their fortunes. Registering with the government in Washington, D.C., he and his sons claimed a 160-acre townsite, the maximum size American law allowed for new settlements. They built a cabin and a mile-long wharf stretching out from the beach, and they cleared a four-mile wagon road through spruce forests and swampland that led to the beginning of the White Pass Trail. He called it Mooresville.

For a decade he lived in lonely isolation. He owned nearly as far as he could see from his cabin door, but it was a barren accomplishment. After all the years spent waiting, after all the brutal winters, his confidence in his success began to fray. He was in his eighth decade, an age when many take stock of their lives, and he found himself beginning to acknowledge his doubts. Perhaps his guiding instinct had been erroneous. Perhaps the Yukon Valley held no treasure. Perhaps Mooresville would forever be a forest and he would die unknown and in disappointment, another humble creature left to decompose in the vast north woods.

Then suddenly they came. The boats spewed them forth by the hundreds, then the thousands. They came charging up from the beaches, pitching tents, cutting trees for shacks. Moore was there to welcome them to his town, but the impatient newcomers had no time for some crotchety old sea captain. With the swagger and the authority of a conquering army, the new arrivals made their own rules. By August a prospectors' committee had laid out the town of Skagway with sixty-foot-streets and thirty-six hundred lots that measured fifty by a hundred feet. It was Moore's land by deed, and a $5 registry fee was collected by the town from anyone who wanted a parcel, but Moore was never consulted and he never received any compensation. Surveyors even condemned his cabin, since it lay in the middle of a new thoroughfare. When they came, all he could do was fight them off with a crowbar as his wife stood sobbing in the doorway.

In the end, the founder of Mooresville moved from the cabin where he'd passed a contemplative decade imagining the day when people would come. Beware of what you wish for, he might have told himself, and then surrendered with a glum resignation. But old age had not dampened his fighter's spirit. He brought his arguments to the courts. It took four frustrating years before authorities in Washington ruled that he was entitled to 25 percent of the assessed value of all the lots so cavalierly carved out of his original townsite. By then he'd also earned another fortune from the fees he'd collected from the boats that docked along his wharf. He ended his days in contentment, satisfied that his vision had been confirmed.

But there were limits to his pride. Even Moore had to concede that the town that took shape in the flatland of his valley had little resemblance to the bucolic village of his imagination. Skagway was from the start a roaring, wide-open town. Its main commercial thoroughfare was only a stretch of black mud grandly christened Broadway Avenue, but four pokey saloons — the Pack Train, the Bonanza, the Grotto, and the Nugget — kept things hopping all day and all night. The whorehouse and the dance halls were just tents, but the painted good-time girls were always busy; there were offerings for every taste. It was a town without rules or law, a spreading tent city of restless, overwhelmed new arrivals who had traveled thousands of hard miles.

Until the steady snow stopped falling and the ice on the trail and the Yukon River melted, the newcomers were stranded in Skagway. People grew insensible with drink and reeled down muddy streets. Deadly fights broke out over insults real and imagined. Piano music and gunfire echoed through the hills day and night. And come November, winter began to take its suffocating hold. The hordes grew impatient, cold, and bored. It was a dark, dangerous season.

"It seemed as if the scum of the earth had hastened here to fleece and rob, or . . . to murder," complained one Englishman who found himself stuck in Skagway late in the fall of 1897. "There was no law whatsoever; might was right, the dead shot only was immune to danger."

It was American territory, but the nearest U.S. marshal lived in Dyea, and he was in no rush to visit. When a Frenchman was caught stealing, the town elected a committee to deal with the transgressor. Justice was swift. The thief was tied to a pole in front of a tent, and a fusillade of bullets pounded his body as he pleaded for mercy. The bloody corpse was left for three days as a warning to other would-be thieves.

When Superintendent Samuel Steele of the North-West Mounted Police crossed the border for a visit, he felt as if he had entered "hell on earth." Bullets ripped through the walls of his cabin, roaring gunfights left mortally wounded victims lying in the streets, and shouts of murder and cries for help were so frequent that quite quickly, he admitted, they ceased to be startling. "Skagway," the veteran Mountie decided, "was about the roughest place in the world."

It was here that Soapy Smith came with his gang.

Soapy booked passage on the *City of Seattle* in August, less than a month after the news from Bonanza Creek reached Seattle. The captain was his old friend Dynamite Johnny O'Brien, and even before they shipped off Soapy asked for a favor. The departure date was the thirteenth. Would Dynamite Johnny indulge a gambler's superstition and delay the voyage for a day? Soapy still vividly remembered the fiasco his previous trip to Alaska had turned into, and he reckoned he could use all the luck he could get. Of course, agreed the captain. How could he refuse to accommodate the stalwart hero who had helped him calm a mutiny?

They were not long at sea before Soapy repaid the captain's courtesy. A passenger had thought to ease the monotony of the voyage by swinging playfully from the halyards as the ship rolled through the ocean swells. But as he swung back and forth, a ten-pound lantern came loose and struck him on the head. He plummeted to the deck, and lay there dead.

The other passengers, already agitated by the overcrowding on the steamer, promptly held a mass meeting. They wanted revenge on the captain and the steamship officials for the unsafe conditions that had resulted in a death. They decided to initiate a $50,000 damage suit against the company.

That was when Soapy intervened. Furious, he announced that the dead man was a stowaway. Then, as the crowd watched in stunned silence, he went through the dead man's pockets. He pulled out a medal and an envelope addressed to Jefferson R. Smith — both of which, he bellowed, had been stolen from him yesterday.

"Now, you scum," he said fiercely, "if you want to stand up for a man who's a stowaway, a cheat, and a bum, I'm off you."

Moments later, the passengers, their anger spent and deflated, dispersed. And Soapy felt restored. He'd let his talents rest dormant for so many months that even he'd had to wonder if he'd lost his touch. But now he had demonstrated to himself — and to his attentive gang members, as well — that he still could manipulate the emotions of a crowd. He could dish out the most preposterous story and the marks would obediently accept it without question. He was once again brimming with confidence. He couldn't wait to get back into business.

This time he was not disappointed. After his first day ashore, Soapy, like the jubilant George Carmack on Bonanza Creek, knew he'd discovered the mother lode. He had crammed a lifetime of plots, scams, and adventures into his hectic thirty-six years, but Skagway would be his golden opportunity. He'd earn both wealth and respect.

The money started quickly rolling in. In three brisk weeks he and the gang had made nearly $30,000. He proudly wrote Mary, "I have had luck in trade" and sent her $1,600.

He had no doubts that this would only be the beginning.

THIRTY-SEVEN

Soapy was king.

In a whirlwind of ruthless ingenuity, Soapy had become, after just a few busy months, Skagway's preeminent citizen. He was monarch over a tent-city empire that included underworld enterprises, saloons and whorehouses, businesses of varying degrees of legitimacy, the best restaurant in the territory, as well as, in one more sign of his complicated ambitions, philanthropic and civic organizations. Soapy's control over the town was total.

He surrounded himself with members of his Denver gang, veterans up to their old tricks in a new, fertile stomping ground. John Bowers was back to wearing his reverend's white collar, once more the pious "grip man" offering fraternal handshakes to newfound friends and lodge brothers as he steered the tenderfeet to Soapy's establishments. "Old Man Tripp" had headed north, too. Now he posed as a benevolent white-haired sourdough who had returned from the Yukon, only the pack on his back carried feathers rather than the prospector's heavy supplies and the mother lode was fleecing a miner who'd already struck it rich. "Professor" Turner Jackson had transformed himself into an authority on the geology of the Klondike bedrock, an erudite adviser to the ignorant and unsuspecting. George Wilder was once again the confident dandy, primping around Skagway's dank saloons in his bowler hat, wing collar, diamond stick pin, and shiny high-buttoned boots, a picture of entrepreneurial success who was only too glad to let a new friend in on a sure thing. "Big Ed" Burns and "Red" Gallagher had come north, too, thugs ready to dish out — as they'd done so effectively in Creede and Denver — savage beatings to any mark who turned belligerent.

In addition, a few new recruits had attracted Soapy's attention with their guile, loyalty, and obedience, and they'd risen to prominent positions in the reunited Soap Gang. "Slim-Jim" Foster possessed a youthful, curly-headed charm that helped make him the perfect steerer. Young Alexander Conlin, who would go on to become one of the most celebrated magicians and mentalists of the 1920s, got his initiation into the art of deception by working three-card monte games in Skagway under Soapy's tutelage. Yeah Mow Hopkins, a veteran of the murderous San Francisco tong wars, would fix people with a sullen, impassive stare, and if that failed to intimidate, he could hurl a hatchet across a room with deadly accuracy. Soapy, who'd an eye for talent, made Yeah Mow his bodyguard.

But beyond his devoted inner circle, Soapy's organization extended, it was estimated, to a loose confederation of about 300, a sizable force in a town that swelled during the winter months to nearly 10,000 people. Operators of shell games, "mechanics" rigging poker games, snatch-and-run robbers, smooth-talking bunco men, madams who'd rushed north with stables of young prostitutes — all worked in Skagway with Soapy's consent and protection. And only after guaranteeing to kick back one-third of each day's take. From all over the West flimflam men, thieves, painted ladies, and hard cases traveled north to enlist in the high-riding Soap Gang. Veteran outlaws like the Moonfaced Kid, Fatty Green, Kid Jimmy Fresh, Yank Fewclothes, and the Doctor got off steamers and immediately went searching for Soapy, eager to acknowledge him as their boss. His sovereignty was undisputed.

The money kept pouring in.

And Soapy was shameless. From the cold reaches of his intelligence, he hatched so many schemes, large and small. The opportunities struck him as endless.

When a steamer arrived, two rows of burly, hard-eyed men would assemble in a ragtag formation along the beach so that newcomers, as if by accident, would be funneled toward any of a dozen steerers. Slim-Jim, though, was the best. His face shining with an angel's smile, brimming with a gee-whiz enthusiasm that could ingratiate itself into the wariest of hearts, Jim would rush up to new arrivals and beg to hear the news from the States. He'd ask where they were from; and, in a truly wonderful coincidence, wouldn't you know it but that was his native state, too. If they had a hometown newspaper, or any paper, for that matter, he'd gladly buy it for a dollar. The cost, he'd confide with an embarrassed modesty, meant little to him after all the gold he'd taken out of the Klondike. And since there was so much news from back home that he was dying to hear, how about, Jim would propose, joining me for a drink. My treat, naturally.

At the saloon, a roulette wheel would be spinning, and a prospector — actually a "capper" working for the gang — would be placing gold nuggets across the board. And winning on every spin. To celebrate, the drinks were on him.

As soon as the newcomer was softened by a couple of free drinks, Jim would make his play. Why don't you try your luck? he'd urge.

The wheel's making people rich today.

If the newcomer placed a bet, he'd win. What'd I tell you? Jim would shout with joy. You're gonna get rich without going to the gold fields. Go on, place another bet, he'd encourage. Only now the mark would lose, and keep on losing until his nest egg was gone.

If prudence, however, prevented his new friend from taking the plunge, Jim would give a discreet signal. A moment later, a fight involving a mess of tipsy prospectors would break out at the bar. In the melee, a solid punch would knock the mark cold — and he'd wake up in an alleyway to find that his money was gone.

Reverend Bowers specialized in another scam. His practiced eye would pick out a prosperous-looking fellow lodge member coming off a boat, and the reverend would approach. Cleary chagrined, distress nearly choking off his words, the reverend would share a tale of woe. Alaska's harsh climate had taken its toll on his frail constitution. The only hope he had of making it through the winter, his doctor had despaired, was if he left Skagway at once for a warmer climate. The reverend needed money to purchase a steamer ticket, but he wasn't asking for charity. He owned a house in town, as well as two adjoining lots, and due to the urgency of his situation he'd sell all three parcels at just a fraction of their true value — say, he'd suggest, $100. But don't take my word for it, the reverend would continue earnestly. Let me show you the properties.

So the two new friends would traipse across Skagway to the house. No sooner would they would walk through the door than a masked man aiming a 10-gauge shotgun would appear. The reverend would shake with fear and plead for his life, while the gunman would proceed with a brusque efficiency. In just moments the thief would relieve the newcomer of his wallet, watch and chain, and any other valuables in his travel bag. Then the robber would rush out the door, disappearing into the crowd filling a nearby saloon. And the reverend, abruptly restored to a stony calm, would declare that since his new friend regrettably no longer had any funds, he'd have no choice but to find another buyer for his properties.

Old Man Tripp was another surefire moneymaker. Posing as a stampeder, he worked the White Pass Trail, and the pickings were easy.

The trail was an arduous climb, a forty-five-mile journey along a narrow, twisting path over slippery slate cliffs, massive jutting boulders, jagged rocks as sharp as spikes, and mud-hole swamps that led toward a high and precipitous summit. This gray-misted peak marked the border between American territory and Canada, and mounted police stationed there enforced a new regulation that increased the struggling stampeders' burdens: It was forbidden to enter the Yukon Territory without a year's supply of food. Along with tents, tools, and other belongings, this added up to over five thousand pounds, more than two tons of goods. So heavy bundles would be packed on prospectors' backs, strapped on overburdened mules and horses, and piled high on sleds. Still, it would take a man twenty or more round-trips to move his outfit to Lake Bennett, and the entire journey could drag on for ninety grueling days. Within months, thousands of packhorses lay dead along the way, their flanks pierced by razor-sharp rocks, or their legs snapped between two boulders, or their bodies crushed by falls after a misstep on the trail above. Their corpses were left to rot, and the strong, raw stench of decomposing flesh seemed to wrap itself around the entire route. Dead Horse Trail, the bitter travelers took to calling the path. All day the solid line of men would trudge slowly forward, a grim, snaking procession climbing upward, their backs bent under the heavy weight of their packs, thick ropes twisted over their shoulders and through their hands as they hauled overloaded sleds.

Old Man Tripp offered a respite from the misery, and a chance to make a boodle in the process. Setting up a tripe and keister on the side of the trail, he'd manipulate three English walnut shells and a single pea. The cappers, packs on their backs as part of their prospectors' disguises, would be betting twenty-dollar gold pieces; and time after time, they'd select the shell hiding the pea. The yelps of joy as they pocketed their winnings would attract the men on the line.

Weary, curious, and often simply bored, they'd pull out of the procession and gather around the old sourdough's keister. Soon enough they'd start betting, too, but the speed and agility of the old man's manipulations were now of a skill that hadn't been previously revealed. They'd invariably lose, and then invariably be prodded into trying to win their money back. Soapy boasted that his share of the take of these games would often run to $2,000 a day. Of course, some of the victims, already testy from the day's hardships, would grumble they'd been gaffed and demand their money back. The cappers would draw their six-guns, and that would discourage most marks. But from time to time the hoodwinked prospectors would be packing, too, and they'd refuse to back down. Then bullets would start flying. In a panic, people on the trail would fall flat to the ground, slip behind horses, and crouch by sleds. On occasion a bullet would hit a gang member, or a gambler, or an unlucky bystander. But Old Man Tripp always managed to duck, and there was never more than a brief interruption to his activities.

While these were bold, old-fashioned schemes, Soapy's Big Store enterprises, as bunco men referred to businesses that were nothing more than fronts for scams, were shrewd inventions. At the Merchants Exchange, newcomers would be informed that the supplies they'd purchased in the States were unsuitable for the Yukon and would be confiscated by the Mounties at the White Pass border summit. The sympathetic folks who ran the exchange, though, were eager to offer assistance. They'd accept the worthless supplies in partial payment for the cost of the new regulation outfit they'd sell. Days later, the "banned" supplies would be resold to a new group of dismayed stampeders who had come north with outfits that, they were advised, would never pass the Mounties' stringent regulations.

Down by the wharves, Soapy ran another "public service" business. There were two cabins, and on each was posted a large sign identifying it as a "General Information Bureau." A man in a somber city suit and collared shirt would oblige the grateful newcomer by providing knowledgeable answers to questions about the conditions of the trails, locations of campsites, and fees for hiring packers. But his real purpose was to collect information, not to offer it. By the end of a polite and breezy conversation, the unsuspecting traveler would've been led to divulge a volume of useful facts. The well-dressed, amicable official would learn who was traveling alone, who carried a firearm, who had a nest egg of cash, and who possessed a well-funded bank account — intelligence that a gang of thieves could put to good use.

On McKinney Street, next door to the town's post office, was the Skagway Real-Estate & Investment Company. The sign on the door detailed the concern's many ventures: "Real estate bought and sold, houses to rent, business chances, investments made for non-residents, special attention paid to the care of property placed in our hands. Mining properties bought and sold & examined. Headquarters for quick cash sales. References, all the prominent men in the city."

It was a wordy advertisement indeed, but all a local had to read was that "non-residents" were offered special attention to know to steer clear. Such information was Soapy's discreet way of communicating that the operation was largely a scam. The businessmen inside would be selling mines that didn't exist, renting houses that were already occupied, and putting cash investors in touch with flimflam artists. It was well known in

Skagway that Soapy Smith preferred to fleece only those who were passing through — unless, of course, the opportunity was too good to resist.

The town's "Cut-Rate Ticket Office" was another of Soapy's operations. It sold tickets back to the States at discounted prices often half of those sold directly by the steamship lines. It was a wonderful deal, except for the fact that the tickets were for steamers that had no intention of ever dropping anchor off Skagway.

The Skagway Telegraph Office was an even more brazen enterprise. For only $5, it promised to send a telegram anywhere in the United States. Stampeders lined up to notify their families that they'd arrived safely and to wire their loved ones that they were deeply missed. A day or so after the telegrams had been sent, the prospector would be informed that a reply had been received. For an additional $5, he could retrieve it from the key operator. The dispatches were terse, but always reassuring. And total fabrications. No telegrams were ever sent from Skagway, and none were ever received. A telegraph line to Juneau would not be strung for another four years.

Skagway's hurrah saloons and gambling parlors were the lucrative cornerstones of Soapy's imperial empire. There were eleven saloons scattered around the town, most with a roulette wheel and faro and poker tables, and Soapy either owned each one outright or had a large piece of the action. He made his headquarters in one of the quieter establishments, a boxy, single-story wood-frame building at 317 Holly Street. A large sign on the roof announced JEFF SMITH'S PARLOR, but the establishment was known throughout Skagway — the entire Alaska Territory, truth be told — as "Jeff's Place."

MOST ELEGANTLY FURNISHED RESORT IN ALASKA, CHOICE WINES AND LIQUORS — HAVANA CIGARS, SPECIAL ATTENTION PAID TO SERVICE, another sign on the front window promised. Inside was a long mahogany bar, and above it stretched an unfurled American flag. Electric lightbulbs hung from the ceiling, a rare convenience in the north country, and at night they shined through the thick smoke wafting from all the pipes and cigars to paint the tight room with a weak yellow glow. Adjacent to the bar was a small restaurant with a few tables covered with oilcloths; oysters and beef steaks were the specialties. But it was in the back parlor, a room the *Daily Alaskan*'s reporter described as "cozy as a lady's boudoir," that Soapy held court.

He'd sit at a round wooden table, his back to the wall, with Yeah Mow at rigid attention nearby. And each night, while sipping from a glass of Canadian rye, Soapy would issue orders, shape new schemes, receive reports from the spies he had working the steamships and the miners' camps, accept the obeisance of his employees and carefully selected newcomers, and count the river of money that was flowing in as steadily as the currents on the mighty Yukon.

Yet Soapy was not content simply to grow rich. He lusted for an achievement that would establish him as person worthy of admiration. He wanted to be recognized as a man whose actions placed him on a lofty pedestal high above the low-life gamblers and two-bit grifters. He wanted to be respected. As a consequence, even while he schemed and thieved, he also performed good deeds.

With an easy charity and a casual benevolence, Soapy would slip a hundred to a prospector down on his luck who needed money for a ticket home. When Reverend Robert Dickey came to town to build the Union Church, Soapy grabbed $200 off a faro table and handed it over as a donation. Since Skagway was overrun with abandoned dogs, mutts brought from Seattle with the hope that they'd be able to pull sleds but who'd proved not up to the demanding work, Soapy organized a program to help. He posted flyers urging every household to take in a stray, and he further demonstrated his commitment by adopting six dogs for his own. After a lawman was gunned down, Soapy told a crowd "it is only right that we should help his widow" and then publicly gave the grieving woman a wad of cash. When plans were announced for a community hospital, his name appeared fourth from the top in the list of benefactors. He was instrumental in establishing the town's fire brigade. And when, in December 1897, Skagway held its first election and a seven-member town council was formed, Soapy was its most ardent and vocal supporter. As a businessman, he insisted, he was all for "the preservation of law and order."

Soapy was untroubled by the obvious inconsistencies in his behavior. He had an actor's ability to slide into different roles. Rationalizations came easy to him. If Yeah Mow or Ed Burns was required to give a brutal pounding to an ornery mark, Soapy had no qualms. "The greatest kindness one can do to such people," he'd explain with a shrug, "is to force them to get out of Skagway and to take the next boat home." Or if a victim of one of his scams was wiped out before even heading into the Klondike, Soapy was unruffled. "Infinitely better," he'd insist, "that any man who is such an infant as to try to beat a man at his own game should lose money here at the seaport, than he should get into the inhospitable Arctic, where such an idiot would lose it anyway or be a burden on the community." His was a stern, unyielding philosophy; and yet it was also generous with Christian charity. He could hold two totally opposing points of view, be both underworld kingpin and the champion of law and order, and navigate with ease through the contradictions. In all things, Soapy was guided by what he believed served him best at the moment.

At the core of his mercurial temperament, though, was a master plan. He still held to the idea that one day, after all his dreary moneymaking shenanigans were no longer necessary, he and Mary and the children would settle down in a big house. In his mind he pictured them living in St. Louis, a comfortable city where his exploits were largely unknown. He saw a day when he and his wife would be granted the respect due to pillars of the community. Like so many of the other gold rush stampeders, he'd come north with the dream of refashioning his life. To his way of looking at things, all his operations, however scampish, were justifiable, activities undertaken in his pursuit of his family's future happiness.

In the meantime, the conventions of lesser men should not restrain him. His success, he felt, was proof of his uniqueness. He'd catapulted above bothersome rules. And even as he vowed his "love to death" in his weekly letters to Mary, he was living in Skagway with another woman.

Nevertheless, Soapy had a politician's instincts, and he took care to polish his image. It caused him a good deal of distress that the *San Francisco Examiner* had it in for him. Not long after he'd arrived in Skagway, it had published an unflattering likeness on the front page, with the caption "Soapy Smith, the uncrowned king of the town of Skagway." Salting the wound, the accompanying article made several snide references about "his ambition to be Chief of Police." So when he learned from one of his many sources that the *Examiner* was sending Edward Cahill, its ace reporter, to investigate the goings-on in Dyea and Skagway, Soapy was there to welcome him when he got off the steamer. Over the next week Soapy wined, dined, and charmed the correspondent with the persistence of a suitor — which, in a way, he was. At Soapy's command, all doors in Skagway opened up to Cahill. The resulting article provided one more proof of Soapy's con man's skills:

"Soapy" Smith is not a dangerous man, and not a desperado. He will fight to very good purpose if he must, but he is not in the least quarrelsome. Cool in the presence of danger, absolutely fearless, honorable in the discharge of those obligations which he recognizes, generous with his money, and ever ready with a helping hand for a man or a woman in distress. . . . Not the least amusing trait of "Soapy" Smith's character is the eager interest which he takes in the preservation of law and order.

But while Soapy could fool some of the people, he couldn't fool all of them. Oscar Dunbar, the editor and owner of the newly created *Daily Alaskan* newspaper, had no tolerance for Soapy's activities. He ran a series of articles warning newcomers about rigged shell games on the White Pass Trail and the "pack of tin horn gamblers" under Soapy's control.

When Soapy had just about enough of the insults, he paid a call on the editor. "I'm sure you're wrong about Soapy Smith," he explained as he shook Dunbar's hand, "because I'm Soapy himself." With his easy charm, he then offered a proposition. Soapy would pay $50 an issue to keep his name out of the *Alaskan.* "That shouldn't be hard to do for that price, should it?" Soapy suggested lightly.

"It shouldn't be," Dunbar agreed.

To seal the arrangement, later that afternoon a gang member delivered two bottles of Mumm extra dry champagne and a box of Havana cigars to the editor. "With Mr. Smith's compliments," the burly messenger explained.

Without skipping a beat, the editor picked up the edition of the *Alaskan* that had just rolled off the presses. "To Mr. Smith, with the compliments of Mr. Dunbar," he said as he handed over the newspaper.

Soapy was livid when he read its editorial detailing how he'd tried to bribe the editor. For a few rough moments he no doubt recalled the thrashing he'd given Colonel Arkins in Denver when that editor had proved insolent. But soon Soapy, who prided himself on learning from his experiences, came up with a more efficient plan. He approached Billy Saportas, a reporter for the paper, and put him on the payroll. After that, the *Alaskan,* at least in Saportas's dispatches, took to singing Soapy's praises.

A few of the gang complained that Soapy was wasting his money. Why pay Saportas when a bullet would quiet Dunbar at a much lower cost? But Soapy shrugged off the expense. Reputation was crucial; it was the bricks upon which his power rested. Besides, the money he was spending was the down payment on the bright future that was shaping up at last for Mary and him.

THIRTY-EIGHT

All through the fall and winter, as the first stampeders rushed north and Soapy established himself in Skagway, George continued to work his site. There was so much to do that he hired a dozen men to help with the underground digging and paid them in gold dust; that way he was able to keep his operation going around the clock. It reminded him of his time at the Treadwell mine where the work had also been divided into shifts. Only now George Carmack was the boss. It was his mine. And it was his gold.

Each day, as another big haul of gold-bearing gravel was added to the dump, he felt that he was getting closer to achieving his dream. In his mind he pictured himself in a well-pressed city suit, the chain of a pocket watch dangling across his waistcoat, a big Havana cigar between his lips, and there he'd be striding into Rose's parlor.

Increasingly he sought refuge in an imagined future. Its possibility became the answer to everything. There was no longer any harmony with Kate. He dismissed her as a tyrant, a shrill squaw unworthy of his companionship.

Kate couldn't understand his behavior. She had no appreciation of the transforming power of greed or how the white man measured success. She was simply angry and hurt. In her resentment, she attacked.

One Sunday afternoon Ed Conrad, a miner who had a nearby claim, heard screams. It sounded to him like a woman calling for help, and he rushed over to the Carmack cabin. He found Kate outside, yelling in Tagish as if intent on alerting the whole countryside.

A moment later George walked out of the woods hauling a sled loaded down with firewood.

"What's going on?" Conrad asked with concern.

"Oh, that woman," George answered lightly, a man accustomed to this sort of drama. "She's just telling me no wood, no fire, no dinner. She thinks her screaming will make me move faster."

In a letter later that winter to Rose, he complained, "My wife had more work than she could do all winter but she is getting too high toned to work now."

Though they were surrounded by great riches, their life on Bonanza Creek had turned into a living hell.

■ ■ ■ ■

Yet even with all his newfound wealth, George was not the richest man in the Yukon. It was the latecomers who'd no choice but to stake Eldorado Creek who reaped the most fantastic fortunes.

There was Antone Stander, for example, a twenty-nine-year-old immigrant from Austria. Stander had worked his way across the continent as a cowboy, sheepherder, farmer, and coal miner before deciding to head to the far north to try his luck at prospecting. Only he didn't have any luck; two years of looking for gold left him dead broke. When he heard about Carmack's find, he rushed up to Bonanza. But he was too late; the creek had already been staked. On an impulse, he decided to explore the country beyond Carmack's site. As the creek twisted south, he followed it into a wooded ravine. Absently, he stuck a pan into the water: The gravel was laced with gold! That afternoon he measured off a claim that would be worth more than $4 million.

As soon as Stander started working the creek, other veterans began to take notice. Jay Whipple, an old sourdough who'd gone broke searching in vain for years in the rough country around Sixtymile; Frank Keller, who'd been a brakeman for the railroad in

California; J. J. Clements, who'd earned the money for his passage north by carrying the mail on horseback; William Johns, a rough-and-tumble former newspaper reporter from Chicago — all struck it rich on Eldorado Creek.

Even the bartender from Bill McPhee's saloon made a killing on Eldorado Creek — without leaving the barroom. Once Stander had staked his claim, he needed supplies to get him through the winter. Clarence Berry helped him out, and got half of Stander's claim in return. It was more an act of kindness than a business deal, yet the bartender wound up making several million dollars from the transaction.

The yield on Bonanza was not as rich; nevertheless, George was not the only prospector to find his fortune along its banks. Louis Rhodes worked a claim a mile or so above George's. After two disappointing months of shoveling through icy muck, he was ready to sell out. He wanted $250 for his claim, only he couldn't find any takers. So he reluctantly kept at it. When he finally reached bedrock, he scooped golden nuggets out of the clay by the handful.

Farther up the creek were the three Scouse brothers. They'd worked in the Pennsylvania coal mines before heading to the Yukon, so they had no misgivings about digging underground. And with the three brothers working in shifts, it didn't take them long to hit bedrock. Only the pay streak seemed to elude them. Day after day, they'd fill big buckets with gravel, but when they washed the loads they found nothing but dirt. Then, on a guess, they crosscut in another direction. When they hoisted the first bucket up on the windlass, there was no need to pan the contents. Gold nuggets lay sprinkled over the gravel like shells on a beach. They would make over $1 million from their claim.

But of all the old sourdoughs who struck it rich, "Big Alex" McDonald, the King of the Klondike, was the shrewdest. When the news of George's strike spread through the Yukon Valley, McDonald didn't have a dime. He was determined, however, not to miss out on an opportunity he knew would be his one chance to turn his life around. So he managed to buy a load of groceries on credit, and then he traded the supplies to a down-on-his luck sourdough for half of a claim on the Eldo-rado. Next, he leased out a section of his half stake to a group of miners for a percentage of their take. He used the proceeds from this "lay," as the practice came to be known, for the down payment on another claim. He continued borrowing to purchase more claims and then leasing them, too. As soon as money came in from one site, he'd use it to make another transaction. He never sold. Within a year, he had interests in twenty-eight claims, and his holdings were worth about $10 million.

Still, no one had forgotten the man whose discovery had started it all. In the Dawson saloons, the sourdoughs would raise their tipsy voices and sing a heartfelt tribute to the man who had changed the course of their lives:

George Carmack on Bonanza Creek went
Out to look for gold,
I wonder why, I wonder why.
Old-timers said it was no use, the water
    was too cold.
I wonder why, I wonder why.
They said that he might search that
Creek until the world did end
And not enough of gold he'd find a postage
    stamp to send.
They said the willows on the creek the
    other way would bend.
I wonder why, I wonder why.

After the second winter's dump was sluiced, in the spring of 1898, George, accompanied by the two rifle-toting Indians for protection, brought the gold into Dawson to be assayed. He found that his take, after the 5 percent tax taken by the Canadian authorities, was worth about $224,000. He could now go home.

His intention was not to leave Bonanza

Creek permanently. There remained a lot more gold to dig up. He'd simply shut the mine down for a spell. And rather than worry about what Kate and his partners were up to, he decided he'd be better off taking them with him. They could stay in Seattle while he traveled south to surprise Rose in Modesto.

But as George began making these plans, a great anxiety came over him. There were no secrets in the north. Everyone in Dawson had heard that he'd taken nearly a quarter of a million dollars' worth of gold out of his claim. Up in the Yukon, the Mounties had a steady control of the territory; he didn't worry much about robbers swooping in to steal the gold he'd mined over the past two years. It wouldn't take long, though, before the word would've spread down to Alaska, and the American district was sheer lawlessness.

Alaska, George imagined, was seething with people who'd jump at the opportunity to steal a fortune of gold. Its port cities were filled with the sort of desperadoes who wouldn't hesitate to cut a man's throat to get what they wanted. He tried to control a sudden surge of panic, but it was no use. He'd heard a story about a prospector who had washed out $30,000 worth of gold, and then became so plagued by the fear of being robbed that he shot himself. For the first time, George understood how the man's mind had skidded out of control. It was truly worrisome. He knew his gold wouldn't be out of danger until it was locked in the safe of a boat steaming to Seattle.

THIRTY-NINE

Charlie Siringo was in Vancouver in pursuit of a bunco artist who had sold a salted Mexican gold mine when he received the telegram informing him that Hiram Schell had escaped. Charlie had been working the phony-mine case for nearly six months; the trail had first led him up to Fort Steele, in British Columbia, then down to northern California, where, posing as a rich Texan, he'd discovered that the crook had used his profits from the caper to buy a sprawling ranch near an Indian village on Canada's Alberni Canal. With the sense that the end of a long chase was finally approaching, Charlie had hurried north and checked into a Vancouver hotel. In the morning, he'd board a steamer for the three-day trip up to Alberni. But tonight he'd been looking forward to sitting down in front of a beefsteak and a bottle of whiskey before tucking himself into a comfortable bed, until the clerk had handed him the telegram.

It was from McParland. The superintendent, never a man to waste words, was particularly terse even for him: Schell escaped. Apprehend.

Standing by the front desk, Charlie studied the message, poring over the three words as if they contained a hidden clue. But no further information was revealed; only a string of questions took shape.

There was no explanation of how Schell had gotten away. Or when. Or where he'd fled. Charlie had no idea if the fugitive was hiding out in Alaska or had run off to the States. For all Charlie knew, Schell might even be in Vancouver at this very moment. And what was Charlie supposed to do about the case in which he was presently engaged? Abandon it, and chase after Schell? Or would it make more sense, since he was so close, to continue on to Alberni, nab his man, and then proceed to locate Schell? Of course, by then there'd be no telling where Schell might've gone. Whatever trail he'd left would've surely grown cold. McParland's instructions were infuriatingly vague. The more Charlie thought it through, the more he began to suspect that this was deliberate. The superintendent was leaving it up to him to decide what to do next.

Charlie mulled the situation. As he did, a series of recollections passed through his memory in a flash: his elation at finally solving the puzzle behind the missing Treadwell gold; the long hunt up and down the Alaska coast in the rainbow canoe; the camp at Chieke Bay where he'd won the confidence of the two thieves; and Schell in handcuffs, the hulking bear of a man surly and defiant, vowing to break out of jail and even the score. And without Charlie's summoning it, in that same instant another image intruded: Mamie. He'd traveled through a despairing time, but in Alaska he'd managed to reach a reconciliation of sorts with all he had lost. As much as any of the events that had shaped the long case, that struggle, too, had been an indelible part.

There was no point in lingering any longer with these memories, Charlie decided as if jolted. A course of action had become clear. He turned his gaze back toward the hotel clerk. Book me a ticket to Juneau, he ordered. I want to leave as soon as possible.

Two days later, as a thin drizzle fell and the air held a warmth that confirmed the spring thaw had arrived, Charlie disembarked in Juneau. Walking down the wharf, he recognized that his predicament was troublingly similar to the one he had faced when he'd first arrived in Alaska more than three years ago. Back then he'd come to solve a theft on a island where a robbery was impossible and there were hundreds of suspects. He'd had neither a clue nor a plan. Now he had to find a resourceful escaped convict who could've vanished into the deep northern wilderness or, no less likely, hopped a steamer for Seattle. Either way, it'd be a daunting manhunt without a single lead to point him in any direction. And once again, Charlie had no well-thought-out strategy to guide him.

All he'd come up with in the course of the voyage from Vancouver was a notion to start off at the U.S. marshal's office. He knew that government lawmen dismissed private detectives as nothing but an interfering bunch of amateurs. Even if the marshal had any information, he'd likely be too wary to share it. But it was the only way Charlie could think of getting started. It'd have to do until he came up with a better idea.

As the detective trudged through the mud that covered Front Street, he couldn't help noticing how much Juneau had changed since his last visit. It was bustling with crowded restaurants and busy supply stores, the good-time music from saloons and dance halls carrying out into the streets, and everywhere he looked there were beaming stampeders, the world their oyster because they were going off to strike it rich in the Yukon gold fields. Charlie had been in Denver when he'd read with interest the first report that a ship carrying a ton of gold had arrived in Seattle. But it was while he was on his way to Gazelle, the sleepy little town in northern California where the sister of the con man who had sold the phony Mexican mine lived, that he'd read the dispatch that had left him truly stunned. It stated that a prospector by the name of George Carmack had started the stampede with his strike on the Klondike River.

Charlie read it through twice and still had trouble believing it. The last time he'd seen Carmack had been on the beach by the Dyea inlet, and the man had been dressed like some ragtag Chinook. Now the paper was saying that Siwash George was a millionaire! Well, if it was true, Charlie reckoned he wouldn't be one to begrudge Carmack his good fortune. The man had shown up in the nick of time in the stamp room at the Tread-well mine. Wasn't for Carmack, he wouldn't be able to draw his old Colt with his right hand. He still owed the man a sizable debt, only there'd be nothing he'd ever be able to do for Carmack now. It seemed that these days the squawman had everything he needed. Well, more power to him, Charlie had silently cheered after reading the news. Since then he hadn't given Carmack another thought. But being in boomtown Juneau, with the silhouettes of the Treadwell mine buildings looming across the channel, brought the whole episode racing back into his mind. Once again, Charlie felt only a surge of happiness at the thought of Carmack's incredible success.

These reminiscences quickly receded, however, as the detective approached the marshal's office. He located the small wood-frame building and strode up to the door. On the steamer, he'd prepared his speech. He'd explain that he was the Pinkerton who had originally arrested Schell and that he was determined to bring him in again. Any information the marshal had on the fugitive's whereabouts would be much appreciated. That was it, short and sweet. He'd deliver it with a brisk authority, though he was perceptive enough to know that it wouldn't serve him well if he sounded as if he were making demands. U.S. marshals were as a rule proud, even prickly sorts. If he had to talk taffy to get what he needed, he was prepared to do that, too. The only thing that mattered, he reminded himself, was seeing Schell back behind bars.

But when Charlie walked into the office, he immediately discovered that all his preparations had been unnecessary. Seated behind the desk was Deputy U.S. Marshal Jim Collins, the very man who had been present with him at Chieke Bay to make the arrests.

Was wondering if I'd ever be seeing you again, the old lawman said with a friendly grin as he shook Charlie's hand.

Gotta say, didn't expect you here, Charlie replied, silently congratulating himself on this bit of luck. In the course of the Treadwell case, he'd earned the marshal's respect. He knew he could count on his cooperation in the hunt for Schell.

Charlie pulled up a chair and Collins started in explaining how he'd come to be sitting in this office. With the whole world, or so it seemed, coming north to look for gold, he said, Washington had decided there should be four full-time deputy marshals to watch over things in the Alaska Territory. They'd pulled him off the traveling man-of-war, and he was now assigned to Juneau. Flocks of newcomers are coming off boats every day and getting into all kinds of trouble, the marshal declared. I've plenty to keep me busy.

Charlie got the marshal's drift and put a quick end to the small talk. Without further preliminaries, he asked, What can you tell me about our old friend Hiram Schell?

Not much, the marshal conceded. One day he was in the Sitka pen, the next day he was gone. Best we can figure, he bribed one of the guards. He was always bragging to the prisoners that we'd never recovered all the gold he'd taken from the mine. We know that wasn't the case, but people down in Sitka had no way of knowing he was gaffing them. Maybe he promised to make some guard rich once he got on the outside. All the guard had to do was leave the cell door open. Or maybe he just walked off when no one was looking.

Could be as simple as that. We just don't know.

Which was damn unhelpful, Charlie thought. Could mean Schell had accomplices on the outside who were hiding him. Or he might be on his own. But Charlie reckoned there was no sense in guessing. All that really mattered was that Schell was at large. Until he found Schell, the details of his escape would remain a mystery.

So Charlie tried another tack. How long has he been on the loose? he asked.

The marshal thought for a moment. Must be more than three weeks by now, he said finally.

That was not what Charlie wanted to hear. With nearly a month's head start, Schell could be sitting in an igloo up by the Arctic Circle. Or he could be on his way to New York. Or he could still be in Sitka and just keeping his head down.

Got any idea where he might've gone? Charlie asked, hoping he didn't sound too desperate.

The marshal hesitated. No, he said at last.

But, Charlie pressed.

Well, this is just a guess, mind you. But I was a crook on the run, first thing I'd want to do is get some money. And the second thing I'd want is to make sure I was among friends. That no one was gonna come sneaking up to arrest me. Only one place this part of the world where a thief could earn the cash he'd need to buy a steamer ticket, if that was what he was of a mind to do, and not have to worry about the law. It's no mystery. Seems like every cutthroat and desperado in the West has made a beeline to the same place. All Schell needed to do was join the party.

Charlie had a dozen questions, but now that the marshal was talking he figured he'd do best by not interrupting. So he was surprised when Collins paused in the midst of his monologue to throw out a question.

Ever hear of Soapy Smith? he asked.

I'm based in Denver, Charlie explained. Can't be a detective in that city without hearing tales of how Mr. Smith had things wrapped up nice and tight for a while. My boss, Superintendent McParland, told me on many occasions that Soapy was the shrewdest operator he'd ever run up against.

Well, the marshal went on, ol' Soapy Smith and his gang have taken up residence in a little boomtown up the coast. Name of Skagway.

You reckon that's where Schell is hiding out?

Might very well be, the marshal said. He'd fit in quite well with that pack of thieves. Hell, I'm sure he wouldn't be the only fugitive in the bunch.

Just up the coast, you say? Charlie said, as if thinking out loud.

Yes, the marshal agreed.

Charlie was quiet for a moment, mulling all he'd just heard. Then he asked, Someone was to go looking for Mr. Schell in Skagway, where'd be a good place to start?

The marshal didn't have to think to give an answer. Jeff's Place, he announced in an instant. That's Soapy's saloon. You hang out there long enough, more than likely you'll see every desperado west of the Mississippi come waltzing into the back room to pay homage to King Soapy.

Once again Charlie sat very still for a few moments. When he was satisfied with the plan that was forming in his mind, he spoke. I reckon I know where I'm heading then, Charlie said. Much obliged.

He got up and once again shook the marshal's hand. He was walking to the door when he turned and asked, Supposing I do find Schell in Skagway. There a marshal in town I can hand him over to?

Yes, Collins answered. Then he hesitated, as if weighing whether to say what was on his mind. I was you, he said at last, I wouldn't leave Schell in his custody.

Charlie didn't understand.

You might as well assume any marshal in Skagway is not just employed by the government, Collins explained. He's also most likely on Soapy Smith's payroll.

Good to know, said Charlie. And then with

a final wave he walked out the door.

There's an etiquette to standing at a bar. In a trail of cow towns from Dodge City to Tascosa, Charlie had come to learn how a cowpoke handles himself in a strange saloon. You plant your boots about a foot or so apart, lean forward a bit from the shoulders, and keep your eyes fixed on your glass of whiskey. You don't go looking anybody in the face or striking up a conversation. A man who pays more attention to who's in the room than to his liquor, or who starts in jawing with someone standing at the bar, is setting himself up for trouble. He's letting it be known that he's a lawman come noseying around, or maybe a flimflam artist looking for a mark. Either way, folks aren't going to take too kindly to him, and that could have some dangerous consequences. In Dodge City one time, Charlie had seen a cowboy get shot just for asking why the lady outside was feeding a couple of doves.

So two nights after his meeting with Marshal Collins, Charlie stood at the mahogany bar in Jeff's Place with his attention fixed on his glass of Canadian rye. He wasn't asking any questions, and in case someone came over to say howdy, he was prepared to ignore them.

Charlie's plan was simple enough, but it would take some time to unfold. Detective work, McParland had often lectured, requires patience, and Charlie was prepared to wait before making any inquiries about Schell. He'd hang out in the saloon for perhaps a week, keeping to himself but letting folks get used to his face. He'd worked out a cover story, the latest in a long list of fanciful biographies he'd adopted in the course of his job, and as the days passed he'd get around to sharing a bit. He'd tell people just enough so that they'd believe he was a Texas outlaw on the run. The name he'd use would be invented, too, another alias dusted off from some distant experience in his rambling life.

Once he was more or less a regular, Charlie predicted, it wouldn't be long before someone would come up nice and casual and invite him into the back room. Soapy's always looking for reliable hands, would be the pitch. So he'd share a drink with the great man himself, and if all went well, he'd maybe be offered an opportunity to do a bit of sly work. And by and by, once Charlie had won the confidence of his new friends, he'd happen to ask if anybody had seen his ol' buddy Hiram Schell. Schell had lent him some money and now that he was flush, he'd like to pay his friend back. Things might get, Charlie knew, a bit scaly; after all, he was setting out to con a passel of con men. But Charlie had been jobbing outlaws for years without getting caught. No reason to think this script wouldn't play out as written, too. And anyways, he didn't have a better idea — or, for that matter, another clue other than the name of this saloon.

Of course, there was one occurrence that could upset his carefully reasoned plan. There was always the possibility, Charlie had to concede, that Schell might belly up to the bar or mosey out of the back room and find himself staring straight into the face of the man who had busted him. That happened, Charlie knew, cover stories and aliases wouldn't do him any good. That was why he wore his Colt strapped to his hip. And he made it a point to keep his coat unbuttoned and his gun hand free. If Schell wouldn't go quietly, Charlie was prepared to shoot it out. Sure, the fugitive might have a room full of friends to back him up, but Charlie had never known a thief or a bunco man who could handle a gun. Soon as he plunked the first one, Charlie reckoned, they'd all back off.

And so Charlie settled in at the bar. But he'd taken only a few sips from his drink before all his carefully laid plans fell completely apart. He reached for his glass and, without meaning to, noticed a man down at the end of the bar. Charlie was surprised, and that was why he made his mistake. He held his glance for a moment longer than he should have. In that instant the man at the end of the bar looked up and recognized him, too.

Charlie hadn't spotted Hiram Schell. He had found a murderer.

The two of them stood alone in the dark on the Skagway wharf. As soon as Charlie had locked eyes with Bill Moore he realized it'd be best if the two of them did their catching up someplace quiet. They went back quite a ways, and there was a lot to talk over. He'd given a small nod of his head, then walked out of the bar. Moore had followed.

In the days when Charlie was a top hand, Moore had run the LX Ranch. Charlie had enjoyed working for him. In his experience, Moore was a born leader of men and one of the best cowmen in the west. But Moore was a complicated fellow; he also was prey to his larcenous heart and killer's temper. All the while he'd managed the LX, he'd been stealing cattle. Finally, he put his own brand on the stolen herd and went off to establish a ranch in New Mexico, down in the American Valley. But Moore's days as a cattle baron didn't last too long. After an argument in a saloon, he shot two men dead. Charlie knew his old boss was now on the run, with a big price on his head.

I heard you're working for the Pinkertons, Charlie, Moore began as the two stood on the wharf. He spoke in a whisper, but the night was so quiet that Charlie thought he might as well be shouting. Don't turn me in, he said with some force.

Charlie had no intention of turning in his old *compañero.* And he'd no desire to draw on him. They'd done too much together for that to be a serious possibility. But Charlie saw no reason to share that with Moore, at least not until he got the information he needed. Course, if Moore went for his gun, Charlie reckoned, he'd have no choice but to go for his, too. He was hoping, however, that Moore wouldn't be so bold. After all, Moore had witnessed the now famous shooting match at the LX when Charlie had matched Billy the Kid shot for shot. If friendship wasn't sufficient to keep things civil, Charlie hoped, then perhaps that memory would discourage Moore.

So Charlie didn't respond to Moore. He simply asked if he'd happened to run into Hiram Schell. Big bear of man with a full beard, Charlie added, trying to prod Moore's memory.

Moore thought for a moment. Lot of folks come to Soapy's place, Moore said, as if making an apology. Maybe. Sounds familiar. But I can't be sure.

Well, I need you to be sure, Bill, Charlie said, his voice turning rough.

Perhaps it was the harsh tone in Charlie's voice that caused Moore to grow anxious.

Look, he offered, I know lots of things. The sort of stuff a Pinkerton might find useful.

I'm only interested in Schell, Charlie said flatly.

But Moore went on, a man bargaining for his freedom. They're planning a robbery, he announced. A big one. A quarter of a million dollars. They're gonna rob some prospector when he takes his haul of gold to the boat to Seattle —

No interest to me, Charlie interrupted.

But Moore was nearly frantic. He couldn't stop. The way he saw it, he was trying to make a deal to save his life. He was on the run for murder and negotiating with a lawman he knew he couldn't beat in a gunfight. All he could do was play the only card he had. So he continued: Old sourdough's name is Carmack. George Carmack. A genuine Klondike millionaire.

Suddenly Charlie was all attention. What was that about Carmack? he asked.

I tell you about the robbery the Soap Gang's planning, you let me go? Deal?

Deal, Charlie agreed.

And for the next twenty minutes, Charlie listened. He heard the secret plan Carmack had devised to get his fortune out of Alaska, and then he heard Soapy Smith's scheme to thwart it.

Back in his hotel room later that night, Charlie began to think through the decision he had to make. No one had seen him talking to Moore. And even if they had, where was the harm? Just two old cowboys talking over better times. He could return to the bar tomorrow night and that would be that. Grateful that Charlie had let him go, Moore had hightailed it for tall timber. He wouldn't be coming back to Skagway for a while. Charlie could continue to hang out at Jeff's Place until either he got a line on Schell or the fugitive walked in.

Or he could warn Carmack.

He was a private detective, not a lawman, Charlie reminded himself. He only worked for people who hired him. Carmack wasn't his client. Besides, he was already on a case. It was the Pinkertons who paid his salary, bought his liquor. He had a responsibility to the agency.

Mamie, he thought silently, as if appealing to a higher judge, what would you do?

It took a while for Charlie to fall asleep. Yet he woke up early and dressed quickly. Then he hurried off to settle an old debt.

FORTY

As Soapy finalized the plans for "the great gold robbery," as it would become known in Alaska, his attention was diverted by the events surrounding a spree of shootings. On the one hand, his concern was a businessman's: The wave of killings would discourage new marks from coming to Skagway. On the other, it was personal: Soapy had reason to fear that the outraged townspeople would lynch him if the murders didn't stop.

His problems had started back in February, after a whore doped the drink of a young prospector. Andy McGrath had been sitting with one of the working girls in the Klondike Saloon, above the Peoples Theatre, a song-and-dance hall over on Holly Street. She was giggling, and that brought back happy memories; Andy hadn't heard a girl's mischievous laughter since he'd left Ohio eight months ago. The next thing he knew, though, he was feeling very wrong. He woke up lying face-down on the wooden floor. When he finally got to his feet, Andy anxiously checked his pockets. His $140 nest egg was gone.

Andy felt foolish. It was a damn steep price to pay for a few peals of naughty laughter. Quickly his embarrassment turned into a red-hot anger. There was no sign of the girl, but he saw Jake Rice, the proprietor, sitting at a table. Andy charged over and demanded that Rice find the girl who'd taken his money. His voice shook with outrage and belligerence.

Rice didn't cotton to the young man's disrespectful tone. Besides, he had no sympathy for anyone naive enough to allow himself to be gaffed by a whore, particularly when the girl was part of his stable and a chunk of the purloined $140 would wind up in his pocket. He signaled to John Fay, the bartender. In an instant Fay and a couple of the boys were all over Andy. Andy put up a fight, but there were three of them. They had done this sort of thing before and always enjoyed taking the prospectors down a peg or two. Once they had Andy on the floor, they kicked away at him. Rice coolly watched his goons punish the young man until he feared that if they kept at it any longer, the prospector would wind up dead. Enough! he ordered. So they dragged Andy out of the saloon and heaved him into the icy street.

"I will come back and settle for this," Andy managed to say as he got to his knees. The three men walked back into the theater without bothering to turn around.

Andy made his stumbling way through the street. He wasn't going anywhere in particular, but then he happened to glance through a window. There was Deputy U.S. Marshal James Rowan, who'd recently settled in Skagway from Dyea, having a late supper in an all-night restaurant. Ignoring the floods of pain caused by each new step, the prospector hurried to the marshal's table. I want to borrow your gun, he said.

Rowan studied the young man. Andy's face was badly bruised, and blood dripped steadily from a cut under his eye. Better I go with you, the marshal said after he'd finished the last bites of his meal.

Andy led the way back up to the saloon. "There's the man," he told the marshal, pointing at Fay.

The bartender shot him. The bullet hit Andy in the groin, and he fell back into a chair. He sat there stunned, a river of blood gushing out of him.

The marshal started to draw his revolver, but Fay fired first. The marshal let out a piercing scream. He'd been hit by a gut shot. As the bullets started flying about the bar, the town fireman reached for his pistol. He aimed at Fay, but he had had a few whiskeys and his bullet wounded another man in the leg. Blood splattered across the floor.

The marshal succeeded in getting to Doc

Daniel Moore's. Gut shots, though, were always a bad business, and he died on the examination table. Andy bled to death in the saloon, his body slumped in the barroom chair. In the meantime, the bartender had fled out the back door.

Fay was in a panic. He reckoned no good would come out of this. He might've been able to talk his way out of shooting the prospector, but a dead marshal was a whole different matter. People would come looking for him for sure, and he suspected they'd be carrying a rope. Fay considered going to Rice for help, but he knew Rice would give him up once he saw a mob marching up the street. Anyways, Rice might run the Klondike Saloon, but he wasn't really the boss. Rice took orders, too. There was only one way he'd have a chance of escaping from this sort of entanglement. He needed to go to the man in charge. Fay ran to Jeff's Place. Then he tucked his pistol into his belt, pulled himself together, and, after wishing himself luck, headed into the back room. His only hope was to beg Soapy for protection.

The next afternoon the church bell tolled. This was the signal for the Committee of 101 to assemble. In the days when Skagway was first established, Major John Strong, a stern former cavalryman, had come up with the notion that since "the United States in its wisdom has seen fit to enact no laws which would give Alaska any measure of local self-government," the townspeople should form a group to protect themselves. He'd organized the local citizens, an assortment of merchants and prospectors, into what he called "a committee of safety, or vigilance committee," and he'd christened the group with a name that'd been first used during the California gold rush.

The men of the Committee of 101 were vigilantes. The code of justice on the frontier was unforgiving, and they took it upon themselves to be judge, jury, and executioners. If they determined that someone had crossed the line, the punishment would be swift: They'd string the culprit up from a high tree. After a U.S. marshal had come to Skagway, though, the committee had pretty much disbanded. Only now the marshal had been shot down, so Strong rang the bell once again summoning folks to a meeting.

A crowd hurried to the church. But even before Strong convened the committee, its actions seemed a foregone conclusion. All that needed to be discussed, most people anticipated, was from which tree to string the rope.

Soapy, however, wasn't of a mind to see Fay hanged. It wasn't that he was particularly fond of the bartender. In fact, he'd no sympathy for the crime; Marshal Rowan had left a widow and an infant son, and that struck a chord in Soapy's sentimental heart. But there was an important principle to be reinforced. He wanted his gang to know that they could count on him. He'd return their loyalty with his own. When Fay asked, Soapy didn't hesitate to offer his protection. And in his shrewd, resourceful way, he quickly came up with a plan that not only would keep Fay safe but would also make it appear as if Soapy were doing the town a favor.

First, Soapy summoned a bunch of his hardest men and sent them off with Fay. No one gets near him, he ordered. You see a crowd, no discussions. Open fire.

Next, he went to the U.S. commissioner in the territory, John Smith. The commissioner, a lawyer from Oregon, was a federal appointee whose primary job was to record real estate transactions and adjudicate property disputes. But since there was no real law in Skagway, he'd often intervene in criminal matters, too.

We want to prevent a lynching, we need to act fast, Soapy earnestly told the commissioner. I want you to deputize my men. They'll make sure Fay gets on the next ship to Juneau.

Commissioner Smith didn't need to consider the suggestion. If it made sense to Soapy, it made sense to him. After all, Soapy was paying him more each month than he received from the government as salary for the entire year. He dutifully followed Soapy to where Fay had been hidden and swore in the Soap Gang thugs. Any actions they'd take to protect Fay would now be legal.

Finally, Soapy went to the Committee of 101 meeting. He let the angry crowd have their say. The discussion drifted between those who wanted to hang Fay at once and those who wanted a jury trial. It would take only minutes to reach a verdict, it was pointed out, and then the hanging could proceed. After the debate had gone on for a while, Reverend Dickey took the floor. With the fervor of an Old Testament prophet, the clergyman argued that it would not be sufficient to inflict vengeance on Fay. It was necessary to bring to justice the people truly responsible for crime in Skagway: the gang of cutthroats who controlled the town.

Soapy decided he'd heard enough. He stood and in a calm voice called for reason. Law and order must prevail if Skagway is to become a civilized community, he lectured.

Voices attempted to shout him down. "Lynch the murderer!" someone yelled. This cry incited the crowd, and the words became a chant: "Lynch the murderer! Lynch the murderer!"

Silence! Soapy thundered above the dim. When the crowd quieted, he resumed talking in his steady way. Commissioner Smith, he explained, as if it were the most normal of occurrences, has deputized twenty of my men to ensure Fay's safety.

A now familiar shout broke through his words: "Lynch the murderer!"

"My men have orders to shoot the first man who approaches," Soapy said with steady conviction. "They're all armed and the law is on their side. They will not hesitate to fire."

After that pronouncement, men began drifting out of the meeting. The next day Fay, surrounded by a cordon of the new deputies, boarded a ship for Juneau without incident. Still, it didn't set well with many in Skagway that Soapy had helped a man responsible for two cold-blooded murders get off scot-free.

A new deputy marshal, Sylvester Taylor, had been appointed and was already on Soapy's payroll when the next murder occurred. Peter Bean, a twenty-five-year-old miner from California, was found lying facedown in the snow on the White Pass Trail, near Porcupine Hill. When the body was turned over, there were powder burns on his face and a .38-caliber slug in his chest. His empty wallet had been tossed into a mound of gray snow.

Coming so soon after the double homicide, the news of Bean's shooting left people incensed. Once again, the church bell tolled and the Committee of 101 gathered. Something has got to be done, Major Strong insisted. The crowd cheered in approval.

The next day handbills were nailed to walls and doors all over Skagway.

WARNING!

A word to the wise should be sufficient! All Confidence, Bunco and Sure-thing Men, And all other objectionable characters are notified to leave Skagway and White Pass Road Immediately. And to remain away. Failure to comply with this warning will be followed by prompt action.

101.

Soapy found one of the notices nailed to the front door of his bar. He pulled it off and begin reading. By the time he finished, he was steaming. He felt as if he'd received a personal threat. Well, if they wanted a showdown, he'd give it to them. His boys would show the committee the meaning of "prompt action."

He started to issue a series of orders, telling his men to outfit themselves with rifles and shotguns, and make sure to pack extra rounds. But by the time the heavily armed men reported back, his anger had deflated. Reason had prevailed. It wouldn't do him any good to go to battle, Soapy had determined. He'd only be killing off the people whose money he was hoping to get his hands on. More than likely, he'd win the war and lose a large portion of his livelihood in the process. There had to be a better way. And as he thought it through, a shrewder strategy took shape: He'd beat them at their own game. Relishing his bit of sport, Soapy crafted a full-page notice for the newspaper.

ANNOUNCEMENT

The business interests of Skagway propose to put a stop to the lawless acts of many newcomers. We hereby summon all good citizens to a meeting at which these matters will be discussed. . . .
Jefferson R. Smith, chairman

The meeting was packed; the entire Soap Gang had reported as ordered. Soapy stood at the front of the room, and when he asked for the crowd's attention a rowdy, enthusiastic roar erupted.

We are the lawful element in town, Soapy proclaimed.

The thugs and crooks cheered.

I hereby christen our committee the Law and Order Society, he continued.

The thugs and crooks cheered even louder.

We are strong in numbers, he said. I expect the press to make full note of this. Why, tonight there are ——. Soapy paused as if to count the assembly. Then he boomed: Three hundred and seventeen law-abiding citizens gathered.

The thugs and crooks let out another cheer, enjoying their boss's joke: 317 Holly Street was the address of Jeff's Place.

The next day the gang members went through Skagway diligently tacking a new handbill to doors and walls.

ANSWER TO WARNING

The body of men styling themselves 101 are hereby notified that any overt act committed by them will be promptly met by the Law abiding Citizens of Skagway and each member and HIS PROPERTY will be held responsible for any unlawful act on their part and the law and order society consisting of 317 citizens will see that Justice is dealt out to the full extent as no Blackmailers or Vigilantes will be tolerated.

THE COMMITTEE

Implausibly, Soapy had declared that villains were heroes. It was as if he'd decreed that up was down or black was white. Yet such was his talent in convincing people that the most improbable lies were God-given truths that he might have gotten away with his brazen utterances if only the killings had come to a halt.

But the bullets continued to fly. Sam Roberts, a gambler, was returning to his cabin with his night's winnings when he was shot at point-blank range. Alexander McLain, a merchant, was robbed outside his home and then gunned down. A prospector was waylaid as he left a gambling parlor and his body tossed from the wharf into the bay. Blood ran in the streets each night.

It got so that many people were afraid to leave their homes. Full of concern, representatives of the Committee of 101 went to Dyea and appealed to the U.S. Army for help. Colonel Thomas Anderson listened, then agreed to dispatch a small squad of soldiers to Skagway.

When Soapy saw the men in blue uniforms marching through the street, he feared that his reign was over. If necessary, he'd been prepared to do battle against the storekeepers and do-gooders who made up the Committee of 101. But how would he ever be able to fight the soldiers of the U.S. Army?

At nine-forty on the night of February 15, 1898, a tremendous explosion rocked the USS *Maine* as it sat anchored in Havana Harbor. Darting flames ignited the five tons of powder stored for the battleship's big guns, and this second blast was catastrophic. As burning oil and fiery wreckage streaked the night sky with a hellish illumination, the seven-thousand-ton warship sank rapidly. Two hundred and sixty-six sailors died that night, and another eight later succumbed to their injuries.

The cause of the initial explosion was never conclusively determined, but for a Congress eager to go to war with Spain in Cuba, facts were irrelevant. They had their justification. On April 25, the United States declared war.

With a similar opportunism, Soapy seized on the war to solve his problems: He created his own army. He announced the formation of the volunteer Skagway Military Company to train soldiers to fight in the war with Spain. And he got the federal government to pay for it; under the Warren Bill, funds were authorized for volunteer units.

Appointing himself captain, Soapy wrote to William McKinley to inform the president that "it is the desire of the company to commence drilling at once, having secured the services of an ex-army officer for that purpose and we wish to know that if we may be furnished with the necessary arms, accoutrements, etc."

A secretary to the president soon responded that the White House had received the letter and "that it has been referred for the consideration of the Secretary of War." It wasn't a ringing endorsement of Soapy's army, but he was not discouraged. After all, the letter on

White House stationery was addressed to "Capt. Jeff R. Smith." Soapy had the letter framed and hung it in his bar for all to see.

By May, the newspapers were reporting that the Skagway Military Company had more than three hundred soldiers. It was an impressive force. Most of the recruits were members of the Soap Gang, veteran criminals who had been outfitted with government-issued rifles and drilled by army officers. Now they embraced military discipline. In the afternoons they marched in perfect formation, rifles at their shoulders, feet pounding in a sharp cadence, through the streets of Skagway. At their head was Soapy, their patriotic leader distinguished by a white ascot decorated with intertwined Cuban and American flags. Their loyalty to him was absolute.

Colonel Anderson decided to withdraw his soldiers back to Dyea. There no longer was a need for the U.S. Army in Skagway.

The church bell now tolled only on Sundays. The Committee of 101 was too intimidated to convene for meetings. The prospect of challenging a well-trained and well-supplied army company was terrifying.

And by the first warm days of June, Soapy had begun to realize that he commanded a militarized force capable of executing a daring gold robbery.

FORTY-ONE

George Carmack was waiting. He'd made up his mind to take his gold to Seattle, and he'd worked out a plan he was convinced would get it there safely. But until the day came to break camp and, along with his family and the two Indians, meet the steamer in St. Michael, he was determined to keep on working his claim. No sense sitting around as long as there still was gold in the ground, he told himself.

So this early June day had started out like any other on Bonanza Creek. George had spent the morning down at the bottom of his shaft, shoveling gravel into the bucket. There was no smoke in the hole; now that the weather had turned warm, the winter burnings were unnecessary. Still, after all the months of blazing fires, the harsh smell of smoke seeped from the dirt walls of the narrow space. George tried not to pay it any mind, but there was no getting around that it was an irritation. Course, that was nothing compared to his fear of a cave-in. Over on Eldorado last summer, the sides of a poorly timbered shaft had given way and some newcomer had been buried alive. George thought that'd be a damn cruel fate: finally to strike it rich, only to get suffocated by your fortune. He was glad when his last bucket had been hauled up and his shift was over. As he climbed up out of the dark hole, the strong sun hitting his face felt like a benediction. It was one of the hired hands' turn to do spadework in the shaft, and George, who liked things to run according to schedule, yelled that he'd better get a move on it. The man hurried over, but from the sour set of his face George could tell he wasn't looking forward to going underground. Not my problem, George told himself, and repeated the brusque order to get moving.

By late afternoon, George was working the sluice box. Sure, $240,000 or so was a sizable fortune, but he was determined that all the newly dug gravel also be washed before they headed back to the States, less than a month from now. When he was off in California, he wanted all his gold locked safe in a Seattle bank and not lying on his dump where anyone could grab a handful.

Sluicing gave him great satisfaction. Whenever George collected nuggets or dust from the wire matting in the dump box, he felt as if he was receiving a reward for all the hard vagabond years he'd put in up north. As a young man, he'd made choices, and each bit of gold he pocketed was his proof that he'd done the right thing. Becoming rich had made him prideful and a bit smug.

He was at the sluice box that afternoon when he saw Jim approaching. The big Indian had been down in Dawson, buying supplies and no doubt picking up more hooch for Kate. Now that they could afford it, she was drinking steadily. At first George had tried to make some sense of her behavior. As best he had it figured, she drank because she was angry, and then the liquor turned her mood even darker, so she drank more. But by now, as long as Kate left him alone, he didn't care how much she drank. Still, George could tell by the look on the Indian's face that there was trouble. He imagined Kate had really tied one on and then had gone off and done something that would require his intervention.

What's wrong, Jim? George asked wearily.

Heard in Dawson someone asking about you. Want to know how get to claim, Jim said.

George was suddenly alert. How many? he asked.

One man.

Indian? White man? A prospector?

White man. But no prospector, they say.

George had been expecting this. Ever since word had gotten out that he'd washed nearly a quarter of a million dollars' worth of gold, he'd known there might be trouble. Odds were, some desperadoes would come by and try to get their hands on it. Another two weeks, though, and his stash would've been on its way to the States. He had it all worked out. Well, he'd just have to deal with things as they were. He already kept his rifle with him at all times, even when he was down in the hole. The encouraging news was that there was only one man. Unless, of course, the stranger was riding point for the gang. Anyways, he was a good rifle shot. And if Jim and Charley got up close, they could probably hit whatever they aimed at. Let 'em come, he thought. We'll be waiting.

Get your gun, George ordered. And tell Charley, too. Go on now!

The three of them were by the sluice box when they saw the man. He was walking along the creek bank, coming up from the direction of Eldorado. And he was out in the open, not trying to keep his head down or stay close to the timberline. He was being very bold, and not for the first time George reckoned he probably wasn't alone. The rest of the gang was just waiting for the signal to come charging out of the woods. It would've made more sense, George knew, for the three of them to have spread out, to form a battle line like they'd taught him in the marines, but he didn't trust the Indians in a gunfight.

He wanted them nearby, where he could tell them what to do. George looked down the barrel of his rifle. If there was indeed only one gunman, George would make short shrift of him.

The man kept coming at a steady, brazen gait. George took aim, his finger resting on the trigger, but the man was still out of range. Another ten yards or so and he'd fire a warning shot over his head. That'd send a message.

He prepared to fire. But as he started to pull back on the trigger, he got a good look at the man's face, and lowered his rifle.

Howdy, said Charlie Siringo as he walked up to the sluice box.

George didn't answer. He was seething. It was that damn phony machine oiler from the Treadwell mine. Only thing George could imagine was that the man had heard about his good fortune and had tracked him down, hoping to get a payoff. This Davis fellow figured he'd pocket a pretty penny in return for not divulging to the authorities that the man who'd started the Yukon gold rush was an AWOL marine.

They wandered, walking and talking; without thinking about it, they kept to a trail that followed the gurgling creek. At first George had led Charlie into the cabin; the miner had figured that if he needed to pay off a blackmailer, it'd be best to do it away from the curious eyes of the hired help. But once they were inside, George had heard the most fantastic story: Davis wasn't really Davis but a Pinkerton by the name of Siringo. And he'd hadn't come to put the screws on him. He'd come to warn George that he'd been targeted by a gang of thieves. George didn't know what to believe, but he did know it'd be impossible to make any sense of all he was hearing if he remained stuck in the cabin. He couldn't breathe, let alone think. And anyways, Kate was there with her bottle. Let's go outside, he'd suggested and led the way.

Charlie was only too glad to follow. He'd slept in caves that were as open and vast as the Great Plains when compared to this pokey cabin. The squaw jabbering in Chinook between pulls on her bottle didn't help make things too hospitable, either. Carmack had ignored her. But then, Charlie had noticed, the man wasn't an Indian anymore. He dressed in proper trousers and gumshoe boots — no more caribou leggings and knee-high moccasins. Who says becoming rich don't change you? Charlie thought with a silent chuckle.

What was no laughing matter, though, was the fact that Carmack was mighty suspicious. It was durn insulting. Charlie was of a mind to wash his hands of the whole matter. He'd done what he'd needed to do, and it didn't set well with him to be thought of as a liar. Soapy Smith wanted to take this fellow's gold, well, Charlie was coming round to thinking, he was welcome to it.

But now that they were outside, it was as if leaving the confines of the tight cabin had opened George's mind up, too. As Siringo kept talking, it became clear to George that the detective, if that's who he really was, already knew a good deal about his plans. A troubling amount, actually. Siringo knew that George had met with the North-West Mounted Police. And he knew the precise route mounted police captain Zachary Taylor Wood had chosen to get his gold out of the Yukon, and then out of Alaska. As well as the very day they'd scheduled for the trip. If this Siringo was working in cahoots with a gang of thieves, it wouldn't make any sense for him to divulge this information. Why not simply use it to make your play? Why let on you knew where and when the gold would be traveling? Unless Siringo was trying to win his confidence. Maybe his plan was to double-cross Smith and make his own move. Or it could be true: Siringo had come to warn him. Years of prospecting had taught George that impossible notions sometimes turned out to be not so impossible. Either way, George reckoned, it was worrisome: Lot of folks knew how he planned to get his gold to Seattle.

The two men walked in silence for a while,

George lost in conflicting thoughts. When they reached a patch of flat ground surrounded by the stumps of several felled trees, George stopped. Why should I trust you? he blurted out, finally getting to the heart of what was bothering him.

Charlie looked him squarely in the face. "I'd be a poor excuse of a Texan, were I to double-cross the man who'd save my gun hand," he said, a stiff edge to his voice.

George considered his words. At last he spoke. Stick around for dinner. Then we'll talk, he decided.

Dinner had been bacon and beans, and Charlie had helped himself to a pull or two of the squaw's whiskey to wash it down. Now they were down by the creek bed, smoking cigars in the bright glow of the Yukon evening.

You were me, what'd you do? George asked. Supposing, that is, I were to believe you.

Charlie rankled at being called a liar in so many words. But, he reminded himself, he *had* lied to Carmack once before: He'd said his name was Davis and that he was a machine oiler. For that matter, he'd even suspected Carmack of being an accomplice in the Treadwell mine theft. So maybe now they were even.

First thing I'd do, Charlie offered, is go see your friend in the mounted police. You need to tell him that there's been a leak. He'd better come up with a new plan.

George agreed that this was the reasonable course of action. But then he went on to ask Siringo something else that he'd come to wonder about. He wanted to know the detective's plans. Now that he'd passed on the information, did Siringo intend to head off straightaway to find his fugitive?

Reckon you might need another gun, Charlie said. Think I'll keep close until your gold is on the boat and steaming to Seattle. If you don't mind, that is.

Long as I don't have to rescue you again, George said without a trace of a smile.

The next day they went to meet with Zachary Taylor Wood. The captain was a proud man: proud of being the grandson of the twelfth president of the United States, and no less proud of being an officer in the North-West Mounted Police. He felt Siringo was impugning both his own honor and that of the Mounties by asserting that the plans he had worked out with Carmack had become known to Soapy Smith.

Charlie let the man have his say, and when the Mountie was done, he asked a direct question: How else would you explain things? It seems pretty clear your secret ain't much of a secret anymore.

That set Captain Wood bristling again, but

in the end he realized he had no reasonable choice, and he picked a new route. They wouldn't take the White Pass, as they'd previously agreed. Instead they'd bring the gold over the Chilkoot and straight into Dyea. The captain would make sure a tugboat was waiting. Once the gold was on board, they'd head to Skagway, where the steamer would be anchored.

When the captain was done sharing his new plan, he abruptly turned grave. There is, of course, another problem, he began. Mr. Smith controls a large and capable force. The Skagway Military Company is under his command.

Well, George said easily, the Mounted Police are a fairly large and capable outfit, too. How about assigning a squad or two to accompany us to Skagway?

Can't, the captain said. It'd be illegal. Once you cross over the summit on the Chilkoot, the Mounted Police have no official authority. It's American territory. I'll make the trip with you. I can let it be known I'm on my way to Vancouver to meet with my superiors. No one's going to make too much fuss about one Mountie. But if word gets back to Washington that an armed squad of North-West Mounted Police came over the trail and marched into Skagway, it'll be seen as an invasion. Might even wind up starting a war between the two countries.

Well, said Charlie. I guess that's it then. The three of us against Soapy's army.

Five, George corrected. My two Indian partners will be there. They know how to shoot — a bit.

It won't come to that, the captain said confidently. There's no telling how Soapy came to hear about the original plans, if in fact he actually has. But now that they've been revised, Soapy certainly won't have any knowledge of the route or the new departure day. Everything will proceed without incident, he promised.

On the way back to Bonanza Creek, Charlie explained that while he trusted the captain, he had too much respect for Soapy Smith not to worry about an ambush. That was why he'd come up with a strategy for evening the odds a bit. There was no point in sharing his plan with the captain, he explained. The Mountie would just get all prickly again.

George listened with attention as the detective detailed his idea. When Siringo was done, he let all he'd heard run through his mind. It'd mean losing Jim and Charley and their guns for the first leg of the journey. But if they got ambushed on the Chilkoot by an army of thieves, two more rifles wouldn't do much good. Either way, it'd be a massacre. And he suspected Soapy wouldn't choose to march his army into combat so far from their home territory — and so close to the Mountie post on the summit. He'd strike closer to Skagway, where he felt safe and invincible. Siringo's plan gave them a chance to put up a good fight along the most dangerous part of the route.

Yes, George told the detective. Might work at that.

George went off to share the plan with the two Indians. They listened, and quickly agreed. Sure, George, we will do it, Jim promised. It was their gold, too, he reminded the white man. Then, without further discussion, the Indians left camp. They'd a lot to do in the two days before the day the gold would be shipped.

In Skagway two nights later, a gang member took a seat across from Soapy. They were alone at the boss's table in the back room. Yeah Mow, the handle of a hatchet sticking out from his belt, stood guard. No one dared approach.

Just got word, the spy announced with excitement. The gold's leaving on a new day. And they're taking a new route.

FORTY-TWO

Once the three men crossed the Chilkoot summit and began their descent into American territory, they went on alert. It was as if they could sense danger approaching.

Earlier on that June morning, after George had told Kate and his daughter that he'd be back to take them to the steamer in St. Michael in a day or two, they had left the camp on Bonanza Creek. It was unseasonably cold, the way it can get in the Yukon when a chilly spring seems reluctant to move on into the full promise of summer. The day was gray and foggy, too; the threat of rain hovered. But they went off without too much apprehension; after all, they were still deep in the Canadian wilderness, far from the reach of Soapy's machinations. Charlie found himself agreeing with Carmack's analysis: The Skagway Military Company wouldn't come marching over mountains and mount a charge across the Klondike River. That'd be too bold a play. They were a crew made up of gamblers, thieves, and outlaws, not frontiersmen. They'd spring their trap when they felt they had an advantage. So the three men — Charlie, George, and the captain — made their way toward the Chilkoot Trail, trying to pretend as if they were out for an early morning stroll. They walked shoulder to shoulder, while George gripped the reins of the string of packhorses that trudged behind them loaded down with a fortune in gold.

Without sharing a word or even a nod, however, they fell into a single line as soon as they started down the Chilkoot Pass and into American territory. The Mountie was in the lead, and he was primed; the latch on his shiny leather holster was now undone. Nevertheless, he was way too lackadaisical a point man for Charlie's comfort. The captain might be full of pluck, yet in the Red River Indian War Charlie had seen too many brave men recklessly steer their outfits into ambushes. Caution and vigilance were traits to be admired as much as courage, Charlie had come to learn. He'd no doubt that should it come to a gunfight, the captain would be a fierce and intrepid warrior. But Charlie feared that Wood was too dismissive of their adversary; he refused to take seriously the possibility that a motley collection of gamblers and outlaws could pose a threat to a ranking officer in the North-West Mounted Police.

Charlie had no such illusions. He was at the rear, and he was on guard. His eyes darted about, trying to spot a telltale movement in the timber or the glint of a rifle barrel protruding from a gap in a rock outcropping. His ears listened for the crunch of boots on the hard ground or the sharp snap of a branch. He wanted to advise Wood to strike a slower pace. He wanted to tell the Mountie that he wasn't invincible. Any man could stop a bullet; and, in fact, despite the morning's thick fog, the blue-and-red Mountie uniform made for an easy target. But Charlie reckoned the proud Mountie wouldn't be persuaded, so he kept his thoughts to himself and his senses tuned to every new moment.

In Skagway, Soapy reviewed his troops. He had devised the attack with a gambler's logic: Raise the stakes high enough, and the intimidated mark will fold. That was why he'd assembled his full force and had made sure they were outfitted for battle, rifles and sidearms for each man. His hope was that Carmack and the Mountie would stare at the well-armed aggressors and realize that to oppose such odds would be suicide. They'd hand over the gold without firing a shot. But if they weren't reasonable men, Soapy had sufficient firepower on hand to wipe them out in the first volley.

■ ■ ■ ■

Wedged in between the Mountie and the detective, George shared the others' silence and kept a very tight hand on the reins as he led the packhorses down the trail. His mood was subdued. He was no stranger to the Chilkoot, but he'd never studied the trail this way before. On previous treks his mind had focused on the physical challenges, the stamina and muscle he'd need to haul himself over the trunks of fallen trees and across the massive boulders that littered the path. Now he saw each new obstacle as a hiding place, a covert from which a gunman might suddenly emerge. Of all his times on the trail, trips made in the harshest of weather, days when the wind shot down from the mountaintop with a fury, when ice froze into slick, perilous sheets and the snow pounded, when rivers of oozing mud flowed, when the risk of falling off the narrow trail and flying to his death five hundred feet below brought a terror to each new step — nothing had left him as apprehensive, feeling as if he were balanced on a razor's edge, as this long journey. Then again, never before had he made the trip hauling nearly a quarter of a million dollars in gold.

Now that his men were assembled, Soapy

selected his advance force. There'd be only seven men, and their role was crucial to his plan. If they performed as instructed, his army wouldn't need to fire a shot. So he chose men who had proved themselves to him in the course of their unruly years together, in adventures in places like Creede, or Leadville, or Denver. He wanted men who enjoyed a good fight, who wouldn't retreat when bullets started to fly, who would charge into the pitch of battle. He wanted killers.

Soapy chose quickly; he'd already given the matter much deliberation. As soon as he finished, he pulled the seven hard cases off to one side and gave them their instructions. When Soapy was satisfied that each of the men understood what was expected, he sent them off.

Then he returned and addressed the remaining troops. Follow me, he ordered.

It was with a sense of genuine relief that Charlie came to the end of the Chilkoot Trail and began the walk across flat ground into Dyea. They were closer to Soapy's territory, but he no longer felt trapped. The trail had offered too many opportunities for an ambush; he'd imagined bushwhackers suddenly surrounding them at any moment. They wouldn't have had a chance. At least now at the first sign of trouble they could take cover in the forest, hunker down, and make Soapy come for them. There were only three of them, but with the trees for protection, they could put up a fight. The bastards would pay with blood if they tried to take the gold.

When the three men got closer to the Dyea beach, George saw his old cabin. No one had claimed it, and it remained abandoned, a relic of a life that had ceased to exist. It belonged to a time when he'd felt he was more of an Indian than a white man. Such sympathies no longer had the slightest sway over him. It was as if all those convictions had been affirmed by another man; which, in fact, he just might well have been, so deeply were those years buried in him. And yet, irony of ironies, here he was once again putting his faith in Jim, in Charley, in the braves who'd been his Tagish brothers. A fortune was at stake, and all he could do was hope the Indians would stick to Siringo's plan.

The skiff was waiting at the water's edge, and the tug was anchored out in the bay, just as the captain had arranged. The fact that they'd made it this far without encountering Smith or his gang had bolstered the Mountie's already brimming confidence. Wood was now certain there hadn't been a leak, and that Siringo, same as all private detectives, was a meddlesome troublemaker.

As soon as they reached the beach, the

Mountie took charge, quickly issuing a flurry of instructions. The two men should unload the bags of gold from the horses into the boat; he'd stand guard. After that was swiftly accomplished, the horses were stabled at the trading post. Then Wood told Carmack and Siringo to go aft; he'd be in the stern working the rudder.

At Wood's command, the sail was hoisted. Then they were under way.

It was just a short sail through calm waters to the tug, but George might as well have been forging his way through a howling storm. His emotions were a tempest. He kept turning his head, looking into the fog behind him, but he saw nothing. Not a trace. Where was Jim? he asked himself with an impatience that left him surprised. Charley? Where were they?

Charlie was not a man prone to worry. His view was that fretting never changed anything. You take what comes, and you deal with it as best you can. That the stiff Mountie was way too sure of himself was irksome. All that meant, though, was that Charlie would need to stay ready, keep his rifle close and his eyes peeled on the horizon. But even Charlie, a steady hand in the tightest of circumstances, couldn't stop his mind from racing with the same question that plagued

George: Where were Jim and Charley? There was no sign of the two Indians, and they were counting on them.

From the Skagway wharf, Soapy watched as his advance force pushed out into the bay. The men were crammed into what was little more than a rowboat. It was an odd vessel from which to mount an attack. Yet they were well armed, and he knew they would not hesitate to shoot to kill. If Carmack resisted, he'd discover that a rowboat could be as murderous a vessel as a man-of-war.

Now that the heavy bags of gold had been transferred from the skiff, the tug set off on a slow pace for Skagway's harbor.

Charlie stood on deck, his rifle cradled in his arms. His eyes searched the horizon, but he couldn't see very far. The fog had thrown a gray veil over the water.

Charlie reckoned that it didn't matter. The Mountie's instincts had been correct. Soapy had no notion that they were delivering the gold to the steamer. There'd be no ambush, no trap sprung. All the precautions had been unnecessary. As for the Indians, it was of no consequence that they'd let Carmack down. They weren't needed.

The Mountie stood at the prow. He was no longer on alert. He had refastened the flap on his holster. The operation had gone off precisely as he'd planned.

George, too, felt that the risk of danger had passed. He'd settled into a calmer mood. Yet he was angry and resentful. What sort of foolishness had persuaded him to rely on Jim and Charley? It was a good thing matters hadn't turned troublesome. Then he'd be in a fix. George blamed himself: He should've known better than to put his trust in a couple of Chinooks.

Charlie saw the boat coming slowly out of the fog.

Three men stood as if at attention in the prow. Each had a rifle aimed at the tug. Crouched behind them were more armed men.

Then he heard a noise carrying from a distance: a loud, mean rumble. In the next instant he was able to see through the gray haze: An army was spread in a battle line across the wharf. Every gun was aimed at the tug.

Surrender! A voice yelled from the rowboat. Follow us in to shore or we'll open fire.

Charlie was confident of his marksmanship. He knew he could hit one of the men standing up in the boat. Perhaps the Mountie

could get another. Carmack's skill was anyone's guess. But as soon they opened fire,
every gun on the wharf would start blasting.
They were three guns against an army. They
didn't stand a chance.

Wait until they get closer, Charlie instructed. The Mountie nodded in agreement.
George took aim. The three men knew that
every bullet had to count, and yet it wouldn't
matter. They would die, but they wouldn't
surrender.

A rifle shot rang out.

Charlie was confused: It came from behind
the tug. He must've been mistaken, but then
he turned and saw the flotilla. There were at
least a dozen canoes loaded with armed
Indians. Now he heard the war cries. It was a
Tagish war party. Jim and Charley had
brought the reinforcements! Just as they'd
planned.

Charlie turned back to face the gunmen.
He cupped his hands and let out one of his
old Comanche yells. It was his way of saying,
You want a fight, now you'll get it.

In the rowboat, the men stared at the swiftly
advancing canoes with astonishment. The war
cries were unnerving. With the guns on the
wharf, they still had the Indians outnum-
bered. But this was not at all what they'd
expected. They'd been counting on easy pick-

ings. Now they were in for a fight, and there was no telling who'd win. Or how many of the gang would die once the bullets started flying.

Turn back! ordered the Mountie. Or we will open fire.

Standing on the deck of the tug, the three men took aim. Three fingers pulled back on three triggers.

The rowboat turned, and headed back to shore.

By the time the tug had chugged up to the wharf, the Skagway Military Company had dispersed. Soapy, however, remained to greet the new arrivals. Welcome to Skagway, he announced without a trace of facetiousness. He was a practical man, and he was prepared to move on. Can I buy you gentlemen a drink? he asked.

The three men walked past him without saying a word.

Later that day, after the gold had been locked in the steamer's safe and George had pocketed the receipt, he decided to leave Skagway. There was no reason to stay. Besides, he had much to do at his mine in the days before he'd board a riverboat in Dawson for St. Michael, and then the steamer to Seattle.

George was not the sort who made friends easily. A prospector's vagabond life is filled with comings and goings; you learn to drift about on your own. He recognized, though, that he owed Siringo a word. He wanted to say something solemn, something heartfelt, but it was not his way. The two men stood opposite each other on the wharf.

Much obliged, he told the detective.

Glad I'd a chance to pay my debt, Charlie said.

Then George turned and headed down to the beach. The Indians were waiting in the tidal flats. Charlie went in the other direction. He walked down the long wooden wharf and on into town. He had an escaped convict to find.

FORTY-THREE

Putting his boot heels hard into the dappled gray gelding's flanks, Soapy galloped up Skagway's Broadway Avenue until he was at the head of the parade. He ignored the elected grand marshal of the Fourth of July celebration and took it upon himself to head the procession. Folks from all over the Alaska Panhandle had come to Skagway for the festivities, and in the aftermath of the failed gold robbery he was not about to pass up an opportunity to demonstrate that he was still in charge.

The long parade moved slowly along streets decorated with red, white, and blue bunting. Children ignited firecrackers. Men drank openly from whiskey bottles. The sporting ladies came out to wave their handkerchiefs at the marchers. A makeshift band had started to play. On every corner a happy crowd milled about, four or five deep.

A flag-trimmed wagon carried a wire cage holding Fitzhugh, Soapy's giant eagle, named in honor of General Fitzhugh Lee, a commander of the American troops in Cuba. Sitting next to the driver, the six-year-old son of the proprietor of one of Soapy's saloons was dressed as Uncle Sam. The troops of the Skagway Military Company, rifles at their shoulders, marched behind the wagon in orderly rows.

Upon reaching a street corner, a sergeant in the company would shout, *Fire!* In unison, the troops would raise their rifles toward the sky and let off a volley. Sitting tall in the saddle, Soapy would congratulate his troops with a grand flourish of his white hat, and the crowd would show their appreciation, too, with a burst of cheers.

It was after the third such volley, as the reports of rifle fire continued to echo, as Soapy waved his hat about and the crowd roared, that Charlie walked up to Hiram Schell and stuck the barrel of his Colt deep into the fugitive's ribs. It was a very discreet gesture, and Charlie spoke in a low voice directly into the big man's ear. You got a choice, Charlie said. Either you come along quietly, or I shoot you down right here.

In the three weeks since he'd returned to the manhunt, Charlie had grown frustrated. He'd not been able to get a lead on Schell and had come to suspect that the fugitive had most likely left Alaska. Schell could be anywhere by now, Charlie had told himself with a heavy measure of resignation. But before abandoning the search, Charlie had decided to make one more attempt. People from all over would be coming to Skagway for the day-long Fourth of July festivities. If Schell was still on the coast, Charlie reckoned, he'd be there, too. So Charlie had shuffled through the crowd, studying the faces, until he'd found his man. Reining in his excitement, he'd waited until there was another burst of gunfire and raucous cheers, and then he'd made his move.

Now Charlie had the Colt jammed against Schell and was wondering if the man would come along or if he'd have to pull the trigger. Charlie waited, and at the same time reinforced his ultimatum by pressing the gun deeper into Schell's ribs.

Schell realized it would be suicide to draw. The moment he reached for his holster, the detective would fire.

Schell turned, and as he did the detective lifted the thief's pistol. Then Schell started walking away from the parade, and Charlie followed right behind, his gun drawn.

Four days later, Schell was back in a cell in the Sitka prison, Charlie was on his way to a village on the Alberni Canal to find a man who'd salted a Mexican mine, and once again the church bell was tolling in Skagway in the middle of the afternoon. The Committee of

101 had reconvened.

For weeks the realization had been growing that there was no reason to be intimidated by Soapy or his troops. If George Carmack, a hardscrabble prospector, not a gunman, could stand up to the Skagway Military Company and walk away with his gold, then they could, too. And now the brazen daylight robbery of John Stewart had given the vigilantes a cause to rally around.

Stewart had been the perfect victim. He'd arrived in Skagway on July 8 with a poke full of Klondike gold dust and the plan to buy a steamer ticket to Vancouver Island, his home. But no sooner had he checked into the Hotel Mondamin than he'd attracted the attention of Slim-Jim Foster and John Bowers. Slim-Jim and Bowers took measure of the prospector and, after exchanging a few sly words, fell into one of their many cons: They were gold buyers for an eastern assaying company.

Why, it'd be plumb foolishness to sell your gold in Vancouver, Bowers told the prospector after introductions were made. We can get you a much better price. You'll return home a rich man. Think how happy your wife will be.

Stewart hesitated.

What's the harm in hearing our offer? Slim-Jim pressed. We can have a drink and discuss it. On us, of course.

So the two well-dressed gold buyers from

back east led the mark to Jeff Smith's Parlor. There was a round of drinks, and Stewart had his caribou poke on the table. I reckon it must be worth about three thousand dollars, said the prospector hopefully. Bowers weighed the sack in his hand. No, he corrected, you've got at least four grand worth of dust. Stewart couldn't believe his good fortune at meeting these two assayers; he'd never receive such a high price in Vancouver. Then an old sourdough came by the table. Want to make sure these eastern fellows ain't cheating you, he said; it was one prospector talking to another. He picked up the poke and hefted it in his hand. Then he dashed out a back door — with the sack of gold dust.

Stunned, Stewart chased after him. But the alleyway behind the saloon was empty. And when he went back inside, the two assayers were gone, too. No one had seen them leave. In fact, no one could even recall having seen Stewart. You sure you got the right bar? someone asked.

Stewart hurried to the marshal's office. Marshal Sylvester Taylor listened. Know the name of the man who took your gold? he demanded. No, Stewart admitted. What'd he look like? An old miner in a mackinaw, Stewart offered, feeling foolish as he said it. Lot of those in town, said the marshal. His tone was suddenly impatient. Look, the marshal said, I suggest you go back to the Klondike and find yourself another poke full of gold. Nothing more I can do, he concluded curtly. The marshal, after all, was taking Soapy's money. He'd no intention of solving a crime that he knew would lead back to the Soap Gang.

Reeling, a year's hard work gone in an instant, Stewart returned to the hotel. He was bereft, a man who had suffered an inconsolable loss. The news quickly spread around town. Hearing his story, the towns-people found it hard not to be affected. And soon the church bell was ringing to summon the 101 vigilantes.

They decided to send a group to meet with Soapy. Judge Sehlbrede, a patrician gentle-man with bushy white muttonchops who may or may not have been a jurist in his native Ohio, was the spokesman. We insist you get your men to return Stewart's poke, Sehlbrede demanded.

Soapy bristled. If any money was lost, the miner lost it in a fair game of chance, Soapy said evenly. He thought that would put an end to the matter.

We insist you arrange for the return of the man's gold, Sehlbrede repeated.

Now Soapy turned angry. It was infuriating that these men thought they could walk into his saloon and give him orders. How dare they question his authority? Yet in the next moment, he asked himself if it would be good business to provoke a confrontation with the committee. Especially if he were to lose. He, too, remembered how his troops had turned and run during the aborted gold robbery. His reputation could not withstand another defeat.

Give me until four this afternoon, he offered. Maybe I'll be able to make amends.

But as soon as Sehlbrede and his group left, Soapy regretted that he had hinted at a compromise. His failure to act defiant would be viewed by the vigilantes as evidence of his weakness. To retain power, he'd need iron in his resolve. It was the committee that must back down, not Soapy Smith.

His gang, though, was apprehensive. Con men had a feel for when the mark was poised to strike back; and vengeance, experience had taught them, could unleash dangerous passions. So Old Man Tripp — who, after all, had been with Soapy through a lot of sticky situations — offered his friend a bit of prudent advice. "People are making such a stink about the job, it would be wise to give the stuff up," he suggested.

Soapy was in no mood to take anyone's counsel. He was beyond engaging the problem with his customary reason. He felt threatened, and that made him aggressive. In a voice loud enough for the entire bar to hear, he shot back at Tripp, "I'll cut the ears off the first man who makes a move to give it back."

And the four o'clock deadline passed.

Soapy was drinking. A bottle of rye and a glass were routine centerpieces on his table in the back room, but Soapy rarely took more than a few sips. The liquor was a gambler's ploy; he'd keep his head clear while others drank. But tonight he needed to drink. His instincts were telling him to run, to leave Skagway just as he'd hightailed it out of Creede and Denver and a dozen other western cow towns. Only now he was in Alaska, at the end of the world, and there was nowhere else to run. This was his last chance. For himself; for Mary; for their future. So he drank, and hoped to find the courage to do what needed to be done.

After the deadline had expired, the Committee of 101 had called a meeting in Sylvester Hall for that evening. People came out in angry droves. At first the speakers demanded "justice for John Stewart." But then Judge Sehlbrede jumped to his feet and declared that the time had come to form a posse to arrest Soapy and his gang. The hall shook with cheers so loud that it seemed as if the log walls would come tumbling down. And as the fiery speeches went on, more and more people continued to arrive. They tried to wedge their way in, but there was no room. At last the vigilantes decided to move the assembly down the street, to the wharf. They would hold their meeting out in the open where the whole town could gather.

Sitting in his back room, Soapy received reports throughout the evening from his spies. And he kept on drinking. At nine P.M., after the crowd had surged onto the wharf, a note arrived from Billy Saportas, the reporter who was covering the meeting for both the *Daily Alaskan* and Soapy Smith: "The crowd is angry. If you want to do anything, do it quick."

Soapy considered the information. There was a stillness in the room; all eyes were focused on Soapy as he struggled to come up with a plan. In the end, it was clear to him that he'd the same two choices it always came down to when things in a town turned bad: He could run or he could fight. He drained his glass, stuffed the note into his pocket, and vowed, "I'll drive the bastards into the bay."

Soapy walked with quick, purposeful strides down Holly Street, on his way to the wharf. He had a derringer up his sleeve, an army Colt tucked in his belt, and a .44–40 Winchester leaning against his right shoulder.

His mind was set. There was no turning back.

A pack of his men followed behind him. But they kept back a good distance. Their boss's dark mood scared them.

Soapy turned south onto State Street, and

into a crowd blocking the way to the wharf. Without breaking his pace, Soapy headed straight toward the mob. "Chase yourselves home to bed!" he bellowed. They parted to let him through. No one dared to speak, or even to look him in the eye.

He continued down the block. His old friend John Clancy, with his wife and son, the six-year-old who had dressed as Uncle Sam for the parade, were waiting there to stop him. They hoped to make Soapy listen to reason.

Soapy pulled the Colt from his belt and waved it at Clancy. "Johnny," he warned, "you'd better leave me alone."

Clancy had no doubt that Soapy, fired up as he was, would shoot him. "You want to get yourself killed, go ahead," Clancy said with frustration. His wife began to cry.

Soapy paid them no mind. He continued on.

He reached the dock. He could see the throng at the end of the wharf. He headed straight toward the crowd. He wanted to put an end to this once and for all.

Four men blocked the way.

"You can't go down there, Smith," barked Frank Reid.

Soapy knew Reid. He'd come north after shooting a neighbor back in Oregon, and had worked as a bartender in a tent saloon and as a surveyor. Now Reid had signed on with the

Committee of 101. "Damn you, Reid," Soapy cursed.

Soapy advanced toward Reid. The two men stood close to each other, only an arm's length apart. Not a word was spoken as they waited to see who would make the first move.

Then Soapy yelled, "I should've got rid of you months ago."

At the same moment, he brought the Winchester down off his shoulder. He used it as a club, slamming the rifle barrel into Reid's arm. Reid grabbed the muzzle with his left hand, and with his free hand he drew a .38 from his pocket.

"My God, don't shoot!" screamed Soapy.

Reid pulled the trigger. The hammer fell with a distinct click, but there was no explosion. The cartridge had been faulty.

With that reprieve, in a single moment that seemed to stretch on forever, Soapy jerked the rifle from Reid's hand, and as he pulled the trigger, Reid fired, too. Two shots exploded, but they sounded as if they were one.

Soapy's bullet smashed into Reid's groin. Reid's hit Soapy in the arm.

But the two men were still on their feet, still firing, still right on top of each other. Gun barrels flashed, once, twice, three times. The noises were rapid and large.

All at once there was silence. Reid had fallen facedown, breathing but with blood and life itself rushing from him. Soapy was on his back surrounded by a spreading circle of blood, a bullet in his heart. The king of Skagway was dead.

He lay there all night, no one daring to touch his body. It was as if the town could not bring itself to believe what had happened. Finally, just before noon old Ed Peoples, the undertaker, came by with a wagon and hauled him away.

With Soapy's death, the gang knew their freewheeling time in Skagway was over. The rubes had reclaimed control. The thieves grabbed whatever money they could, and went on the run.

The vigilantes came after them. Racing through the streets, committee members called on everyone to join the manhunt. Brandishing Winchesters, pistols, and coils of hanging rope, a mob fanned out.

The hunting was easy. Skagway was blocked by a wall of mountains on one side and endless water on the other. The Soap Gang was trapped.

Reverend Bowers and Slim-Jim were caught as they slinked through the tall timber on the way to the White Pass Trail. Old Man Tripp lived on berries in a forest outside town for two long days before he decided he had endured enough deprivation. "We should have been hanged twenty years ago," he conceded to one of the boys before returning to Skagway to take his chances. The vigilantes arrested Tripp as he was devouring the last bites of a large restaurant meal with great satisfaction. Marshal Taylor was pulled from underneath his bed.

Within days the jail was packed with gang members. There were so many arrests that the committee had to put new prisoners in city hall. When that was full, suspects were wedged into the second-floor space above Burkhard's hardware store.

And now the town demanded justice. "Hang them! Hang the whole gang!" nearly one thousand people screamed as they converged on the makeshift jails. People were waving ropes. Many were drinking. The situation was out of control. Violence seemed inevitable.

John Tanner, the new deputy marshal, who had been appointed by the authorities in Juneau after Taylor's arrest, went out to face them down. "Let law and order rule," he yelled at the crowd as he cocked his Winchester. "You want to hang someone, you'll have to hang me, too!"

His courage was remarkable. And no one doubted his resolve. The crowd continued to mill about for a while, but his grit had dulled their mood. Soon they dispersed. By the week's end, the ringleaders of the Soap Gang had been sent to Sitka to stand trial. The rest were put on steamers bound for Seattle. You return to Alaska, they were told, you'll be sorry you did.

As his men were rounded up, Soapy was buried. Only five people followed the cart with Soapy's coffin to the overgrown field outside town. There were three of the lawyers who had worked on his many businesses, his mistress, and a member of the vigilante committee who wanted to make sure this wasn't one last trick and that Soapy was truly dead. "The way of the transgressors is hard," Reverend Sinclair reminded the mourners as the body was lowered into a small, stony grave.

Soapy hadn't been buried for more than a month before people in Denver were lining up to pay a nickel to view a wax impression of Soapy's face that had been molded in the mortuary. After Denver, the promoters took the relic from town to town across the West. Paying customers pushed and shoved and elbowed their way to get a good view. The death mask was a fake, but no doubt this detail wouldn't have troubled Soapy at all.

■ ■ ■ ■

EPILOGUE: AFTER THE GOLD RUSH

■ ■ ■ ■

Mary wanted proof. She refused to believe that her husband had been killed. Over the years, there had been dozen of reports of Soapy Smith's death. He'd perished in Klondike avalanches, stormy shipwrecks, barroom gunfights — and all of these accounts had turned out to be tall tales. "Never believe I'm dead until you see me in the morgue," Soapy had written her only weeks before she'd read the article in the St. Louis newspaper detailing the fatal shooting on the Skagway wharf. So Mary had paid it no mind. But as days passed without a letter from her husband, she began to worry. By the end of the month, his silence had become a torment. Mary decided to go to Skagway.

Accompanied by eleven-year-old Jeff Jr., she arrived in Skagway in August. Wearing a crepe bonnet with a veil that reached down her back, Mary wandered about the town asking questions. She was a polite woman and comported herself with a prim reserve.

People would remark that she was nothing like her husband. They were very solicitous.

It didn't take Mary long to establish that Soapy was dead. Dressed in widow's black, she and the boy walked through the town to the rocky hill where her husband was buried. Mary stood by Soapy's grave for over an hour, her head bowed. She didn't cry. She didn't say a word. She was lost in the rush of memories, a marriage of joys and disappointments. She was also deeply hurt. Without ever asking, she'd learned that her husband had been living with another woman. Had Soapy's love for her, for their family, been one more false pledge in a life built out of illusions? Now she would never know. All Mary knew with any certainty was that the betrayal left a coldness in her heart as piercing as her husband's death.

The money was gone, too. She met with one courteous lawyer after another. She appealed to John Clancy, the friend and partner who'd been appointed executor of Soapy's estate. She confronted the men who now ran the saloons and dance halls that had previously belonged to Soapy. Each of them offered a version of the same vague and perplexing explanation: Your husband unfortunately had a gambler's sense of economy. He spent all he earned.

But what about the businesses, the real estate? Mary demanded, her outrage building

612

each time she found herself asking the same obvious questions. There must be something. A deed? A mortgage? A bill of sale?

Time after time, the responses were apologetic yet adamant. Searches of the town records have been conducted, the men told her. Not a single document confirming either your husband's ownership or his interest in any business has been found. We'd like to be more helpful, Mrs. Smith, but without the necessary legal papers, our hands are tied.

But there must've been a bank account? Or cash? He was sending me money every month, Mary would challenge.

No one knew anything. But finally John Clancy offered some modestly encouraging news. It seemed that, yes, $148.60 had been discovered in her husband's room.

By law, that money's mine, Mary declared emphatically. As soon as she blurted it out, she realized she must've sounded terribly greedy. But she'd used her savings to buy the two steamer tickets to Alaska. She was concerned that she had no way to pay for the trip back home.

Yes, Clancy agreed, the money was rightfully hers. However, the costs for the funeral, the inquest, the autopsy, and probate had amounted to $191. The town had claimed the $148 in cash and then had ordered the sale of Soapy's personal property to cover the remaining $42.40.

In the end, Dynamite Johnny, the steamship captain Soapy had stood with against a mutinous crew, offered his assistance. He gave Mary and the boy free passage on his ship to Seattle. She left Skagway without saying any good-byes.

As the ship bounced through the Pacific waves, Mary, dressed for deep mourning, stood by the rail. She was a small, pale woman, and the boy was by his mother's side holding her hand. He sensed her despair, and tried to get her to talk. But Mary was locked in her own thoughts. She stared out at the vast gray expanse of ocean as if to wonder whether all the seas on the planet would be sufficient to wash away the lies that had so soiled her life.

It was raining money. One after another, half-dollar coins flew out of the fifth-story hotel window. Coins bounced on the sidewalk and rolled clanging into the street. All at once streetcars came to a screeching halt, and the passengers and even the conductors jumped off to scramble after the loose change. Word spread quickly through downtown Seattle, and people flocked to the sidewalk outside the hotel. It was pandemonium. And the money kept raining down.

Tagish Charley was enjoying himself. Sitting in the hotel room with Jim and Kate, the three of them happily passing a bottle around, it had occurred to him that it would be a lark to see the white men fight over something as meaningless as money. Besides, he'd more than he needed; why not give it away? So he'd summoned the bellboy and handed him $500. Get me half-dollars, he'd instructed. And more whiskey.

When the bewildered bellboy returned from the bank with the one thousand coins, the Indian began tossing them out the window. Kate and Jim joined in, too. The three of them were pouring money down on Seattle when the police arrived. They would've been arrested for disturbing the peace if George had not returned in time from the meeting with the lawyer he'd hired to make his long-standing AWOL arrest warrant disappear. Only after offering profuse apologies did George manage to persuade the police to overlook the Indians' odd behavior.

The next time, however, George was not in town to intervene. He had traveled to northern Washington for a few days to inspect a mining property another new lawyer had suggested as an investment. Kate remained in Seattle with Jim and Charley, and they grew bored. There was nothing to do in the hectic, noisy city but drink whiskey. Inevitably, things got out of hand. The *Seattle Post-Intelligencer* reported:

Mrs. George W. Carmack, the Indian wife

of the discoverer of the Klondike, slept last night in the city jail, charged with being drunk and disorderly and disturbing the peace of the city of Seattle. Under the same roof in the men's ward Skookum Jim, her brother, found lodgings as a plain drunk. So much for the debasing tendencies of great wealth and the firewater of the white man. . . .

Domestic happiness has not been the lot of the Carmack family or its collateral branches since the wealthy squaw man and his relations came down from the north a few months ago.

George bailed them out, but he was furious. Why did I ever get involved with these Chinooks? he reprimanded himself. Now that he was wealthy and respected, a man with lawyers, bank accounts, and investments, he refused to remember that his life had ever been lived another way.

It had been George's intention to leave the Indians in Seattle while he went to California for his long-awaited reunion with Rose. He now realized that this was not possible. There was no telling what would happen if they were left on their own.

He told Jim and Charley that they would need to return at once to the Klondike. They were glad to go. They'd had enough of Seattle. They missed vast spaces and solemn

quiet. They had no connection to this unnatural world. If this is what gold bought,
then they were only too glad to throw their
money out the window.

George took Kate and their daughter to his
sister's ranch. He'd anticipated his return,
he'd imagined all the things he would say to
Rose, but the reunion turned out to be a
disappointment. He'd been away for too long.
What had once bound them together no
longer existed. They were strangers to each
other.

Kate's behavior was no better in Modesto
than it was in Seattle. She would disappear
for days, only to be brought back to the ranch
reeking of alcohol by a chagrined neighbor.

George had no sympathy. He was repulsed.
Misery was all they shared. When it came
time to return to his mine, he announced that
he'd be traveling to the Yukon alone. Kate
could stay with Rose if she wanted.

George was in Dawson, now a booming
gold rush city, when he met Marguerite
Laimee. Only twenty-six, Marguerite had
spent some time in the silver-mining camps
in Coeur d'Alene, Idaho, and then had
moved on to the gold fields in South Africa.
From there, a man she'd met had taken her
to Sydney, Australia. When that didn't work
out, she'd decided to head to the Klondike.
She'd opened a cigar store in Dawson, but
also spent a good deal of time on the second

floor of the Green Tree Hotel, where a group of young women entertained the miners.

George didn't care about Marguerite's past. He liked the way she tilted her head back when she laughed. He appreciated the way her silk dress curved around her torso. He thought she was the sort of woman who would look good on the arm of a middle-aged millionaire. Marguerite thought so, too. When George asked her to marry him, she accepted.

He wrote to Rose. He wanted his sister to tell Kate he wouldn't be coming back. "I can't ever live with Kate again . . . I will send her some money," he explained. And that was that. After all, they weren't, he pointed out, officially married.

George and Marguerite's union was joyful and prosperous. They settled into a twelve-room white-frame house in Seattle with a garage in back for his kerosene-burning Mobile Steamer. He was one of the first men in Seattle to own an automobile, and he was very proud of the vehicle. Marguerite was a good businesswoman, and she directed her husband's money into real estate. He owned office buildings, apartment houses, and hotels. He grew fat; the once-skinny prospector weighed well over two hundred pounds. With the passing of the years, his fortune multiplied, too.

Yet George could never stop looking for

gold. He worked several claims in California, on the western slope of the Sierra Nevadas, and in the Cascade Mountains east of Seattle. "I am convinced that there are enormous gold deposits in the Cascades and gold will be found when somebody with nerve enough to dig deep goes after it," he told a reporter. Marguerite was not as optimistic. "Lovie, stop spending your money on the mine or we'll go broke," she chided.

George paid her no mind. He was determined to find another mother lode. He'd all the money he needed, but he nevertheless spent the last decades of his life attempting to re-create the exalting moment of discovery he'd experienced as a young man on Bonanza Creek. He kept trying, but he never succeeded. When he died at sixty-two, he was working a new claim.

Charlie Siringo found the man who'd sold the phony Mexican mine, and then hit the trail for other adventures. He spent months posing as an outlaw in Hole-in-the-Wall, Wyoming, while attempting to track down Butch Cassidy and the Sundance Kid. He went after Kid Curry, the outlaw who'd robbed the Union Pacific. He spent eight months in the hills of Kentucky questioning moonshiners about the whereabouts of the kidnapped son of a Philadelphia millionaire.

He had lots of cases, and along the way

there were women, too. Charlie tried to put Mamie behind him. He married Lillie in Denver, and they had a son. But within a year or so, the mother and child went off to California, and he never saw her again. On a case up in Oregon, Charlie met Grace. They married, and she came to live with him on the ranch he'd purchased in New Mexico. But this didn't work out, either. He headed off to South Dakota on an investigation, and when he returned to Santa Fe, Grace was gone.

Back in the warm sunshine of his Sunny Slope Ranch, spending his days riding Rowdy, his favorite saddle stallion, Charlie got to thinking. There was just no point in trying to re-create what he'd experienced with Mamie, his child bride. Why search for something that was not lost, he told himself. So he settled in comfortably with the memories of their shared life. In that way, his past would be his future.

Now that his mustache had turned white, Charlie found that he was rethinking his youthful cowboying days, too. When he'd signed on with the Pinkertons, he'd done so in part because the West had been won. An era was over. He'd needed to move on with the changing times. But after twenty-two years as a detective, chasing all sorts of disreputable types, after he'd traveled around a new industrialized America, Charlie was no longer so sure. He'd come to believe it had been a mistake to break faith with the past. Courage, self-reliance, and backbreaking work were the cowboy way. A firmness of character and a boldness of vision had tamed the West. If America was to succeed in this new century, it would do well to reconnect to this heritage.

So when he retired from detective work, Charlie sat down to write. He told stories that re-created a time in the West when men faced impossible odds and yet persevered. He wrote about heroes and villains. And when Charlie was in his mid-sixties, Hollywood discovered him.

William S. Hart, who had made his reputation performing Shakespeare on the New York stage, had moved to Los Angeles in 1914 and helped make cowboy films enormously popular. He was the tall, chiseled hero who rode into town with his Colt strapped on, the man audiences knew they could count on to set things right. He played on-screen a version of the life Charlie Siringo had lived. After seeing a few of his films, Charlie wrote him a fan letter. Hart, who admired Charlie's books, wrote back and asked if they might meet.

That was how Charlie wound up advising Hart on the production of *Tumbleweeds*. It was a film about the Oklahoma Land Rush of 1893, and Charlie had lived in nearby

Caldwell when it was a wide-open cow town. He was glad to help. To his delight, he even got to work as an extra.

At sixty-eight, his back was still ramrod straight as he sat tall in the saddle, a bandanna knotted around his neck, his white broad-brimmed hat firm on his head, and his big Colt in the holster at his hip. When the camera started rolling, Charlie gave his horse some spur and galloped off into the distance, the last American cowboy.

And what of Ed Schieffelin, the millionaire prospector who'd commissioned his own steamship to take him up the broad Yukon River years before Carmack or any of the stampeders? What had become of him after he'd grown discouraged and decided that there was no gold up in the frozen north?

Schieffelin returned to the States, but he never gave up prospecting. He was in the forests of Oregon when the discovery was made on Bonanza Creek. Some men might've cursed their luck after hearing the news, but not Schieffelin. He kept on panning.

The world was heading to the Yukon, but he stayed in Oregon. He was sure he was on to something. And one morning as he washed off his gravel, he saw that it was laced with bright gold. After all the years of searching, he'd found the mother lode. He rushed back to his cabin, eager to get into town to file his claim. As he reached his door, Schieffelin suddenly grabbed his chest; and then he collapsed. His heart had failed, and he was dead.

Some folks said it was a tragedy, to die like that just when he'd struck it rich. But the old sourdoughs knew better. Schieffelin had died a happy man, and, after all, there weren't many prospectors you could say that about.

A NOTE ON SOURCES

Deep into the rich unfolding story in Larry McMurtry's *Streets of Laredo,* the sequel to his incomparable *Lonesome Dove,* there's a small moment when Woodrow Call, the dour former Texas Ranger who personifies the heroism and grit of the men who civilized the Wild West, pays a visit on a prosperous cattle rancher, Charlie Goodnight. McMurtry writes:

Call had been inside the Goodnights' house just once, to visit them. He had not paid much attention to the books, but Goodnight had one that had just come in the mail a few days before. It was called *A Texas Cowboy; or, Fifteen Years on the Hurricane Deck of a Spanish Pony* — on its cover, it had a picture of a man sitting on a pony that was clearly not Spanish. The book was by Charlie Siringo, a kind of ne'er-do-well who had cowboyed a little and rangered a little, while gambling and drinking steadily, at least in the years when Call had been aware of him.

It was a surprise that such a man had written a book, but there it was.

"I want you to read it and tell me if you think there's anything true in it," Goodnight said. "I think it's all yarns, myself."

Call read the book and agreed with Goodnight. It was all yarns, but what else would anyone expect from a braggart like Siringo?

Now, *Streets of Laredo* is a novel. Call and Goodnight (at least as he appears in this book; there was, indeed, an early Texas cattle baron by that name) are fictional characters; that they live and breathe on the page with such an affecting complexity is a tribute to McMurtry's genius. And this exchange is only a brief aside, a quick diversion from the gallop of the novel's narrative. Further, the record demonstrates that Call had it wrong, at least about a couple of things: Siringo never was a Texas Ranger, and he wasn't much of a gambler, either. Nevertheless, I read this passage with some concern. It is a stinging indictment of the veracity of Charlie Siringo and his books (especially if one supposes that the person going out of his narrative way to do the condemning isn't a fictive character but, rather, the best living writer about the American West). It's something an author setting off to write a true story centered around Siringo had better keep in mind.

And it wasn't only Charlie Siringo's truthfulness, I quickly discovered as I began to mull the book that would become *The Floor of Heaven,* that provoked concerns. Another of the main actors whose story is central to my tale is also brought to task by a reliable judge. Jeff Smith, the great-grandson of Soapy Smith, has written an exhaustive biography of his ancestor that is always proud and loving, and often exculpatory. Yet even he has to throw up his hands at one convoluted point in his history and concede, "The thing about that story, though, is that not only was it likely true; it is quite likely also untrue, or at least in part." That's how it is with Soapy: His version of events — in remarks to friends or reporters, diaries, letters to his wife — is unashamedly a very subjective stew. The truth is whatever serves him best at the time. The con man's persuasive malarkey that allowed him without compunction to pass off McGinty as a genuine archaeological find and to set up a telegraph office before telegraph lines had been strung ran deep.

Then there's George Carmack. Prior to his momentous discovery on Bonanza Creek, many of his fellow prospectors had taken to calling him "Lying George." And even after his success, a few, such as the understandably bitter Robert Henderson, never abandoned the pejorative. Carmack's reputation suggested that there might be a problem for a nonfiction author trying to get at what actually happended in 1896 along the tributaries of the Klondike River. Whom should one believe? While there's *My Experiences in the Yukon,* Carmack's self-published first-person account of his find and the events leading up to it, there are also several revisionist tellings of the story. For example, in 1949 Jennie Mae Moyer published a pamphlet *(Early Days at Caribou Crossing and the Discovery of Gold on the Klondike)* that was a transcription of another take on the events, one delivered as a lecture in the waiting room of the White Pass and Yukon Railway Station at Carcross, in the Yukon Territory. There seventy-three-year-old Patsy Henderson, Tagish Charley's brother, had insisted that it was Charley who should be credited with the find that ignited the stampede to the Yukon. According to this angry account, the white man is once again the usurper of something that by right belonged to an Indian.

Clearly, anyone setting off to tell a true story about the lives and times of these three men would need to make his way through a deep and murky historical swamp. He'd face the genuine danger — "probability" is undoubtedly more accurate — that he'd soon be knee-deep in a morass of fanciful yarns, self-serving fabrications, and, too often, blatant lies. To write a factual account, he'd need to tread gingerly through some rough historical country. No source — not even a first-person account, or contemporaneous newspaper articles, or, for that matter, an article in a scholarly journal — could be accepted at face value. For example, there are at least six accounts of Soapy's attempt to rob the gold shipment protected by Captain Zachary Taylor Wood of the North-West Mounted Police. There's a telling in Reverend Robert Dickey's *Gold Fever,* a contemporaneous report rediscovered in 1997 by the resourceful Klondike Press; another mention in the reverend's diaries now at the Yukon Archives in Whitehorse, Alaska; a 1983 article by G. S. Howard in the *Quarterly,* published by the Royal Canadian Mounted Police; a passing reference in *Forty Years in Canada,* the 1915 memoir by Wood's boss, Colonel Samuel Steele; a fast-paced account in a 1957 edition of the magazine *Fury: Exciting Adventures for Men;* and several oblique references in the papers of the Pinkerton National Detective Agency stored at the Library of Congress. Significantly, each of these "true" accounts offers a conflicting version of events.

This is not to say, however, that all these epistemological problems took me by surprise. I knew what I was getting into: Yarns and tall tales are the stuff that has helped keep the Wild West and the far north alive in our imagination. In fact, these sources were my inspiration, too: I hoped to pay tribute to this proudly inflated yet iconic heritage.

I wanted to write a character-driven story about the intrepid men who traveled from one newly civilized frontier to a place that remained excitingly dangerous, a fierce and lawless land. I wanted to tell a story about people so squeezed by the economic hardships of the times that they were willing to do or try just about anything to fill their lives with the prospect of something better. I wanted to write about the heroes, villains, and dreamers who joined the great stampede to the frozen north. I wanted to capture the boldness, self-reliance, and tenacity of the men and women who helped shape a still vibrant strand in the American character. I wanted to tell an engaging tale that contained both high drama and a perplexing mystery. And I wanted to write a true story, to boot.

So, I read. I made my way through piles and piles of books, articles, pamphlets, and monographs. Spreading across my long, light-filled writing room were, to give only a few examples, such diverse mountains of knowledge as scientific treatises on gold mining and metallurgy; tales and histories of the Yukon gold rush; photocopies of 1890s newspaper articles from Denver, Skagway, and Juneau;

collected pioneer letters and diaries; and first-person reports of cattle drives up the Chisholm Trail. I gave myself an extensive education — and I knew I was only skimming the surface. I also traveled, going to Matagorda County, Texas, then up along the Alaska Panhandle and into the Yukon Territory; and I even made a quick jaunt up I-95 from my home in Connecticut to Yale University, where the Beinecke Library holds an extensive collection of court records, photographs, and letters involving Charlie Siringo (a treasure trove whose location is not so surprising as it might seem when one considers that Howard R. Lamar, a former president of Yale, is the author of the well-researched and readable *Charlie Siringo's West,* published by the University of New Mexico Press in 2005).

Once I'd completed these preliminary researches, after I'd seen with my own eyes many of the places I'd be writing about, I sat down to map out the narrative architecture of this book. I was determined to make this a factual account, but I also had no plans (or, I admit, the abilities or the expertise) to make this a scholarly historian's tome; I am, after all, a journalist by training and inclination.

I have tried to establish myself, with my previous eight nonfiction books, as a storyteller. So, I would need to make choices. I would need to make judgments about which versions of the past made the most sense to me, which seemed the most reliable. I didn't want to disrupt the flow of the large story I was offering up to my readers with a litany of caveats squawking that while one authority says this is what happened, another source begs (or, more often, insists) to differ.

Further, I wanted to tell a fast-paced story and to make my characters come alive in the reader's mind. I wanted to share what they were thinking and feeling with, I concede, a novelist's immediacy. I wanted the reader to be involved with Siringo as he tried to solve the mystery of the stolen gold; with Carmack as he dipped his pan wishfully into the waters of Bonanza Creek or struggled through a brutal Alaskan winter; with a down-and-out Soapy as he struggled to find the will to bounce back with a vengeance. And, again, I wanted it all to be true.

No doubt about it, I was setting out to make my way across a narrow literary tight-rope. It would be easy (and tempting!) to take a false step. So I knew that the only way I could keep my authorial balance would be to set some rules. Let me share them.

When dialogue appears in quotes, these are words that can be directly attributed to an actor in this drama. They are taken from either one of the principal's own writings — books, letters, diaries — or a contemporaneous newspaper or literary account. For example, when Soapy Smith first sets up his keister in Denver, I introduce this event with a long monologue spoken by the con man. The words are not a writer's invention. My source was George T. Buffum, a witness to the occasion who then set it down on paper (*Smith of Bear City and Other Frontier Sketches,* Grafton Press, New York, 1906).

When I describe what someone in this story is thinking or feeling, these are thoughts and emotions that were first reported by the individual. For example, Siringo's whirlwind courtship of Mamie and his devastation after her death are poignantly detailed in his own books (*Riata and Spurs: The Story of a Lifetime Spent in the Saddle as Cowboy and Detective,* Houghton Mifflin Company, Boston, 1927, and *A Cowboy Detective: A True Story of Twenty-two Years with a World-Famous Detective Agency,* W. B. Conkey Company, Chicago, 1912). When I share George Carmack's thoughts as he heads over the Chilkoot Pass or mourns a lost love, these are ruminations I found in his letters and diaries that are now stored in five large boxes at the University of Washington or from his self-published pamphlet describing his prospecting days.

When a location or an incident is described in this story, the details are grounded in my research. For example: Siringo's own amazed description of the Treadwell mine on Douglas Island in *A Cowboy Detective* was further fleshed out by my reading of a 1902 tour of the mine reported by Charles Palanche in volume 34 of the *American Geologist* and the observations of the members of the Harriman Alaska Expedition, in a book of the same name (Doubleday Page, New York, 1904); my description of the Panic of 1893 was informed by my readings in at least a dozen sources, but most significantly Richard Timberlake's essay in *Business Cycles and Depressions* (Garland Publishing, 1997); and the details of Carmack's experiences as a sheepherder were also shaped by William Douglass's *Sheepherders of the American West* (University of Nevada, 1986).

Yet, as I have previously stated, this is not an academic work. I set out to tell a story, to write a narrative history. Therefore, I don't feel it would serve much heuristic purpose to list the hundreds of books and articles I consulted as I put this story together. However, the interested reader who would like to delve deeper into the characters that run through this story and into the times in which they lived might enjoy spending further time with (in addition to the invaluable primary sources I list in the opening Note to the Reader) the works I found myself returning to most frequently: Pierre Berton's *The Klondike Fever: The Life and Death of the Last Great Gold Rush* (Basic Books, 1958) is the best book I've read on the events surrounding the rush to the north; at times the writing is lyrical. Tappan Adney's *The Klondike Stampede,* a compilation of his experiences as a reporter for *Harper's Weekly* during the gold rush and first published in 1900, is a keen-eyed report with a good deal of valuable observations about the mechanics of gold mining (UBC Press, Vancouver, 1994). *George Carmack: Man of Mystery Who Set Off the Klondike Gold Rush* (Epicenter Press, Fairbanks, 2001) by James Albert Johnson is a lively and well-researched account by the man who providentially found Carmack's papers in a secondhand bookstore and who later graciously donated them to the University of Washington. While there is a small library of books on Soapy Smith, the only one an interested reader needs to make his way through is Jeff Smith's exhaustive *Alias Soapy Smith: The Life and Death of a Scoundrel* (Klondike Research, Juneau, 2009). Nevertheless, Jane G. Haigh's *King Con: The Story of Soapy Smith* (Friday 501 Media, Whitehorse, Yukon, 2006) is a carefully researched and written biography. And for an engaging tour through aspects of the gold rush days that are too often ignored in standard histories, both Lael Morgan's *Good Time Girls* (Epicenter Press, Fairbanks, 1998) and Claire Rudolf Murphy and Jane G. Haigh's *Gold*

Rush Women (Alaska Northwest Books, Anchorage, 1997) are essential.

Finally, let me share below, chapter by chapter, the main sources of information for each chapter of this book.

Prologue: Pierre Berton, *The Klondike Fever* (KF); Tappan Adney, *The Klondike Stampede* (KS); Alaska History and Cultural Studies, Chapters 4–9: River Transportation, www.akhistorycourse.org; A. C. Drysdale, "From Tombstone to the Yukon: Ed Schieffelin's Alaskan Expedition," *Alaska Journal,* vol. 13, no. 3, Summer 1983 (TTY); Frank C. Lockwood, *Pioneer Days in Arizona,* Macmillan Co., New York, 1932; Jeremy Rowe, "Following the Frontier from Arizona to Alaska: The Photographs of Charles O. Farciot," http://vintage-photo.com/reference/ChFarciot; C. L. Andrews, *The Story of Alaska,* Caxton Printers, Caldwell, ID, 1938 (SOA); Walter Noble Burns, *Tombstone,* Doubleday, Doran & Co., Garden City, NY, 1929; M. H. E. Haynes and Taylor H. West, *Pioneers of the Klondyke,* Sampson, Low, Marston & Co., London, 1899 (POK); C. H. Hamlin, *Old Times in the Yukon,* Wetzel Publishing Co., Los Angeles, 1928 (OTY); W. J. Loudon, *A Canadian Geologist,* Macmillan

Company of Canada, Toronto, 1930 (CG); Edward Burschall Lung, *Black Sand and Gold,* Vantage Press, New York, 1956 (BSG); Frederick Palmer, *In the Klondyke,* Charles Scribner's Sons, New York, 1899 (ITK); Warburton Pike, *Through the Subartic Forest,* Edward Arnold, London, 1896 (TSF).
Chapter One: Charles A. Siringo, *A Texas Cowboy; or, Fifteen Years on the Hurricane Deck of a Spanish Pony,* edited with an Introduction by Richard W. Etulain, 1885; reprinted by Penguin Books, New York, 2000 (TC); Charles A. Siringo, *A Cowboy Detective,* facsimile of the 1912 edition, University of Nebraska Press, 1988 (CD); Charles A. Siringo, *Riata and Spurs,* facsimile of the 1927 edition, Sunstone Press, New Mexico, 2007 (RS); Howard R. Lamar, *Charlie Siringo's West: An Interpretive Biography* (CSW); J. Marvin Hunter, ed., *The Trail Drivers of Texas,* University of Texas Press, Austin, 1985 (TDT); Beinecke Library, Yale University, Western Americana Collection, Box 2–3; E. C. Abbott and Helena Huntington Smith, *We Pointed Them North: Recollections of a Cowpuncher,* Lakeside Press, Chicago, 1991; Charles D. Peavy, *Charles A. Siringo: A Texas Picaro,* Steck-Vaughn Co., Austin, 1967 (TP); Donald F. Worcester, *The Chisholm Trail,* University of Nebraska Press, 1980 (CT);

Raymond W. Thorp, "Cowboy Charlie Siringo," *True West* vol. 12, 1965; Orlan Sawey, *Charles A. Siringo,* Twayne Publishers, Boston, 1981 (CAS).

Chapter Two: Jeff Smith, *Alias Soapy Smith* (ASS); Jane G. Haigh, *King Con* (KC); William Ross Collier and Edwin Victor Westrate, *The Reign of Soapy Smith, Monarch of Misrule,* Sun Dial Press, NY, 1938 (RSS); Frank C. Robertson and Beth Kay Harris, *Soapy Smith: King of the Frontier Con Men,* Hastings House, NY, 1961 (KFCM); Lyle W. Dorsett, *The Queen City: A History of Denver,* Pruett Publishing, Boulder, 1977 (QC); Carl Abbott, Stephen J. Leonard, and Davis McComb, *Colorado: A History of the Centennial State,* University Press of Colorado, 1994 (HCS); Smith family letters as cited by Jeff Smith (SFL).

Chapter Three: James Albert Johnson, *George Carmack: Man of Mystery Who Set Off the Klondike Gold Rush* (GC); Carmack letters and diary, University of Washington Collection (CLD); KF; KS; William Douglass, *Sheepherders of the American West,* University of Nevada, 1986 (SAW).

Chapter Four: CD; TC; RS; CSW; Charles A. Siringo, *History of "Billy the Kid": The True Life of the Most Daring Young Outlaw,* facsimile of the 1920 edition, Steck-Vaughn, Austin, 1967; Robert R. Dykstra, *The Cattle*

Towns: A Social History of the Kansas Cattle Trading Centers, Alfred A. Knopf, New York, 1968; Jon Tuska, *Billy the Kid: His Life and Legend*, Greenwood Press, Westport, CT, 1985.

Chapter Five: George T. Buffum, *Smith of Bear City and Other Frontier Sketches*, Grafton Press, New York, 1906; ASS; KC; RSS; KFCM; QC; SFL; *Rocky Mountain News* archives, Denver Public Library (RMN); Robert L. Perkins, *The First Hundred Years: An Informal History of Denver and the "Rocky Mountain News,"* Doubleday, Garden City, NY, 1959.

Chapter Six: GC; CLD; SOA; BSG; TSF; H. H. Bancroft, *History of Alaska, 1730–1885*, A. L. Bancroft & Co., San Francisco, 1886 (HOA); Bruce Miner, *Alaska: Its History*, G. P. Putnam's Sons, New York, 1899 (AIH); Joseph Grinnell, *Gold Hunting in Alaska*, David C. Cook Publishing Co., Elgin, IL, 1935 (GHA); James Michener, *Alaska*, Random House, New York, 1988; Andrei Grinev, *Tlingit Indians in Russian America, 1741–1867*, University of Nebraska Press, 2008 (TI); Nore Dauenhauer, *Russians in Tlingit America*, New York, 1960; E. R. Scidmore, *Alaska: Its Southern Coast and the Sitka Archipelago*, D. Lothrop and Co., Boston, 1885 (ASC); George C. Shaw, *The Chinook Jargon and How to Use It*,

Rainer Printing Co., Seattle, 1909.

Chapter Seven: CD; RS; CSW; Frank Moran, *"The Eye That Never Sleeps": A History of the Pinkerton National Detective Agency*, Indiana University Press, Bloomington, 1982 (ENS); James D. Horan, *Desperate Men: Revelations from the Sealed Pinkerton Files*, G. P. Putnam's Sons, 1949 (DM); Horan, *The Pinkertons: The Detective Dynasty That Made History*, Crown Publications, Inc., New York, 1967 (DD).

Chapter Eight: ASS; KC; KFCM; QC; SFL; RMN; CD; RS; CSW; ENS; DM; DD; Registry of Pinkerton National Detective Agency, prepared by Michael McEldering, Manuscript Division, Library of Congress (RPNDA).

Chapter Nine: ASS; KC; RSS; KFCM; HCS; SFL; Robert K. DeArment, *Knights of the Green Cloth: The Saga of the Frontier Gamblers*, University of Oklahoma Press, Norman, 1982 (KGC); Leland Feitz, *A Quick History of Creede: Colorado Boom Town*, Little London Press, Colorado Springs, 1969; Feitz, *Soapy Smith's Creede*, Little London Press, 1973; Museum of Hoaxes, www.museumofhoaxes.com; Judith Ries, *Ed O'Kelley: The Man Who Murdered Jesse James' Murderer*, Stewart Printing & Publishing, Marble Hill, MI, 1994; *Creede Candle* archives, Denver Public Library.

Chapter Ten: GC; CLD; SAW.

Chapter Eleven: CD; RS; CSW; RPNDA; ASS; KC; QC; HCS; RMN; Louisa Ward Arp, *Denver in Slices,* Sage Books, Denver, 1959; Clyde King, *The History of the Government of Denver,* PhD Thesis, University of Pennsylvania, 1911; Thomas J. Noel, *The City and the Saloon: Denver, 1858–1916,* University of Nebraska Press, Lincoln, 1982; Lewis Stone Sorley, *History of the Fourteenth United States Infantry, from January, 1890–1908,* privately printed; CSW; CLD.

Chapter Twelve: Richard Timberlake, *Business Cycles and Depressions;* Douglas W. Steeples and David Whitlen, *Democracy in Desperation: The Depression of 1893,* Greenwood Press, Westport, CT, 1998; Clement Juglar and DeCourcey W. Thom, *A Brief History of Panics in the United States,* Cosimo, Inc., New York, 2006; W. Jett Lauk, *The Causes of the Panic of 1893,* online facsimile of 1907 edition; Lucy G. Barber, *Marching on Washington: The Forging of an American Political Tradition,* University of California Press, Berkeley, 2004; Jacob S. Coxey, *The Coxey Plan: A Cure for Hard Times,* Massillon, OH, 1914; SOA; KF; HOA; AIH; GHA; Jim DuFresne, *Alaska: The Complete Guide to the Last Frontier,* Lonely Planet

Publications, Victoria, Australia, 1983 (ACG).

Chapter Thirteen: CD; RS; CSW; RPNDA; ENS, DD; Trevor Davis, *Looking Back on Juneau: The First One Hundred Years*, Miner Publishing, Juneau, 1979.

Chapter Fourteen: CD; RS; CSW; RPNDA; David and Brenda Stone, *Hard Rock*, Vanguard Press, New York, 1957 (HR); Edwin Kible, *The Birdman of Treadwell: Diary of a Treadwell Gold Miner*, Doubleday & Page, New York, 1924 (DTGM); Charles Palanche, *American Geologist*, vol. 34, 1904 (AG); *Harriman Alaska Expedition*, Doubleday & Page, New York, 1904 (HAE); GC; CLD.

Chapter Fifteen: GC; CLD; KF; Ernest Ingersoll, *Gold Fields of the Klondike and the Wonders of Alaska*, W. W. Wilson, New York, 1987; Thomas Wiedemann, *Cheechako into Sourdough*, Binfords & Mort, Portland, OR, 1944; Roy Minter, *White Pass: Gateway to the Klondike*, University of Alaska Press, Fairbanks, 1987 (WP); Walter R. Curtain, *Yukon Voyage*, Caxton Printers, Caldwell, ID, 1983 (YV).

Chapter Sixteen: GC; CLD; KF; KS; GHA; TI; TSF; ITK; BSG; TTY; POK.

Chapter Seventeen: GC; CLD; TI; TSF; Patsy Henderson, *Early Days at Caribou Crossing and the Discovery of Gold on the*

Klondike, 1949, University of Washington Archives (EDCC); George W. Carmack, *My Experiences in the Yukon,* 1933, University of Washington Archives (ME); Kan Sergei, *Shamanism and Christianity: Modern-Day Tlingit Elders Look at the Past,* http://books.google.com; Morton Klass and Maxine Wiesgrau, eds., *Across the Boundaries of Belief: Contemporary Issues in the Anthropology of Religion,* Westview Press, Boulder, CO, 1999.

Chapter Eighteen: ASS; KC; *Seattle Times,* online archive; RSS; KFCM; SFL; RMN; Della Murray Banks, "Homer's Gold Seekers: A Game of Bluff," *Alaskan Sportsman,* October 1945 (HGS).

Chapter Nineteen: CD; RS; CSW; RPNDA; HAE; AG; DTGM; HR.

Chapter Twenty: CD; RS; CSW; RPNDA; HAE; AG; DTGM.

Chapter Twenty-One: CD; RS; CSW; RPNDA; Jim Gibbs, *Alaska Maritime,* Schiffer Publishing, Atglen, PA, 1997 (AM); Marcus Backer, ed., *Geographic Dictionary of Alaska,* Government Printing Office, Washington, DC, 1906 (GDA); ACG.

Chapter Twenty-Two: CD; RS; RPNDA; GC; CLD; ME; EDCC.

Chapter Twenty-Three: ASS; KC; SFL; HGS; Milton A. Daby, *The Sea Saga of Dynamite Johnny O'Brien,* Lowman & Hanford, Seattle, 1933.

Chapter Twenty-Four: CD; RS; CSW; RPNDA; AM; GDA; ACG.

Chapter Twenty-Five: CD; RS; CSW; RPNDA; AM; KS; KF; Mike Leahy, "Gold Smelting," http://www.pbs.org/weta/roughscience/series3/big_smelt/smelting.html; "Gold Mining & Gold Prospecting," http://www.e-goldprospecting.com; HR; BSG.

Chapter Twenty-Six: ME; KF; KS; EDCC; CLD; GC.

Chapter Twenty-Seven: ME; EDCC; CLD; KF; GC.

Chapter Twenty-Eight: CD; RS; RPNDA; AM; KS.

Chapter Twenty-Nine: ME; CLD; EDCC; KF; POK.

Chapter Thirty: CD; RS; RPNDA; CSW.

Chapter Thirty-One: ME; KF; EDCC; GC; CLD; POK.

Chapter Thirty-Two: ASS; SFL; KC; RMN, *Seattle Times* archives.

Chapter Thirty-Three: ME; CLD; GC; KS; KF; HR; BSG.

Chapter Thirty-Four: ME; CLD; GC; KS; KF; William Ogilvie, *Early Days on the Yukon,* John Lane Co., New York, 1913; POK; James Wickersham, *Old Yukon,* Washington Law Book Co., Washington, DC, 1938.

Chapter Thirty-Five: ASS; *Seattle Post-*

Intelligencer archives; KF; KS; Sharon A. Boswell and Lorraine McConaghy, *Raise Hell and Sell Newspapers: Alden J. Blethen & the Seattle Times,* Washington State University Press, Pullman, WA, 1996; GC.

Chapter Thirty-Six: KF; KS; GC; Will Chase, *Reminiscences of Captain Billie Moore,* Burton Publishing Co., Kansas City, MO, 1923; Arthur Dietz, *Mad Rush for Gold in Frozen North,* Los Angeles Time-Mirror Printing and Binding House, 1914; Hamlin Garland, *Trail of the Goldseekers,* Macmillan Co., New York, 1899; ASS; POK; Clarence L. Andrews, *The Story of Alaska,* Caxton Printers, Caldwell, ID, 1938; Andrews, "The Real Soapy Smith," *Alaska Sportsman,* November 1947; Gerald L. Pennington, *Klondike Stampeders Register,* Windsor Associates, San Diego, 1997; Mabel Pearce Reed, *Skagway Memories,* self-published, 1988; Robert L. S. Spude, *Skagway, District of Alaska, 1884–1912,* University of Alaska, Fairbanks, 1983.

Chapter Thirty-Seven: ASS; KC; RSS; KFCM; KF; SFL; Lael Morgan, *Good Time Girls;* Samuel H. Graves, *On the White Pass Payroll,* Lakeside Press, Chicago, 1908 (OWPP); Will Irwin, *The Confessions of a Con Man,* B. W. Huebush, New York, 1913; Archie Satterfeld, *Chilkoot Pass,* Alaska Northwest Books, Portland, OR, 2004;

Harriet S. Pullen, *Soapy Smith: Bandit of Skagway,* Skagway Tourist Agency, Skagway; Shea and Patten, *The Soapy Smith Tragedy,* Daily Alaskan Print, Skagway, 1907; Howard Clifford, *Uncrowned King of Skagway,* Sourdough Enterprises, Seattle, 1997.

Chapter Thirty-Eight: GC; CLD; KF; KS; POK.

Chapter Thirty-Nine: CD; RS; RPNDA; DM.

Chapter Forty: ASS; SFL; KC; *Seattle Times* archives; Harry L. Suydam, "The Reign of Soapy Smith," *Frank Leslie's Popular Monthly,* vol. 51, 1901 (RSS); KF; R. M. Dickey, *Gold Fever* (GF); Dickey, Diary (DD).

Chapter Forty-One: GC; CLD; CD; RPNDA; G. S. Howard, "Badman of Skagway Meets Insp. Wood," *Quarterly,* Royal Canadian Mounted Police, vol. 48, 1963 (BOS); ASS; Samuel Steele, *Forty Years in Canada,* Jenkins Press, Toronto, 1915 (FYC).

Chapter Forty-Two: RPNDA; BOS; ASS; FYC; Philip Godsell, "Skagway Terror," *Fury: Exciting Adventures for Men,* October 1957.

Chapter Forty-Three: ASS; SFL; RSS; KF; KC; *Seattle Times* archives; Frank Clancy, "I Was Just a Kid," *Alaska Sportsman,* October 1955; James M. Sinclair, *Mission: Klondike,* Mitchell Press, Canada, 1978;

Calvin H. Bardull, "I Saw Soapy Killed," *Alaska Sportsman,* June 1952; Hazel Stewart Clark, "A Man of Honor," *Alaska Sportsman,* March 1958; OWPP; "Soapy Smith Skull: An Ironic Monument to a Two-Gun Tyrant," *Literary Digest Magazine,* September 1927.

Epilogue: ASS; SFL; KC; GC; CLD; *Seattle Post-Intelligencer* archives; Claire Rudolf Murphy and Jane G. Haitch, *Gold Rush Women;* CD; RSS; CSW; RPNDA; Robert S. Birchard, *King Cowboy: Tom Mix and the Movies,* Riverwood Press, Burbank, CA, 1993; Diana Serra Cary, *The Hollywood Posse,* University of Oklahoma Press, Norman, 1995; William K. Everson, *A Pictorial History of the Western Film,* Citadel Press, Secaucus, NJ, 1969; KF; TTY; POK.

ACKNOWLEDGMENTS

When I was a young boy growing up in a wooded area of the north Bronx, my friends and I used to chase around playing cowboys and Indians. Hiding behind rock outcroppings and clumps of tall, ancient trees, we devised intricate games that involved ambushes and ferocious shoot-outs with our cap guns. Then the developers came — and the Wild West that was our corner of New York City began to disappear. We had no choice but to move on to other pursuits. And so I soon discovered basketball and books.

But the memory of my early "cowboy days" and their abrupt end stayed with me over the years. In time, I decided to write a book that would focus on the last days of the Old West and the decision by some intrepid men and women to move on to the far north to search for adventure and fortune.

When I first began the intellectual journey that would become this book, I turned to two people for guidance. First, I shared my plan with Lynn Nesbit. Lynn has been my agent for more than two decades, and in that time she has become literary adviser, friend, and confidant. Once again, she gave me encouragement and wise advice; and once again, I owe her enormously.

Then I spoke with Rick Horgan, my editor at Crown. Rick is someone who cares about books and cares about editing them. He improves everything of mine that he marks with his stern pencil. And, not least, he's a man who always — always! — does precisely as he says. That's a rare quality in any field, and I'm grateful to be able to work and publish with him.

As the book moved forward, I was also helped and encouraged by many people at Crown, including Tina Constable, Molly Stern, and Nathan Roberson. And the team at Lynn's office whom I pestered too often were a godsend: Cullen Stanley, Tina Simms, and Lenore Hoffman.

Once there was a manuscript, I shared it with my longtime friends Bob Bookman and Stuart Manashil at CAA, and their help in trying to bring this story to the screen has proven invaluable. At *Vanity Fair,* both Graydon Carter and Dana Brown gave me wise advice. Alan Hergott, as always, served as a friend and a wise counselor. And Christopher Mason gave the manuscript a thoughtful read.

While writing the book, I also relied on a circle of friends: Susan and David Rich; Sarah and Bill Rauch; Irene and Phil Werber; John Leventhal; Bruce Taub; Pat, Bob, and Mark Lusthaus; Gary Cohen; Beth De-Woody; Adrienne Riso; Bob Mitchell; and, not least, my sister Marcy.

My children — Tony, Anna, and Dani — were a source of constant joy and immense pride.

And Ivana helped to make it all worthwhile.

ABOUT THE AUTHOR

Howard Blum is a contributing editor of *Vanity Fair* and the author of eight previous critically acclaimed bestselling nonfiction books. His most recent book, *American Lightning,* was a *New York Times* bestseller and an Edgar Award winner, was chosen as a Best Book of the Year by the Independent Booksellers Association, and is being made into a major motion picture. Blum lives in Connecticut.

The employees of Thorndike Press hope you have enjoyed this Large Print book. All our Thorndike, Wheeler, and Kennebec Large Print titles are designed for easy reading, and all our books are made to last. Other Thorndike Press Large Print books are available at your library, through selected bookstores, or directly from us.

For information about titles, please call:

(800) 223-1244

or visit our Web site at:

http://gale.cengage.com/thorndike

To share your comments, please write:

Publisher
Thorndike Press
10 Water St., Suite 310
Waterville, ME 04901